Rethinking Language Policy

For three activist couples: Joshua and Gella Fishman for Yiddish, Toni Waho and Peni Poutu for Maori, and Wayne and Agnes Holm for Navajo

Rethinking Language Policy

BERNARD SPOLSKY

EDINBURGH
University Press

Edinburgh University Press is one of the leading university presses in the UK. We publish academic books and journals in our selected subject areas across the humanities and social sciences, combining cutting-edge scholarship with high editorial and production values to produce academic works of lasting importance. For more information visit our website: edinburghuniversitypress.com

© Bernard Spolsky, 2021, 2023

Edinburgh University Press Ltd
The Tun – Holyrood Road
12(2f) Jackson's Entry
Edinburgh EH8 8PJ

First published in hardback by Edinburgh University Press 2021

Typeset in 10/12 Times New Roman by
Servis Filmsetting Ltd, Stockport, Cheshire

A CIP record for this book is available from the British Library

ISBN 978 1 4744 8546 3 (hardback)
ISBN 978 1 4744 8547 0 (paperback)
ISBN 978 1 4744 8548 7 (webready PDF)
ISBN 978 1 4744 8549 4 (epub)

The right of Bernard Spolsky to be identified as the author of this work has been asserted in accordance with the Copyright, Designs and Patents Act 1988, and the Copyright and Related Rights Regulations 2003 (SI No. 2498).

Contents

Preface

When you study something as complex, dynamic and chaotic as language policy, you should not be surprised to keep finding new elements and seeing new connections. I have been struggling with this ever since I started working in the field during the year that I spent as a fellow at the National Foreign Language Center in Washington, where Richard D. Lambert and his colleagues and some other visiting fellows were starting to explore the concept and where I realised that educational linguistics was part of a larger field. My first effort, in discussions with Elana Shohamy, was to try to draft a language education policy for Israel. In the process, we developed the notion that language policy was more easily understood by looking at three separate but related aspects: the actual language practices of a speech community, the beliefs or ideology that members of the community have formed about language and language choice, and any efforts by individuals or institutions to modify the practices or beliefs of the community. This model was the basis for the research that we conducted for the Israeli Ministry of Education and for the book that we wrote (Spolsky and Shohamy, 1999).

Over the next few years, I continued to learn and think about the topic, publishing my evolving notions in two more books, (Spolsky, 2004) and (Spolsky, 2009a) and in a number of articles. I learned a lot more when I edited a handbook (Spolsky, 2012b), in which forty-seven scholars reported on various aspects of the topic and I used this added knowledge when I wrote more papers.

Though I had by this time come to believe that writing another book would be too much for me, I was tempted by a suggestion from a colleague that I do so in a growing series with the title 'Rethinking . . .' This book is the result. Most of it was written while sitting quietly at my desk in Jerusalem, but a visit to India and learning about the problems of designing a language policy for that complex developing nation led to further thought and the eventual shaping of my ideas.

It is appropriate to thank the many colleagues and students who have shared in this quest and to recognise the family and friends and doctors who have supported me and kept me able to carry on with it. I am also grateful to publishers and editors and readers who have helped to shape my experience and thoughts. Language policy and management remain critical if we are to survive in a world threatened by pandemics, climate change and irresponsible governments.

Introduction:
The Non-Linguistic Environment

Human habitats

Language policy does not exist in a vacuum, but in the complex array of environmental conditions that encompass human life. In making this point, I am arguing against what I call *linguicentrism*, the notion that language is independent of its environment. In this introductory chapter, I will sketch a number of relevant non-linguistic features – physical geography including characteristics that encourage human residence such as agricultural and mineral resources and that constrain it such as mountains and seas and climate, demographic forces such as intensity and diversity of ethnic settlement and movement, progress in technology, events such as modernisation and globalisation, civil and external wars and epidemics and corruption that hinder the implementation of policies – which can be shown to have an effect on language practices and ideology and management. This is obviously a task better undertaken by a scholar such as Jared Diamond, whose books explore the relationships between geography, anthropology and linguistics (Diamond, 1997, 2005, 2013). But even a brief sketch will be useful in avoiding the error of isolating language policy from the people and the world we live in.

I grew up in New Zealand, a country happily located in the temperate zone with ample soil and rainfall and separated by sea from close contact with other people and languages. When I was a teenager, few Māoris were still speaking their heritage language – and those that did lived in villages, towns and suburbs distant from me. There were few immigrants speaking other languages until after the war – my own parents grew up speaking English and my grandparents spoke it too. It seemed an ideal place to live comfortably and monolingually.

When later I spent a few years in Montréal teaching and working on my doctoral dissertation, I wondered, during the first winter as the snow continued to pile up at the side of the roads, why people lived there, but I was also learning to live in a bilingual city. In much the same way, after I moved to

Israel I wondered how the Bedouin could manage living in a hot waterless desert and when I taught for some years in New Mexico and carried out a research programme with the Navajo people, I wondered how they could survive in their barren and mountainous land. In all three, I learned to live in a multilingual society, but one where my heritage English had high status.

The lesson I learned from my different countries of residence is that human beings are capable of managing in diverse conditions of physical geography and climate. But physical geography does have its effects on culture and language practices. Although we no longer assume as some did once that phonetics and the shape of the mouth and tongue are modified by the environment in which people live, it is clear that physical geography sets important constraints on the development of language policy. The most important effects involve the possibility of contact: islands, mountain ranges and jungles all foster the isolation that permits the evolution of new varieties and the maintenance of different languages. Sea coasts and rivers permit the contacts between peoples that lead to the building of multilingual cities and towns. They also provide a way for raiders or conquerors to enter. But the geographical barriers are not absolute: as Kulick (1992: 2) argues, it is not isolation that explains why Papua New Guinea has so many tiny languages – 35 per cent of its recognised languages have fewer than 500 speakers – but the fact that the villagers cultivate linguistic difference as a boundary-marker. Human attitudes can overcome physical conditions.

Human geography

Human communities are particularly attracted by good conditions for agriculture and by the availability of mineral resources. The sparser vegetation of mountainous regions is likely to result in pastoral exploitation and less intensive settlement; the alluvial soil and ample water of floodplains allows more intense agriculture and settlement. But floods, now exacerbated by climate change, interfere with settlement and can force movements of population.

Climate change threatens to have even more serious effects: an increase in the power of storms, flooding of the low land on which many major cities are built, higher temperature of seas causing loss of fish supplies and higher temperature of land causing destructive fires. All of these have potential effects on the language practices of exposed communities. Again, there is interaction with human behaviour, such as the development of slavery to provide labour for the plantations established in colonies. The wealth produced by mineral resources might be used for the public good or diverted to build the fortunes of corrupt officials. Thus the human and the natural are intertwined.

Demography

A good number of the non-linguistic factors that affect language policy can be derived from looking at human geography and specifically at demography.[1] In a pioneering effort to determine the cause of language maintenance in the United States, Kloss (1966) argued that many factors worked both for and against maintenance; one factor clearly supporting it was religio-societal insulation, which results when a group 'withdraws from the world'. Although demographic features such as time of immigration and the existence of language islands are important, Kloss stressed that greater numerical strength and smallness of the group are ambivalent in their effects.

Looking beyond immigrant groups in the USA and studying minority languages[2] in a number of multilingual nations,[3] I found that the number of speakers is not the determining factor that one might expect: there are tiny language groups that are classified as vigorous and large groups considered to be threatened.[4] Other factors, such as the upward socioeconomic mobility that Joshua Fishman recognised, or the valuing of a language for heritage identity or for employment and economic success that Heller and McElhinny (2017) and others see as critical, turn out to be more important than purely demographic factors. But demography remains significant, in setting the fundamental basis for the natural intergenerational transmission or the school language policy on which language shift and maintenance commonly depend.

Demographic isolation accounts for the language situation of indigenous tribes in the Amazon; it is only those tribes that have been protected from any contact with others that are safe from pressure to shift to a more valuable language (Spolsky, 2018b). Language shift depends first and foremost on contact.[5] Even an isolated Papua New Guinea village like Gapun, two days walk through the jungle from the next village, proved susceptible to the incursion of the Tok Pisin brought back by young men who had worked on plantations: children had switched to it without their parents noticing (Kulick, 1992). Contact remains a significant demographic factor; just as individual bilingualism depends on contact of two languages in the repertoire of a speaker (Weinreich, 1953), so societal multilingualism depends on the existence of multilingual repertoires[6] used by a social unit, family, village, city or nation, as well as on the attitudes to the varieties.

Expanding repertoires

Changes in linguistic environment are important. Grosjean (2019) has recently published an account of the expansion of his personal repertoire:

> François Grosjean takes us through his life, from his monolingual childhood in a small village outside Paris to the long periods of time he spent in Switzerland, England, France and the United States, becoming

bilingual and bicultural in the process. During his life, his dominant
language has changed many times between English and French and
he has also acquired and subsequently lost, other languages, including
American Sign Language.

Although I myself added a little Hebrew to my repertoire through religious
life in my home and some French, Latin and less German during schooling,
it was the time that I spent living in French-favouring Montréal and later in
Hebrew-dominant Israel that led to useful proficiency in other languages.

Just as an individual's language repertoire is modified by moving to a new
environment, so a community's repertoire is influenced by a change in location and a consequent change in demography. Villagers, whose language
situation was stable as long as they were isolated, undergo a major change
when they move to a city, for cities are marked by demographic complexity
and associated linguistic diversity (Cadora, 1970).[7] Obvious examples are the
shift to English of Māori speakers who left their villages in the first half of the
twentieth century, or the major changes produced by urbanisation in China
(Seto, 2014). Urbanisation, a kind of internal migration, is a major cause
of language shift, depending on the extent of social and economic contact
between the various groups in the new location. Intermarriage, education
and employment provide the greatest contact; residential and religious or
ethnic segregation slow down the amount and likelihood of intercourse and
so the likelihood of language shift.

Even before a local educational system starts to forcibly expand the repertoire of children beginning school,[8] neighbourhood children in a linguistically
diverse community introduce new varieties to the children they play with,
producing the peer influence that Harris (1995, 1998) argues is potentially
as strong as parental models and challenging the effects of family language
policy. Schools in a village commonly work to introduce the dominant
national or regional variety, but in the city, they provide a language of wider
communication among the linguistically diverse intake as well as a valued
language of instruction.

But it is oversimplifying to assume that the village did not include some
diversity, such as the gender-marked varieties produced in cases of exogamous marriage preference or the caste-related diversity of Indian villages
(Gumperz, 1958) or the chiefly varieties of Tongan (Haugen and Philips,
2010) and other Polynesian varieties. And although it is true that modern
cities are increasingly diverse (Blommaert, 2013), they echo the linguistic
complexity of medieval sea-ports, so that the term 'superdiverse' is probably superfluous (Pavlenko, 2017). However, the process of urbanisation has
important effects, as the Muslims who moved from the villages to Christian
and Jewish Baghdad found (Blanc, 1964) and as the villagers moving to
Chinese cities demonstrate (Xu, 2015).

Birth order and density

Although it is true that the number of speakers is not the most critical feature in accounting for the success of language management, there are other demographic criteria that are influential. Within the family, for example, the number and pattern of members is important: the vast number of family patterns ranging from a couple through an elaborate collection of parents, grandparents, significant others and children makes it impossible to arrive at a simple definition of family and a classification of family language policies. A couple may or may not share the same language variety and may have the same or different attitudes to each language in their repertoire.[9] Significant others include relatives such as recently arrived grandparents or uncles and aunts speaking a heritage variety, or various types of caretakers or household servants speaking other languages (Lorente, 2017). Families with only one child (as mandated in the People's Republic of China (PRC) until recently) are more likely to maintain a single variety than families with several children where older siblings regularly introduce the school variety to younger ones.

At levels of demographic organisation beyond the family, the diverse social patterns have important effects. Linguistic diversity in a neighbourhood or region provides pressure for shift.[10] Similarly, social networks such as those described by Milroy (1980) are important: when family members continue to work and associate with relatives living outside the home, networks are established which support language maintenance. The development of telephones and computer-based social media such as WhatsApp and Zoom enables language maintenance at a distance.[11] The residential intensity of linguistic, ethnic and religious groups has important effects. Food preferences as well as social support encourage the development of ethnic and religious concentrations that provide an environment for language maintenance.[12] In the same way, proximity to churches, mosques and synagogues encourage demographic intensity.

At the same time, socioeconomic, religious, ethnic and linguistic variation sets up barriers between groups and limit intercommunication. When we lived in the Old City of Jerusalem, we were often asked whether our children played with the Arab children living on our street and replied that they did not play even with the Jewish children attending the other Jewish religious school. Thus, demographic variation within a community is a significant factor in language maintenance. Even more influential are changes in the demographic pattern as the results of migration and urbanisation. The two are closely related, for the movement from rural life to the city can produce the same alteration in linguistic and social environment that the forced or voluntary movement from one country to another produces. In each case, an individual speaker, family, social or ethnic group may be separated or isolated from the new community. It is the change in demography that becomes the significant factor.

Whatever the reason, whether it is movement forced by government policy such as the population shifts required by the Babylonians in the ancient world or by Nazi Germany, the Soviet Union and China in the twentieth century, or produced by economic and ethnic pressure in the late twentieth and twenty-first centuries, or the voluntary search for greater freedom or economic success producing Jewish or Chinese or Indian diasporas over the centuries (Spolsky, 2016b), or the religious intolerance that motivated settlers moving to North America, or the economic pressure that has continually encourage urbanisation, it is environmental demographic change that produces conditions for language shift.

Technological developments

Agriculture and exploitation of minerals were both influenced by developments in technology and affected language practices especially as machines replaced human labour. I recently learned that my grandfather's migration from Scotland to New Zealand in 1906 was the result of the formation of the British American Tobacco company; the cigarette makers recruited from Eastern Europe by the British company were made redundant by the cigarette-making machines added by the American component.

In the same way, the development of the machine loom led to changes in employment patterns. Recent progress in communication has been even more striking. When I grew up, we communicated locally by telephone and received news from abroad by mail and radio; now we have instant communication with family and friends and colleagues and businesses throughout the world by computer and smartphone and can watch television events on the moon and hold virtual meetings on Zoom. The immediacy and cheapness of these methods of communication is a major component of globalisation, a process which started with trade (the Silk Road and the various empires supported by sea and land routes), but was greatly increased by being connected internationally.[13] The number of smartphone users worldwide was projected to amount to nearly 3.5 billion in 2020, with over 300 million in India, providing oral and visual contact to nearly half of the world population.

When computers were developed, it was assumed that they would only be efficient for the Latin alphabet – we had trouble entering Navajo text into the computer in 1970 (Spolsky et al., 1973) – but the standard system, Unicode, now handles over 150 scripts, meaning that speakers of many languages have a way of using the increased communicative power. Improved translation systems mean that communication is also possible between writers (and speakers) of different languages. Technology thus supports linguistic diversity.

Interference with language management by non-linguistic forces

As we will discuss in Chapter 12, the governments of modern nation states tend to prefer monolingual hegemony and try to encourage the use of a single national language. We shall be studying the policy counterforces to this, but there are also many non-linguistic factors that work to defeat attempts at the implementation of language policies which generally depend on education. These will be explored in more detail, particularly in Chapter 7 dealing with the linguistic fate of colonies before and after independence; they include wars, droughts and other climate effects, corruption and other phenomena which hinder funding support for education.

All of this then provides the background in which language policy – practices, ideologies and management – develops and helps to account for the difficulties and failures of implementing even well-designed national language policies. Driving around India and seeing the size and complexity of the country, the uneven development of the road system – as virtually unformed and bumpy sections alternated with superhighways with toll systems – and the vast range of poor villages alongside new universities and suburbs, one quickly realises how non-linguistic forces and concerns can interfere with the implementation of language policies. Linguicentrism obscures this; language policy depends on many non-linguistic factors.

Notes

1. The section on demography is based on a paper written originally at the invitation of Wei Li and appeared as Spolsky (2019f).
2. For a useful presentation of definitions for terms like 'minority' and 'indigenous' in Europe and South Asia, see Rautz et al. (2008). For discussion of contribution of applied linguistics to indigenous language revitalisation, see McIvor (2020).
3. I have looked closely at Vanuatu in the Pacific, India in Asia, the Russian Federation in Europe, Brazil in the Americas and Nigeria in Africa. All are highly multilingual. See Chapter 9.
4. 'Vigorous' on the scale (Expanded Graded Intergenerational Disruption Scale (EGIDS)) used in *Ethnologue* (Lewis et al., 2016) applies when a language is 'used for face-to-face communication by all generations and the situation is sustainable'; 'threatened' means that it is losing users. More serious is 'shifting', where the language is no longer being transmitted to children (Lewis et al., 2016).
5. Rodríguez-Ordóñez (2019) shows how contact linguistics should take into the account the ideologies that lead to language shift and maintenance.

6. I find the notion of repertoires to be more useful than named languages (Benor, 2010; Gumperz, 1965; Laitin, 1992; Lüdi, 2006).
7. Or as in American Samoa or the Amazon jungle, when road building led to contact of the rural with the urban, something I first learned in the case of Navajo (Spolsky, 1974b).
8. Over 40 per cent of children attend a school using a language of instruction that is not their home variety (Walter, 2003). I will repeat this worrying fact regularly for it shows the basic inadequacy of much language education.
9. See, for example, Bahalwan, 2015; Cheng, 2003; Johansson, 1991; Novianti, 2013.
10. See, for example, Leventhal and Brooks-Gunn, 2000; Ma and Herasimchuk, 1971; Vicino et al., 2011.
11. There was a session reporting research on digitally mediated communication in contemporary multilingual families in Finland, Norway and Switzerland at a symposium on family language policy at the Institute of Education, University College London, 5–6 September 2019. The coronavirus has doubtless increased the significance of digital messaging.
12. A classic study of such a neighbourhood is the bilingual barrio in New Jersey studied in Fishman, Cooper and Ma (1971).
13. My journey from Australia to Great Britain in 1957 took six weeks by ship; there will soon be direct flights.

1   The Individual in Language Policy and Management

Seeking a model

In the two decades since my first paper on the topic of language policy (Spolsky, 1996),[1] I have found it necessary to keep adding to the complexity of the model that I postulate in order to account for the many different cases I have come across. Working with a colleague, Elana Shohamy, our first concern was the challenge of proposing a language education policy for Israeli schools (Spolsky and Shohamy, 1999); in tackling this, I was able to build on my earlier experiences with Navajo (Spolsky, 1975) and Māori (Spolsky, 1989) and my long interest in language education (Spolsky, 1974a). In designing the Israeli policy (Spolsky and Shohamy, 1999), we proposed a model which defined language policy as consisting of three interrelated but independent components. These were language practice (the choices of language variety made by speakers in a community), language beliefs and ideology (what people think should be the language of the community) and language management (efforts by people or institutions inside or outside a community to modify the beliefs and practices of members of the community) (Spolsky, 2004). This was and remains the basic model.

As I continued to work with the model and tried to account for common failures of national policies (Spolsky, 2006a, 2006b), I found it necessary to consider language policy at different levels, ranging from the family to the nation and beyond and in different domains ranging from home to government (Spolsky, 2009a) and recognise that these policies at other levels could impede a national policy. After a study of many cases, especially former empires and their successors (Spolsky, 2018b, 2019c), I extended the model to include non-linguistic situations and events interfering with the implementation of language policies (Spolsky, 2019e). More recently, I have been persuaded of the significance of the individual, both for establishing practices and through self-management,[2] for resisting external management and expanding individual and group linguistic repertoires. This in brief is where I came from and how I got here: as a result, it seems appropriate to rethink the topic of language policy by reversing the normal order of presentation, with its historical focus on state language policy (Jernudd and Nekvapil, 2012) and to start with the individual speaker instead of the nation.

An important initial qualification is that just as not all states are interested in developing a formal language policy – the United States is an obvious example (Spolsky, 2011a) – so most speakers are probably unaware that their own repertoires are changing as a result of external experiences and pressures.[3] In a homogenous monolingual society like the one I grew up in, it was my family's Jewish religious observance that first revealed to me that there was another language (Hebrew) that we used for prayers at home and in synagogue. My Protestant peers probably had to wait until high school offered us a French class and even that remained an academic exercise until we saw a French movie or went on board a visiting French navy ship. My own contact with languages other than English in vernacular use came first when I taught classes that included Māori students in a Gisborne high school and later when I lived in Israel and Québec. But anyone growing up in the normal multilingual environment of modern cities, with parents or grandparents or peers using a complex repertoire of varieties, becomes aware early on of the values attached to each variety and the costs and advantages of modifying their own repertoires.

Languages or repertoires

I now speak of repertoires, avoiding the problem of oversimplification that comes of references to named languages. The value of talking about repertoires (individual or collective) is argued in Benor (2010) and Spolsky and Benor (2006) and is in line with contemporary doubts about named languages.[4] Using the concept doesn't mean giving up on naming languages, difficult as it is to define them linguistically, for they are essentially dependent on political or social decisions. How does one define English, with all its national and dialectal varieties? Or why does one distinguish (other than politically) among the recently separated varieties of what under Tito was Serbo-Croatian, each now recognised as distinct by the International Organization for Standardization (ISO) even though it claims that its first criterion is mutual unintelligibility? When does a regional dialect like Friesian or Afrikaans become a separate language from Dutch, and why is Catalan a language even without political independence, and why are mutually intelligible varieties of Scandinavian languages accepted as languages, but mutually unintelligible topolects of Chinese are all lumped together?[5] Languages are varieties named politically[6] or in popular usage.[7]

Children develop and expand their language repertoires depending on the varieties that they hear in their environment. A child with both parents speaking the same variety will start off with it, but may later add the language of significant others, like grandparents or caretakers and the older siblings who bring home a language from school, or the neighbourhood peers they play with. Studying this normal development is a sub-field named family language policy and the home is probably the most important domain for language maintenance (Spolsky, 2012a, 2018a): languages are endangered when a language is no longer passed on to babies and young children.

But there are two other important processes to note at the level of the individual speaker. The first is accommodation, the not necessarily conscious modification of one's repertoire to that of one's interlocutor, and the second is self-management, the conscious effort to modify or add to one's linguistic repertoire in the belief that it is advantageous. Accommodation theory is based on evidence that 'an individual's speech patterns are in part dependent on the person to whom he is talking' (Giles et al., 1973: 177). Speakers make linguistic adjustments based on their perception of their interlocutor's social status,[8] age and presumed knowledge of the topic. They also learn what is appropriate when talking to various audiences: avoiding swear words when talking to their mother, or using an immigrant variety with their grandparents or a recently arrived aunt, or switching to a more formal style in public. Giles (1971, 1973) suggested that convergent accommodation occurs when speakers modify their accent in order to obtain social approval; to express disapproval, they modify their accent in the opposite direction (divergence). At a group level, a minority group's divergence might lead to language maintenance, as Fishman (1966) has shown in the case of Hasidic use of Yiddish. Much the same process is recognised by the theory of language socialisation (Duranti et al., 2011; Ochs, 1986; Ochs and Schieffelin, 2011), an ethnographic approach which traces the way in which children's and adults' linguistic and cultural adeptness develops as they move into expanding speech and cultural communities with different linguistic codes and semiotic systems.

Some of the important evidence of the nature of accommodation refers not to language shift, but to the modification of dialect differences, as suggested by Giles's initial reference to accent. For example, Kerswill (2003) explains the loss of localised features in British English to be the result of geographical diffusion, with a spread from more populous and economically developed locations to surrounding cities and later to rural areas in between and he associated individual face-to-face relations with what Cooper (1982) calls 'adopters', those who accept innovation. The second mechanism, he says, is what Trudgill (1986) called 'levelling', another result of speech accommodation. Hornsby (2007) finds dialect levelling in both Britain and France, which he associates with urbanisation. Dialect levelling has also been studied in Tunisia (Gibson, 2013) and recently in Israel (Cerqueglini, 2018). In Israel, the traditional distinctions between mutually unintelligible urban, rural and Bedouin dialects of Arabic still maintained by people over the age of seventy are being lost among younger people working in public institutions and educated in Standard Arabic, Hebrew and other modern languages. The values associated with speakers of more standard varieties then lead to changes in individual and community repertoires.

Looking at the actual language practices, whether of an individual or a larger community, it is useful to describe linguistic repertoires in place of named languages, for just as the idealised language studied by the followers of Chomsky is a useful myth, so the communication proficiency of a speaker or a community of speakers is better studied as a repertoire. Named languages occur not in practices, but in beliefs: their existence is a first belief of speakers and linguists; they are also the focus of management, which depends on values assigned to identified named language varieties.

Beliefs

This influence of beliefs shows up also in accounting for successful second or foreign language learning. Gardner and Lambert (1972), based largely on their studies of French Canadian, French American and English students in Canada, drew attention to the importance of attitudes and motivation as a critical factor in acquiring a language in school; they proposed a distinction between integrative motivation (learning a language as reflecting a desire to be like representative members of the other language community or to be associated with that community) and instrumental motivation (a desire to gain social recognition or economic advantage). This model was in time challenged by Dörnyei (1999; Dörnyei and Ushioda, 2009), who brought the study of language learning motivation in line with developing psychological interest in cognition and of people situated in a specific sociocultural context. The motivational self-system as it applied to second language learning now has three components: the ideal self, the ought-to self and language learning experiences.[9]

An individual's language repertoire (equivalent to the language practices of a community) depends on the languages to which he or she is exposed; an individual's language beliefs or ideology depend on his or her responses or attitude to speakers in the environment and to their potential usefulness. For a young child, significant speakers are caretakers (parents or others); later it means peers including older siblings and friends from the neighbourhood; and in due course, it adds teachers and actual or potential employers. A growing repertoire results from meaningful exposures and the associated values assigned to the people and the language varieties. In addition, it is liable to be influenced by management efforts of authorities, such as teachers and employers or the state. Immigrant mothers or fathers may try to preserve a heritage language or encourage the adoption of the local dominant variety. Each new domain or level, calling for communication with an increasing array of speakers, adds new sources of language proficiency.

The three-component model that I started with is useful in accounting for the development of individual language repertoires. First in importance are the language practices of the individual's environment. In the home, the choice of languages that household members address to each other and, even more important, the choice of meaningful utterances addressed to the growing child, helps to establish an initial repertoire. These choices depend on two essential features: first, that others are willing to speak to the individual and secondly that the utterances are meaningful.[10] There are societies such as the Kaluli in Papua New Guinea where adults see little point speaking to babies and children (Ochs and Schieffelin, 2001). In such cases, a child's first exposure to meaningful utterances will be speech from older siblings. And there are cases, such as that attested in another New Guinea village (Kulick, 1992), where adults produced meaningless sentences in their local language for babies, but later started using Tok Pisin, the pidgin variety brought back by men from the plantations and adopted in time by women, to give instructions to the children. The result was that children under the age of thirteen were not acquiring the village variety, but shifting to Tok Pisin.

What this suggests is the importance of beliefs or ideology, especially the values that are associated with a variety. A baby recognises that the mother's variety is associated with food and comfort; a pupil recognises that the teacher's variety is associated with success in school; a working adult believes that an international language provides access to better paid work. These beliefs about the value of varieties play a major role in determining the continuing expansion of an individual's speech repertoire.

Self-management

This brings us to the notion of self-management, a concept developed in research on voluntary language learning in international businesses (Nekvapil and Nekula, 2006). In such situations, a worker will notice the need to add a different variety to guarantee promotion: Czech workers in a German-owned factory who wished to become foremen or managers realised that they should learn German and were willing to take private lessons.[11] Self-management occurs when an individual sets out to learn a valuable variety, providing support for the growing global language teaching industry.[12] When collectivised, this can lead to the demand that the public school system teach the language: this is obvious in Asia, with the growing interest in English language teaching (Kweon and Spolsky, 2018) and in the Australian language policy that encouraged the teaching of Chinese and Japanese (Lo Bianco and Wickert, 2001).

Self-management has many similarities to accommodation theory (Giles et al., 1973), but although it is usually considered a positive action, it too can share a negative approach, as in resistance to language learning or to one or more of the efforts of language managers. This shows up in the research

on attitudinal effects on language learning; the research usually finds that
favourable attitudes to the language or its speakers result in better language
learning, but the opposite is also true: unfavourable attitudes act as a block
to success.[13] The decision to succeed in school second language learning or
the decision of an individual to seek an alternative method of acquiring the
language is self-management, influenced by values assigned to the language
and its speakers.[14] Within any speech community, there are likely to be a
number of individuals who select their own repertoire expansion and others
who resist the efforts of language managers, internal or external, who seek to
influence their practices or beliefs.

Belief in the value of proficiency in English is associated with what has
been called the English divide, something which Terasawa (2017) identifies
in Japan, whereby an elite group of citizens in virtually every country of the
world are the ones who develop a high level of proficiency and fluency in
English, which establishes their status. It is a common belief in many countries that, without this proficiency, one is excluded from the highest levels of
employment (Block, 2018).

The individual's potential effect on language management

As one explores the various levels and communities in which language policy
occurs, it will be important to be reminded continually that there are individuals (and often groups of individuals) who have their own beliefs, leading
them to develop individual repertoires different from the majority. Thus, the
language practices and beliefs of a community will always be diverse, producing a sort of chaotic pattern that will constantly challenge simple analysis.
Starting like this with the individual, although it leaves gaps to be filled by
other domains and environments, will provide a better understanding of the
way in which a person's linguistic repertoire expands, as they move into new
and more demanding situations, and the way in which putative managers
at various levels attempt, succeed or fail to shape community repertoires.
Ultimately, the fate of a language policy depends on the ability and willingness of individual members of the speech community to accept it; although
perhaps many speakers are unaware of the importance of language and language choice, without acceptance by members of a speech community, any
attempt at language management is doomed.

Notes

1. My introduction to the field of language policy was while I held a Mellon
   Fellowship at the National Foreign Language Centre in Washington
   founded and directed by Richard D. Lambert. Lambert, a historian by
   training and introduced to languages by the army programme during

the Second World War, saw language policy as the field driving foreign language education.

2. For a while, I was uncomfortable with the notion of self-management proposed by Czech linguists (Neustupný and Nekvapil, 2003) but, as this chapter shows, I have now been convinced of the importance of the individual.

3. Harrington et al. (2001) showed from a study of Christmas broadcasts how Queen Elizabeth's pronunciation changed from year to year, matching similar changes among other English speakers.

4. It was also inspired by the personal policy of our middle grandson, who while he was young, insisted on using English when his older and younger siblings had already shifted to Hebrew.

5. Topolect is a better translation than dialect for *'fāngyán'* to refer to the regional varieties like Cantonese and Hokkien (Mair, 1991). *Ethnologue* (Lewis et al., 2013) recognises thirteen separately coded 'member languages' of Chinese (zho is its ISO 693-3 coding).

6. 'A shprakh iz a dialekt mit an armey un flot' ('a language is a dialect with an army and a navy'), Weinreich (1945) was told by a Bronx high school teacher who was attending one of his classes.

7. The recognition by speakers of significant varieties is the subject studied by perceptual dialectology (Preston, 1999).

8. Languages such as Samoan (Ochs, 1988) and Indonesian and Korean (Chang et al., 2018) have styles using honorifics that mark social relationships.

9. Siridetkoon and Dewaele (2018) show how this can be applied to a third language learned, providing an explanation for multilingualism.

10. Krashen (1981) wrote about the importance of meaningful comprehensible input in language acquisition.

11. Gouin et al. (1892) provide a fascinating account of a French scholar preparing to study in Germany who tried various methods of learning the language (using phrase books, memorising a grammar book and a bilingual dictionary) before discovering his own method (the series) of language learning.

12. The *Global Digital English Language Learning Market Size, Status and Forecast 2025*, published by Wise Guy Reports (Qy Research, 2019), predicts continued growth in the market especially in Asia.

13. I suspect that my own failure in German at university in 1951 was influenced by my growing awareness of the Holocaust.

14. In Israel, there was resistance to the learning of English in the first years after the end of British occupation during the Mandate, finally overcome by the attractions of globalisation.

2 The Family and the Home

Significance of the home

For children not raised in an institutional or collective setting such as an orphanage or a kibbutz children's house, the family home provides the first linguistic environment and its language policy is thus critical. The growing literature on the family, which includes Caldas (2012), Haque and Le Lièvre (2019), Schalley and Eisenchlas (2020), Schwartz (2010) and Spolsky (2012a, 2018a), has been a significant addition to understanding language policy. To appreciate the complexity, it is important to note the diversity and dynamism of the family.

One recent attempt is Walsh (2012), which shows that it is difficult to define a 'normal' family because of the variations found in patterns and size: the nuclear US family considered typical in the 1950s replaced the diverse and varied residential and kinship systems of earlier years but now must be looked at alongside single sex couples and other models, as a result of the changes in gender roles and relationships (such as one and two earner families and non-working males), the diversity of increasingly multicultural societies, the growing disparity in socioeconomic situations and the diversity in arrangements of family life (2012: 10). There is much diversity and change in the USA, with even greater variety when one looks internationally and includes the extended families in Nigeria and elsewhere in sub-Saharan Africa (Oni, 1995) and the child-headed families that Kendrick and Elizabeth (2016) found in Uganda. Everywhere, change is rapid, with an increase of cohabitation without marriage, single parenting, single sex partnerships, changing roles of mothers and fathers, increasing rates of divorce, more children born out of wedlock, changing percentage of step-parents as a result of maternal death, decline in fertility and death rate, continuation of poverty, increases in migration and weakening of religious belief and practice (Abela and Walker, 2014).

What is a family?

This diversity raises a serious problem in attempting to explore family language policy, as families range from a married couple to a group of people living in the same residence or village. Perhaps, it might be best to use a language-related definition, such as the first environment in which a child acquires language. But this misses the childless family, a couple living together and accommodating to each other's speech.

The customs and rules of a couple living together (including a pair of the same sex) vary also from place to place and from time to time. Bumpass and Sweet (1989) report that the US 1987–1988 National Survey of Families and Households showed that nearly half of the persons in their early thirties and half of the recently married had lived together before marriage. There are also traditional communities in which parents arrange marriages and pre-wedding meetings must be in public places; I regularly see ultra-orthodox Jewish courting couples sitting uncomfortably in hotel lounges in Jerusalem.

Often both partners in a married couple come from the same linguistic background, but increasingly in modern diverse cities, they may vary in dialect or in dominant language. In such cases, the accommodation described in the first chapter will be relevant. My wife (from the USA) and I (from New Zealand) both grew up speaking English, but with lexical differences and different accents: I noticed that over time my original pronunciation of medial 't' changed to my wife's 'd' in 'butter'. Any variation, especially in cases of linguistically mixed marriages, sets a need for family language management. This is especially true in societies that practise linguistic exogamy (Fleming, 2016; Jan et al. 2016). Just as there are many societies with incest bans on close kin, and other such as Navajo that forbade contact between those in the same clan,[1] so there are some that do not permit marriage between speakers of the same variety. The published research on family language policy deals mainly with the results of linguistically mixed marriages, produced most commonly by migration including urbanisation.

Migrating families

Migration, Navarro and Macalister (2016) point out, now affects millions of people, who have to face the challenge of integrating into a new language and culture. This is a common focus for studies of family policy. For example, Schüpbach (2009) collected life stories and held interviews with fourteen Swiss German families who had migrated to Australia at different times, finding less transmission of the heritage language at more assimilationist times. Yates and Terraschke (2013) interviewed thirteen newly arrived immigrants to Australia who had married English-speaking partners, finding a greater likelihood that their children would lose the heritage language. The loss of migrant heritage languages is a common finding in research on home language policy.

Exogamy

There has been an increasing number of studies dealing with the importance of family language policy in resisting the rapid shift from indigenous languages (Hale, 1992; Krauss, 1992) and the field is now well established (Schalley and Eisenchlas, 2020; Spolsky, 2008a, 2019a). Most scholars in the field would agree with Fishman (1991: 92) that intergenerational language transmission, a family concern, is the critical factor in ensuring the survival of a language. I have so far concentrated on external pressures, but have also mentioned linguistic exogamy, producing linguistically mixed marriages. With the enormous increase in migration and the relaxation of many traditional constraints on marriage, linguistically mixed marriages (or couples living together) have become increasingly common. An early problem for such a couple is their choice of a language for communication. The formation of a dyadic group is facilitated by ease of communication, so that marriage is most commonly between people speaking the same language, but there are many exceptions (Thibaut and Kelley, 1959). The choice for a bilingual dyad of what to speak to each other depends often on the environment in which they met or in which they live. In a rare small study of five couples one of who was a speaker of Swedish, Johansson (1991) reports that they chose the father's family when living in his country, but code switching was common. For a mixed couple, language choice is an important issue, especially when it come to choosing which language to pass on to offspring. The language policy of mixed marriages has thus become a widely studied question for over a century.

In one of the earliest studies, Ronjat (1913) reported on the development of the one person, one language approach in a family with a French-speaking father and a German-speaking mother. Barron-Hauwaert (2004) surveyed a hundred bilingual families around the world that followed this approach and found reports of success and failure, noting the influence of siblings and school. She lists other strategies, such as speaking the minority language at home, providing support for the language least likely to be learned,[2] or setting a time and place for each.

There are many studies of mixed marriages. Bahalwan (2015) describes an Australian–Indonesian mixed family, noting that children in the same family differed in language preference. De Klerk (2001) studied ten Afrikaans–English mixed marriages in South Africa, finding differing outcomes. Curdt-Christiansen (2013) looked at a number of mixed English–Chinese families in Singapore, noting the various strategies that parents employed. Döpke (1992) observed differences between mothers and fathers in six mixed German–Australian families, noting that environment became increasingly important. In explaining loss in use of Hakka in Taiwan, Jan et al. (2016) found that intermarriage was a major cause. Noting shift from the heritage language, Morris and Jones (2007) described the first stage of a longitudinal study of ten mixed language families in Wales. Novianti (2013) investigated the language policy of Sundanese–Minanghabau merchant families in Bandung, where each parent tried to pass on their culture, but the father was dominant. Comparing mixed marriages in Catalonia and Québec, O'Donnell (2000) noted that linguistic exogamy was favourable to Catalan in Catalonia, but marginally disadvantageous to French in Québec. In Australia, Yates and Terraschke (2013) reported that exogamous immigrants were at a disadvantage. Cheng (2003) studied several generations of mixed marriages of a Chinese family in Singapore.

One special case is the Deaf. If either parents or children are deaf, an appropriate language policy is needed. Pizer (2013) investigated the problem of families with deaf parents and hearing children, which requires the use of both a spoken language and a signed language to maintain successful communication. Although a small set of families included in the study varied in language practice, leading to differences in proficiency in Sign, avoiding language barriers seemed to be a common ideology. McKee and Smiler (2016) considered the problems of a family with a deaf child, who need to develop a policy (with preference for sign or speech or cochlear implants) both within the family and in choice of schooling.

Diasporas and urbanisation

Extensive migration produces diasporas, an important trigger for language shift. One of the largest and most widespread diasporas is of migrants from China (Li, 2016b), but within the borders of the PRC, there is also evidence of a major effect of internal migration and urbanisation on family language policy. The language situation of China is made more complex by the nature of Chinese as a set of topolects, virtually distinct languages united by a long tradition and a common writing system. These topolects have been brought into contact by a 'scale of urbanisation in China ... without precedent in human history' (Seto, 2014); she goes on to report that 'in 1950 13% of people in China lived in cities. By 2010, the urban share of the population had grown to 45% and is projected to reach 60% by 2030'. Migrants from the villages and small towns are exposed to the city topolect, and their ideology and language practices outside and within the home are also under pressure from the State policy promoting Mandarin as Putonghua, the national standard language (Li and Li, 2015b; Spolsky, 2016a), and from the practices, ideology and management of the school. Bingbing et al. (2015) describe schools in Shanghai for migrants from Anhui and other provinces; the teachers almost all supported government policy on Putonghua, but given mobility and lack of financial support for the schools, the students' proficiency in Putonghua remained low.

In the widespread Chinese diaspora (Li, 2016b), the pressures working against a family maintaining the heritage variety come from three sources: the local language situation, the mixture of topolects among the migrants and the fact that any Chinese language education is likely to be in Putonghua. In introducing this topic, which he notes has been little studied, Li (2016a: 8) notes that most Chinese migrants came from regions speaking topolects other than Mandarin, such as Cantonese, Hokkien and Haka. The migrants did not attempt to teach their heritage language to others, but learned the local language; a period of multilingualism was commonly succeeded by loss of the stigmatised heritage variety. When they learned Chinese in school, it was Putonghua and not their heritage topolect.

Many studies look at these diaspora communities.

Studying ten Chinese immigrant families in Québec, Curdt-Christiansen (2013) found that sociopolitical and economic pressures influenced family ideologies, encouraging the learning of English and French, but Chinese remained an identity marker and the way of maintaining Confucian culture. An ethnic Chinese family in Indonesia shifted over three generations, using nine varieties. Ng and He (2004) studied Chinese–English code switching in families in New Zealand and found it more common in grandchildren than in their parents or grandparents. A three-generational shift was also found in the Irish Gaeltacht (Antonini, 2002) and among Malays in Malaysia shifting to English (Burhanudeen, 2003). In Singapore, Curdt-Christiansen (2016) notes, the Chinese community, usually speakers of various topolects like Hokkien, make up 75 per cent of the population, but the state policy declaring English, Mandarin, Malay and Tamil official has led to a double shift: from topolect to Mandarin and from Mandarin to English. Parents now tend to use English and Mandarin to each other, and half of the siblings in the families studied use English to each other; a third use the two varieties. Translanguaging is thus the norm.

Another large diaspora comes from India (Oonk, 2007a), also a hugely multilingual country.

> Modern India, as per the 1961 count, has more than 1652 mother tongues, genetically belonging to five different language families. Apart from them 527 mother tongues were considered unclassifiable at that time . . . The number of multilingual populations is also remarkable. They constitute 19.44% of the total population in India. (Mallikarjun, 2004)

Mahapatra (1990) noted that based on the 1981 census, the fifteen scheduled languages accounted for 95 per cent of the households and Hindi for 40 per cent.

There have been few studies of family language policy in India. One studied three middle or upper class communities speaking Hindi, Bengali or Tamil and living in Delhi; in that case, Sahgal (1991) noted the invasion of English into the home domain. About half of those studied used their mother tongue, but there was little use of Hindi in the Bengali or Tamil families, a result of the greater economic attraction of English (Azam et al., 2013). At the same time, there have been reports in some cases of increased emotional commitments to the mother tongue, not reported before the middle of the nineteenth century (Mitchell, 2009).

In the Indian diaspora, with differences depending on region of origin and local situation, many of the 20 million migrants from South Asia want their children to prosper locally and so encourage them to learn the new language, but some prefer them to maintain their heritage culture and language and marry speakers of their heritage variety (Oonk, 2007a). In the USA, Telugu speakers try to maintain their children's knowledge of the heritage language but find them reluctant to do so (Bhat and Bhaskar, 2007). In East Africa, Oonk (2007b) found, Gujarati was maintained by the second generation of migrants from India, but lost by the third. In the north of England, Conteh et al. (2013) report, Punjabi and Urdu-speaking families take multilingualism for granted, setting up Saturday classes to encourage continued use of the home language.

There have been other studies of mixed families and migrants. Exploring the family language policy of Azerbaijanis, the majority population of the Iranian city of Tabriz, Mirvahedi (2016) found that Azerbaijani was severely challenged by the strength of state and educational language policy requiring Farsi, the national language. This supports the ecology of language paradigm proposed by Haugen (1972).

Family language policy is negotiated and shaped by a combination of internal and external factors (Macalister and Mirvahedi, 2016). Noro (1990) learned that different language ideologies affected the policy of two groups of Japanese immigrants to Toronto, a group that arrived earlier and a later community of those who came under the relaxed immigration law of 1966 together with an increase in the number of Japanese businessmen employed at overseas branches of Japanese firms. The earlier arrivals were supportive of a government-sponsored heritage language programme, but the latter group expressed support for their heritage language by establishing a Japanese Home Classroom and later a Japan Academy. The result is that Japanese children in Toronto show a wide range of Japanese proficiency.

In a study of fourteen Swiss German migrants, Schüpbach (2009) noted that those who migrated during a more assimilationist period in Australia were less likely to pass on their heritage language. The Soviet conquest of Lithuania, Latvia and Estonia introduced large numbers of speakers of Russian and, in over twenty years of independence, there has been a marked change in language use in these families, with increased use of the local language in private and public domains: there is a growing tendency to speak Lithuanian at home and to send children to Lithuanian schools, although Russian remains the most common home language (Ramonienė, 2013). In Scotland, however, religious differences (most Lithuanian immigrants were Catholic and the churches maintained the language) were not strong enough to prevent third-generation loss of language among a comparatively small Lithuanian immigrant community (Dzialtuvaite, 2006). Religious language policy, however, shares with the school support for Irish maintenance in the Gaeltacht (Antonini, 2002). Religion is also an important influence on home language policy among the Fulbe families in the Northern Cameroons studied by Moore (2016) and in immigrant families in New Zealand (Revis, 2016).

External pressures on family policy

External pressure on family language policy comes from a number of sources. Perhaps most relevant is the linguistic environment. In several publications, Harris (1995, 1998, 2011) argued the importance of nurture over nature, describing how peers bring the local language into a household: she presented as evidence the observation that children often speak the heritage language with the same accent that their non-heritage friends use when they learn it at school. She advised parents that the best way to assure that their children do well in school is to choose a neighbourhood where education is encouraged. There are other studies which show the difficulty of parents fighting the environment. The Caldas family, living in Louisiana where there has been a shift from Cajun French (Valdman, 1997) to English, wanted to bring up their three children to be bilingual speakers of French and English, encouraging the process by speaking French at meals. This was far from successful with their son, though his younger sisters were more easily influenced because they were in a bilingual programme at school. What made the difference for their adolescent son were summers spent in Québec; in an environment where French was the dominant language, he would address his father in French in place of the English he used in Louisiana (Caldas, 2006, 2008; Caldas and Caron-Caldas, 2000, 2002).

Former Soviet immigrants in Israel provide a major source for recent studies of family policy. In the 1990s, mass immigration from the Soviet Union to Israel brought in a million migrants, building a Russian-speaking community that made up a fifth of the Israeli population.[3] The immigrants were able to build a Russian social and voluntary educational life (Remennick, 2002), but the pressure of Hebrew hegemony that came from the state educational system encouraged language shift (Spolsky and Shohamy, 1999). In a detailed long-term study using ethnographic observation and interviews, Kopeliovich (2006, 2009, 2011, 2013) looked at the language practices, beliefs and management of one community of immigrants, concentrating on a family whose ten children gave evidence both of parental efforts and of the individual responses of a wide age-range of the children. The parents wanted their children to maintain their heritage Russian alongside their school-mandated Hebrew; the mother did this by urging them to speak Russian, but the father took a neutral but more effective approach by reading them stories in Russian regularly. As the children grew older, they saw less value in Russian, though they accepted that the baby needed to learn it, until in late adolescence, about the time they went into the army, they regretted their low proficiency: the eldest daughter volunteered to work in Russia with potential migrants in order to improve her Russian.[4]

The diversity of cases shows that one cannot deal with family language policy as a closed domain without noting all the external influences that are brought to bear on the home. One internal factor is the mixed marriage. Also internal are choices made in the family, whether by the individual or by the parents or significant others, to select another language. The unmarked case is the language of the parents, with a mixed marriage necessitating a decision on a policy to be followed with offspring. The presence of a significant other may give children a chance to add another variety, such as the heritage language brought by a grandparent, or the language of a servant. For a variety of reasons, parents might decide to add another language, such as a religious variety, or a heritage language, or an international language believed to be economically advantageous.

There are also many external influences that may lead to a different family language policy, such as the language of the environment in the case of urbanisation or migration, where local languages are introduced by the children's peers or schools. Religious leaders may insist on another variety, as in the case of Hasidic rebbes who want their followers to speak Yiddish. Another important influence is provided by the school teachers or social workers who try to persuade parents to use the dominant language. Or some institution or group – an activist movement, or the local or national government – may be trying to modify family language policy. For example, the Māori Language Commission, realising the importance of the family, made influencing home usage a high priority and called on tribal organisations to focus on this task. Because of the importance of the family in establishing the language choice of children, any agency or group aiming to manage language is likely to fail if it does not take the family into account.

Beyond this, the family can attempt to support its language policy outside the home domain. One obvious method is selecting the external linguistic environment: Harris (1995) suggested the best way to influence one's children was choosing a good neighbourhood. This was borne out by the influence of summer visits to Québec by the Caldas family in encouraging their children to speak French (Caldas, 2006). It is the motivation for South Korean 'sojourner' families such as those who go to the United Kingdom (Moon, 2011) or Singapore (Bae, 2013) for a short time, or Korean fathers (*gireogi*

appa or wild geese) who send their families to live in English-speaking countries while they themselves continue to work in Korea (Lee and Koo, 2006).
It was also common for Samoan parents in New Zealand to send their children to family during vacation periods (Spolsky, 1991b). Another strategy is
for a family to send their children to community language weekend schools
(Conteh, 2012; Conteh et al., 2013; Curdt-Christiansen, 2013; Nolan, 2008;
Schwartz et al., 2011).

The importance of the family in language management

Weekend and afternoon schools and other attempts by family members to
find language support for home policy will be discussed in later chapters.
But it is clear that the language policy of the home is an extremely significant
factor and accounts for the difficulties faced by managers at other levels.
The critical importance of the family is shown by the factor of natural intergenerational language transmission, the teaching or the belief of the need to
teach a heritage family variety to babies and young children, as the optimal
condition for language maintenance. In the scales for language survival, this
and the choice of a language of instruction in school are perhaps the two
most powerful predictors of whether a language will continue. Decisions of
the family to use a variety provide the environment in which young learners,
the most flexible and pliant acquirers of language proficiency and fluency, can
most easily expand and develop their linguistic repertoire. Although family
language policy may be challenged by peer pressure and by school policy,
it lays a firm foundation for later language practices. Language managers
and advocates at other levels – teachers, religious leaders, activist groups
and agencies – are coming to realise this and often attempt to influence the
family to select a favoured variety. Speech communities where parents avoid
communication with their offspring are likely to find that their children
have shifted to another variety. Thus, the home policy, strengthened when
the family members unite to provide exposure to their heritage variety, but
strong enough to be effective even when they are unaware, sets a major challenge to management at other levels. Whatever other influences there may
be, it is the language policy of the family and home that sets the basis for an
individual's linguistic repertoire.

Notes

1. Anglo school teachers assumed that the reason Navajo boys and girls
   were reluctant to hold hands was the gender rule they themselves had
   learned; they worked to break it down, which was why older traditional
   Navajos complained that schools led to incest.
2. I am reminded of a Moroccan Jewish head of family who insisted that

Hebrew be the language of the Sabbath meal while the family was still living in Morocco, but who after they had moved to Israel, expected Judeo-Arabic to be spoken.

3. The migrants included speakers of other Soviet languages like Ukrainian and Georgian, most of them bilingual in Russian.

4. Kopeliovich (2013) continues to work with children in the community to encourage bilingualism.

3 Education

Influence of school language

After the family and home, the next domain that attempts to modify an individual's linguistic repertoire is the school, taking advantage of the comparative ease of pre-adolescent language learning. Starting when the child enters pre-school or first grade, the next years expose a child to the school's selected language of instruction, the language or languages used by fellow students and the foreign or additional languages included in the curriculum. Given the impact of this exposure, perhaps the major factor in language shift, a significant question becomes who determines school language policy: the manager may be the national or regional government, a local school board, a religious authority, the parents or the teacher. Each of these can have a different ideology and goal.

I was uncertain as to whether education or religion should be the chapter after the home until I remembered that schools were commonly established to teach literacy in sacred languages in order to pass on religious beliefs. The Mesopotamian scribal schools such as those in Sumer were intended for bureaucrats (Foster, 1982), but they were later charged with the preservation of sacred texts (Tov, 2018). Jewish, Christian and Muslim schools were all under religious control, starting with teaching the appropriate sacred language. The return to secularised education in Christian Western Europe can be dated to the French Revolution, when Church schools were taken over by the State. The fading of religious observance especially in Western Europe has left an ideological gap that is being filled by nationalism, with subsequent influence on choice of language of instruction. In this chapter then, I will include religious schooling for children, leaving the focus on religious language policy for adults to a later chapter.

Language education is a vast topic – I have edited an encyclopaedia (Spolsky, 1999) and a handbook (Spolsky and Hult, 2008) as well as a two collections on bilingual education (Spolsky and Cooper, 1977, 1978) and many articles and chapters on the topic – so this chapter will be limited to an overview of the main issues and some illustrative cases. I start, as the three-component model suggests, with a sketch of the current situation, then consider relevant beliefs and ideologies and try to sum up approaches to management. This will of course require moving outside the educational system to explore other managers, but the key focus will be on the education system which constitutes the first major challenge to family language policy as well as serving as the favourite tool of language managers. What then is the overall picture?

Importance of school language of instruction

In two important studies, Walter (2003, 2008) has summarised evidence that the choice of language of instruction has a major effect on the effectiveness of schooling. He estimated that for at least a third of the children in school (ignoring the increasing mass of children without schooling living in or migrating from war-torn or dangerous countries), school is conducted in a language that they do not understand. Walter and Benson (2012) make this even clearer. There were, according to Grimes (1996), 6,833 spoken languages in the world, but no more than 599 languages that are used in education (Walter and Benson, 2012: 283). As a result, more than 2.3 billion people, nearly 40 per cent of the world's people, are 'potentially negatively affected by official policy on language use in education' (Walter and Benson, 2012: 282).

The largest effect of language education policy is that it forces children to learn a new variety in order to understand their teachers, something which research shows can take up to seven years (Levin et al., 2003; Shohamy et al., 2002). Adding to this are differences in dialect; children in Belgium come to school having grown up with a local Dutch or French dialect and need to learn the standard Dutch or French of the school (Aunger, 1993).

The effectiveness of a school language policy may be weakened by the need or willingness of many teachers to ignore official policy and use the local variety. I first observed this gap between policy and practice on a trip to Micronesia where I was told that the teaching was in English; as I walked around a school, I heard teachers conducting their classes in Ponapean, though their textbooks were in English. Palestinian teachers are reported to use the spoken variety and not the Classical or Standard Arabic laid down. This disregard for official policy is made possible by the normally impenetrable classroom – four walls, a teacher and a bunch of students, invaded occasionally by a principal who uses a loudspeaker system to listen to what is happening. When teachers switch to the children's variety – and they are now being encouraged to do this by scholars who favour what they call translanguaging (García and Li, 2013; Li, 2018a; MacSwan, 2017; Otheguy et al., 2015) – the school is opened to the languages of the home. Otherwise, the situation is what I observed during my first visit to a huge Bureau of

Indian Affairs boarding school in the middle of the Navajo Reservation: the Anglophone teachers speaking English and the Navajo children, 90 per cent of whom had never heard that language before they came to school (Spolsky, 1970), not listening.[1] Walter and Benson (2012) estimate that many major languages, forty-five of the ninety-seven languages with over 10 million speakers amounting to over a billion speakers in all, are not used in schools.

International or global languages like English, French, Standard Arabic, Spanish, German and Portuguese are supported at all educational levels, including where they are not the language spoken at home (Coupland, 2011). Other major languages like Dutch, Russian, Mandarin Chinese, Turkish, Japanese, Korean and Japanese are languages of instruction in their own countries, but increasingly challenged by international languages (especially English) at the higher levels of education (Ammon, 2001). The lowest categories (undeveloped national languages like Aymara and Malagasy; subnational languages like Ilocano and localised oral languages like Otomí in Mexico or Yi in China) are rarely used in education; this, Skutnabb-Kangas and Phillipson (2010) argue, is probably the main cause of language shift and death, especially in the case of indigenous languages (Magga et al., 2005).

Variation in school language practice

When we ask what are the language practices of schools and the educational establishment, we need to consider the differences among communities and sub-domains. Pupils in the playground commonly continue to use their home language or the local neighbourhood variety, though Rampton (2014) has drawn attention to what he calls crossing, 'the use of Panjabi by adolescents of African-Caribbean and Anglo descent, the use of Creole by adolescents with Panjabi and Anglo backgrounds'. In the classroom, the teacher is expected to use the school language, though there are many exceptions and the pupils are required to speak it too when called on. After years of being praised for speaking – parents celebrate the child's first word – a child is expected to learn that at school the teacher controls turn-taking and language. In some schools, such as in former British colonies, a local language is allowed as language of instruction for the first few years, but generally, by the secondary level at the latest, the standard language is officially prescribed. At some stage, usually the secondary level but increasingly earlier, under the pressure of globalisation and ambitious parents, one or two foreign languages may be added to the curriculum for a few hours a week. At the university level, more and more courses may be taught in a global language. Underlying this highly varied set of practices, there are a number of common beliefs and ideologies. Summarising these will help understanding of the complexity of language policy.

Scribal elite schools and Hebrew popular literacy

But first some historical background. I have already mentioned two religious educational goals: the bureaucratic training of scribes and providing access to religious texts for lay-people. Both focus on a form of language other than the common speech. The scribal schools trained a small number of clerks able to keep records of laws or property, or transmit decrees or other official documents. There were in the ancient Middle East nine law codes, like the Hammurabic code, written in cuneiform in a number of languages including Sumerian and Hittite (Westbrook, 1985). In Egypt, the writing was hieroglyphic script and scribes recorded stocks held, taxes, court proceedings, contracts and wills. All this was a key part of the bureaucracy that enabled the working of the kingdoms. Training a scribe took several years and was restricted to an elite (Williams, 1972).

There were also scribes in Biblical Judah, trained probably in scribal schools and responsible for copying (and perhaps editing and composing) the Biblical and other texts, including those found at the Dead Sea (Tov, 2018). Wang (2014) reports the contribution of scribes to the development of ancient states in China, the Near East and the Americas. Scribes were not just trained in literacy, but also in accounting (Ezzamel, 1997) and mathematics (Trouche, 2016). The administrative value of literacy was recognised in nineteenth-century Tonga and quickly applied to sending out royal decisions (Martin, 1817; Spolsky et al., 1983). In China, the Imperial Examination system for 2,000 years controlled entry to an administrative elite (Elman, 2000).

Popular literacy education was rarer. One of the most notable cases was when, in the period after the destruction of the Temple by the Romans, literacy in Hebrew was set as a goal for all male Jewish children. Until the destruction of the Temple, Jews had two ways to observe their religion: by sending a sacrifice to the Temple or by studying the written Law. After the Romans destroyed the Temple, only the second was possible. The rabbis then called for all six-year-old boys to be taught to read Hebrew. In practice, this was limited to those whose families could afford to spare them from farming tasks and who could share in paying a teacher. As a result, whereas in the first century there were nearly 6 million Jews, by 650 CE just over 1 million remained; the massive demographic change was also partly explained by massacres and forced migration. But literate Jewish males were able to benefit professionally and commercially especially with the growth of cities and trade (Botticini and Eckstein, 2012). Ability to read the Qur'an was of value in Islam, but memorisation was emphasised. In Christian communities, literacy was for a long time restricted to clerics and popular literacy developed much later.

Traditional Indian and medieval European schooling

In India, the earliest Vedic system of education focused on oral learning of the religious texts; later, schooling was restricted to the Brahman caste and conducted in Sanskrit. Buddhism established large monasteries in which monks were admitted on the basis of personal merit, ignoring caste; the language of instruction was usually Pali, a classical liturgical language, or one of the Prakrit languages. There was limited education for common people. Under Muslim rule, there were *maktabs* in which younger children were taught Arabic and Persian Language and script and *madarsas* for advanced education; other languages were not used. The main goal of education was religious and education became compulsory for boys (Sharma and Sharma, 1996).

In the Western world, with the gradual replacement of Latin by the vernaculars, universal literacy (male at first) became a general goal, but the Classical languages were replaced by the official standard languages, producing new barriers for speakers of non-standard varieties. In France, the promotion of the Parisian standard was encouraged by Richelieu as a means of supporting central rule (Cooper, 1989) and the same political ideology underlay the policies of the Jacobins during the French Revolution and of French governments since. Wright (2012: 62) cites a speaker at the Convention in 1794: 'Chez un people libre, la language doit être une et la même pour tous [For a free people, the language must be one and the same for all].' Schooling was to be in standard French only, although it took almost a century for there to be enough qualified teachers to implement the goal. The same policy was applied in the French colonies, where only a minority benefited (Spolsky, 2019c). By the nineteenth century, a common definition of a nation was a state with one people, one territory and one language. This obviously worked as a counterforce to diversity and to any individual or family or ethnic group that wanted to maintain its heritage variety.

Economic pressure on schooling

There were economic motivations for monolingualism. At the national level, language diversity lowers the efficiency of communication, so that choosing a single language is assumed to be economically advantageous (Grin, 1996a, 1999). Because different states have different national languages, firms that wish to do business internationally need to have employees with proficiency in customer languages. Grin et al. (2010) developed a model that shows both the economic advantages of other language skills in multilingual Québec and Switzerland and the value of multilingualism to businesses. This belief in the potential value of skills particularly in English but also other dominant languages accounts for the pressure that parents put on school systems to teach their children a global language even at the cost of the local variety, though as Bruthiaux (2008) noted, in poorer countries local languages and regional varieties are of more use in the informal economy in which half of them will be employed.

Grin et al. (2010) argued that the cost of language education should probably be shared between individuals, businesses and the state depending on the benefit accrued. In a study of the cost-effectiveness of mother-tongue education in Africa, Alidou et al. (2006) estimate a start-up cost of 1 to 5 per cent of the national education budget, but point out that over time these costs will be absorbed and made up by lowering the rate of pupil retention and class repetition. But costs are difficult to estimate and Grin (2005: 13) concluded, 'It follows then that even a high-cost policy can be perfectly reasonable on economic grounds, if the outcome is "worth it"; and paying for something which is worth paying for is a quintessentially sound economic decision.' But without government or other support, setting up parent-run language schools or programmes is neither easy nor cheap.[2]

National unity and heritage identity

A common modern motivation for choosing a language for a national school system is unity. Deciding to have one language in a nation is a first step; the second is which language it should be. In the unmarked case, it is the dominant language, the language spoken by the majority. But often, it was the language of the ruling group that was chosen – thus, Parisian French was chosen by Richelieu, Castilian Spanish in Spain, Urdu in Pakistan, High German in Germany and Austria, the Mandarin topolect in China, Amharic in Ethiopia and Kiswahili in Tanzania. This choice, backed by patriotic and historical claims, left the excluded language speakers to form activist groups calling for recognition and inclusion in school policy – Breton and Occitan in France, Catalan and Basque in Spain, Sindhi and regional varieties like Punjabi in Pakistan (and the speakers of Bengali seceded to form Bangladesh), other topolects like Cantonese and Haka in China, Tigrinya and Oromo in Ethiopia, Bantu and Nilotic languages in Tanzania. In many cases, a non-local language was chosen to avoid granting power to the speakers of a large local language: this accounts for the choice of Malay in Indonesia and the pressure for English in India.

In rare cases, a nation chooses to be bilingual (English and French in Canada, Afrikaans and English in the apartheid Union of South Africa) or multilingual (nine African languages added in South Africa; Dutch and French and German in Belgium; French and German and Italian and Romansch in Switzerland). In each of these cases, there is likely to be pressure for bilingual or multilingual education, often limited regionally. Belgian language policy is territorial, with only Brussels bilingual; each region chooses one of the standard languages for education, although children commonly speak the local dialect. Switzerland too is territorially divided and India was sub-divided into states to match the major linguistic patterning, setting the basis for the three language policy developed in 1957 but seldom implemented (Mohanty et al., 2010).

With recent growth in nationalist feelings, national language policy reflects the political situation: just as the Scandinavian nations created national varieties from mutually intelligible varieties, so after the break-up of Yugoslavia, each of the new states chose to replace Serbo-Croatian with its own renamed modified variety as the national language. National pride was a source of language policy in the nineteenth century, leading to the propagation of new national languages for countries achieving independence from former empires (Wright, 2012). This was challenged by globalisation (Wright, 2016) promoting English and other international languages. In many postcolonial nations, choosing a local language was prevented by the inertia that maintained colonial languages in education and as official, something that was true especially of African countries (Kamwangamalu, 2016). This helped those leaders who had benefited from the elitist colonial schools to maintain power (Myers-Scotton, 1993). The struggle between colonial French and nationalist Arabic continues in North Africa (Daoud, 2011; Sirles, 1999). In Southeast Asian postcolonial nations like Vietnam (Wright, 2002) and Malaysia and Thailand (Kosonen, 2009; Rappa and Wee, 2006), local national languages were re-established as official and as languages of instruction, though challenged by globalisation and English. Wee (2003) discusses the development in Singapore of what he calls 'linguistic instrumentalism', and the local languages, once seen as representing cultural and traditional values in contrast to the English which is valued on economic and technological terms, are now seen as commodifiable resources (Heller, 2010a) and so economically valuable.

An alternative motivation for language education policy is the belief in the value of a heritage traditional language (or language and culture) associated with an ethnic or regional group, with a goal of reclaiming or maintaining identity. This is expressed by the language activist movements for schooling in Basque, Catalan, Yiddish, Irish, Māori and many other languages and will be discussed in Chapter 10. It is often behind the efforts to provide schooling in threatened and indigenous varieties and was particularly strong during the 1960s and 1970s (Fishman et al., 1985), leading to a flourishing but temporary bilingual education movement (Crawford, 1999; Fishman and Lovas, 1970; Lewis, 1980; Paulston, 1988; Spolsky, 1978).

Schooling that pays attention to the language needs of minority groups is supported also by belief that it is a universal human right. This is set out in some regional and international charters, such as the 1992 European Charter for Regional or Minority Languages (Oellers-Frahm, 1999) and the Universal Declaration of Linguistic Rights (Phillipson and Skutnabb-Kangas, 1995; Skutnabb-Kangas and Phillipson, 2017). These rights are also written in many national constitutions (Covell, 1993; Halaoui, 2000; Jones, 2002; Shabani, 2007). Rights will be discussed in Chapter 11.

The home–school language gap

Research has produced convincing evidence for the value of including the student's home language in the school. Collier and Thomas (2004; Thomas and Collier, 2002) showed this for the United States. Walter (2003, 2008) presents evidence of the importance of the language of instruction and Walter and Davis (2005) report on how this works in Eritrea. Benson (2000; Heugh et al., 2007; King and Benson, 2003) reports on similar evidence from Mozambique, Bolivia, Ecuador and Ethiopia. Teaching initial reading in Navajo led to improved educational outcomes in a school in the USA (Holm and Holm, 1990; Rosier and Holm, 1980). Some systems have chosen this belief as a guide, but it is opposed by those who choose the use of elite languages (Walter and Benson, 2012: 287). This common ignoring of the value of initial education in the child's home language means, as mentioned earlier, that 40 per cent of children come to school not knowing the language in which their teachers will speak to them. Given the evidence that it takes on average six or seven years for a non-school-language speaker to become fully proficient in the school language, these children are permanently behind in their studies and so discriminated against.

Different beliefs are held by the many stakeholders in the educational system, ranging from the individual teachers and the school's parents to those international organisations with concern for human rights. However, as Lo Bianco (2008: 113) argues, educational systems are

> principally the property of states. Even if authority is devolved to semi-autonomous bodies such as religious, ideological, regional-ethnic, or other parent-controlled agencies for the delivery of schooling, or higher or specialised education, states typically license, authorise, fund or certify educational practices.

He suggests that states tend to have eight language-related aims at the secondary school level: to add proficiency in reading and writing to the repertoire of the majority of the children, to add standard language norms to non-standard speakers, to teach academic registers and styles, to teach the national standard language to immigrants and indigenous groups, to add specialisation in the disciplinary variety of particular fields, to provide standard language proficiency for children with special needs such as deafness or blindness, to occasionally make concessions to learners with non-standard backgrounds and to teach prestige, strategic or status languages. The relative weight attached to the implementation of these goal varies from nation to nation.

Although there are exceptions where the national government recognises bilingualism or multilingualism as an educational goal, it is generally the case that its first concern is with literacy and proficiency in the national standard language, with a second priority being given to economically important global languages. This is obvious in Europe, where members of the European Community favour their own national language, but then assume that the first foreign language will be English. For this reason, the European Union calls for teaching a second foreign language. A few countries recognise indigenous minority languages but the European Union has not yet recognised the many immigrant languages starting to change the demography of European nations.[3]

An important question is how strong and effective is central management of language education. In English-speaking countries, it is generally assumed that the standard language can be taken for granted, though there are groups in the USA that would like English to be established constitutionally or legally, fearing the effect of continuing large-scale Spanish-speaking immigration. Many countries have established their standard language in this way, following the example of France which has struggled to weaken regional varieties and dialects since the days of Cardinal Richelieu. But the persistence of regional varieties, like Breton and Occitan and Catalan and Basque in France and of Basque and Catalan in Spain and of Welsh and Gaelic in Britain and the survival of indigenous languages in the Americas, show that central policy is not easy to implement (Spolsky, 2006a, 2006b).

Who sets policy for schools?

Even in totalitarian countries like China (Spolsky, 2016a) and Russia (Grenoble, 2003), support for non-standard varieties continues to challenge national monolingualism. But, as will be detailed in Chapter 10, there have been powerful language managers at the head of states: Cardinal Richelieu in France, Kemal Ataturk in Turkey, Reza Shah Pahlavi in Persia, Lee Kuan Yew in Singapore, Manuel L. Quezon in the Philippines and Kim Il-sung in North Korea; each of them set out to establish new language policies including school language policy. But usually, language education policy at the national level is under the purview of a minister of education, unless there is a national agency for language policy, like the State Language Commission in the People's Republic of China or the State Language Inspectorate in Latvia, two examples to which the term 'language police' is applied. Sometimes, authority over education is passed by the constitution or the central government to a state or provincial government. This can lead to major differences: in India for example, where the states are responsible for 90 per cent of the costs of education, the low level of national literacy (65 per cent in 2001) is accounted for by six large northern states which include 75 per cent of the children out of school or that have below five years of elementary education (Mehrotra, 2006). The weakness of public education helps to explain why so many children are sent to private schools – one sees private English-medium schools in every town in India, though the quality of teaching is not guaranteed – which have slightly better results (Goyal and Pandey, 2009).

In the USA, states are constitutionally responsible for education and set standards and policy, but the federal government has worked to influence schools by funding, such as through the Bilingual Education Act. But there is further decentralisation: in the 2002 Census of Governments (US Census Bureau, 2004), the United States Census Bureau found over 13,000 school district governments as well as nearly 180 state-dependent school systems and 1,330 local-dependent school systems. In Canada, each province is responsible for public education and is divided into educational districts governed by a superintendent and a local board of education. In Germany, education is the responsibility of the Länder (the states). In England, there are over 150 local authorities for education and in Wales there are over twenty. In New Zealand, each of the 2,550 state schools now has its own board of trustees.

Regional or local governments and local school boards may be permitted to choose language education policies that support or contradict those of the central government. There are other sources of interference with state policy. At the beginning of the chapter, I mentioned religious influences. Often, schools come under the direct control of religious authorities. Jones (1983) describes the problems of Muslim schools in Java, which require the teaching and learning of Arabic in Arabic script, Javanese (the native language of 40 per cent of the population of the island of Java) in both Arabic and Javanese script, Javanese in Arabic script, Malay in Arabic script and Indonesian in Latin script. Leibowitz (1970) traces religious influences on American education: until the end of the nineteenth century, when public schools stopped teaching German immigrants in German, parochial schools were established to continue the language policy, leading to political struggles especially in Illinois and Wisconsin. Lutherans maintained German until the 1920s when state governments started making English the compulsory language of instruction.

Opposition to Asian immigrants affected schools in the USA. In Hawaii until 1920, many private schools (Christian or Buddhist) taught in Chinese, Japanese or Korean. A 1920 Act limited this to one hour a day and required all teachers to be proficient in English; attacks on these schools continued. Japanese schools survived in California, but were closed after Pearl Harbor. Spanish schools, often parochial, in New Mexico, California and Texas were similarly under attack. The Catholic schools in California opposed the imposition of English but in 1870 English was required in all schools. When Mexico ceded the territory to the United States, New Mexico recognised Spanish, but in 1891 all schools were required to teach in English, as part of a struggle over power and land between Anglo settlers and Mexican

Americans. In colonial situations like the French and Portuguese and British Empires, missionaries often supported the use of local vernaculars in religious schools, but were soon overruled by administrators.

Jewish religious education started early and priests were responsible for teaching literacy, but the rabbis argued that it was a father's responsibility to teach his sons to read Hebrew. This became particularly important after the destruction of the Second Temple and a widespread educational system developed, with boys at the age of five or six brought to small local schools for instruction in the Hebrew of the Bible and the Hebrew-Aramaic of the Talmud; at the age of sixteen, many would go on to yeshivas in large cities for further Talmudic study (Jacobs, 1893). The language of instruction would be the local Jewish vernacular (such as Yiddish or Ladino or Judeo-Arabic), but the goal was literacy in Hebrew and Hebrew-Aramaic. The major religious goal for Jewish language education was access to texts in the sacred languages, but an effect was the training of literate adults able to conduct business.

There are other sources of language management and advocacy in the schools. Armies, navies, air forces and intelligence agencies have language needs that lead them to develop their own schools and training programmes. We will deal with this in detail in Chapter 6, but here we will note some cases of efforts to influence language teaching in the schools and universities. During the Second World War, the US Army, influenced by congressmen whose colleges and universities were suffering from the recruitment of male students, persuaded the army to start the Army Specialised Training Program which included a well-publicised but ultimately ineffective programme to teach a number of foreign languages on college campuses to soldiers. Few of the graduates were employed in the many languages they learned because of the demands for infantry in Europe (Spolsky, 1995). After the shock of the Soviet success of Sputnik, the US Congress responded with the National Defence Education Act which aimed to support the teaching of relevant foreign languages in US schools and colleges. One goal was to replace the traditional study of French and German with the teaching of languages like Russian and Chinese (Brecht and Rivers, 2000, 2012; Brecht and Walton, 1994). An outstanding case of military support for school language teaching is provided by the continued encouragement of the teaching of Arabic in Israel (Mandel, 2014).

The industrial and business communities also play an important part in influencing school language policy. Ball (2012) analyses the efforts of the business community to encourage educational reform in England with the goal of producing literate employees. One of the clearest examples of economic motivation for school language policy is provided by Singapore, where the choice of English and Mandarin was part of a policy of economic development (Silver, 2005). In Australia, a national policy on languages that focused on multiculturalism was replaced by a policy that concentrated on teaching Asian and Pacific languages with assumed economic benefit (Liddicoat, 2009). Wright (2002) shows how economic and political pressures led to changes in Vietnam from teaching Russian to teaching English. In the twentieth century, the centrality of the USA to the world's global economy established English as a global language and meant that most foreign language teaching became teaching English as a foreign language.

There has in contrast been a widespread tendency to decentralise control of education. The 1988 Education Reform Act in England and Wales maintained local management but kept central curriculum control; at the same time, it increased a commercial approach to education (Bowe et al., 2017). In the same year, there was a major change in New Zealand, with each primary school coming under the authority of its own local school board (Lange, 1988), but central curriculum control was maintained. Parents were generally satisfied but school principals found funding inadequate and staffing a problem (Wylie, 1997).

The New Zealand reform was perhaps in part inspired by the example of Māori parents who had since 1980 been setting up pre-school and primary level programmes as part of an effort to regenerate the language which was no longer being spoken by children (Spolsky, 2005, 2009b). The first two steps in that process were an adult level revival programme, *Te Ataarangi*, intended to teach young university students their heritage language and a pre-school programme, *Kōhanga Reo*, which used grandparents to teach the language to their young grandchildren. When these children were ready for regular school, the parents looked for a local state school that would continue immersion in Māori; failing this, some started independent schools (*Kura Kaupapa Māori*) to do this. The reform which established local control of primary schools allowed these schools to be come charter schools funded by the state.

Language education policy working

New Zealand afforded one example of schools that took on the task of language revitalisation. Another example is Scotland, where a Gaelic revitalisation programme began in elementary schools in 1985, producing a tiny group of new Gaelic speakers (Dunmore, 2019). There are many others, some described in a collection of papers from a 2005 symposium (Hornberger, 2008). In Norway, starting in 1959, community pressure led to a series of educational reforms that brought the Sámi language into schools, reversing a century or more of Norwegianisation; the language is now used in three kinds of schools, maintenance, transitional and foreign language (Hirvonen, 2008). But Huss (2008) found the results depressing, as there continued to be strong opposition to Sámi in many regions.

In Latin America, where indigenous peoples make up about 10 per cent of the population, by the 1990s there was recognition of indigenous culture and language, with pressure from communities for intercultural bilingual education leading to some success but also arousing opposition. At the same time, there have been attempts at building a plural society, marked in Bolivia in 2005 by the election of an indigenous person who is now in his fourth term as president (López, 2008). In New Zealand, the Māori-medium programme has had significant success in its twenty years of operation, but important challenges remain (May and Hill, 2008). In Mexico, there has been considerable progress in bilingual education programmes for indigenous groups, but the example of Hñähñö, large numbers of whom have migrated to Mexico City, shows the great problems produced by discrimination and lack of resources that block successful bilingual education (Recendiz, 2008).

Kamwangamalu (2008) sums up developments in Africa. Except in Somalia, Ethiopia and North Africa (and to a lesser extent in Tanzania and Madagascar), attempts at vernacularisation, replacing the former colonial languages with indigenous African languages, have largely failed, with instrumental economic arguments outweighing cultural values. Spolsky (2008b) argues that the success of Hebrew in Israel maintained for 2,000 years as a sacred and literary language and revitalised by school policies has not been repeated in other cases: school can help, but strong support in the home and community are needed. McCarty (2008) agrees with Spolsky that schools cannot do it alone, but with other social institutions can help to keep heritage languages alive.

But school systems can also resist efforts to recognise the languages and language preferences of pupils and parents. One detailed study of private schools in Quetta, Pakistan (Manan et al., 2016) shows how this works. Few pupils bring Urdu or English from home, where 90 per cent of the children speak sixty different languages, but by severe management intervention – notices, wall paintings, penalties and occasional punishment – the pupils are forced to accept the school and state policy. The use of punishment to suppress stigmatised languages in school has been reported often and in many places (Sallabank, 2011: 281) – the Welsh stick to beat a child heard speaking the language (Byram, 2018: 37), the washing out the mouth of Navajo children (Spolsky, 1975), Breton (Adkins, 2013) and Occitan (Manzano, 2004) in France, are some attested cases. In English-medium private schools in India, students are said to be punished for speaking in their home language (Mohanty, unpublished). The Havana Declaration on Indigenous Languages[4] includes the following:

> We denounce the punishment and supposed 'correction' practices perpetrated on indigenous children and teenagers for speaking their mother-tongues and being themselves, as well as the poverty, the imposition of a single language and culture, the forced assimilation, epistemic and linguistic violence suffered by indigenous peoples.

Schools have played a major role in the shift from Navajo to English. Lee and McLaughlin (2001) pointed out that only 10 per cent of the schools with Navajo pupils are under control of local Navajo communities or of the Navajo Nation. Of these, only half a dozen have had an emphasis on Navajo language maintenance, the most successful being Rock Point where children were taught literacy in Navajo before English (Holm and Holm, 1990; Rosier and Holm, 1980) and Rough Rock (McCarty, 2002). But, as Holm and Holm (1995) admit, this did not lead other schools to follow them. Most schools on the reservation come under the control of the appropriate state department of education;[5] as a result, although the teaching staff is now largely Navajo,[6] the curriculum is under non-Navajo control. Even when there are Navajos on the school board, the school is under state law and policies. As a result, only 10 per cent of Navajo children are now being taught in their heritage language or about their culture. There is a Navajo immersion programme at Fort Defiance (Arviso and Holm, 2001; Benally and Viri, 2005) showing better results for pupils in the bilingual than those in the monolingual programme.

A similar tendency is shown in the loss of Spanish by Puerto Rican pupils in New York City schools (García et al., 2001). Puerto Ricans make up a large but unidentified part of the 355,000 Latino students in the schools, 100,000 of whom were reported in 1992 to be English learners (García et al. 2001: 67). In the 1970s, there were transitional Puerto Rican bilingual programmes, but by the end of millennium, most had been replaced by Dual Language programmes where the goal was to use native speakers of English to make the rest of the class proficient in English; most of the English-speakers in these classes were reported to be second- and third-generation Puerto Ricans fluent in English and the remainder Dominicans, Mexicans and Central and South Americans. By 2000, a high school certificate would only be awarded to a student who pass the English Language regents' examination.

A secular Yiddish school movement in the USA was at its peak in the early twentieth century, but by the 1970s most Yiddish language secular study was restricted to university and adult programmes (Avineri, 2012). Among ultra-orthodox Jews, however, Yiddish remains the language of instruction in many Hasidic schools, where boys are expected to start using the language at the age of six. Under full control of their communities, these schools often downgrade or neglect the state school curriculum, teaching Talmud using Yiddish. In Israeli Hasidic boys' schools, Hebrew is used a little in early grades and sometimes for secular subjects, but girls' schools mainly have Hebrew as language of instruction and teach classes in Yiddish (Bogoch, 1999). Schools play an important role in maintaining the Yiddish language in Haredi communities in Antwerp, USA, Israel and Britain.

Québec schools provide an interesting example of the complexity of language education policy. In Canada, each province establishes its own system. In Québec, the government mandated two religiously associated school boards, one Catholic and one Protestant. Before Bill 101 was passed in 1976, each had its own language policy. The Catholic schools used French as language of instruction, but there was a small number of schools for Irish Catholics using English, and the Protestant Board ran English-medium schools, with some schools using French for Huguenots. Each taught the other language as a foreign language. In the 1960s, a group of parents of children in a Protestant school in the St Lambert district of Montréal felt that the teaching of French in the schools was inadequate and wanted their children to become bilingual. With advice from two professors at McGill University (Wallace Lambert in Psychology and Wilder Penfield from the Neurological Institute), they managed to persuade the school board to allow them to start an experimental immersion programme; in 1965, the first experimental kindergarten class started with twenty-six pupils. Continued parental pressure led to the spread of the programme to higher grades with a follow-up programme in high school and reports of success led to its diffusion throughout Québec and in many other provinces (Genesee, 1988). A second set of pressures on Québec schools was political: in 1976, the pro-independence Parti Québécois passed Bill 101, the Charter of the French Language, as a way of raising the standard of the language and reversing the ongoing shift of Francophones to English. This law and a series of later legislation restricted attendance at English-medium schools to those whose parents had attended such schools in the Province, thus preventing Francophones and immigrants from choosing English education. Combined with other legal requirements, such as use of French in businesses and publicity, the government intervention in the schools guaranteed the survival of the French language in the Province (Bourhis, 1984).

The power of a school system to lead to language loss is widely attested. 'Schooling in Spanish is probably the main cause of language shift', writes Lastra (2001: 152), describing the major Mexican language, Otomí. In Africa, 'The educational domain was and still is, a major arena for the language shift pull . . . many children who have been to school have completely shifted away from their mother tongues to the English language' (Adegbija, 2001: 285). 'Ainu is not taught in any primary or secondary public schools of the Japanese educational system' notes Maher (2001: 341). And school-based instruction in order to preserve a language is doomed to failure, unless there is a society in which the language can function '*before* school begins, *outside* of school during the years of schooling and afterwards' concludes Fishman (2001: 471). 'Schools cannot successfully counter social, economic and political force' (Paulston, 1988: 3).

But parents and linguists and language activists who believe that they can help are the main agents who advocate and work for language maintenance. Although most agree that the policy of the home is critical, revitalisation movements usually focus on the school. However, a generation of children taught Welsh and Māori in school do not seem to speak it outside or pass it on to their own children (Sallabank, 2011: 282).

Standard versus vernacular language in schools

A first significant question in schools is which language is chosen as language of instruction and target. One dimension of this issue is the choice between standard language and vernacular. It is common for the school to mandate use of the standard language even though students (and often teachers) normally speak a stigmatised vernacular variety. Only rarely do you find a case like Norway, which mandated teaching literacy in two standard varieties (Bokmål and Nynorsk) without interfering with the pupils' local dialects; more common are cases like Fiji where the missionaries chose to develop literacy in the easternmost Bauan dialect producing problems for the speakers of the many other dialects, some with fewer that 60 per cent cognate words (Schütz, 1985). This difficulty is faced by Iraqi Kurdish activists in trying to develop a standard that will be acceptable to speakers of the two major varieties. A similar problem is faced by Quechua activists in Peru, where there are two major varieties (Coronel-Molina, 2008, 2015). One of the main reasons for choosing Classical Arabic over Egyptian or other local varieties was Pan-Arabism (Suleiman, 1994, 1996). In New Zealand, in contrast, the Māori Language Commission aiming to develop tribal support of home language use encourages the tribes to discover and recognise dialect differences. But choosing among unstandardised vernacular dialects as the school language is often a major problem.

Bilingual education

There developed many kinds and patterns of bilingual education to deal with the need to maintain home languages while teaching the school standard. Mackey (1970) described the theoretically possible models: 'medium (single *vs.* dual) maintenance, transfer (acculturation *vs.* irredentism) and transition (gradual *vs.* abrupt)', each further divided by 'five types of school-home relation and nine types of school-environment relations'. The first set of distinctions refers to the two kinds of time allocations to each language: the number of hours per week (ranging from immersion – 100 per cent use of a language – to once a week) and the number of years in the educational pattern (starting in pre-school or school year and lasting until which school year). But in the USA, now, bilingual education has been outlawed in some states and replaced by programmes which aim to produce monolingual English competence.

A key factor in choice of school language policy is who is the manager or how successful are the language advocates (Spolsky, 2020b); this will be discussed further in Chapter 10. Lacking direct authority over the school system, parents and communities can build support for home language policy by providing out-of-school activities. When parents or the community set up their own language maintenance or revival programmes, one common model is the pre-school programme, as exemplified by the New Zealand Māori *Kōhanga Reo* (J. King, 2001). Another is the after-school or weekend community school, associated principally with religious groups, such as the Hebrew schools in diaspora communities (Spolsky, 2016b) or the Greek Orthodox (Bailey and Cooper, 2009) schools in the USA or the Muslim schools in Britain (Meer, 2009). There are also the diaspora ethnic schools such as the Chinese (Li, 2005) and Japanese (Shibata, 2000) diaspora schools in the USA and the afternoon and evening programmes for the children of former Soviet immigrants in Israel (Schwartz, 2008; Spolsky and Shohamy, 1999: 241).

Another out-of-school pattern is the summer camp, such as the Hebrew summer camps in the USA (Benor et al., 2020); some of them originally aimed to develop the Hebrew proficiency of campers, but now the Hebrew language component shows only in the use of appropriate Hebrew loanwords in the spoken and written English. Hinton (2011) mentions summer schools for Native American languages (Miami and Keresan in the USA) and for Karaim in Lithuania.

The many types of bilingual education listed by Mackey (1970) deal with the time available to each language on two dimensions: how many hours in each week and how many years in the whole school programme. At one extreme are two absolute monolingual programmes: the state language only as in pre-1979 France and its empire (which may be designated 'submersion') and the minority language only approach, immersion, used in the first years of British colonial education and practiced by Māori revitalisation schools. In between are all the possible sharings of time of bilingual programmes, including those that put two teachers each using a different language in the classroom, as in the Rock Point Navajo programme or in a few Hebrew–Arabic bilingual programmes in Israel. The pattern may be repeated every school year (a maintenance programme) or varied in the case of transition from the home language to the state dominant language. In the classic St Lambert pattern in Montréal, immersion in the target language was replaced by a sharing of time in later years; in the normal British colonial policy, teaching in an indigenous language gradually transitioned into teaching in English, usually accomplished by the secondary school.

Whatever the pattern, one problem is to find teachers who are proficient in the target language and as language teachers. At first, the Māori pre-school programmes found a solution by using grandparents still fluent in the language, but untrained as teachers. A master–apprentice programme started in California for indigenous languages spread through the USA and to Australia, Canada, Brazil and Spain; masters were trained in a two to five day programme (Hinton, 2011: 303). The state school-based Māori immersion classes in New Zealand were staffed commonly by senior women teachers still fluent in their childhood language; they invited older relatives to help with their classes (Spolsky, 1989). The Hebrew revitalisation teachers in the agricultural villages of Ottoman Palestine were proficient in the language of the sacred texts to which they added the modernising terminology of codes of Jewish practice (Glinert, 1987). A major part of the Navajo revival effort was the training of Navajos as teachers. In many programmes, fluent native speakers were employed as teacher aides. In Hawaii, the Kahuawaiola Indigenous Teacher Education Program was accredited in 2001 to support the language revitalisation efforts: it requires fluency in the language, six weeks intensive living in an immersion setting and a year of student teaching. As well as a teacher's licence course, there is also an MA and a PhD (Wilson and Kawai'ae'a, 2007). Reid (2004) describes and compares two indigenous teacher education programmes, one in Saskatchewan, Canada and the other in New South Wales, Australia; she discusses the contributions of the two, but notes the conflict between indigenisation and community support.

The importance of teachers in supporting school language policy is shown by the French case; although the requirement to teach only in standard French was set during the French Revolution, it was late in the nineteenth century before there were enough teachers qualified to achieve this. Since 1979, there have been schools teaching Occitan in France. These Calandreta schools, over sixty at the primary level and three colleges, are provided with teachers by Aprene, the Occitan Higher Education Institution at Besier, which is part of networks of schools for Basque, Alsatian, Breton and Catalan, all of which offer immersion programmes and some teacher training in their heritage languages (Sumien, 2009). But the provision of qualified teachers fluent in endangered languages remains a major problem.

The school as a major instrument of language management

To sum up, the school has potential to be the major force in language management after the family. In the revernacularisation of Hebrew, the spread of standard English, the establishment of Indonesian and in many other similar cases, education has been the major force behind language shift. Because of its importance, it is subject to pressure from all stakeholders active as advocates or managers of its policies: it is the major focus of conflict between the state with its insistence on the official language and the family and the community which may support the maintenance or revitalisation of heritage ethnic languages; it is used by religious institutions to provide access to the sacred language; it is seen by the business community as providing workers proficient in economically relevant languages and language skills; it may be used by armies and intelligence agencies as a source of personnel speaking the languages they want.

But school by itself cannot impose major changes for it depends on the cooperation of all the other social levels influencing language practice. The choice of language of instruction is an important force. By not using the language of the pupil's home variety, it ensures that minority children are severely discriminated against: as mentioned earlier, some 40 per cent of the children who go to school are held back by this policy, until after six or seven years they become at ease in the selected language. And of course, the many children who lack schooling are even more likely to be condemned to lower economic status. And schools are the normal place to add proficiency in classical or foreign or religious languages and so to preserve varieties that are not spoken to young children.

This power then explains why so many sectors and agencies try to dominate the educational system, ranging from the central government to activist parents. Although the strange way in which adult teachers are locked in a classroom with a number of children gives extra control to teachers, many of whom ignore the requirement to use the official language of instruction and shift to the vernacular, it is usually forces outside the classroom that set curriculum and lay down language policy. But of course, inadequacies of teacher selection, training and proficiencies mean that formal language policies are often not implemented.

With all these interferences, including the non-linguistic factors blocking implementation of even good policies that take into account the complexities of levels and domains, school is probably the second most significant source of language management, able even to overcome the effects of home policy.

Notes

1. Webster (2010a) gives a revealing description of the effects of language policy in Navajo schools.
2. When we conducted a Jewish day school in New Mexico, we could not persuade the local Jewish Community Council that adding students cost more money. In much of the world, education is underfunded.
3. Versteegh (2001) reported over 200,000 inhabitants of Moroccan birth in the Netherlands.
4. Elaborated by the participants in the III International Colloquium of Studies on Native Cultures of America held in Havana, Cuba, in October 2018.
5. The Navajo Nation occupies portions of four states, Arizona, New Mexico, Colorado and Utah, each with its own department of education.
6. A major programme in the 1970s with federal government funding was aimed at training a thousand Navajo teachers.

4 Neighbourhoods and the Workplace

Peers and parents

Even before children go to school, they may be influenced by young friends from the neighbourhood who come to play. Other potential invaders are radio, television, computers and phones. In what was acclaimed as a revolutionary study, Harris (1998, 2011) argued that peers had more influence on a child than parents and that choosing a neighbourhood where other immigrants from your homeland have already settled is the easiest way to help your children by providing an environment that will ease integration and growth. The language practices of the neighbourhood and the language policy of the workplace can be major challenges to family language policy and powerful determinants of the language repertoire of an individual. Describing an individual's external linguistic environment is then an important task for students of language policy.

Sometimes, the repertoires of home, schooling, neighbourhood and workplace overlap. There can, however, be a significant gap for an individual or family that has moved to a new place of residence as a result of urbanisation or immigration and is living in an environment that is ethnically or culturally or religiously different; this why people moving try usually to live close to others from the same background, often forming an alien or otherwise noticeable cluster whose culture and speech is similar. Obvious examples are the Chinatowns in many Chinese diasporas (Li, 2016b), or the ethnic or orthodox Jewish sections of many cities.

Even in monolingual villages, there are dialectal differences, as Gumperz (1958, 1964) showed in villages in North India and Norway, with caste or class the determining factor. For immigrant communities, the date of arrival will produce differences in the rate of shift to the new language. In town and cities, as early as Jerusalem in the Second Temple period (Spolsky and Cooper, 1991) and echoed 2,000 years later (Spolsky, 1993), there was marked multilingualism, now referred to by some scholars as superdiversity.

Superdiversity, a term coined by Vertovec (2007) and applied to language repertoires by Blommaert (2013) seems to suggest that this is a modern development resulting from the huge increase of immigration, but does not do justice to the multilingual diversity of ancient and medieval port cities. But it is true that modern cities are highly diverse, as a result of immigration, urbanisation and the forced and voluntary resettlement that affects millions in the world today. A major task for language policy is how to capture and describe these complex sociolinguistic environments.

Describing the sociolinguistic repertoire of a neighbourhood or a work-place calls for the application of several methods.[1] In studies of Indian and Norwegian communities, Ferguson and Gumperz (1960; Gumperz and Blom, 1972) made use of the customary method of ethnography, participant obser-vation. Fishman et al. (1971), on the other hand, depended on analysis of answers to elaborate questionnaires. During the year that they were working together on the Jersey City study, Fishman and Gumperz sometimes argued and each would ask the other to present their evidence: Fishman would bring sheets of computer printout from his study; Gumperz would say, 'Last night I was at a party . . .' Lambert, in his study of practice and attitudes in bilingual Montréal, argued for long semi-structured interviews (Lambert et al., 1975). In our work in the Old City of Jerusalem, Cooper and I combined interviews, street observations and photos of public signage. Similarly, in a study of a bilingual Hungarian–German town, Gal (1978) used both questionnaires and observation to establish that social network membership accounted for the choice of variety.

Each method has different costs and benefits: questionnaires tend to bias the results towards the investigator's assumptions and the short questions used in language censuses lead to confusion – how does one differentiate between the results of a question about home language use or first language use or dominant language? Ethnographical observation requires dealing with the presence of an observer, which is why it is better to use a trained local person rather than an alien scholar, reducing the likelihood of observer effect (Spolsky, 1998: 8). Interviews require selecting and finding a willing and representative number of subjects and produce a large amount of text that needs transcription and analysis. Each of these methods can produce differ-ing results, so multi-method studies are preferable.

Public signage in the neighbourhood

One simple method that has become popular is taking pictures of public signs. The ease of using cell phones to collect evidence of public signage has encouraged a new field, now known as linguistic landscape (Backhaus, 2005; Ben-Rafael et al., 2006; Spolsky, 2019d), with its own journals and academic conferences. Public signs are easy to photograph, but not easy to interpret: without knowing the agent who selected the language of the sign, their full sociolinguistic meaning is hidden (Malinowski, 2009). Moreover, signs are in the written language and can be misleading because they do not represent the normal spoken language of the area. In the Navajo Reservation in the 1960s, for instance, the normal spoken language was Navajo, but almost all literacy was in English (Spolsky and Holm, 1973).[2]

Street signs, their language determined by national or local government, echo historical change as in the three periods of government – British, Jordanian and Israeli – accounting for the bilingual and trilingual ceramic signs in the Old City of Jerusalem (Spolsky, 2020a; Spolsky and Cooper, 1991). Backhaus (2007) found that in Tokyo the local government regulated street signs, requiring English to be added in neighbourhoods where tourists were common. Transnistria, the unrecognised state of Pridnestrovian Moldavian Republic between Moldova and the Ukraine, that is trilingual in Moldovan, Russian and Ukrainian, showed its claim of independence from Moldova by the fact that most of its public signs are in Russian (Muth, 2014). Senegal adopted French as its official language on independence in 1960 and half of the shopkeepers use it for their signs, but a quarter now add Wolof, a widespread lingua franca (Shiohata, 2012). Although France considers French its dominant official language, street signs in Toulouse consistently show loyalty to a heritage language by adding the regional Occitan (Amos, 2017).

Shops and stores vary in language choice. In neighbourhood stores, the shopkeeper is often local, although there are ethnically marked food stores – I grew up with 'Chinaman' as the term for the local fruit and vegetable store. Signs in local stores include printed national and global labels which may not be in the local language. Globalisation is shown by the inclusion of English loan words in Asian and European advertising signs (MacGregor, 2003; Schlick, 2003; Soukup, 2016). In markets that support bargaining, prices are seldom if ever marked, but, increasingly, laws require the detailing of contents, weight, sale-by date and price, adding value to literacy for a shopper.

Local stores and marketplaces are an important part of a neighbourhood, both in revealing the local language practices and in encouraging the integration of new arrivals who need to learn how to shop. The service encounter in local stores is a topic of a number of studies. Bailey (1997) describes miscommunication between Korean shopkeepers and Afro-American customers: Ryoo (2005) describes how Korean shopkeepers work to overcome this and establish relations with Afro-American shoppers. Shively (2011) traces the way foreign students in Spain learned their role in the encounter. In our study of the Old City (Spolsky and Cooper, 1991), we were told Arab shopkeepers recognised Israelis and tourists by their failure to start conversation with polite family health enquiries and immediately asking about price. Normally, shops wishing to cater to foreign tourists advertise their linguistic skills ('English spoken here'), but the cover of Spolsky (2009a) shows a sign by a Philadelphia shopkeeper reserving the right to refuse service to anyone not speaking English! A recent study by Webster (2014) has shown that although the Navajo Tribal Council mandated that the newly required street signs be in English so that non-Navajos could read them, a large number are in Navajo, often misspelled.

These linguistic landscape (or better, cityscape, except in the case of Navajo) studies, easily captured by the cameras built into smartphones, miss the spoken language of the neighbourhood, obvious in the culturally determined greetings of one resident to another. And the smartphones are destroying the greeting: 'Social life, street life and attention to people and things around one have largely disappeared, at least in big cities, where a majority of the population is now glued almost without pause to phones or other devices . . .' (Sacks, 2019: 28).

Knowing how to greet in public was an important social skill: I recall my satisfaction at learning to say 'Good night, sir' to a school master when leaving high school in the late afternoon and now know how and when to add a 'Good month' in Hebrew to my morning greetings in the streets of my Jerusalem neighbourhood. Carrying out research on the spoken practices of a community is more difficult than taking photos of signs. In the Jerusalem study, we had students walk along a set route in the market and make notes of the age and appearance of anyone they heard speaking and the time, place and language. Arabic, Hebrew and English accounted for about three-quarters, a different result than for signs (Spolsky and Cooper, 1991: 97–8). Spoken language was closely related to dress, explaining how shopkeepers could guess which language to address to a tourist passing by.

Thus, studies of linguistic landscape add to surveys of spoken language in showing the repertoire of a neighbourhood, but do not by themselves give an accurate picture.

What is a neighbourhood?

A first methodological issue is the difficulty of selecting the boundaries of a neighbourhood: lacking any size definition for the concept of speech community (Gumperz, 1968; Horvath and Sankoff, 1987; Xu, 2004), the choice of the area to be described is a key factor. In our study of Jerusalem, we selected the area known as the Old City, surrounded by the walls built by the Ottomans in the sixteenth century. We noted the division into uneven quarters (more accurately, *quartiers*) by the British, with the tiny Armenian quarter consisting of the Convent with its own walls, the Jewish quarter redefined after 1967, the Christian quarter consisting of churches and other institutions and the remainder known as the Muslim quarter. Even within these named areas, there were further distinctions, such as the Gypsy complex in the Muslim quarter, the difference between lay and clerical residents of the Armenian quarter, the division in the Jewish quarter in preference for synagogue and school and the division of religious institutions between Greek Orthodox, Latin, Coptic and other churches in the Christian quarter. When we were asked by visitors if our children played with their Muslim neighbours, we replied that they didn't even play with the children who attended the other Jewish religious school. There was a major distinction between streets that were residential, those that were commercial making up the *shuk* (market) and those with public and religious institutions. Thus, it turned out to be difficult to establish the Old City as a neighbourhood, but better to see it as a series of urban spaces increasingly learned by a young child. Additionally, the gates and walls, once clear boundaries with guards, no longer closed off the area; the area of East Jerusalem outside Damascus Gate blends with that inside, as does the area of West Jerusalem with that inside Jaffa Gate.[3]

Other studies found similar difficulty in defining a neighbourhood. William Labov in his master's study selected an island community, Martha's Vineyard (Labov, 1962), but noted the differences in residential patterns among farmers, fishermen and summer tourists. For his doctoral dissertation, he first chose the lower and higher floors of some New York department stores to illustrate social distinctions in pronunciation and then selected a number of blocks in lower Manhattan where he found similar social influence on linguistic features (Labov, 1966). Joshua Fishman for his study of a Puerto Rican neighbourhood selected an area in Jersey City (Fishman et al., 1971). In studies of Jerusalem, he and his team looked at the signs and observed the speech of a mixed commercial residential street in the centre of the city (Rosenbaum et al., 1977). Cooper and Carpenter (1976) explored the choice of language in a multilingual market in Ethiopia; in this area, as we later found in the Old City (Spolsky and Cooper, 1991), it was usually the seller who learned the buyer's language. For a study of bilingual signage, Backhaus (2005) looked at streets in Tokyo where tourists were common and where the city council required bilingual signs.

With the sociolinguistic diversity of neighbourhoods, an individual's linguistic repertoire is likely to expand as contacts increase, producing a regular process of language socialisation (Ochs and Schieffelin, 2011). Even if one's immediate neighbours use the same language, there can be dialect differences, leading to modification or addition to one's repertoire. In recreational spaces and school playgrounds, children are exposed to different varieties. The shopkeepers from whom they buy food might be immigrants, their teachers will usually try to use a standard variety and their employers are likely to encourage socially or commercially desirable practices.[4]

Language socialisation

Governing this expansion of the linguistic repertoire is socialisation. Riley (2011) has described the ideologies and beliefs that effect language socialisation. One is the belief that young children are less proficient in communication and benefit from being taught, though there is cultural variation in how and when this guidance is to be given. For instance, the Kaluli of Papua New Guinea believe that parents and older siblings must 'show' children how to speak, modelling correct utterances, unlike Anglo-American working and middle class parents who do this with names for things. Western Samoans do neither, but encourage practice in etiquette formulas. Rural African Americans assume that children will imitate their elders. In Samoa, parents teach respectful language and in Thailand, teachers teach children the politeness particles to be used addressing someone of higher status. In US law schools, professors tell first-year students how to speak in court.

In many communities, ideology assigns values to the diverse means of communication, generally preferring literate to oral modes, middle class speech to lower class, white to black dialects and, of course, the dominant language variety to all others. Thus, New York Puerto Ricans are reported to rate what they call 'Spanglish' lower than standard English. Also in New York, there is a popular belief that each borough has a distinctive accent, though Becker and Newlin-Lukowicz (2018) have now shown this to be a myth. And since Cardinal Richelieu, most French speakers accept the superior status of standard Parisian French. The common belief in the existence of a correct version of a language variety is considered a norm by Bartsch (1987), who supports the notion that normalised correct language aids comprehension, but in many societies, a speaker is not judged on correctness but by persuasiveness.

Although these ideologies may be relevant at all levels of society ranging from the home to the state, there is special relevance to the neighbourhood and the workplace. There are rare cases where the national government declares certain kinds of language illegal, as in the Turkish ban on the speaking of Kurdish and the US ban on mailing obscene matter. Obscenity was defined in the USA as depending on local community standards until the Childhood Online Protection Act was ruled unconstitutional for applying this to the Internet. In Britain, a 1959 law bans obscene publication, but there are exceptions and a decreasing number of successful prosecutions under the act. In the USA, some state governments and local authorities have banned obscene language, together with 'fighting words' in Georgia. The call for political correctness has led to bans on racist terms such as 'nigger' and 'wop' and an ongoing campaign continues against sexist language, complicated by grammatical gender and the lack of neutral terminology (Coates, 2005; Fasold, 1987). In the 1990s, a counter-movement by neoliberals and conservatives challenged this process as a university-based movement of repression (Berman, 2011; Fairclough, 2003).

Language in the workplace

Local stores constitute a natural bridge between the neighbourhood and the workplace, especially when they are family businesses. Larger stores on the other hand usually need to employ salespeople from outside the neighbourhood and some language management is then necessary (Hamp-Lyons and Lockwood, 2009; Holmes and Stubbe, 2015; Macias, 1997). A first requirement is that staff be able to understand the owner's instructions, though in some workplaces this problem is solved by the hiring of bilingual supervisors, as is the case of foreign labour in Israeli agriculture and construction (Drori, 2009).

Nekvapil and Nekula (2006) have studied language management in Czech foreign-owned enterprises, describing methods adopted to handle the communication needs of German-speaking senior staff and Czech-speaking employees. In a number of pioneering studies, Grin (1996a; Grin et al., 2010) has explored the economics of the multilingual workplace, concentrating on Switzerland and Québec. Bordia and Bordia (2015) discuss the willingness of employees to use a foreign language in multilingual businesses. Kingsley (2013) explores the local policy developed by employers in ten Luxembourg banks with international business and the language practices of the employees. Another study of the multilingual workplace in Luxembourg was undertaken by Wille et al. (2015). Damari et al. (2017) surveyed the foreign language skills required by 2,000 US firms; although most valued the ability of employees to work with foreign customers and businesses, only 10 per cent required new hires to speak a language other than English.

One effect of globalisation has been the development of English as a corporate language in international businesses. However, Kankaanranta et al. (2018) see a distinction between the standard language used in official publications and Business English as a lingua franca used in practice.

A need for language management has arisen with the opening of call centres in foreign locations. To change a hotel booking recently, we spoke to agents in Estonia, Thailand and Italy and the hotel in Israel. In each case, the agent was able to converse in English. Employees in call centres are expected and trained to modify their accents in the direction of either American or British English (Rahman, 2009), with the result that they are globalised (Aneesh, 2012).

The workplace then has an important effect on the expansion and shaping of the language repertoire of employees, as studies of the economics of multilingualism by Grin (1996b) and Chiswick (1994) have shown. Brecht and Rivers (2005) suggest that these linguistic needs should drive language teaching policy instead of the current practice continuing to teach the traditional foreign languages. But, as Neustupný and Nekvapil (2003) noted, often the correction of linguistic insufficiency depends not on government policy but on individual self-management.

Language management in the workplace as a factor

Commonly, although home language policy is driven by identity and herit-age preservation, the workplace can establish the importance of economic factors. If a job requires proficiency in a specific variety, as Arabic-speaking Palestinian programmers need Hebrew to talk to their Israeli employers and English to communicate with their counterparts in California, then the hiring policy will often take language into account and ambitious indi-viduals will self-manage and find a way to acquire the needed language skills. Additionally, ambitious parents like the South Korean 'wild geese' who sent their families to an English-speaking country, or the New Yorkers who hired Mandarin speaking nannies for their children, will modify home language policy to switch from heritage to economic goals. The workplace, then, has an important role in determining the language policy of a modern speech community, something that we will continue to explore in Chapter 8.

Notes

1. See also Chapter 10 of Bradley and Bradley (2019).
2. In a recent paper, Webster (2014) describes the major changes taking place in signage in the Navajo Nation since the Tribal Council mandated street signs for any road with at least four dwellings.
3. The Mamillah Mall outside the Jaffa Gate of the Old City of Jerusalem is full of international stores and used by tourists, Arabs and Jews but it also provides easy access to the Western city.
4. Including a ban on using a language not known by customers.

5 Public Institutions for Communication, Culture, Religion, Health and Law

The interconnection of levels

An advantage of the structure that I have chosen for this book, starting with the individual and ending with the nation state, is that it reflects the gradual and continual expansion and refinement of a speaker's sociolinguistic repertoire, as they move from private to public domains. But there are problems with the approach, the major one being the interdependence of the various levels and domains and the way in which managers or advocates on a higher or wider domain or level often attempt to influence or succeed in influencing speakers at another level. Thus, governments commonly try to manage family language policy and compete with religious, economic, ethnic or other putative managers. Nor does the approach necessarily capture the sequence or progression of the contacts of an individual: the institutions described in this chapter might influence an individual at different times and in diverse orders, or might never apply. I have already treated of some important institutions – the family first and the school next, followed by the community and the workplace. Here, I set out to consider some of the other public or private institutions which influence repertoire expansion, but the order in which I treat them does not necessarily apply to all speakers.

Media

I start with communication media, some of the various agencies that, although they are public, enter the home and so constitute a major potential force to lead to modifications in the sociolinguistic repertoire of children as well as adults. Radio broadcasting began in California in the early twentieth century and by the 1920s had spread through the USA and Europe. The first commercial station in the USA was launched in 1920; the British Broadcasting Corporation was formed in 1926, followed by other national stations in Europe. For forty years, radio 'provided one of the primary means of negotiating the boundaries between public life and the private home' (Hilmes, 2002: 1) and so it exposed children to the dominant language of the community. As radio spread, it began to broadcast in an increasing number of languages, something taken advantage of by the US Office of War Information during the Second World War to match the English language broadcasts of the Nazi government (Doherty, 2000); foreign language broadcasting became a significant instrument in spreading propaganda. In peacetime, because local stations (especially FM) were comparatively cheap, they were available to support indigenous languages.

Indigenous language FM stations supported minority languages in Latin America. It has been argued that

> Radio is a veritable medium which has provided a good access to communication for a large number of people, both literate and non-literate. Its advantage over other media lies in its relative simplicity, cheapness and ubiquity without dependence on electricity supply. (Oyero, 2003: 185)

In a survey of indigenous listeners to a Lagos FM station, Oyero found that most preferred to hear radio in their native language. Similar success was reported in South America: in Columbia in 2002, fourteen indigenous radio stations began operating reaching nearly 80 per cent of the national indigenous population (Rodríguez and El Gazi, 2007). Navajo radio broadcasting played a role in language maintenance (Klain and Peterson, 2000); although the music played on the stations was country western in English, the announcers used Navajo.

Printed matter – newspapers, magazines, books – entered the home earlier than radio of course and literate homes helped to enrich the language repertoire of children and adults. Newspapers started in Britain in the late eighteenth century, but circulation was low, about one paper for every 300 inhabitants, but by 1938, it had risen to one paper for every four people (Aspinall, 1946). Book ownership too grew gradually and steadily and public libraries provided greater access. Many agencies and people tried to manage what could be published, with widespread censorship developed for books and newspapers for religious and political reasons and to avoid obscenity (Ahmed, 2008). There was also control of the language: Tavárez (2013) reported that the Inquisition banned vernacular translations of the Bible in sixteenth-century Latin America; Mizuno (2000) describes US Government pressure blocking Japanese publications after Pearl Harbor; and Fishman and Fishman (1974) complained about the Israeli Government's limitation of paper supply for Yiddish publications.

Publication in vernacular languages has had an important role in language maintenance. The classic study of language loyalty in the United States (Fishman, 1966) provides a chapter reporting non-English and ethnic group press followed by another on foreign language broadcasting, two critical measures of the sociolinguistic repertoire, and its chapters include brief notes on television, which as Glazer (1966: 366) notes, already had an important role in teaching English to immigrants.

Another early public medium was the theatre. Drama and theatres developed in ancient Greece, providing an important source of entertainment especially in cities, though the medieval and later development of touring companies allowed those living in the provinces to share. Though plays are generally performed in the standard or literary language, indigenous languages have been used in what Desai (1990) labels 'popular theatre', encouraged by Paulo Freire and spread throughout Africa. Indigenous language theatre is reported in a number of countries, including Canada (Smith, 2017), India (Kapadia, 2016) and Australia (David, 2016).

Movies are another influence on community sociolinguistic repertoires. Before television, the local movie theatre played a major role in recognising and signalling the language practices of a neighbourhood. The number of countries producing movies was limited but there were two ways to adapt a film to make it locally understandable, dubbing and subtitling. Once talkies began, the international sale of movies required dealing with the limitation of the language of the original. Dubbing, adding synchronised speech in another language, was expensive but preferred in Western Europe;[1] subtitles, with the problem of timing, were more established in Scandinavia (Tveit, 2009). The languages used for subtitles was a reflection of the local speech repertoire: I recall a movie theatre I went to in Jaffa, a heavily immigrant neighbourhood in Israel, in the 1950s, where English-language films had subtitles in Hebrew and Arabic on the main screen and two hand-written side screens each with half a dozen other immigrant languages. The local movie theatre lost much of its audience with the development of television.

Television, spreading after the 1950s, invaded the home domain bringing the dominant language with it (Glazer, 1966: 367). It opened the Navajo Nation to the outside world, producing a major change and driving language shift (Lee and McLaughlin, 2001). Strong efforts by supporters of endangered languages sometimes managed to exploit the medium. Because television is more expensive than radio, its use for minority languages requires government subsidy. There was pressure for minority language television in Wales, Scotland and Ireland in the late 1990s (Hourigan, 2007). Only after a major campaign was Māori television launched in 2004; it is now playing a significant role in the revitalisation of the language (Smith, 2016) and in raising its status.

Computers and smartphones now have invaded private space with consequent language effects. Holton (2011) presents the technological problems in adapting Internet technologies to the preservation of minority and endangered languages. At first, there was an assumption that the web and the smartphone were instruments for globalisation, forcing all users to adopt Latin letters and English. I still recall the problem we had in transcribing

Navajo texts for computer analysis (Spolsky et al., 1973), until we adopted the convention of work-arounds using letter combinations developed by Werner et al. (1966). But there was rapid advance, as Anderson (2004) pointed out in his concept of the Long Tail, showing that computer technology allowed adaptation to smaller languages: Unicode can now handle most of the world's writing systems. Although many smartphone users still prefer Latin or Hebrew letters to write Palestinian Arabic or Pinyin for Chinese, the availability of dictation systems and the continued expansion of Unicode make it possible to handle minority languages.

All these communication media may of course appear at all levels ranging from the individual to the global; they play a key role in globalising the various local levels, as they encourage the expansion of individual and social repertoires. There are attempts at all the levels to manage them – a totalitarian nation like China for instance can block or censor them (Chen, 2020) and there are programs for parents to block their children's access to what they consider unsuitable sites. But it turns out that the system as a whole is out of control, as shown by the failed attempts to jam the videos made by the right-wing terrorist while he murdered over forty people in a mosque in New Zealand in March 2019. Thus, potentially, they now provide an open neighbourhood to anyone with Internet access.

Religion

I turn next to religion, already mentioned in Chapter 3 as often managing and influencing educational establishments. For the observant, its influence can come in the home (as young children are taught to pray) and be repeated regularly in public worship, ranging from the five times a day a Muslim is expected to pray or the three times a day of Jewish religious services or the weekly Sunday morning church service of the moderately observant Protestant.

Religion affects language policy in various ways and at many different levels. At the individual level, there are traditional prayers with set language and formulas, like the recitation of the Rosary by Catholics, which may have begun in the vernacular and was translated into Latin (Winston-Allen, 2010: 17), or the mantras in Vedic Sanskrit recited by Hindus, or the Hebrew blessings that observant Jews teach their children.[2] In contrast, there is the spontaneous prayer in the vernacular of a believer faced with illness or some problem. At the family level, there are the prayer and bible readings of some Protestants, or the rituals associated with family meals among observant Jews. It is in the neighbourhood that one finds the churches, mosques and synagogues associated with regular public prayer. Here, the pattern and language of worship is laid down by authority or tradition, often with a sacred language (Latin,[3] Arabic, Hebrew[4]) established for hymns and prayers and sacred text readings, with the local vernacular regularly used for sermons. The switch from Latin to the vernacular was a critical innovation of Protestantism and from Hebrew to the vernacular a mark of Jewish Reform. Muslim immigrants in Britain are reported to be using English in their rituals. Given the importance of sacred languages, teaching them to children is a major contribution to the expansion of their sociolinguistic repertoire in the family or the neighbourhood. Important studies on religion and language include Omoniyi and Fishman (2006), Pandharipande et al. (2020), Paulston and Watt (2011) and Sawyer (2001).

The health field

The domains of medicine and health also have their own language policies. Doctors and nurses and other health professionals need to be able to communicate with each other and with their patients (Elder et al., 2012). Read et al. (2009) report the requirement of English proficiency set for immigrant health professionals in New Zealand. In the last half-century, there has been recognition of the importance of doctor–patient communication (Korsch et al., 1968), now made easier by the provision of interpretation services (Bührig and Meyer, 2004). Medical interpretation has grown since the passage in the USA of the Civil Rights Act of 1964, Title VI of which called for the use of professional interpreters for patients with limited English proficiency (Angelelli, 2004: 1), replacing family members, including children (Cohen et al., 1999).[5] Angelelli's pioneering book discusses the problems of medical interpreting before describing details of the interpretation services at a California hospital that provides both face-to-face and speakerphone interpretation.

Jacobs et al. (2018) argue that professional interpreters, although expensive (ranging from $45–$150/hour for in-person interpreters, to $1.25–$3.00/ minute for telephone interpreters and $1.95–$3.49/minute for video remote interpreting), lead to better and more efficient care.[6] McEwen and Anton-Culver (1988) describe the special problems faced by the Deaf in dealing with healthcare practitioners. Even with professional interpreters, doctors find many communication problems, especially giving detailed instructions in what to do after the consultation (Karliner et al., 2004).[7] As a consequence of concern about the ability of foreign doctors to communicate with their patients, many countries are now developing special tests of their language proficiency (Boulet et al., 2001). In Australia, an English test has been developed for health professionals (Elder et al., 2012).

From the point of view of the managers of health services, a principal issue is the pressure to communicate with patients who lack proficiency in the dominant language that professionals use. This shows up also in public signage in a hospital, where it is difficult to provide signs in all the languages of patients: Schuster et al. (2017) note that a study of ten Israeli hospitals showed that signage was mainly in Hebrew, though there were a few in

English and Hebrew too.[8] From the point of view of doctors and nurses, the limited proficiency of patients hinders developing an accurate history and giving instructions.

But the problem is wider than language choice. The medical profession has built up a major body of knowledge and accompanying terminology not known by laymen. As Foucault (1975) pointed out, medical patients, like school pupils, undergo regular examinations and tests; this produces the kind of knowledge that enables doctors and teachers to develop a discipline which gives them authority. But patients, even when they know the same language as the doctor,[9] do not know their terminology or professional language. As a result, it is common for patients to ask the nurse 'What did the doctor say?' (McCarthy et al., 2012). On the other hand, for the computer literate, the proliferation of popular and professional medical sites on the Internet means that it is now possible to check a doctor's recommendation.

In sum, the health domain sets a number of challenges to a community's speech repertoire, calling for what McCarthy et al. (2012) call health literacy, which focused in their study on the recall of spoken instructions. Even proficiency in the dominant language is not enough, as this is a case of professional–lay communication; the professional who recognises this will make the effort to accommodate a patient who is not health literate. But there are growing efforts to overcome this problem, not just in providing interpretation services but also in preparing professionals to talk to their patients.

Police and law

The police and the legal domains also have communication difficulties, whether in choice of language variety or in special rules. The participants in the police domain may be classified as cops, robbers, victims and witnesses: one of the first problems faced by police arriving at a crime scene can be to decide the status of the people involved (Spolsky, 2009a: 124). In San Diego in the 1970s, noting that police who could not communicate with Vietnamese and Cambodians at a crime scene simply arrested all the bystanders, a volunteer telephone interpreter service was set up. This later developed into the AT&T Language Line which continues to offer online video and telephone services to police and others: the video service is available in thirty-six languages (including American Sign) and phone interpretation in another 240 languages. Prices range from $1.45 to $3.00 a minute.[10]

But problems continue: there are studies of services to minority people in Glasgow, of domestic violence to Arab American women and Sudanese immigrants and of language barriers in the delivery of police services to Hispanics. The cost of providing services is a major problem: South Korean police need to advise foreign suspects of their rights in thirteen languages and British police reported a major increase in spending on interpretation services. To deal with this, some police departments include language proficiency in their hiring and promotion policies: New York Police Department reported testing employees in forty-five languages. The Berlin police department wanted to hire 10 per cent of new recruits from ethnic minorities able to speak Turkish, Arabic, Polish, Russian and Serbo-Croatian. Police departments in the USA have been selecting or training officers with proficiency in Sign. Prison officers in the UK have also noted difficulties with interpretation.

The legal field has its own set of language policies (Spolsky, 2009a: 116–24). The task of the courts is to interpret and implement written laws using oral debate between professionals (lawyers and judges) who pose questions in defined forms to lay witnesses. Lawyers who do not follow the rules of the court are rebuked by judges, as are lay witnesses who do not follow instructions to answer Yes or No.[11]

Apart from the professional–lay problem, the most common language issue in the legal field is the choice of language. The fact that many defendants or witnesses are not proficient in the dominant language laid down for the courts produces a serious problem, ideally remedied by interpreters. The requirement for interpreters is based on the sometimes uneven implementation of a civil rights principle that accused persons have the right to know what they are accused of and what evidence is being given against them. Amendment VI in the US Bill of Rights (1791) laid down this policy; it echoed the 1362 decision in the English Statute of Pleading which established the use of English in courts, in place of French which had formerly been used or Latin in which records were still written. But full implementation took a long time: in 1650 under Oliver Cromwell there was a requirement that statutes be written in English and in 1731 legislation established that all statutes and court proceedings should be 'in the English tongue and not in Latin or French'.[12]

In the twentieth century, this principle was laid down in the International Covenant on Civil and Political Rights, adopted in 1966 by the United Nations General Assembly and included in the constitutions of many newly independent states: any person charged in a criminal case should be informed 'in detail in a language which he understands of the nature and cause of the charge' and also have the 'free assistance of an interpreter'. In the USA, Congress passed the Court Interpreters Act; in 1988, there were reported to be 46,000 dockets in federal courts requiring interpreters (Benmaman, 1992). There remain problems in the training and certification of court interpreters (Wallace, 2019). Especially in immigration courts, where it is often impossible to find an interpreter for a minority or indigenous language, the lack of trained interpreters often leads to incorrect decisions.

Nolan (2020) describes the problems faced by immigrants from Guatemala in immigration courts in the USA, 250,000 of whom have been apprehended at the US border. At least half do not speak Spanish, but one of a number of Mayan language varieties and dialects. Mam, a recognised language with many dialects, was the ninth most common language used in immigration courts. There are few qualified interpreters and they face problems in finding Mam equivalents for lexicon like asylum, stipulate or credible fear. In many cases, the government uses telephone translation services with unqualified interpreters. A former immigration court judge pointed out the special problems of rare-language speakers who only speak K'iche' or Q'anjob'al or Chuj.

The legal domain is another example of the difficulty of ignoring higher levels, for its managers and advocates come from the levels of national governments and supranational supporters of civil and human rights. This helps to explain the spread of interpretation services to courts in many countries, such as Japan (Takeda, 2009), Argentina, Australia, Austria, Germany and South Africa (Mikkelson, 2016). But the need to find interpreters for a huge range of languages and to certify their competence (Salimbene, 1996) leads to the high costs that many court systems are now facing.

The influence of language management in public domains

Each of these public institutions with their own language practices and policies potentially add to the speech repertoires of individuals who come in contact with them. Watching TV shows, you can develop an idealised or dramatised notion of the special language of hospital workers, policemen and lawyers. In these domains, the policy goes beyond choosing a named language to knowing the special jargon and customary pragmatics of the profession, so that there is scope for the intervention of agencies and groups concerned with the discriminatory effects of the language gaps.

Notes

1. Though I recall my shock at hearing fluent French coming from an Australian actor in a movie set in Central Australia.
2. Just as Western parents teach their children to say thank you, observant Jews train their children to say a blessing. I once heard one mother saying to child given a sweet, 'Say thank you and say a blessing.'
3. Required in Roman Catholic churches from the sixteenth-century Council of Trent until Vatican II.
4. With the exception of a few traditional Aramaic prayers.
5. While waiting for attention in an emergency ward, I was fascinated to hear a Palestinian doctor using English with an interpreting family member of an elderly Russian immigrant patient. At least this was an adult, but imagine a child required to tell her mother she had cancer!
6. One in forty malpractice suits were said to result from misinterpretation.
7. Spolsky (2004: 1) cites the case of a Turkish woman who was refused a heart operation in Germany because the doctors assumed she would not

understand their post-operation orders; the State Minister of Health said that in future they must find a better solution.

8. I observed a few handwritten signs in Russian in one Jerusalem hospital.
9. In the eighteenth century, doctors were expected to know and use Latin; the requirement continued into the twentieth century.
10. Keeping down the cost, interpreters may be volunteers or part-timers working from home.
11. Rosen (1977) sets out the problems of an anthropologist as a professional witness who does not know the rules established in courts.
12. One English court continued to use French in its records until the middle of the nineteenth century.

6 Military Language Policy and Management

The Bronx high school teacher auditing Max Weinreich's class in 1944 who defined a language as a dialect with an army and a navy (Weinreich, 1944) not only set off a long dispute as to who said that[1] but provided a useful suggestion about the requirements for recognition of a named language. But it also hints at the many intriguing aspects of military language policy and management and of military influences on language policy. In this chapter,[2] I first sketch language management as resulting from the communication needs of armed forces and in the next chapter look at the effects of military conquest in colonies and empires.

Military language policy

Military language policy might usefully be classified by the specific communication problems faced by various ranks in an army, ranging from the recruit who needs to understand his immediate commander to the chief of general staff who wants both to be able to pass orders to all units under his command and to understand what the enemy are saying. Although the military is normally under the control of the central government (and in many countries runs the government), often its requirement for communication or security leads to an independent language policy.

The recruit's problem might best be exemplified by the French Foreign Legion, which, following French national language policy, uses only French. The policy is described by Lyons (2009), who learned French as a volunteer in the Legion and further develops the notions on identity of legionnaires as a band of brothers (Lyons, 2004). The Legion at the time consisted of 7,800 volunteers, of 117 nationalities, 60 per cent of whom were mother-tongue speakers of French. Most of its officers were French speakers and all instruction and orders were given in French. Classroom teaching of French took place in a stressful and violent environment, with recruits *traumatisé* by slaps or punched by their instructors. The Legion used bilingual Francophone soldiers who worked with recruits during the four months of training inside and outside the classroom and who helped them learn songs which taught technical terms and formulas.

The Roman Army, which recruited widely outside Italy, was polyglot, but commonly officered by speakers of Latin as a first or second language. Adams (2003), who produced a major study of bilingualism in the Roman Empire, devoted a chapter to the Roman Army. In Egypt, it had units of soldiers from Palmyra in Syria, who spoke Palmyrene, a western dialect of Aramaic with a historic alphabet in which inscriptions were written between 100 BCE and 300 CE. The soldiers in Egypt left trilingual inscriptions, in Latin (the main language of the Roman Army), Greek (the language of the eastern Roman Empire) and their heritage Palmyrene. Greek was the normal vernacular of Roman soldiers in the Byzantine Empire and many documents were written in it, though at senior levels, officers used Latin. There were units in the army that used only Greek, but there was pressure to learn and use Latin, so that 'the army was undoubtedly the most potent force during the Roman Empire behind the learning of Latin by speakers of Greek and vernacular languages and behind the consequent spread of bilingualism' (Adams, 2003: 761).

The British Army in India required its British officers to learn Urdu and the language of their troops. Because promotion for officers in the regular British Army was by purchase, it was less affluent middle class and professional men who sought commissions in the Indian Army.[3] They were more committed as soldiers and they made the effort to learn the language of those under their command (Omissi, 2016: 104). Communication was also assisted by the appointment of bilingual Indian officers, under the authority of the British officers. Urdu (later called Hindustani) was set as the official language of the Indian Army in 1864 (R. D. King, 2001), but the sepoys spoke many other languages. After India became independent, the British Indian Army was divided into three: one part became the Indian Army, a second part the army of Pakistan, and the Brigade of Gurkhas remained part of the British Army. The Indian Army now uses Hindi; the Pakistani Army uses Urdu; and the Brigade of Gurkhas offers English courses for Gurkhas and Nepali courses for British officers.

The problem faced by the Israel Defence Forces after the creation of the State in 1948 was that many of its recruits, new immigrants from Europe or the Arab world, did not know Hebrew. It was said that a sergeant needed to wait until his orders were translated into ten languages! As a result, the Israeli Army quickly developed an Education Corps which taught Hebrew and later offered basic and secondary education to recruits. All new recruits were tested for Hebrew literacy and only those who passed the test were permitted to take advanced courses and be promoted. The Hebrew teachers were young women soldiers, high school graduates choosing to spend their two-year period of compulsory service as teachers and given brief preparation by training college lecturers doing reserve army duty. The programme continues, faced with the challenge in the 1990s of the immigration of a million Russian speakers and 75,000 Jews from Ethiopia. It now also offers courses preparing non-Jewish Russian immigrants for conversion (my grand-daughter did her army service in this way). Another task of the Education Corps was teaching other languages, such as Arabic for the Intelligence Corps and English for officers selected for training overseas (this was my own army service).

During the First World War, the United States Army made use of Choctaw soldiers as speakers on telephones to pass information in a language that the enemy could not understand (Meadows, 2002: 18). In the Second World War, the policy was revived, with the use of Navajo code talkers by the Marine Corps (Paul, 1998); they developed their own Navajo terms for military items. In that war, the US Army also use Comanche soldiers as code talkers (Meadows, 2002). The USA made use of other native speakers: German refugees were sent to the Military Intelligence Training Camp at Camp Ritchie in Maryland and were used after the invasion of Europe to interrogate prisoners of war. Second-generation Japanese-Americans (Nisei) mainly from Hawaii were recruited into the US Army and formed the 100th battalion; a good number were also used by military intelligence as interpreters and translators. Some 2,000 linguists were trained and played a significant role in the Pacific campaign (MacNaughton, 1994).

During the Second World War, the US Army was persuaded by members of Congress to make use of now deserted college campuses for part of the training. The Army Specialised Training Program was tasked in three areas: engineering, emergency medical training and a well-publicised but ultimately ineffective project for giving proficiency in the language and culture of the militarily significant regions of the world to recruits. Re-evaluation of the Foreign Language and Area Studies programme suggests that the programme was of little real value to the army, skimming off 150,000 highly qualified recruits from more useful tasks (Cardozier, 1993; Keefers, 1988). It helped the colleges make up for the wartime loss of male students and gave trainees a welcome respite before they were sent, as most were, to regular infantry units where their language skills and cultural knowledge were not required. Although many recruits benefited personally from their learning of an uncommonly taught language, the need for reinforcements in the final days of the European campaign meant that few if any were used by the army as interpreters. The programme employed linguistic scientists who worked with native speakers to teach many languages that had not previously been taught in the United States and also had an influence on the development of foreign language teaching. The enthusiastic publicity about the success of the intensive teaching had some effect on approaches to language teaching in the universities: some universities doubled the number of hours in first-year courses, but generally, intensive programmes did not fit into university curricula.

Intelligence

The shock of the success of Russian space mission Sputnik in 1957 drew US attention to the weakness of its foreign language education system and a group of Congressmen combined to pass the National Defence Education Act a year later. Language teaching was supported by the Act and the latest panacea, the audio-lingual method, was encouraged. Intensive graduate programmes for Russian and other critical languages were opened at a number of universities. Although the programme was not successful, in 1991 the National Security Education programme mandated the Secretary of Defence to offer scholarships and fellowships to students studying languages and areas critical to US national security and to enable universities to develop programmes of study in these areas. There continued to be arguments based on defence needs for improvement in the teaching of foreign languages but funding remained low: $114 million in 2007 compared to one $4.65 billion contract for outsourced translation in Iraq and Afghanistan. As Brecht and Rivers (2012) sum up in their review of US foreign language education with support from the Defence establishment, the absence of encouragement from the Department of Education was a source of continued weakness.

Another example of security influence on language education policy has been described by Mendel (2014) as underlying the teaching of Arabic in Israel. Before the State of Israel was established, Arabic was learnt by many Jews in British Mandate Palestine because it was the lingua franca of the region. However, as a result of the conflict between Arabs and Jews, from 1948 onward, the main pressure for the teaching of Arabic in Jewish schools came from the military and intelligence establishment without support from the Department of Education. Especially after the 1967 and 1973 wars, teaching Arabic became both normal and urgent. One of the results, as Mendel points out, was that what he calls Israeli Arabic became not a bridge to communication so much as a point of division, with Palestinians suspicious of any Jews speaking Arabic. The suspicion arose, Mendel believes, because of the importance that the intelligence agencies assign to linguistic proficiency.

This is also the point made by Footitt and Kelly (2012a) in a pioneering study of the role of language in military conflict. They note the problem faced by intelligence agencies in balancing the need for trust and security in their employees with the need to use people acquainted with the languages and culture of the enemy. Hiring native speakers of enemy languages is risky, so efforts are made to develop language teaching methods and centres to provide the needed courses for trustworthy candidates. In their book, they concentrate on two case studies, the long-term preparation of Allied intelligence forces for the invasion and occupation of Europe and the Second World War, and the use of interpreters in the Bosnia-Herzegovina conflict in the 1990s.

In a pioneering collection of conference papers, Footitt and Kelly (2012b) provide a wider view of language in the military, starting with the example of the French Army in the eighteenth century and moving on to cover the Franco-Irish campaign against Britain at the end of the eighteenth century, the problems of the allied coalition in the First World War, the Italian Army in Slovenia in 1915 to 1917, German problems in Finland in the Second World War, British forces in Bosnia in the 1990s, untrained interpreters in the Korean War, the British Army's contact with refugees, the Irish language in the Northern Ireland conflict, language problems in Cyprus, Serbo-Croatian in Yugoslavia, language in the Imperial War Museum and the role of the British Council.

The break-up of Yugoslavia in the 1990s led to the surfacing of a number of language issues, as each of the newly independent states tried to establish their own language variety as a replacement for the Serbo-Croatian that had been mandated by Tito. Kelly and Baker (2013) provide a detailed case study of this in Bosnia-Herzegovina and the problems faced by the United Nations (UN) forces, lacking knowledge of the local language, in working as peace-keepers. As a result of the inadequacy of improvised language services, the North Atlantic Treaty Organization (NATO) forces established a Linguistic Services Branch. Local interpreters were often resented as representing occupation forces. Problems of ethnic identity plagued them and the military. The multilingualism of the NATO forces also led to miscommunication.

Training for military and intelligence

Another case study by Footitt and Tobia (2013) looks at the role of language in the British effort during the Second World War and after. The book starts with a sketch of the limited role played by pre-war foreign language education in providing the proficiency that was soon seen to be needed. It goes on to describe the linguistic skills needed in understanding intelligence material, including the results of code breaking that started to become available. It deals with the proficiency needed by those in face-to-face contact, whether as interrogators or as spies. It then describes the role of language in the psychological warfare conducted especially by radio. Another chapter describes the preparations for the invasion of the continent, followed by one which deals in particular with the training of military interpreters for the war trials. With the conclusion of hostilities, two areas continued to be important: communication with war refugees and preparation for the Cold War which required the training of Russian speakers.

Armies often develop their own language policy. One interesting case of an independent policy is Canada. From the establishment of the Canadian Armed Forces in 1868, they were predominantly Anglophone, with English as the working language and used in all the technical services. Around the turn of the century, there was a suggestion that officers should know French, but the fact that fewer French than English Canadians served in the army seems to have justified neglecting this suggestion (Preston, 1991: 158). However, by the time of the Korean War and with the developing government support for bilingualism, it was decided in 1951 to open a French language military college in Québec. A 60–40 mix was proposed; Francophones received initial instruction in French, but they required English in the units to which they were posted. Military training was more important than linguistic training. Basically, Francophones were learning English or dropping out in the third year, but Anglophones were not developing French proficiency.

In 1966, the Canadian Prime Minister made a statement favouring bilingualism and three steps were proposed to implement it in the armed forces: Francophone schools for the children of soldiers which would encourage their parents to volunteer, a French language military training centre and French language units in the army, navy and air force. A directorate was set up to handle implementation of the policy, but both the air force and the navy were reluctant and, by the 1990s, it was clear that the programme was a failure (Bernier and Pariseau, 1994). The government policy could not be implemented.

Summing up, armed forces have special language needs, with the dominant issue the need for a common language of communication. The inclusion of recruits speaking other varieties and the overseas service of many soldiers, sailors and airmen means that the armed forces become a means of increasing the linguistic repertoire of those who serve. All of this justifies the recognition of military language policy as a significant field.

Notes

1. See the Wikipedia article on the sentence: some to whom the statement has been misattributed include Antoine Meillet, Hubert Lyautey and Joshua Fishman.
2. This chapter follows closely the chapter 'Military language management' in Spolsky (2009a).
3. James Roach, appointed after the First World War to be assistant examiner at the University of Cambridge Local Examinations Syndicate and who developed the Cambridge English examinations, told me that his father, a clergyman, suggested he join the Indian Army at the outbreak of war as he could not afford to buy him a commission in the British Army or support his expenses. He did this and although under age, served in the Middle East.

7 Imperialism and Colonialism

Although the armed forces of a state are commonly under the control of a minister or department of defence, they are historically likely to be used in offence, in campaigns of conquest that lead to the spread and imposition of imperial language varieties. Not just the empires of the past, but as Phillipson (1992a) claims, 'military dominance worldwide and the neoliberal economy constitute a new form of empire that consolidates a single imperial language'. In this chapter, I will explore some imperial languages spread by conquest and often maintained after independence: in the next, I will consider the claim that linguistic imperialism continues as a result of economic power.

Colonies in the ancient world

One of the earliest attested imperial languages was Aramaic which, together with Akkadian, became an official language of the Neo-Assyrian Empire in the mid-eighth century BCE, until it was replaced by Greek during the Seleucid Empire in the fourth century BCE but continued as a major spoken language until the Islamic Conquest in the seventh century CE which spread Arabic over the region. Although none of these empires enforced the use of the imperial language as a vernacular, the major ethnic deportations of the Neo-Assyrian period and the spread of Islamic religion led in time to the adoption of the invading language by the conquered peoples. Rochette (2011) says that Latin was never imposed by force in the Roman Empire, the eastern provinces of which continued to use Greek, but was spread by the army, by retired legionnaires and by its use in the courts. Nor did Islam insist on Arabic as a secular lingua franca; although Arabic was the language of the conquerors and of their religion and culture and ultimately replaced Aramaic in much of the Middle East, many regions continued to use their local languages. Persia, Turkey, the Sudan and the Berber areas of North Africa continued to use their vernaculars.

The Portuguese Empire

But the imposition of imperial varieties was associated with conquest and religious conversion, as was shown with one of the first Western empires, the Portuguese colonies in South America, Asia and Africa, which form the basis of a modern Portuguese-speaking confederation.[1] The Portuguese Empire, founded at the end of the fifteenth century, lasted until the Carnation revolution of 1974, when soldiers and civilians protested the cost of fighting wars against independence movements. Although the Empire was intended to exploit the colonies for trade in slaves and goods produced by slaves, without success at sending settlers except to Brazil, the long period of rule helped to set Portuguese as the only official language in the territory, so that it subsequently could serve as a unifying force in independent African communities (Chabal and Birmingham, 2002). Portuguese resisted globalisation and the spread of English, so that it is now the fifth most common language on the Internet (Martins, 2014). Its official status dates from the reign in the fourteenth century of the poet-king, Dinis I (Ferreira, 2005).

In Portuguese colonies, the meagre education provided for the indigenous people was left to the Roman Catholic Church and its missionaries, some of whom saw value in using the local languages to teach the catechism, but this policy was banned by colonial administrators. In Africa, the artificiality of borders established by the European powers dividing up the continent meant that attempts of activists to use indigenous languages were vitiated by the multiplicity of varieties within the newly independent states and the lack of standardisation; as a result, political leaders and parties chose Portuguese as a unifying force, which meant that the imperial language was carried over into postcolonial language policy. As a result, the previous Portuguese colonies now form Lusofonia, a linguistic union of the homeland, Brazil and the former colonies with nearly 200 million speakers.

Portuguese colonialism hid behind *lusotropicalism*, an ideology proposed by the Brazilian sociologist Gilberto Freyre. He suggested that the Moorish origin of the Portuguese prepared them for life in the tropics and for the merger of European and Black cultures (Freyre, 1938). Plantation society was patriarchal with most of its settlers male. In the absence of female settlers, the planters married local or enslaved black women. The ideology sanctioned Portuguese colonisation as a non-exploitative fusion. These ideas were welcomed by dictators (Getúlio Vargas in Brazil and Antonio Salazar in Portugal) in the 1930s and not rejected until the 1974 Revolution. They continued to provide a post hoc ideological basis for the maintenance of the imperial language in the successor states and formation of an imaginary territory of cultures and a symbol on the basis of which to build a political union.

Brazil

The language situation in the colonies was complex. Take Brazil for instance. Before its conquest, it was occupied by indigenous tribes. Portuguese colonisation started in 1530, with administrators and Jesuits arriving later in the century. For two centuries, there was a steady expansion of the territory occupied by settlers. When a short attempt to enslave local Indians to work in the plantations failed, the colonists began to bring slaves from Africa. Between the middle of the fifteenth century and the end of the nineteenth, Brazil brought in one third of the nearly 10 million slaves that came to the Americas (Curtin, 1972). The discovery of gold in 1690s encouraged new male European settlers. The Brazilian colony became independent early: in 1807, fearing a Napoleonic invasion, the Portuguese royal court moved from Lisbon to Brazil. Ten years later, to justify remaining in Brazil, a United Kingdom of Portugal and Brazil was proclaimed; when the Royal Court moved back to Lisbon in 1821, the Brazilians refused to become a colony again and independence was recognised in 1825 (Schultz, 2001).

Brazilian colonial language policy dates back to the 'Directory of the Indians' published in 1757 which banned the use of indigenous languages and made Portuguese obligatory. Only white settlers knew the language and there was little if any schooling for Indians and slaves (Massini-Cagliari, 2004). Even after independence, Brazilian language policy continued to ignore the fact that Brazil was becoming one of the most diverse language areas in the world (Lewis et al., 2016). Over the centuries, diversity was augmented by the many languages brought by the slaves from Africa and by the introduction of four important immigrant languages: German with 1,500,000 speakers, Italian with 50,000 speakers, Japanese with 380,000 speakers and Spanish with 460,000 speakers (Rodrigues, 1986). Brazilian Portuguese, influenced in part by the other languages of the country, has now become the recognised standard for Lusofonia. In recent years, as in much of Latin America, there has been some recognition of multilingualism and some support for the threatened indigenous languages (Hamel, 2013). But essentially, the colonial language policy and the sizable number of settlers from Portugal resulted in the dominance of the imperial language even after two centuries of independence.

Portuguese colonies in Asia

Even in Asia where the Portuguese were traders, initial colonial policy was to enforce the imperial language. However, in Malacca, the Moluccas, Goa and Macau, political changes after independence have left only minimal Portuguese influence on the language pattern. The exception is Timor-Leste, influenced by the fact that it was invaded and ruled successively by the Dutch, the Japanese and Indonesia, until the United Nations sent in Australian soldiers and finally granted independence. Under Indonesian rule, Portuguese was banned and Indonesian was the language of instruction in schools. The occupations – Portuguese, Dutch, Japanese, Indonesian, Australian – and globalisation have had major effects on the sociolinguistic repertoire, setting a complex challenge for language policy. After independence, Portuguese and an indigenous variety, Tetun, were made official; English and Indonesian remain working languages (Taylor-Leech, 2009).

Portuguese colonies in Africa

Africa was different. The Portuguese Empire in Africa was one of the earliest, dating back to the explorations of the fifteenth century. The West African colonies traded with Brazil, providing slaves for the colony. In the nineteenth century, products grown by the forced labour of African slaves were traded with other nations as well. Other European powers competed for territory in Africa, leading to a major conference in 1884–5. King Leopold II of Belgium persuaded France and Germany to invite thirteen European nations to establish a policy for the sharing of Africa (Förster et al., 1988). Meeting in Bismarck's official residence in Berlin, the conference first resolved to end slavery. It agreed which European states had a rightful claim to which regions and established the principle of effective occupation, which required a ruling nation to negotiate treaties with local rulers, to fly a national flag, to police the territory and to exploit it economically. This principle applied to coastal areas, but the European nations later claimed interiors of which they had not yet taken control.

The Berlin conference granted Portugal territory between Angola and Mozambique, which Britain later occupied. It set boundaries between French and British and between French and German territories. It established the Congo Free State as the personal possession of King Leopold of Belgium. The Niger and Congo rivers were declared free for travel. By 1902, the scramble for Africa had brought 90 per cent of the continent under European sovereignty, divided in ways that ignored the existing ethnic and linguistic zones and thus produced the fragmented states of which Angola was a prime example.

In the Portuguese colonies in Africa, schooling was largely left to religious missions, though there were commonly bans on teaching in indigenous languages. Like the French, the Portuguese conferred citizenship – the status of *assimilado* (civilised) – only on those natives who had achieved Portuguese linguistic and cultural proficiency, a rare phenomenon. In Mozambique, with a population of 31,255,435, only 4,500 Africans ever reached this level.

Independence came to these former slave colonies in 1974, but in all cases, Portuguese remained the official language, though there have been movements for bilingual education in Angola and Mozambique. Angola has thirty-five indigenous languages, but over half of the population uses Portuguese as a second or third language (Makoni and Severo, 2015). Cape Verde, without an indigenous population, was an important site for the slave trade and is now inhabited by half a million *mestiços* and former slaves. Education remains weak; Portuguese has few native speakers, but it is the only official language; the majority speak one of two dialects of Kaberverdianu, a stigmatised creole. São Tomé and Principe was similarly settled only for the slave trade; official Portuguese is spoken as a second language by speakers of the three unrecognised creole varieties.

Mozambique had a good number of Portuguese settlers who exploited the slave trade, but most left after independence. However, the ruling Front for the Liberation of Mozambique chose Portuguese as official, aiming to 'make the language of the enemy our instrument of combat' (Stroud, 1999: 347). There are over forty indigenous languages spoken there, mainly of Bantu origin, and knowledge of Portuguese is weak. The preference for the colonial language, together with serious political and economic problems, has prevented the development of a workable language education policy.

Guinea-Bissau has many ethnic groups and seventeen indigenous languages. Portuguese, with few native speakers, is official, but Kiriol, with a quarter of a million native speakers and another 600,000 second language speakers, is widely spoken but not recognised in the educational system; few children complete elementary school.

The basic pattern of Lusophone Africa, now formally united as *Países Africanos de Língua Oficial Portuguesa* (PALOP), can be summed up as early settlement by a small number of Portuguese men who married local indigenous women or slaves, producing a mixed population and a creole. The colonial rulers exploited slavery or forced labour for agriculture or mining and required that any education be in Portuguese. It was accepted as language of unity in the postcolonial state, which suffered continued poverty, civil wars and corrupt dictatorships.

The French Empire

French colonies were also created for the benefit not of the indigenous conquered peoples but of the home country.[2] Their borders were set for political convenience and produced a jumble of ethnicities, languages and cultures. Exploitation was the main aim of colonisation and there was generally no attempt to find a practical educational solution to the local diversity.

During French rule, a small elite of the colonised people was assimilated, having been educated in French and convinced of its value. Local languages and creoles were stigmatised and banned from school use, reducing their status in the eyes of their speakers. After independence, the French-speaking locals replaced the colonial rulers, applying much the same language policy or in a few cases attempting to establish hegemony for a local variety. However, centralised language policy failed to change widespread traditional language practices: it was not just the pressure of other interest groups, but even more the effects of economic, demographic and political pressures that hindered producing a French-speaking population. Thus, it is not just the competition of various levels of language management, but political and economic weakness that continues to prevent the solution of the language problems first recognised half a century ago.

The French experience was similar to the Portuguese, but with important differences. The second French Empire started later than the Portuguese, with less time to have an effect. And although in the early years the French too depended on the Church for education, after the French Revolution, the school systems were secularised. But like the Portuguese, the French proclaimed a civilising role, which meant the imposition of the metropolitan language and culture with no regard or respect for indigenous local sociolinguistic patterns. Again, except in those cases where there was large-scale European settlement, accompanied by land grabs, slavery, forced movement or murder of indigenous residents, the monolingual ideology was implemented by ignoring indigenous languages and teaching the metropolitan language to an elite minority.

The earliest documentary statement of French language policy, the *Ordonnance de Villers-Cotterêts* issued in 1539 required French in place of Latin in court documents.[3] A centralising language policy was reaffirmed by Cardinal Richelieu, who, in the early seventeenth century, fought against *dérèglement*, disorder, threatened by powerful regional nobles: he set out to assert central rule through imposing a standardised Parisian version of the French spoken by the royal court (Cooper, 1989). The language policy that Richelieu instituted was continued and enshrined by the Jacobins in 1793 during the French Revolution, when they passed a decree, Article 7 of which required that, throughout the Republic, instruction was to take place solely in French (Ager, 1999: 21). The policy was implemented by a decree calling for the appointment of a French teacher in those areas where a regional language was still spoken: Brittany, Alsace-Lorraine, Corsica and the mountain regions. Other language laws followed during the nineteenth century: the Guizot law in 1833 ordered primary teaching in French and a decision of 1881 made primary schooling free, compulsory and secular. However, full implementation of French as a language of instruction took many years because of the shortage of qualified French-speaking teachers.

In the twentieth century, the Deixonne law did allow for some teaching of four regional languages – Basque, Breton, Occitan and Catalan – in school, but only for one hour a week. The primacy of the French language was finally incorporated into the French Constitution of 1992, as one of the amendments felt necessary because of the Maastricht Treaty which established the European Union. It was confirmed by the Toubon Law of 1994.

Language policy applied to all territory under French rule, so that the colonies too were part of the monolingual hegemony. Even after they became independent, most former French colonies maintained an official status for French, which helps to account for the development and name of Francophonie, an organisation of over forty independent French-speaking nations. There were exceptions in North Africa (with Arabisation) and Asia (in former French Indochina), but in sub-Saharan Africa and elsewhere, French remains strong in former colonies. The ideology was clear. Peripheral territories had been included in the idealised home territory – Occitan in the south, Basque and Catalan in the west, Breton, Flemish and Breton in the north; others were added (Alsatian German and Corsican) by later conquest. The same policy was then applied to overseas colonies. In each, government policy called for forced educational assimilation, although local pressure for language maintenance was finally if partially recognised by the Deixonne law, allowing some limited teaching of the local language in schools. In a classic lecture, Renan (1882) defined the French notion of nationalism – a voluntary association of citizens, one and indivisible, secular and based on universal principles of liberty, equality, fraternity and the rights of man. This was consistent, Ager (2001: 19) says, with the notion of 'one language, one culture, one territory, one political conception' with a hegemonic language as the centre of the nation state, and accounts for the policies that aimed to impose a single language on the diverse regions that made up France with their assortment of local languages and varieties.

The notion of unification through language was applied to the colonies: 'during the height of the colonial period between 1880 and 1960, the same education was provided for (some) children in Africa as for those in Lille: the same textbooks were used . . .' (Ager, 2001: 18). In the colonies, there was a strong belief in the civilising function of French rule. It was during the Third Republic (1870–1940), Conklin (1997: 1) asserts, that France declared its unique mission to civilise the people it was conquering and colonising. It assumed the superiority of the French, the primitive nature of the indigenous peoples that they were now ruling, the perfectibility of humankind and the special qualifications of France, after the Revolution, to take on the task. But the time allowed proved to be too short in most cases, so that what happened was a change in ideology; French proficiency was confined to a privileged few who benefited from the school system. However, because the leaders of the independence movements and the rulers of the newly independent successor states came from this elite, the ideology was preserved and the notion of the hegemony of a standard French language was continued in most former colonies.

An important force behind this continuation of the colonial metropolitan language was labelled by Myers-Scotton (1990, 1993) as *elite closure*, a process, she suggests, by which those in power maintain their privileged position by language choice. In particular, it occurred in those colonial African societies where only a small group acquired the colonial language, but they used it to maintain their leadership and power in the postcolonial state. In French African colonies, Bokamba (1991) estimates, no more than 20 per cent acquired proficiency in the French language, maintained as the only official language by those leaders who had benefited from the limited educational systems.

It is useful to distinguish between the major varieties of colony: colonies of occupation, where an army conquers and sets up what they hope will be continuing rule, and settler colonies where significant numbers of settlers are sent from the homeland to the conquered territory (Johnston and Lawson, 2000). An even earlier stage were trading colonies, where a handful of settlers were accompanied by missionaries and later defended by French military force. The French settlements in North America and in Algeria became settler colonies, leaving significant numbers of speakers of French in Canada and the United States after the French had lost control and resulting in the expulsion and repatriation of many settlers and other French speakers (Jews and Christians) when the North African colonies became independent. The other settlements in Africa and those in Asia were largely occupation colonies, initially conquered for trade and later developed as plantation colonies, necessitating the importation of slaves or forced labour. In some of these, because locals had remained the majority, it was feasible for the indigenous peoples to attempt to restore their traditional culture and language after independence.

French colonies in North America

In North America, French settlers began to arrive in 1604. A long period of conflict with the British concluded with the surrender of Montréal in 1760 and the Treaty of Paris of 1763 when New France became the Province of Québec and its inhabitants became British subjects.

However, the Québec Act (1764) granted rights to the defeated French. The legislative assembly of Lower Canada used both English and French, but the Act of Union (1840) favoured English. The British North America Act (1867) established the Dominion of Canada as a confederation of four provinces, Ontario, Québec, New Brunswick and Nova Scotia; the Act set English and French as official languages, both of which could be used in federal parliament and courts. Provision and control of education was left to the provinces and allowed for denominational schools. Some provinces did not maintain linguistic equality: for instance, Manitoba in 1890 abolished French in schools and the legislature (Conrick and Regan, 2007). The Act set official languages only for Québec, but in 1969, with the passing of the Official Languages Act, French and English were both required for government use at federal level. Over the years, there was an increase in the number of non-English, non-French immigrants, who made up a third of the population by 1971: 45 per cent of the population were of British origin and 29 per cent of French origin; in 2011, 21 per cent of the Canadian population were native speakers of French. But only English and French were supported.[4]

In the 1960s, a growing shift to English led to attempts by the French-speaking majority in Québec to remedy the low status of their language, directed by a movement called the Quiet Revolution (Gagnon and Montcalm, 1990). In 1976, a separatist political party came to power and one of its first steps was to declare French the only official language of the Province (Genesee, 1988).

Bill 101, passed in 1977, known as the Charter of the French Language, mandated the use of French. Names of towns, rivers and mountains were changed from English to French; non-Francophone professionals had to pass French proficiency examinations; only children of Anglophone parents who had attended an English school in Québec could attend an English-medium school; all commercial advertising and public signs had to be in the official language; all films had to be dubbed in French; courts and the legislature could operate only in French; all municipalities must conduct their business in French; all businesses must have French names and if they employed more than fifty staff members, must conduct internal business in French; and quotas for Francophones were set for every level of administration. A large number of Anglophone residents and businesses left the Province in consequence (Fishman, 1991: 310).

In spite of unevenness in the level of national bilingualism and continuing conflicts over the method of implementation (Mitchell, 2016), the number of French-speaking settlers and the history of the federation has produced in Canada an English-speaking community that respects the rights of minority French speakers and has permitted in Québec the creation of a Francophone Province that enforces the position of French. Here, it was not imperial French language management, but the continuing existence of French speakers living in close contact and maintaining religious and educational institutions, translated into political power and threatening secession, that forced Canadian recognition of what had become a minority language. And it was political power and the threat of withdrawing from the federation that forced the Canadian Government to accept a national bilingual policy and to overcome the effects of conquest.

In the United States, the situation was different. French Canadians moved to New England in large numbers from Canada in the nineteenth century, living in ethnic communities held together by the Catholic Church, which established over 280 parishes to which were appointed French speaking clergy in spite of the opposition of Irish bishops who argued for assimilation. By 1912, children could study in 123 Franco-American parochial schools that taught originally in French but that slowly shifted to English. In 1911, there were seven French daily newspapers, though only one survived until 1960. For many years, there were close relations with French Canada and continued immigration but, gradually, the second generation adjusted to accepting permanent settlement, shifting to English and intermarrying. Less time was devoted to French in the schools and the parishes shifted to teaching in English. Although there remained a few who resisted, by the 1960s most were giving up on French language and ethnic traditions (Lemaire, 1966).

Louisiana was different. The region was claimed as a French colony in 1722 and slaves were brought from West Africa. After the Seven Years War, in 1763 Louisiana was ceded to Spain, but Francophone immigration continued, with an increase in 1765 when settlers were expelled from Arcadia (now Nova Scotia) by the British. French and Spanish settlers and African slaves continued to move into the region. At the end of the eighteenth century, a scheme to persuade women to go out to Louisiana failed, so the French Government started to ship out women criminals and prostitutes (Zug, 2016). In 1800, Napoleon reacquired the colony, but in 1803, the French sold Louisiana (which included Missouri and Illinois) to the United States. Lower Louisiana became the US state of Louisiana and Upper Louisiana became the states of Illinois, Indiana and Missouri.

This history helps to explain the complicated language pattern that developed. In Upper Louisiana, a variety identified as Missouri French existed for a while but is virtually extinct (Carrière, 1941). In what is now Louisiana, a number of varieties developed: standard French, a Louisianan variety developed from Arcadian Canadian French (Cajun) and a number of varieties of Louisiana Creole forming a continuum as is common with creoles (Valdman, 1997). By the end of the twentieth century, Louisiana French and Creole were being replaced by English, only people over the age of fifty still being fluent speakers and generally using the language only in the family and with each other. In 1968, influenced by the ethnic revival (Fishman et al., 1985), the Louisiana State Government established the Council for the Development of French in Louisiana which supports university scholarships for studying French, immersion programmes and other community language programmes. Louisiana shares with other former colonies a low level of education and poor socioeconomic status as well as authoritarian local government (Associated Press News, 2019). It was perhaps this poverty and poor education, resulting in less than normal upward social mobility, that kept some speakers of Creole continuing to use their heritage language, but certainly without any significant contribution from French language management.

French colonies in Asia and the Pacific

In Asia, French Jesuit missionaries arrived in Vietnam in the seventeenth century and European trade started in the eighteenth century. In the middle of the nineteenth century, France sent a naval fleet to Vietnam in order to protect its missionaries; it captured Saigon in 1859 and began to accumulate territory used mainly for trade and plantations. In the 1880s, following victory in a war with China, four protectorates (Annan, Tonkin and Cochinchina – together forming the current Vietnam – and Cambodia) were united as French Indochina, with Laos added in 1893.

The Japanese occupied Indochina during the Second World War and French forces reoccupied it after the war; however, the Viet Minh continued fighting and the French were forced to withdraw as part of the Geneva Accords of 1956, a major defeat for the Second French Empire. French Indochina had been considered a *colonie d'exploitation économique* and not a *colonie de population*, so that, by 1940, only about 34,000 French civilians lived there (compared to over 1 million in North Africa). Nevertheless, French was the language of instruction in schools. The educated elite, especially in Vietnam, started to use it, but local populations continued to speak over 100 languages. Wright (2002) notes that only a tiny minority were educated in French; most Vietnamese were uneducated and used a Vietnamese–French pidgin to communicate with their employers. After independence, Vietnamese became the official language and the role of English grew.

There were French colonies in Polynesia too. French Polynesia is made up of over 100 islands and atolls, 67 of them inhabited, and has a population over 285,000, mostly of Polynesian origin, spreading over 1,200 miles in the South Pacific Ocean (Paia and Vernaudon, 2016). The most populous island is Tahiti, the city Pape'ete serving as the administrative centre of what is now an overseas collectivity of France. Only French is an official language in French Polynesia; although Tahitian is taught in the Sorbonne, it may not be used in the assembly, but in 1981, a decree added it to those languages permitted under the Deixonne law. In 2007, 68 per cent of the population reported speaking French at home and 24 per cent reported they spoke Tahitian; in the 2012 census, most people over the age of fifteen claimed French, but 85 per cent said they spoke a Polynesian language (Paia and Vernaudon, 2016). In Polynesia under continued French rule, language policy has been successful in establishing the French language, though it competes with religious and commercial support of English.

Its existence reported originally by a Portuguese explorer in 1606, New Hebrides was rediscovered by the French explorer Louis Antoine de Bougainville in 1768. In 1825, a trader found sandalwood there and brought in Polynesian workers who later clashed with the indigenous Austronesian people, the Ni-Vanuatu. Originally most settlers were British from Australia, but by the twentieth century they were outnumbered by French settlers. The community remained more or less independent, with locals divided in preference for annexation by Britain or France. The British–French Condominium that was set up ignored education until the 1960s when the British opened some English-medium primary schools in rural areas and a secondary school and a training college in Port Vila. To compete, the French started French-medium schools. Neither system used or permitted local languages or Bislama,[5] a pidgin which has been creolised. Renamed Vanuatu on independence in 1980, the national language is now Bislama; it is official together with English and French. There are another eighty languages spoken in Vanuatu, most with fewer than 1,000 speakers. Vanuatu shares with other former colonies pressure to maintain the imperial language, with the dispute between English and French taking attention away from the recognition of indigenous varieties and even the appeal of a widespread local creole, Bislama, used as a lingua franca by most people.

New Caledonia is a special collectivity still under French rule pending a third referendum in 2020.[6] The archipelago, including the main island and a number of smaller islands in the south-west Pacific Ocean, has a population of over 250,000. Discovered by James Cook in 1774, early trading focused on sandalwood and blackbirding (seizing native Kanakas to work in Australian plantations). The London Missionary Society and the Roman Catholic Marist brothers started missionary work in the 1840s. In 1854, the French Navy under orders from Napoleon III took possession and founded the city of Nouméa. The mission schools taught in the indigenous languages, but in 1919, came under the control of the Education Service; use of indigenous languages was banned and the mission schools closed (Léonard, 1996). Pressure for use of indigenous languages re-emerged in the 1970s and in 1984, the ban on Kanakan languages was relaxed. Under French rule, the government continues to be reluctant to recognise the needs of the speakers of the local languages and, as a result, the level of educational achievement of the indigenous population remains low (Léonard, 1996).

French colonies in the Caribbean

The first permanent French settlement in the Caribbean was founded in 1635 on the island of Martinique. A company was set up by Cardinal Richelieu to develop the region and colonies were established in Guadeloupe, Grenada, Dominica and Trinidad. Martinique and Guadeloupe are currently overseas departments; St Martin and St Barthélemy form overseas collectivities. Haiti was once French; Dominica and Saint Lucia became British before they became independent.

The history of French Caribbean conquest and colonies is complicated: many were fought over and occasionally lost to other imperial powers and they became independent at various times. But they share in the fact that they were mainly plantation colonies, with West African slaves brought in to replace the Caribs and other indigenous peoples who were commonly slaughtered or wiped out by introduced diseases. Those colonies that became independent entered a period of instability, caused by misrule or natural disasters. They also share a common linguistic fate: the indigenous and African languages were replaced by a number of varieties of French-based creoles, which were also ignored by colonial and independent governments and usually kept out of the education system. Whoever ruled, the linguistic ideology continued to assume the importance and centrality of French, as language of government and public life, controlled and used by a small educated elite.

Haiti is a special case. When he proposed the term 'diglossia' for the situation he discovered in Arabic-speaking countries in which two related languages divided up functions, one serving as the prestige formal, written and official language and the second being widely spoken as the vernacular, Ferguson (1959) presented a number of typical cases: Switzerland (with High German and Swiss German), Greece (with *katharévusa* and *dhimotí*) and Haiti (with French and Creole). Haiti shares the western portion of the island of Hispaniola with the Dominican Republic. Many creole linguists do not see the situation as diglossia, but as two separate linguistic communities, a minority Creole/French bilingual elite and the majority urban and rural Creole-speaking masses. Also, whereas the leading scholar, Albert Valdman, once believed that all French-based creoles were related dialects, he now understands that each is a fully autonomous language, differing significantly in structure and role (Valdman, 2015: ix).

Originally conquered and settled by Spanish explorers, Haiti was ceded to France in the seventeenth century and grew using the labour of slaves brought from Africa into a major producer of sugarcane. During the French Revolution, the slaves revolted and defeated the French, becoming independent in 1804. Many whites were killed or emigrated, leaving a largely black population of over 700,000. In 1915, American forces took over control of Haiti and were withdrawn only in 1934, after which the Dominican dictator Trujillo ordered the killing of Haitians on the Dominican side of the border. In the 1950s, François Duvalier became dictator. Succeeded by his son in 1971, disorder followed the latter's ousting in 1986 and democratic government was only established in 1994. In the twenty-first century, there have been a series of tropical storms, cholera outbreaks and earthquakes and the political situation remains unstable. There are high levels of corruption and poverty. Foreign aid is necessary. The two official languages are French, said to be spoken by 40 per cent of the population and used in government, schools and business, and Haitian Creole spoken by all as a vernacular (Valdman, 1968, 2001). The long debate over the standardisation of Haitian Creole (*Kreyòl*) reflects various ideological positions on Haitian individual and national identity (Schieffelin and Doucet, 1998).

Dominica became a French colony in 1727. In 1763, France ceded the island to the British; French remained the official language, but the population generally spoke Creole. In 1861, the island became a crown colony and formed part of the Windwards. In 1978, it became independent, but was soon threatened by mercenaries; with US help, this was averted and parliamentary government restored. English is now the official language, but most speak *Patwa*, an Antillean creole based on French; some speak an English-based creole, *Kokoy*. Island Carib is extinct. English is the official language of government and urban life; Patwa (*patois*) has been the normal vernacular of rural areas (Paugh, 2005).

Although it is located in South America and borders Brazil, Guiana, its official name, is often associated with the French Caribbean. With a population of over 250,000, two-thirds of them with French nationality, it is an overseas department and the second largest region of France; it is the most prosperous territory in South America, with a 2015 gross national income near $10,000, much of its economy supported by the European Space Agency. There were originally five Guianas; Spanish, now part of Venezuela, British now Guyana, Dutch now Suriname, Portuguese now part of Brazil, and French. Given the linguistic diversity and the general failure of the educational system to handle it, the level of education in French Guiana is the lowest in all of France, with half of the children not completing high school (Migge and Léglise, 2010).

French colonies in Africa

Although the development of French colonies in Africa is mainly associated with the scramble for Africa in the nineteenth century and so included in what is called the Second Colonial Empire, there was a French presence in West Africa as early as the fifteenth century, when various European powers started to send traders and to compete. In the 1850s, the French began to occupy the mainland, one of their goals being to abolish the slave trade conducted by the many native kingdoms. There was gradual settlement, with preference for more developed areas (Huillery, 2011).

The present population of Senegal, which was granted independence in 1960 and almost established federation with the French Sudan, which broke away to form the Republic of Mali, is over 13 million. The largest of the twenty or so ethnic groups are the Wolof (43 per cent) followed by the Fula (24 per cent) and the Serer (14 per cent). The official language is French, which 10 per cent of the population is said to know well and another 10 per cent of males and 2 per cent of females to know partially. Wolof is the lingua franca, said to be understood by 80 per cent of the population (Eberhard et al., 2019).

Mali had a long history as the centre of a Muslim empire which flourished from the thirteenth to the seventeenth century. Islam was introduced into West Africa early and flourished during the Mali Empire – Timbuktu was a centre of Islamic learning during the empire: three madrassas formed what is now known as the University of Timbuktu. The people of the town speak one of several varieties of Songuay, a Nilo-Hamitic language, but Arabic was the language of Muslim scholars. The empire was divided into three warring states in the seventeenth century and conquered by the Bamana (Bambara) Empire in the middle of the century. This empire lasted until conquered by the Toucouleur, speakers of Fula. Internal and external slavery was common.

Mali came to be known as the French Sudan as it was gradually occupied by French forces starting in 1879; the occupation was completed in 1890. It became independent as part of the Mali Federation in 1959, but this only lasted two years. In 2012, Tuareg rebels formed a breakaway state, which was recaptured by Malian and French forces a year later. The rebels destroyed many of the manuscripts in the libraries, but others were saved. As a result of the fighting and of chronic food shortages, hundreds of thousands of Malians were displaced. There is still a high proportion of child labour and the state remains a centre for internal and international human trafficking. Marked now by the second highest rate of infant mortality in the world and with a low level of literacy, the population of Mali is estimated to be 17.5 million. Ethnically, 34 per cent are Bambara, 15 per cent Fulani, 10 per cent each Sarakole and Serufo and there are several other ethnic groups. The official language is French, but nearly half the population are reported to speak Bambara; in addition, there are now thirteen recognised national languages. The large majority of Malians continue to be Muslim.

Summarising the effect of French colonial language education policy in French West Africa, Bokamba (1991) concluded that it had produced the highest level of illiteracy in the region, the highest school dropout rate and the least well-developed lingua francas in Africa. This was the result of the application of the French-only rule in all colonies, with the requirement of French reinforced by regular banning of the local languages, such as in the 1911 decree setting up primary schools in Senegal. Only a small number of natives were educated: in 1960, only thirty-one Malians received a bacca-laureate. But the value of French for the elite few who learned it was high, serving as the qualification for upward mobility, so that continuation of the language policy by the government was assured after independence. Since independence, the former French colonies have spent a large proportion of their budget on education but most of the money has gone to teachers' sala-ries. The new states have continued the French notion of elitism in education; promotion to a higher class depends on performance in French and those subjects taught in French and, as a result, about 25 per cent of children in Mali schools are required to repeat a class level.

At the end of the nineteenth century, the French invaded Mauritania, defeating the existing emirate by 1912. The French incorporated Mauritania into French West Africa. During colonial rule, 90 per cent of the population remained nomadic. In 1960, Mauritania became independent and chose a new capital city, Nouakchott. Many other sub-Saharans moved in, usually French speaking and thus qualified to become government employees. The French Army continued to fight the northern Hassane tribes. Dominant elites work to Arabise Mauritian law and language. Ethnic discord continues and Amnesty International is concerned that laws against slavery are not observed (Alt, 2013). Since 1999, Arabic has been the language of instruc-tion initially in primary school, with French introduced in the second year and used to teach science. Arabisation was a reaction to the French policy of replacing the existing Muslim culture and Arabic language with French civilisation (Ahmed, 2012). The Arabisation movement became more focused in 2010, in speeches given by the country's prime minister and culture minister. As in many former colonies, social conflict and political struggles have blocked any attempt to develop and implement a workable language education policy.

Originally part of various West African empires, central Guinea was active in the slave trade from the sixteenth century and an Islamic state from 1735 to 1898. In 1898, the French defeated Samouri Touré, Emperor of the short-lived Wassulu Empire. Guinea achieved independence in 1958, refusing autonomy in the French Community and Sekou Touré became president, aligning the new state first with the Soviet Union and then with the People's Republic of China. The official language is French, with nearly 3 million second language users. Pular is a de facto language of national identity, with 2.5 million users; Maninkakan is a language of wider communication with 3 million speakers; other major languages are Kissi (280,000) and Sussu (900,000). There are over thirty-four languages altogether (Lewis et al., 2016).

In marked contrast to Guinea, Ivory Coast achieved a high level of economic development after independence, although it too suffered from authoritarian rulers and civil war. With a complex ethnic and linguistic mix of over sixty languages (Delafosse, 1904), it continued the French language hegemony of the colonial empire and, with its indigenous African languages discouraged, is now marked by the unplanned development of a local French creole (N'Guessan, 2008).

The French invaded what is now Burkina Faso in 1894 and made the area part of the Upper Volta colony. It was later included in French West Africa, but after the Second World War became a territory in its own right. It became an autonomous republic in the French Community in 1958 and was granted independence in 1960, as a one-party state. In 1983, a *coup d'état* led to a change of dictator; the following year, the name of the state was changed to Burkina Faso ('land of incorruptible or honourable people') (Englebert, 1996). A short war with Mali followed. There are over sixty languages, with Mòoré (also known as Mossi) spoken by 40 per cent in the central area and the capital city; Jula (Djoula) is spoken by the Mande and other major languages are Fulfulde (also known as Fula) and Gourmanchéma (Gourmanché). The official language is French, used in administration and legal services. Education is expensive; Burkino Faso has one of the lowest literacy rates in the world (https://www.africa.undp.org/content/rba/en/home/ourwork/povertyreduction/successstories/burkina-faso-illiteracy.html).

A major slave trading area in West Africa, Togoland became a German Protectorate in 1886. After the First World War, it was divided between Britain and France; British Togoland become part of Ghana in 1957 and the French section became the independent Togolese Republic in 1959.

Corruption, coups and a thirty-eight-year-long dictatorship followed. The situation is claimed to be improving recently. Togo has forty ethnic groups and forty indigenous languages. French is the statutory national language and many people are said to speak it as a second language.

The French conquest of Dahomey began in 1872; after a second war in 1894, Dahomey became a French protectorate and part of French West Africa in 1904. A port and railroads were built and Catholic missions opened schools. In 1946, it became a French overseas territory and gained independence in 1960, followed by many coups and different forms of government. It was renamed Benin in 1975, a Marxist–Leninist state which lasted until 1990, when it became a multi-party state. A third of the population is reported to speak French, mainly as a second language. French is a mark of prestige and needs to be employed in administration and in the city. All printed material is in French. A local variety called *français d'Afrique* has developed. The most widely spoken indigenous language is Fon, spoken by a quarter of the population. Tossa (1998) found that in the cities, especially the largest (Cotonou), the three main languages are Fon, French and a mixed variety. All indigenous languages are considered national languages and, following a national literacy and adult education policy adopted in 2003, may also be used in pre-school education. Benin is listed as one of the two African countries that support pre-school education in African languages, but there is a lack of resources to support the programmes (Dossou, 2002).

A landlocked territory, Niger is at the bottom of the UN Human Development Index (United Nations Development Programme, 2015) and the literacy rate is the lowest in the world. Niger was conquered by the French after a long struggle starting in 1889 and completed only in 1922 when it became a French colony; the last resisters were the Tuareg, a Berber people. It was granted limited autonomy in 1958 and became independent in 1960. French is the official language, spoken by the educated elite, with 6,000 native speakers and 2 million estimated second language speakers. Hausa is the main trade language, used by 8 million. The 1989 constitution listed a number of national languages, showing the existence of pressure for indigenisation; they are spoken by some residents, are occasionally used on radio and television, and might be used in a few experimental school and adult education programmes and in post-literacy activities. The constitution refers to the task of restoring value to these languages, but there is a huge gap between sociolinguistic reality (with French the status language) and the ideologically favoured promotion of indigenous languages (Wolf, 2003).

Although Arab traders visited the island of Réunion earlier, the first Europeans there were Portuguese, who landed in 1507, but left it virtually untouched. The French arrived in 1638 and brought out convicts, but civil settlement dates from 1664. The French settlers imported African, Chinese and Indian slaves and indentured workers. The island was occupied by the British in 1810 but restored to France in 1815. Slavery was abolished in

1848. In 1860, a Franco-British convention allowed the bringing of 6,000 indentured labourers a year from India. French is the only official language, but many people speak Réunion Creole. This is a continuum, with French and Malagasy as its main sources, but not mutually intelligible with French or with Mauritian Creole (Corne, 1993), developed on the basis of colonial varieties of French (Beniamino, 1996).

In 1638, the Dutch established a settlement on an uninhabited island 1,200 miles off the south-eastern coast of Africa, naming it Mauritius. They abandoned it in 1710 and the French took it over five years later and named it Isle de France. In 1810, it was conquered by the British who allowed the settlers to keep their land and language. It became a sugar-producing colony and developed as a tourist resort. There is no official language, but both English and French can be used in parliament and in official administration. The constitution is in English and the Civil Code in French. Schools use both English and French and pupils must learn both. But most people speak Mauritian Creole (Morisyien, Kreol) as a native language and language of wider communication.

There is no official language in Djibouti either, but both English and French can be used in parliament and in official administration. In 1977, a third referendum voted almost unanimously in favour of independence, which was granted and the first president was in office for twenty years, when, after an armed conflict, a power sharing agreement was reached in 2000. But soon there was only one party, the opposition having boycotted the 2005 and 2008 elections. In 2013, an opposition party was allowed again. There are French and US military bases. The two largest languages are Somali (500,000 speakers) and Afar (300,000), but the official languages are Arabic and French, presumably so as not to favour one of the two major indigenous languages (Appleyard and Orwin, 2008).

A department and region of France, Mayotte is an archipelago in the Indian Ocean between Mozambique and Madagascar. The islands were populated by Bantus and later came under Islamic rule through a succession of sultanates. It was purchased by France in 1841 and voted in 1971 to remain part of France; it became a department in 2014. Polygamy is common and women are unlikely to be employed. Recent problems include a growing population of illegal immigrants, a water shortage and a crisis in education. Mayotte is claimed by the Comoros. The economy depends on French aid. France sees the archipelago as a useful possession, but Comoros claim that they speak the same language. Free immigration to the EU complicates the claims (Muller, 2012). Regnault (2009) discusses the problems that being a French department produces in a society with strong cultural identity. With a population over 200,000, most speak a Bantu language, Comorian (Shimaore), related to the language of the neighbouring Comoro Islands; the second major language is Bushi (Kibushi), a variety of Malagasy. A quarter of the population are immigrants from the Comoros.

Most are Muslims; sharia law still applies. French is the official language, but not widely known.

Visited by Arab traders as early as the tenth century and with Bantu migration in the Middle Ages, French trading posts were set up in Madagascar in the seventeenth century. A local kingdom was recognised by the British in the early nineteenth century and the London Missionary Society translated the Bible into Malagasy. Foreigners were later banned and French incursions fought off, with a series of wars that were ended by annexation by France at the end of the century. Plantations were established. Education between the ages of six and thirteen focused on French. Railways and roads were built by forced labour. During the Second World War, an independence movement became more influential and an autonomous state within the French Community was set up in 1958; full independence followed two years later. Four republics ensued: the first with strong French involvement, the second a socialist–Marxist military government, the Third Republic lasted from 1990 to 2010 and the Fourth was set up in 2010 with a democratic constitution. The population of about 23 million includes many ethnic groups all speaking Malagasy, an official language alongside French and a macrolanguage with many varieties. Under French rule and during the First Republic, French teachers were brought in to implement what was a strong educational system, but they were expelled during the Second Republic and there was a process of *malgachisation*, an attempt to use Malagasy in schools, and a lowering of standards.

Chad, a landlocked basin in Central Africa, has been inhabited and farmed for 2,000 years. Important empires developed there, including the Kanem in the Middle Ages, a third of whose population was slaves. France invaded the area in the late nineteenth century, forming the Territoire Militaire des Pays et Protectorats du Tchad in 1900 and incorporating it in French Equatorial Africa in 1920, but doing little to develop it. Education was neglected; the south was treated as a source of cotton and untrained labour. The French opened only one school in 1921 and by 1933 there were only thirty-three qualified teachers (Mays, 2002: 20); most funding went to the Sara ethnic group in the southern region, producing future leadership (Mays, 2002: 20). After the Second World War, Chad became a French overseas territory and was granted independence in 1960. The official languages are Standard Arabic and French; Chadian Arabic, and its varieties, is the most widely used lingua franca. The quality of education is low. Chad is listed as a failed state by the Fund for Peace, with high corruption, and is ranked as the seventh poorest country in the world in the United Nations Human Development Index. The weakness of the education system can be blamed in part on the French failure to deal with the complex ethnic and linguistic system, imposing its language on a society even though lacking the resources to develop proficiency in it.

The French established their first outpost in Central Africa in 1889 and integrated it into the French Congo in spite of disputes by 1900. It became a separate colony in 1903 and part of French Equatorial Africa in 1910 and later became an overseas territory in 1937. The official languages are French and Sango (or Sangho), an African-based creole with French loanwords (Samarin, 1986) or a simplified form of the base African language, Ngbandi (Diki-Kidiri, 1998). Samarin (1986) reported that standard French was being taught and was perceived as the white man's language; Sango, seen as the language of the Republic, had not been standardised. Public education is poorly funded and fewer than 50 per cent of children are enrolled. Child labour is common. Human rights violations are rampant and human trafficking is at a high level (Central Intelligence Agency, 2017). The Central African Republic is another rare example of a nation which includes an African language (a lingua franca) alongside French as official, but the civil strife and weakness of the educational system has reduced the effect of this recognition.

Also in central Africa, with access to the Atlantic Ocean, Congo-Brazzaville was part of the French colony of West Africa. Originally inhabited by Bantus, it came under French rule in 1880 and was exploited for its natural resources. It was the capital of Free France during the Second World War. It was separated from French West Africa in 1958 as Middle Congo, renamed the Republic of Congo and granted independence in 1960. *Ethnologue* lists sixty-two languages; French is official and Kituba and Lingala are statutory languages of national identity; both are creoles that developed at the end of the nineteenth century (Samarin, 1991). French is the only language of instruction in schools (Galisson et al., 2016).

Originally inhabited by pygmies (Mbenga), the territory of Gabon had already been conquered by migrating Bantu when Europeans arrived in the fifteenth century. In the eighteenth century, there was a Myeni speaking kingdom and the French established the town of Franceville. In 1885 Gabon became a colony and was incorporated into French Equatorial Africa. Independence was granted in 1960 and Léon M'ba was elected president and set up one-party rule; he survived a coup with the intervention of French soldiers who are still there. About 10,000 native French live in Gabon. Many other Gabonese know some French, with 30 per cent of Libreville claiming to speak it natively; 32 per cent speak Fang as mother tongue. French is the language of instruction in schools, but English is taught as a second language. In Gabon you are only considered bilingual if you know two European language (English and French). Children who acquire French at home are considered early bilinguals; those who acquire it at school are considered late bilinguals (Mbokou, 2012).

Germany conquered the Cameroon region in 1884, but after the First World War it was divided between the British (Cameroons) and the French (Cameroun) with a mandate granted to each by the League of Nations in 1922. Cameroun became a *Commissariat de la République autonome*, teaching French in the schools and imposing French law with the aim of eliminating German influence. During the Second World War, it was under Free French rule and afterwards became a United Nations Trust as part of the French Union. Agricultural development was encouraged and roads built. About 10 per cent of the 3 million population were settlers and there were some 15,000 workers connected to the administration. In spite of the establishment of a representative assembly, a war of independence started in the 1950s and there were heavy casualties in a long conflict. In 1960, the Republic of Cameroun was granted independence, but the civil war continued. At the same time, the British Cameroons was divided, the northern Muslim half joining Nigeria and the southern joining the French sector to form the Republic of Cameroon. The official languages of the Republic are French and English. In spite of the government's aim being bilingualism in these two languages, it is seldom achieved. Some 300,000 speak or learn German still. There are several lingua francas.

French in North Africa and Arabisation

In North Africa, the war of independence in Algeria, which had been one of the earliest conquests of the Second French Empire, turned out to be the straw that broke the camel's back, responsible for the repatriation of nearly a million French settlers, the Christian *pieds-noirs*, but also the expulsion of the Jews who had lived in Algeria for two millennia. It also led to the decision of France to grant autonomy or independence to most of its other overseas possessions.

The French first conquered the city of Algiers in 1830 and slowly overcame resistance in other regions. Their goal was overseas settlement colonialism (Benrabah, 2013): hundreds of thousands of settlers (*colons*) were allocated confiscated land, becoming successful in agriculture and making up in time half of the population of the cities of Algiers and Oran and a fifth of the population of Algeria. Algeria was administered as a department of France and major investments were made in French schools, with the goal of assimilating the original inhabitants culturally. There was tension between direct and indirect approaches to colonisation, between imposing European models and maintaining indigenous traditions. Both approaches were supported by different administrators (Lawrence, 2016). In the early period, rule was through the existing Arab leadership, but this was accompanied by aggressive military action against any resistance. In the next period (1848–70), there was a combination of civil and military policies; the fact that the Arab Bureaus supported indigenous institutions angered the settlers. Gradually, rule changed from military to civilian, with consequent policy changes. But educational policy maintained a policy of assimilation: traditional Islamic schools were closed, so that the level of literacy fell from 50 per cent to less than 25 per cent; this was not remedied by government schools which Muslim parents distrusted for their secularisation (Benrabah, 2013). French language, methods and curriculum were imposed, but Arab resistance combined with lack of resources for private schooling meant that only a minority of Algerian school age children were in school (Heggoy, 1973). Resentment came to the surface in the outbreak of the Algerian War in 1954 and hundreds of thousands were killed in bitter fighting (Horne, 2012). In 1962, after the Evian agreement, Algeria became independent and a million settlers returned and Jews emigrated to France.

The remaining population of Algeria, Arabs and Berbers, is about 40 million. The official language is Modern Standard Arabic, though most people speak Algerian Arabic (Darja). Berber (Kabyle, Amazigh, Tamazight) has been a national language since 2002, spoken by about 30 per cent; it became official in 2016. French continues as a co-official language, introduced in primary schools. It is claimed by about 60 per cent of the population and is the language of advanced education and the elite.

There was opposition to Arabisation from the French-speaking elite and from the Berbers. It faced other problems; Benrabah (2004) argued that, instead of producing national legitimacy through Islamicisation and Arabisation, the policy led to conflicts between groups. Algeria has thus suffered as a result of two major efforts at language management by governments: the French colonial attempt to wipe out Arabic and ignore Berber and replace both with the metropolitan language, and the postcolonial policy of imposing Standard Arabic on an Algerian Arabic speaking majority and a Berber-speaking minority.

Originally Berber, Tunisia was conquered and populated by Arabs from the eighth century and, with the exception of a short period of Norman rule in the twelfth century, remained under Arab rulers until seized by Ottomans in the sixteenth century. In the later part of the nineteenth century, a French Army of 36,000 invaded and forced the Bey to accept a Protectorate. French officials were appointed at all levels and French law applied. French colonists arrived, 34,000 by 1906 and 145,000 by 1945. A unitary Franco-Arab school system established French as language of instruction and taught Standard Arabic as a second language, but no more than a fifth of eligible pupils attended school.

Tunisia became independent in 1956 and a republic a year later. Modern Standard Arabic is the official language but most people speak Tunisian Arabic. A small minority speak Berber languages. Two-thirds are said to know French, used in secondary and tertiary education, by the press and in business. English is becomingly increasingly important, but Berber is not supported. The situation remains in flux: Arabisation, Daoud (2011) suggests, has run its course and there is an increasing movement toward French, weakened now by the incursion of globalising English.

Earlier a Berber state, Morocco became a Roman province in 44 CE but was reconquered by the Berbers in the third century. Islamic conquest in the eighth century brought Arabic to the region, and from the eleventh century there were a series of Berber Muslim dynasties, replaced by Arabic dynasties in the sixteenth century. An independent Moroccan kingdom signed a treaty with the United States in 1786. In the nineteenth century, both France and Spain developed interest in Morocco, and Spain established a protectorate in the coastal areas. In 1912, France established its own protectorate as well. Thousands of settlers arrived and pressured the French Government to increase its control. A school system was set up and slavery was abolished in 1925. In the 1920s, French and Spanish troops put down a Berber rising. Morocco became an independent kingdom in 1956 (Zouhir, 2013). Modern Standard Arabic and Tamazight are now statutory national languages. French is taught as a compulsory language in all schools and used in government and commerce. After independence, an Arabisation programme was intended to replace French, but has not yet succeeded.

French colonies in the Middle East

In the Middle East, the Levant came under French rule as one result of the Sykes–Picot Agreement which in 1916 divided the region between France, Britain and Russia; a League of Nations Mandate confirmed this after the war. France granted some autonomy to Syria in 1936. During the Second World War, Syria was under Vichy rule until the British and Free French occupied it in 1941 and it was granted independence in 1944, though the French Army continued to maintain control until 1946.

Chaos followed: there were twenty governments and four constitutions between 1946 and 1956, followed by several military coups. A civil war began in 2011, which has so far resulted in about 200,000 killed and 500,000 Christian refugees. About 10 million Syrians have been displaced and nearly half of them are refugees outside the country (Deane, 2016).

Standard Arabic is the official language, but there are a number of local dialects spoken. With Syrian cities under siege and bombardment and so many Syrians in refugee camps in neighbouring countries (Deane, 2016), Feldmann (2016) finds that the 'colonial legacy in education had a large negative impact on secondary school enrolment in both Spain's and France's former colonies in the recent past – that is, long after the end of colonisation'.

Lebanon developed into a centre of Christianity under the influence of a monk called Maron in the fifth century. In the seventh century, the Syriac speaking Maronite Christians maintained autonomy even after the Islamic conquest. The Druze faith emerged in the area in the eleventh century. Conquered by the Mamelukes, the region came under Ottoman rule; the Maronites were supported by Frankish Crusaders who were finally defeated by the Ottomans. Lebanon continued to be under Ottoman rule until after the First World War, when it was incorporated into the French mandate of Syria and Lebanon.

In 1920, France established Greater Lebanon and in 1926 the Republic of Lebanon. At the end of the Second World War, Lebanon became independent and French troops withdrew in 1946. The constitution says that 'Arabic is the official national language. A law determines the cases in which the French language is to be used.' Most people speak Lebanese Arabic, but 40 per cent also use French, the main second language taught in 70 per cent of schools; English is taught in the other 30 per cent. Deane (2016) says that among the problems faced by Syrian refugee children in Lebanese schools is the fact that in Lebanon English and French are treated as second languages but in Syria they are foreign languages; the refugees are educated separately, with Lebanese children in school in the morning and Syrian children (paid for by international funds) in the afternoon.

To summarise French colonial policy, there are major regional differences. The North American settler colonies left behind large French and Spanish minorities in what became English-speaking nations; in Central and South America, the colonial languages Spanish and Portuguese remained dominant, even though there has been some recent recognition of minorities; in North Africa, in spite of Arabisation, the colonial language continued to play a significant role even when it lost official status; in Asia, it was replaced by indigenous languages and challenged by English; and in the rest of the African colonies, French remained the dominant elite language of education and government, although it was rarely learned by more than half of the local population. In plantation and slave colonies, a pidgin or creole developed and sometimes spread, occasionally being recognised.

Colonial language policy

Having looked at these two empires for evidence of the results of conquest and the nature of colonialism, it is possible to develop a first model that we can check with the shorter cases that follow. The basic pattern starts with military conquest, either of adjacent European territory or of non-European territory on another continent, or with trade to non-European territories, followed by military conquest. The new space may be incorporated and assimilated politically, religiously and educationally and used sometimes for settlement but always exploited economically. If local labour is not available, slaves or indentured workers will be imported to work in plantations. Education in the imperial language will be provided for settlers and minimally for indigenous populations. When the financial and military cost of maintaining colonial rule becomes excessive, independence is granted, but the new leadership, elite speakers of the imperial language, maintain the colonial language policy as the independent state struggles to overcome the damaging effects of colonial exploitation.

The Spanish colonies

The Spanish Empire followed shortly after the Portuguese, but expanded to conquer great land masses and many civilisations containing millions of non-Europeans: it imposed its language, faith and culture on its colonies. For 200 years it occupied territories in Europe, Africa, America and Asia. This made it the greatest world power in the sixteenth and seventeenth centuries, but involved it in continuing conflicts that led to its downfall (Maltby, 2008). Having reconquered Iberia from the Muslim invaders, it ruled Portugal from 1580 to 1640 and governed Naples and Sicily at the same time and the Netherlands from 1556 to the middle of the seventeenth century. When its European possessions were lost, it was restricted in Europe to Iberia, where Castilian Spanish began its struggles with Catalan, Basque, Aragonese, Asturian, Roma, Extremaduran, Galician and a few others. Spain quickly emulated Portugal in establishing overseas colonies.

The Spanish overseas empire began at the start of the fifteenth century, with nobles taking over portions of the Canary Islands and with royal conquest at the end of the century. Originally occupied by the Guanches, genetically similar to the Berbers of North Africa, Spanish rule involved colonisation, settlement and the importation of slaves for sugarcane plantations; with other immigrant settlers, the linguistic result was a distinct dialect (Samper-Padilla José, 2008). The dialect was carried to Louisiana where it is virtually extinct (Coles, 1993); the territory was granted limited autonomy in 1882.

In 1492, Columbus's arrival in America led to the development of several Spanish colonies, starting in the Caribbean and spreading as a result of the defeat and conquest of the Inca and Aztec empires in the early six-teenth century. As many as 70 million of the 80 million indigenous people were killed by the diseases introduced by European settlers (Totten and Hitchcock, 2011).

Slavery and exploitation contributed to the economic success of the Spanish American colonies and trade continued to grow, though agricultural development was uneven and inefficient and poverty was widespread. Spain lost Brazil to the Portuguese in the mid-eighteenth century and the Empire was threatened by Russian, French and British competition. It ceded its Western North American territories to the United States in 1819.

In the early nineteenth century, the remaining Spanish American colonies began to press for independence and they won freedom from Spanish rule throughout the century, producing a number of new states ranging from Mexico in the north to Argentina and Chile in the south, with Cuba and Puerto Rico holding out until nearly the end of the century. The new states, which maintained Roman Catholicism and Spanish, were ruled by locally born pure Spanish and *mestizos* (born of mixed Spanish and Indian blood).[7] In only a few countries was political stability achieved.

Spanish remained the official and educational language and each of the independent states set up an academy that collaborates with the Royal Academy in Spain, which provides the President and Treasurer of the Association of Spanish Academies. The association is responsible for the preparation and publication of dictionaries and grammars of Spanish.

Most of the new states had large numbers of non-Spanish immigrants, from Germany, Italy and Japan especially. The many indigenous languages were long ignored or suppressed,[8] but recently under the pressure of international rights treaties, there has been some government support for indigenous language maintenance or revival. In a review of a large number of recent books, Restall (2007) concludes that what Kamen (2004: 512) called the 'unrelieved desolation' of how millions experienced Spanish colonial rule was not particular to Spain, but equally true of the colonial world developed by European powers in the sixteenth to twentieth centuries.

The Belgian colonies

Among the colonial powers, Belgium produced one of the worst cases of destruction of the existing peoples and their culture. 'Repression, murder, forced labour, racism and exploitation were intrinsic dimensions of the Belgian rule in the Congo, as they were in all colonial enterprises', writes Vanthemsche (2006: 90), in an account challenging a Belgian schoolbook praising the way that the colonial administrators 'civilised the black population' and 'greatly improved the living conditions of the indigenous people'.

The Belgian Congo under the personal ownership of the King Leopold II exploited the colony as a business: 'The local population was forced to work in a most inhumane way in order to boost rubber "production" and export. Arbitrary executions, repression and even mass killings were common things in Leopoldian Congo' (2006: 90). International pressure finally forced the Belgian Government to turn it into a colony in 1908 and some efforts were made to repair the damage. But as Kent (2015) concludes, 'The Belgians had made little effort after the Second World War to prepare their African territory for a future as a self-governing state.' The title of Ewans (2017) *European Atrocity, African Catastrophe* describes the result clearly and the absence of educated leadership in the state that became independent in 1960 guaranteed the civil strife and dictatorships which followed.

One of the most multilingual countries in Africa with over 215 indigenous languages, the official language of the Democratic Republic of the Congo, as it was named in 1964 after the assassination of Patrice Lumumba, remains French, with Koongo, Congo Swahili, Lingala and Luba-Kasai recognised as provincial official languages in certain regions (Lewis et al., 2016). This continued a colonial policy which encouraged use of indigenous languages in the early years of schooling. This was reversed, Bamgbose (2004) says, by a further policy that Bokamba (2008) called 'authentic nationalism', under the Presidency of Mobutu Sese Seko from 1965 to 1971, during which time the state was known as Zaire. The policy of one national and four regional languages is said to have lowered ethnic tension and to have led to stable multilingualism rare in Africa. But the former colony continues to have major problems: a major Ebola outbreak, a measles epidemic, continuing civil strife with a hundred armed groups said to be operation in spite of 16,000 UN peacekeepers, widespread rape and sexual violence, massive human rights violations and extreme poverty.

German colonialism

German efforts at conquest in Europe reached a high point in the twentieth century, with the Nazi government combining efforts to seize all German speaking regions and later to expand conquest, applying an ideology of *lebensraum*, a notion developed in the nineteenth century to claim living space for a racially superior German people and carried to its extreme by the policies of Adolph Hitler and his supporters. An earlier result of population pressure was large-scale emigration; between 1820 and 1920, some 6 million German emigrants left Europe, with major migrant communities established in the USA, Argentina, Brazil, Chile, Paraguay and other South American states.

Outside Europe, the German colonial empire was launched in 1884 during the scramble for Africa, building the third largest empire in Africa as well as several colonies in the Pacific, all of which it lost after the First World War. The former colonies in Africa covered areas that are now Cameroon, Nigeria, Chad, Guinea, Central African Republic, Ghana, Togo, Namibia, Burundi, Kenya, Mozambique, Rwanda and Tanzania; in the Pacific, they included Papua New Guinea, Palau, Micronesia, Nauru, Northern Mariana Islands, Marshall Islands and Samoa.

There is dispute about German colonial policy, with the Herero genocide being regularly cited (Gewald, 2003). Language education in the German African colonies allowed an important place to local languages, perhaps because the Germans were reluctant to share their culture and language with racial inferiors (Obeng and Adegbija, 1999). Little remains of the influence of Germany in what were its overseas colonies. After the failure of its overseas empire, German turned its attention to the attempt to expand in Europe (Young, 2016: 2).

The Italian attempts at empire

Italy too sought overseas colonies, losing out on an attempt to occupy Tunisia in 1881, but granted a toehold in the port of Massawa in Eritrea in 1886 and seizing territory that would become Italian Somaliland. A first effort to conquer Ethiopia in the 1890s led to military defeat. In 1898, Italy failed to gain a coaling station in China, but three years later acquired a concession there. In 1912, after a war with Ottoman Turkey, it gained Libya and the Dodacanese Islands. It was not rewarded with overseas territory for joining the Allies in the First World War.

Under Mussolini, Italy claimed territory in Dalmatia and the Balkans. Between 1935 and 1937, Italy invaded and finally conquered Abyssinia. In 1939, it seized Albania. In its various possessions, the key Fascist policy was Italianisation, the spread of Italian language and culture, combined with repression of rebellion and colonisation by settlers (Andall and Duncan, 2005). During the Second World War, in alliance with Nazi Germany, it attempted further expansion but was defeated in Africa and lost all its overseas possessions in 1947. Because of the relatively short time of occupation, there was minimal influence.

The British Empire

The British Empire lasted much longer and left major effects on its colonies. Starting in the late sixteenth century, the British established the largest empire in the world; in the period before and after the First World War, it governed a quarter of the world's population and of the earth. Most colonies became independent after the Second World War, but many have joined the Commonwealth of Nations and share a queen.

In the seventeenth century, Britain established a number of colonies in North America, sending settlers to what is now the United States and Canada. At the same time, it occupied and settled islands in the Caribbean, developing plantations and bringing slaves from Africa to work them. Bases were built in Africa to handle the slave trade, which flourished into nineteenth century. During this time, the British East India Company began trade with India and Asia, competing with the Dutch until the end of the century; during the eighteenth century, the major competition was with the French.

Towards the end of the eighteenth century, a large section of British North America achieved independence as the United States of America, but Canada remained British after the defeat of the French.

At this time, exploration of the Pacific led to the development of Australia at first as a convict settlement, with the slaughtering of indigenous Aboriginal peoples and later growth as a free settler colony. New Zealand was acquired at the middle of the nineteenth century by a treaty with the indigenous Māori chiefs. For a time, settlement continued peacefully, but in 1860, land seizure led to the New Zealand Wars and a policy aiming at assimilation and language shift.

The nineteenth century saw the growth of British power, with major colonies added in Asia and Africa. Responsible government was later granted to the white colonies: Canada for all except foreign affairs in 1867 and Australia and New Zealand in the 1900s. At the turn of the century, conflict between Dutch and British settlers in South Africa led to the Boer War and British sovereignty, completing British rule of colonies from Cape to Cairo. South Africa was granted some autonomy in 1910 and independence in 1931.

Just as there was no clearly stated language policy in the United Kingdom, but a gradual and undirected acceptance that all needed English (though areas of Wales and other peripheries could choose to maintain a heritage language provided they also mastered English), so there was a spread of English to the colonies. It was most obvious in the countries where there was heavy settlement – Canada, Australia, New Zealand, South Africa[9] – though in Canada (especially Québec) there was a conflict with Francophone settlers that forced a bilingual compromise and in South Africa there was a long struggle with Afrikaans. Only in New Zealand was there early recognition of the language of the indigenous population: from 1840 until the 1870s and again after 1980, Māori was recognised in schools. In the other countries, the languages of the indigenous peoples were essentially suppressed, until South African independence led to nominal recognition. In the other colonies, there was major controversy over language policy, with a disagreement between those who argued, like the French and the Portuguese, for teaching only the imperial language and those, labelled Orientalists in India, who were supporters of the indigenous local languages.

The Macaulay Minute

A key document in the setting of British colonial language education policy was a minute written by Thomas Macaulay, serving in India from 1834 to 1838 on the Supreme Council of the Governor-General, Lord William Bentinck (Macaulay, 1920). He wrote about the language of instruction for schools, noting that half the committee favoured Oriental languages (Sanskrit and Arabic) and half favoured the imperial language, English. His judgement was based on the greater usefulness of English:

> I have no knowledge of either Sanskrit or Arabic. But I have done what I could to form a correct estimate of their value. I have read translations of the most celebrated Arabic and Sanskrit works. I have conversed both here and at home with men distinguished by their proficiency in the Eastern tongues. I am quite ready to take the Oriental learning at the valuation of the Orientalists themselves. I have never found one among them who could deny that a single shelf of a good European library was worth the whole native literature of India and Arabia.

He cited the case of Russia, which by teaching Western European languages to its elite, 'civilised Russia'. Teaching English in India, he argued would 'do for the Hindoo what they have done for the Tartar'. Spending money on the Sanskrit and Arabic colleges would be supporting 'false texts and false philosophy'; why, he asked, do students need to be paid for learning these languages when they learn English without pay? He realised that there was not enough money to educate 'the body of the people' but there was enough to form a 'class who may be interpreters between us and the millions whom we govern'. He concluded that if his advice were taken, he would be happy to continue as chair of the committee, but if not, he could not continue in support of a 'mere delusion'. The Governor-General agreed that 'the great object of the British Government ought to be the promotion of European literature and science among the natives of India'.

Macaulay's ideological position was similar to that proclaimed by the French and Portuguese colonial rulers, that the purpose of colonial education was to civilise the ignorant natives and that this could only be done through teaching a Western language and culture. It is noteworthy that the unwillingness of the colonial governments to spend too much money in the colonies made it impossible to think of educating all the people, something that explains the willingness of the British Mandatory Government of Palestine to leave the running of schools to the two ethno-religious communities. Although there were some in India who objected, arguing that abolishing the Sanskrit and Arabic colleges would alienate important sectors of the population, Macaulay's arguments were accepted (Thirumalai, 2003) and influenced the development of language education policy throughout the British Empire. Educating the 'body of the people' in the first few years of primary school could be in the local indigenous language,[10] but the elite who continued through primary and secondary school should do so in English, the Western language of civilisation and power.

How this decision affected local languages can be seen from the history of Māori schooling in New Zealand. Christian education antedated the British conquest, conducted by Christian missionaries brought to New Zealand by Māori chiefs. The mission schools used Māori and their success can be shown by the publication of Colenso (1872), a book whose title was *Willie's first English book, written for young Maoris who can read their own Maori tongue, and who wish to learn the English language.* But the mission schools that taught in Māori were replaced after the New Zealand Wars. The Native Schools Act in 1867 (Simon, 1998) set up village schools that emphasised English; some of these schools shifted to English-medium after the Education Act of 1877 established free compulsory schooling. The Native Schools Code of 1880 allowed continuation of initial use of Māori, but required rapid transition to English. In 1903, the Inspector of Native Schools in 1903 banned the use of Māori.

In British colonial schools, then, the transitional model was initial teaching in the vernacular, favoured by missionaries as the best way to teach Christianity, but replaced as soon as possible by the civilising teaching of English promoted by Macaulay and accepted by many local leaders. Advanced education (which meant secondary school and higher) was restricted to an elite, but they were the leaders who ruled in the independent states that followed British rule. So again, with rare exceptions, British conquest and colonialism meant English. Even in independent India, where the constitution allowed ten years before English was to be faded out, the strength of English and the unwillingness of non-Hindu states to accept Hindi have meant it continues to be dominant.

The development of globalism and the economic value of English, supported by political and business interests (Phillipson, 2017), added to the effect of the colonial policy and explains why most former British colonies, and not just those with English-speaking settlers, have continued to treat English as their most useful language. English struggled against French in Canada and Afrikaans in South Africa and although both are still reasonably strong in terms of numbers of speakers and official status, English is dominant. Tanzania, the most advanced in acceptance of an African language, has adopted Kiswahili as an official language and now has a policy of using it at all levels of education, but even there, there remains serious doubts about the implementation of the policy (Tibategeza and du Plessis, 2018).

The colonial language heritage

From this survey, one can see that, except in a number of Asian countries, European colonialism regularly worked to weaken and replace indigenous languages with the language of the conquerors. Among the justifications offered for this was the number of competing local language varieties and their low level of development; commonly, they lacked a writing system and a lexicon capable of dealing with modern concepts and objects. But as the Macaulay Minute showed, even languages with a major well developed literature, like Sanskrit and Arabic, could be considered useless. Although most colonial governments claimed that their goal was civilising the native peoples, thus asserting their own superior culture, their most common interest was exploitation, gaining land to be used for plantations or for settlement of surplus home populations. Their main expenditure was for military costs and the limited resources for education give the lie to the claim of civilising. Some effort was made to provide basic education to the masses, offered by some (the British and the Germans, for example) in some of the local languages; more advanced education, provided for a limited elite, was always in the language of the conqueror.

Thus, the international languages (English, Spanish, Portuguese, French, Russian) were given a wide currency, building for the later stage when they were supported by trade and globalisation. There were similar processes in Asia, with Japan (until its defeat) and China insisting on their national language as the required colonial language.

The end of colonial rule did not lead to a major change; commonly, the rulers of the newly independent states had been members of the elite who had learned and shifted to the colonial language and accepted the linguistic ideology and repertoire. Phillipson (1992b) and others were justified in their statement that colonialism was a major cause of language shift.

Notes

1. This section is based on Spolsky (2018b). I go into the Portuguese and French Empires in some detail, but only sketch other cases.
2. This section is based on Spolsky (2019c).
3. The language clause was one of 192 articles in the *Ordonnance* and appears to be the only one still in effect.
4. The figures are from Statistics Canada reported by the Canadian Official Languages Commissioner.
5. Bislama (*bichelamar* in French) is based on English lexicon and together with Tok Pisin (New Guinea) and Pijin (Solomon Islands) forms Melanesian Pidgin. 'National language' is the term in the English version of the Constitution; the French version is 'La langue véhiculaire nationale'. It developed among Ni-Vanuatu working on plantations in Queensland and Fiji and spread to workers from various parts brought to work on plantations within the New Hebrides. During the war, it further spread in contact with American troops. It serves as a lingua franca in most of Vanuatu.
6. Both the 1987 and 2018 referendums rejected independence.
7. As in Brazil, marriage of male settlers with local Indian and slave women was common, but the racially pure had higher social status.
8. A notable exception is the widespread informal speaking of Guarani in Paraguay.
9. Rhodesia too had a large white population, but not enough to delay the achievement of independence and Black rule.
10. It is to be noted that Macaulay did not touch on the issue of teaching in the vernacular, but opposed expenditure on colleges teaching the classical languages of Hindu and Muslim sacred texts.

8 Economic Pressure and Neoliberalism

Motivation

Why do people learn new languages and expand their linguistic repertoires? In their studies of second language learning, Gardner and Lambert (1959, 1972) proposed a contrast between two kinds of supportive attitude for learning a language, which they labelled *integrative* and *instrumental motivation*. Integrative motivation referred to acquiring a language in order to belong to the group speaking the language, as a result of assigning a high value to the identity with which it was associated. My expansion of language competence by adding Hebrew was at first to establish my identity as a Jew and then as an Israeli. Instrumental motivation referred to learning a language for some practical purpose: I learned French, Latin and German at school and university in order to pass examinations. Although more recent work by Dörnyei (1999, 2009; Dörnyei and Ushioda, 2009) and others have produced more complex models,[1] these two contrasting motivations remain at the head of those explaining choice of language. It is useful to consider them also as the principal explanations for language shift: faced by a situation where there is a choice of languages, the two competing pressures are most likely to be heritage and identity on the one hand (integrative) and occupational and economic success on the other (instrumental).

From the examples of language shift that will be examined in the next chapter, it seems a useful simplification to suggest that, provided there is contact with more than one variety, a first necessary condition for language choice, each variety's value for integration and economic success will serve as the best explanation of language preference for the individual and the community. Speakers of minority and less powerful languages will be attracted to dominant and more powerful languages, both to be assimilated and integrated into the associated community and to benefit from the results of employment depending on competence. This justifies recognising the relationships between language policy and economics; the 'market potential of multilingualism' has been labelled *linguanomic$* by Hogan-Brun (2017).

Real and assumed value

There are two separate but related questions that arise: what is the market value of knowing a specific language and what do people think is the value of knowing a language? The first is a question for economists; the pioneering studies have been those by Grin and colleagues (for instance Grin, 1996a; 2005; Grin et al., 2010) and by Chiswick and his colleagues (for instance Chiswick, 1992; Chiswick and Miller, 2002; Chiswick and Repetto, 2000). The second is commonly discussed in studies of attitudes and values of language proficiency (for instance Grin, 2001; Paternost, 1985; Te Puni Kokiri, 2002).

In the first chapter of this book, I dealt with individual choices of language, including the process referred to by Nekvapil (2012; Neustupný and Nekvapil, 2003) as self-management; the specific cases they worked with were Czech employees of German businesses in the Czech Republic who chose to take private classes in German in order to improve their prospects for promotion. But this motivation also applies to the decision that parents make to have their children acquire one or more languages to make them employable in firms requiring specific language competence. There is much evidence for this: the pressure on school systems throughout the world to teach English as the first foreign language, the attractiveness of English-medium schools in India and elsewhere, the Korean fathers who send their families abroad to learn English, the willingness of some American parents to hire Mandarin speaking domestics, the traditional foreign language nannies and the preference for Russian-medium schools in the USSR. All of these point to the assumed value of a dominant language.

The global attraction to English, blamed by Phillipson (1992b, 2003) on British and American government policy and the spread of colonial languages attributed by Skutnabb-Kangas and Phillipson (2010) to governments and businesses can perhaps better be explained by the power of economically valued languages (Mufwene, 2005a, 2005b). Unless there is strong ideological willingness to resist language shift, such as in the case of religious groups like the Amish and some Hasidim who choose social and cultural isolation or of ethnic minorities like Catalans and Māoris who seek to bolster their ethnic identity, the attraction of the locally dominant variety with its promise of access to jobs and markets is a significant cause of linguistic shift.

This can be seen in studies of marketplaces. In Ethiopian markets, Cooper and Carpenter (1976) found that it was sellers who learned the language of buyers. Similarly, in the Old City of Jerusalem, Arab merchants learned Hebrew and English and other languages to deal with local Jews and tourists (Spolsky and Cooper, 1991). Signs boasting of language knowledge ('English spoken here') show the importance of language proficiency in attracting the business of tourists (MacGregor, 2003). The addition of English to street signs in Tokyo (Backhaus, 2006) and elsewhere confirms the assumed added value of a global language (Phillipson, 2017). Studies in linguistic landscape (Ben-Rafael et al., 2006; Gorter, 2006; Pütz and Mundt, 2019) commonly deal with commercial signs and provide evidence of the economic value of some languages.

Establishing economic value

To quantify these anecdotal examples turns out to be difficult. One of the earliest studies of the economic value of language proficiency was Migué (1970), who explored the difference in earning between Anglophones and Francophones in Québec, though it turned out that this resulted from ethnic group difference and not language proficiency. Vaillancourt (1980) distinguished between language as an ethnic marker and language as human capital. He went on to argue that individuals prefer to purchase goods using their strongest language (usually their native language) and that they will generally seek employment in jobs that respect their skills, including language proficiency. Firms seek to employ individuals whose language skills signal their ability to deal with their customers and clients and will choose languages for internal communication according to the language skills of employees. As a result, he argued that in a bilingual economy, bilingual employees are preferred; although those who speak the employer's language are more likely to get better jobs, those who know the language of technology will also be preferred.[2] In a study using data from the Canadian 1971 census and excluding women (not well represented), speakers of languages other than French and English and industries like fishing and agriculture where language is less important, Vaillancourt (1980) found that in Québec there were three distinct groups in terms of gross earnings: unilingual Francophones at the lower end, bilingual Francophones next and unilingual or bilingual Anglophones at the top. The differences were most striking in jobs in management and next in jobs in sales. Although Francophones made up 80 per cent of the population of the Province, it was clear that English was then the more economically valuable language. And this remained true when other factors such as education and experience were taken into account. In politics, however, French was more valuable, which led to the change in language policy in the Province in the 1960s. By 2000, however, after the passage of laws supporting French in Québec, the situation had changed and the relative position of unilingual Anglophones was now close to that of bilingual Francophones. The position of Allophones (usually immigrants) had dropped relative to Francophones (Vaillancourt et al., 2007). There was also evidence of differences according to industrial sectors (Grin et al., 2010: 63).

Language value in multilingual societies

Canada has proved a good case to study. A second major set of studies have been by Grin and his colleagues and students in Switzerland, a nominally multilingual nation where four languages are distributed territorially and recognised constitutionally. In spite of this, with a few minor exceptions, each region is monolingual, with German, French, Italian or Romanche recognised as official locally. Because the regions do not coincide with political units (cantons or municipalities), trade sets up a widespread need for cross-linguistic communication, so that even firms with domestic business can see the value of multilingual proficiency. Grin (1997) found that bilinguals, whether men or women, always earn more than unilinguals, the difference in the case of French-speaking men exceeding 25 per cent. Similarly, analysing data from the 2000 census, it appeared that men and women with excellent English skills earn over 40 per cent more than those with no English competence; 'good' skills were worth 8 per cent (women) and 16 per cent (men). However, this finding needs to be modified to take into account education and the fact that English has a greater effect in German-speaking than in French-speaking regions. But the evidence of the earning value of foreign language knowledge remains clear (Grin et al., 2010: 69).

Grin (1996a, 2001, 2003; Grin et al., 2010) discussed how to discover the economic value of language proficiency. An early conference paper (Grin, 1998) argued that the various linguistic areas of Switzerland maintained clear linguistic boundaries with each other, but were held together by the myth of multilingualism: only three cantons were bilingual and only one trilingual. Another study noted that 97 per cent of Swiss report only one mother tongue (Grin and Korth, 2005). Earlier, Grin and Sfreddo (1998) established that Swiss speakers of Italian as a first language were disadvantaged. Grin and Korth (2005) dealt with the growing importance of English as a foreign language in Switzerland. Grin (2001) showed the high reputation that English and its economic value hold in Switzerland, where English skills resulted in a wage premium of between 12 per cent and 30 per cent. Grin et al. (2010), a three-year research study funded by the Swiss National Science Foundation, studied the economics of the workplace. Recognising that there are other approaches to multilingualism, such as from sociolinguistics, psycholinguistics, geography, political science and law, they set out to explore the mutual influence of linguistic and economic variables. In the first of three parts, they set the background by describing multilingualism and the relevant principles of economic theory. In the second part, which they consider the core, they look at and redefine the theory of the firm by including language variables as determinants of key economic variables such as productivity, costs and profits. In the third part, they discuss policy implications. Appended are details of the economic models and procedures they use. They point out that most of their data come from Switzerland and Québec, as there is little if any comparable data from other countries.

But there are some studies of immigrants. Chiswick (1994, 1992; Chiswick and Miller, 1992; Chiswick and Repetto, 2000) has shown the economic value of immigrants' acquisition of the dominant language in Canada, the United States and Israel. In Israel, Chiswick and Repetto (2000a), using data from the 1972 census, reported that 'those who speak Hebrew on a daily basis as a primary or only language and who can write a letter in Hebrew earn about 20 percent more than those who do neither'. They also found that 'English speakers earn about 15 percent more and Arabic speakers earn 2 percent less than Hebrew speaking immigrants who speak neither of these languages.' Other variables considered, Hebrew added about 13 per cent to earnings and English about 15 per cent. For immigrants, the cost of five months[3] attending a full-time Hebrew ulpan (including lost earnings) would lead to a return of 20 per cent over a lifetime of work. But there is no evidence of the specific value of an immigrant's knowledge of their various first languages, nor of the value of languages other than Hebrew or English.

Language as commodity

Notwithstanding the sparseness of hard data, scholars continue to explore the political and economic aspects of language policy, pointing out its relevance to colonialism and capitalism. Commodification of language, it has been pointed out, can be seen in service industries (Cameron, 2000). In service situations, customer care is a common goal, which raises the importance of being able to communicate in the customer's language. Where this becomes particularly relevant is in the staffing of call centres, which function in multilingual states and internationally (Rahman, 2009).

Heller (2010b) suggests that in late modernism and late capitalism, language has taken on new importance in tourism, marketing, language teaching, translation, communications (especially call centres) and performance art. It has become increasingly significant in managing the expansion of markets. It has also served to preserve neocolonialism. As we saw in Chapter 7, for many reasons newly independent states continued to use the imperial language even after the formal colonial ties were broken. Duchêne and Heller (2012a, 2012b) expand on these notions and Heller and McElhinny (2017) argue that language plays a crucial role in producing and maintaining social inequality. In colonies, the education required to develop proficiency in the official language was available only to the elite, who thus were advantaged in access to employment and government. In the postcolonial states, this inequality continues.

Another recent book connecting language and political economics is Block (2018), adding detailed studies of the Spanish situation to a general survey of the field. Block opens by citing an earlier study by Irvine (1989) which discusses the connection between language and political economy. Irvine noted a change from the Saussurean separation of the sign from the material world which she finds in William Labov's use of socioeconomic class as predicting the distribution of some linguistic variants. Following others like Hymes (1974) and Gumperz (1983) who saw speaking as a social and cultural activity, she goes on to consider the role of language in the political economy. Her first point is that 'linguistic signs denote objects, the natural world and economic skills and activities' (Irvine, 1989: 250). The second is the sociolinguistic notion that there is a connection between linguistic and social diversity, so that specific varieties and repertoires are associated with specific social groups. Labov (1966), who showed the relevance of certain variants to identifying socioeconomic class in New York City, is the obvious example. This leads, she argues, to the commodification of linguistic features. She illustrated the resulting multifunctionality by describing the use of compliments and praise in Wolof.

Block (2018) goes on to describe political economy and develops from this an account of neoliberalism, a complex phenomenon (an economic regime, a political ideology, a way of life and so on) which underlies current concern in politics and linguistics for the study of social stratification. He argues therefore that sociolinguists should develop an interest in political economy.

History of language and political economy

This is the particular approach of the work of Monica Heller. In a review article, Heller (2010a) summed up work on the commodification of language, arguing that with the globalisation associated with late capitalism, the salience of language as a commodity had been increasing. Heller and McElhinny (2017) carried this further. In a historical approach, they start in the fifteenth century with the beginning of colonialism and the debate in the century that followed about whether to use indigenous or colonial languages for religious conversion of the conquered peoples. The development of comparative philology in India was a project that established hierarchies of language. There were three challenges to this: evolutionary approaches which made it possible to rank languages and the speakers along scales of progress, the study of pidgins and creoles which did not fit the pattern, and criticisms of evolution and racism by Boaz and other anthropologists who tried to separate race from language. They trace the development in the nineteenth and twentieth centuries of the nation state and the fascist, communist and universalist responses to the contradictions that the nation produced. They look at the development of nations as markets, dealing with industrialisation and European imperialism. They next consider challenges to bourgeois imperialism in the invention of international auxiliary languages like Esperanto, the Soviet search for a science of language compatible with Marxism, the fascist development of extreme nationalism and reaction to the perceived contamination of colonialism.

Heller and McElhinny go onto deal with the aftermath of the Second World War and the beginning of the Cold War, with the continuing struggle between capitalist and communist ideologies challenged by the decolonisation of the 1960s. During this period, structural and generative linguists were building a universalist model of language that ignored society; this coincided with proposals for machine translation and government support for the development of linguistic departments,[4] and the development of technology that supported persuasion and propaganda. Scholars seen as communist, anti-racist or pro-indigenous or who studied the languages of communist countries were silenced or seen as suspect. Developments in theoretical linguistics with emphasis on syntax separated language from its social context. In contrast to this mainstream development, there also grew a field of sociolinguistics and an associated study of language policy and planning. Starting in the United States, sociolinguistics also sprouted in Europe, relevant to a simultaneous mobilisation of linguistic minorities such as those in Catalonia, the Basque country and Wales.

Neoliberalism developed, following the end of the Welfare State in the 1980s, the collapse of the Soviet Union, the extension of globalisation, and the dismantling of the regulatory and government basis for the Welfare State and control of big business. There was increasing surveillance and censorship, with citizenship more closely tied to labour and increasing commodification. Growing disparity of wealth is now connected to language differences and the inequalities of race, gender and sexuality. Heller and McElhinny conclude by summarising late capitalism and the associated development of white supremacist, nationalistic and dictatorial governments. They see some hope in movements that challenge these developments.

What I find significant about this review of the political relevance of language is its breadth: instead of focusing on a single cause, such as imperialism or big business, they attempt to cover the full development of language as a source of power over the period of modern history. This argues for a close connection not just between society and economics, but also between language and economics.

The significance of economics

Although there are many questions raised by the limitations of current economic theory, such as its assumption that society is driven by self-interest, there are good reasons to look at economic considerations driving language policy, with languages commodified and valued for providing access to a livelihood. Similarly, one should note that the economic weakness of a nation blocks or at least interferes with its ability to tackle language problems and to implement policies that might solve them. Even without the kind of detailed data that economists like to work with, there is good reason to see the influence of economic factors on language choice and policy.

Notes

1. Dörnyei and Clément (2001) list seven broad dimensions of motivation; the first two are the affective/integrative and the instrumental/pragmatic; these are followed in order by macro-context, self-concept-related, goal-related, educational context-related and significant others-related. Macro-context would seem to be sociocultural environment; the others can be subsumed under integrated or instrumental.
2. My daughter, the chief executive officer of a logistics start-up in Israel, told me that she needed to hire engineers and programmers whose English proficiency enabled them to converse with professionals in their field in the USA.
3. The Hebrew ulpan course was set to last five months because the Israeli teachers hired to teach them were entitled to two months holiday a year in regular schools, and not for any pedagogical reason.
4. Noam Chomsky's work at the time was supported by grants from the US Air Force.

Endangerment and Language Shift

Language endangerment?

This brings us to considering what happens to language varieties that lack economic value. Since the publication of papers by Krauss (1992) and Hale (1992), more and more linguists have drawn attention to the many of the world's languages that are being lost, as their speakers are forced or choose to shift to a larger and seemingly more powerful variety. At the same time, Fishman (1990, 1991, 1993, 2001) took a more positive approach, looking at 'a baker's dozen' cases of attempts at resistance to language shift. Thus, language endangerment became a major policy topic, in parallel with the wider concern about climate change.

In their introduction to a collection of papers on the topic of endangerment, Duchêne and Heller (2008) drew attention to the twenty-first-century proliferation of texts, many produced by the United Nations Educational, Scientific and Cultural Organization (UNESCO), that offer estimates usually ranging from 5,000 to 6,000 of the number of languages currently spoken and of the number of years (20 to 100 usually) before half of them will disappear. Many of these texts explain the reason for their alarm with an appeal to the value of linguistic diversity, either as related to biodiversity or to the world's cultural heritage; all assume the political right of speakers to defend their languages.[1] Duchêne and Heller (2008) said they did not accept these arguments at face value; they were doubtful about the number of languages, how to count them and how to recognise their death. They asked whether linguists and anthropologists might not be making these claims to justify their expertise and to show the social legitimacy of their professions.

Why do speakers of endangered languages abandon them? Grenoble and Whaley (1998: 22) put it simply: adapting to 'a situation where use of that language is no longer advantageous to them'. In a footnote, they recognised 'dramatic exceptions in which entire speech communities are eliminated through war, disease or genocide . . .' This was the fate of Native American languages wiped out by European diseases, of Yiddish whose speakers were killed by the Nazis, of Tasmanian aboriginals and Californian and Amazonian tribes murdered by settlers and of speakers of Tibetan, Uyghur and now Mongolian being re-educated in Mandarin. Others, however, seem to assume that language death (or what they call linguicide) is always the fault of governments and big business (Skutnabb-Kangas, 2000). The lack of government support for indigenous languages is noted by Bhuiyan (2017); even in Bangladesh, a nation created by concern for the refusal of Pakistan to recognise Bengali, speakers of indigenous languages are discriminated against and their languages stigmatised.

There have been many attempts, Grenoble and Whaley pointed out, to characterise the nature of endangered languages; one of best known is Fishman's Graded Intergenerational Disruption Scale (Fishman, 1991: 91ff).[2] They found a more useful typology in Edwards (1992), who groups minority (and not just threatened) language situations on a table with two parameters: eleven perspectives by which human groups can be character-ised such as demography, economics and religion, and the three scopes to which these characteristics can be applied (speakers, languages and settings): this gives thirty-three cells in which questions can be asked, permitting the development of a model for predicting the continued use of the language. They then suggested some additions to Edwards's model. One is to add lit-eracy, a feature regularly debated as a factor in language maintenance, with most activist linguists claiming that adding literacy to a variety strengthens it, although others fear that it weakens a variety by providing access to the schooling that is a major cause of language shift. Second, they argued that setting needs to be expanded to distinguish among areal, national, regional and local settings. Thirdly, they argued that the variables need to be ranked hierarchically; they suspect that if this is done, the economic perspective will turn out to be most influential.

Grenoble and Whaley used this complex model to explore three specific regions. In sub-Saharan Africa, they noted, in all cases but one, the threat to minority languages comes not from former colonial languages but from other indigenous languages. Although the European languages are firmly entrenched as elite languages and although there was colonial suppression of indigenous languages, there are few signs that the European languages will ever be adopted by the general population. One factor is the absence of extensive European settlement. A second is the density and number of indig-enous languages. A third is the ideological acceptance of multilingualism. A fourth is the pan-Africanism which leads to resistance to non-African lan-guages. Finally, the poverty and scarcity of economic resources (and I would add, other related factors like war, civil strife, corruption and disease) have blocked the development of efforts to promote local languages.

The second case they chose is the former Soviet Union, with much the same multilingualism and multi-ethnic pattern as sub-Saharan Africa, but a dif-ferent outcome as minority languages were being replaced by Russian. Here strong centralised language management, such as the literacy campaigns of the 1920s and the favouring of Russian in the education system, worked to make it more valuable than the local languages. Thirdly, they summarised the situation of Māori in New Zealand, noting the shift resulting from European settlement, the shift in language of school instruction to English and urbanisation, and the ideological force behind the recent revitalisation movement.

They concluded stressing three significant factors: economics, access and motivation. In studies of Africa, it is clear that the lack of economic resources to support the successful teaching of the former colonial languages to the full population is a major factor inhibiting shift to those languages, thought to be pragmatically attractive for employment, something which individuals must deal with through self-management. It is the economic advantage assumed to come from proficiency in Global English that explains English being the normal first foreign language except where another global language (Mandarin, French, Spanish, Russian, for instance) has national or regional relevance. By access, Grenoble and Whaley meant access to the endangered or the majority language, including such dimensions as language density, isolation, age and numbers of speakers and especially access to media.

A more complex model

Edwards (2019) responds to reactions to his model. He first argues against the simple approach that says there are big languages like English threatening small ones, pointing out that there are many languages like Swahili which pressed on Bemba and a number of other languages while at the same time being threatened itself by English; similar chains are English–French–Cree in Québec and Russian–Georgian–Ossetian and Spanish–Quechua–Aymara.[3] Although the Brueghel picture is labelled 'Big fish eat little ones' it shows 'Bigger fish eat smaller ones' setting up a chain.

Edwards argues against binarism and calls for a more nuanced description than typologies permit. He starts with geographical context, distinguishing indigenous from immigrant varieties,[4] and within each, those minorities that have majorities elsewhere (for instance Russian in Israel, Spanish in the USA, French in Canada), those that are scattered like the Chinese topolects or concentrated and those that have speakers of the same variety across a border but close, something common in Africa with the artificial boundaries drawn by imperial powers, but also noticeable in the border areas of India and Nepal and of Brazil and Peru. Next, he refers to his 1992 typology, which considered speakers, languages and setting under eleven disciplinary conditions; an expanded version proposes three questions for each of the thirty-three cells. He then lists some applications of the model and some modifications such as the suggestion by Darquennes (2013) to add a historical dimension to each of the disciplines and to replace speakers with group. Edwards concludes that a comprehensive typology 'could be a heuristic for further and more systematic investigations and could perhaps permit predictions to be made concerning language shift and/or maintenance outcomes'. The fact that nobody has yet taken up the challenge reflects the complexity and expense of such a study and perhaps its low priority for funders.

Loss or evolution

Mufwene (2005a), in contrast, expressed doubt about the statements on endangerment by many scholars, who, he said, oversimplify reality and

> have generally reduced globalisation to a process that makes the world more and more uniform by the world-wide diffusion of intellectual, linguistic, military, technological and other cultural products associated with hegemonic regimes such as the USA, the United Kingdom and Australia. In other words, they equate globalisation with what would be the westernisation of the world and talk about indigenous languages as if indigeneity were no longer a relative notion and such languages were to be found only in the Americas, Asia and Australia.

He pointed out that language loss has proceeded at different rates. He also criticised the tendency to express concern about languages and not speakers.[5]

Globalisation, he believed, involves both a speeding up of communication and logistics and the replacement of imperial rule by the power of multinational corporations. It leads to multilingualism, but not necessarily to the minoritisation of non-imperial languages that marked colonialism. Trade colonialism did not lead to language shift, but enriched linguistic repertoires by adding pidgins; it was the next stage that was critical, depending on whether the colony that developed was based on settlement or exploitation. Settlement colonies developed in two ways, either as plantation colonies with imported slaves or as farming industrial colonies with European indentured servants. Generally, European settlers and immigrants established nationally segregated communities until the early twentieth century, but later (as in USA and Brazil) shifted from their heritage German or Italian or other European language to the dominant national language. In the plantation colonies, the pidgins evolved into creoles and new slaves adopted the creoles and gradually gave up stigmatised African languages.

In exploitation colonies, such as India was under the Raj, the indigenous languages remained as the L variety of a triglossia, with the European variety (English in India) used by the educated elite in different domains from the indigenous lingua francas and vernaculars. The European language was used in new communicative domains, but even the elite who acquired it continued to use indigenous varieties or lingua francas for the marketplace or to maintain ethnic identity. This evolution, Mufwene argued, was not new, but similar to the way that Vulgar Latin was spread by Roman conquests.

Many local languages remain strong. In Botswana, for instance, Khoisan is being replaced by Setswana, with English not a threat. Most minority languages in India are more threatened by regional or local languages than by Hindi or English. Bilingualism associated with expanded linguistic repertoires does not necessarily lead to language shift. It is all more complex than many scholars suggest. And there is egalitarian multilingualism in much of the world.

Mufwene went on to question the arguments presented for fighting endangerment. 'One must ask whether linguists or would-be speakers of the relevant languages are not the ones benefitting (the most) from the exercise', he remarked (2005a: 40), echoing Duchêne and Heller's views above. He also expresses doubt about the notion that the loss of language means loss of a precious heritage language, citing Sapir's statement that language and culture 'are not wedded like two sides of a coin' (p. 41).[6] He cited an economist who says that multiplicity of languages is 'inhibitive to economic development'. Language shift is an individual matter, he suggested: 'Noticing that a language is endangered is largely a retrospective outlook on evolution, particularly because language loss is the cumulative result of individual decisions that have been made independent of each other' (p. 42). He asks, would the speakers want to go back to their traditional community?[7]

Mufwene concluded by saying that neither language endangerment nor globalisation are new phenomena. Each case needs to be looked at separately. 'While it is certainly regrettable that some languages are vanishing, it is undeniably evident that the socio-economic ecologies in which speakers have evolved have changed to points of no return' (p. 46), he concluded. But as he said, many linguists and some anthropologists continue to advocate fighting language endangerment and shift.

The linguists' case for diversity

In a paper first given at a conference (Krauss, 1991) and published a year later, Krauss (1992) raised the battle cry that loss of language diversity was 'significantly comparable to' endangerment of biological species in the natural world. He gave estimated and imprecise statistics, finishing with the calculation that 'the coming century will see either the death or the doom of 90% of mankind's languages' (1992: 7). He called on professional linguists to try to preserve the field in which they work. Introducing the same issue of the journal of the Linguistic Society of America, Hale (1992) repeated and confirmed this plaint and plea for action. He argued that the kind and speed of loss was now different and part of the 'loss of cultural and intellectual diversity in which politically dominant languages and cultures simply overwhelm indigenous local languages and cultures' (1992: 1). He also compared this to the loss of biological diversity. His paper led the journal issue in which Krauss and others report specific cases, Hualapai in Arizona, indigenous languages in Nicaragua, Native American languages in Guatemala and Mayan, highlighting cases where there were attempts to maintain or revitalise the threatened languages and concluding with another essay by Hale that made the case for the loss of intellectual diversity resulting from the loss of languages.

About the same time, Fishman (1991) expanded an earlier paper (Fishman, 1990) to explore what he labelled 'reversing language shift', surveying 'a baker's dozen' of successful or failing cases of attempts to ameliorate the situation of threatened languages. The examples he selected were Irish, Frisian, Basque, Navajo, Spanish in the USA, Yiddish,[8] Māori, Australian immigrant and aboriginal languages, Modern Hebrew, French in Québec and Catalan.[9] These are not the endangered indigenous languages that Krauss and Hale were dealing with, but they enabled him to present and explore the Graded Intergenerational Disruption Scale, later expanded in Lewis (2009) to classify the present state of the languages of the world.

Since then, there has been an outpouring of expressions of concern and reports of situations and efforts to reverse language shift. Two handbooks deal with endangerment, Austin and Sallabank (2011, 2014), but although the former includes two dozen chapters on various aspects of the topic starting with a review by Grenoble (2011), there are no detailed studies. The second, which focuses on beliefs and ideologies, also includes details of language practices and management. It opens with seven case studies: Irish, Arabic in Cyprus, Ladin women in the Dolomites, Kven in Norway, Gamilaraay and Yuwaalaraay in Australia, and the Arapesh languages in New Guinea. This is followed by a section on reversing language shift activities with chapters on Guernésiais on Guernsey, the Sumu-Mayanga Indians in Nicaragua, Provençal and Scots, Māori, seven languages in the Lower Fungom region of Northwest Cameroon, Wangkatha in Australia, the Baining language family in Papua New Guinea, Rama in Nicaragua and Francoprovençal. The whole question of language documentation is reviewed by Austin (2013) and its role in preserving endangered languages is shown in Jones and Ogilvie (2013).

Basically then, we have linguists in conflict. There are those who are alarmed and those who see it as a normal evolutionary development. Among the first are many who set out to help, encouraging or joining the efforts of activists to maintain the larger minority languages like those listed by Fishman or the smaller indigenous varieties dealt with in McCarty (2012) and McCarty et al. (2015).

Bradley and Bradley (2019) ask the significant question: what can linguists do about language endangerment? They first outline a dozen ways of scaling or estimating the nature and degree of language loss[10] and then cover the full field of activities, including working in a community and recognising its attitudes; they set out a scheme for describing the pattern of language use, knowledge and the sociolinguistic setting; they summarise the field of language planning and management; they define and explain the various kinds of language reclamation; they illustrate the various methods of studying an endangered community; and conclude each section with an detailed account of a particular case. They combine theory and practice and make clear that the decisions must be those of the community and not the linguist who is an outsider.

To help clarify the many different situations, in the next sections I look at the situation of a number of minority languages, attempting to tease out the factors affecting shift or maintenance.

Minority languages in India

The minority languages of India are endangered languages in a constitutionally multilingual nation. Pandharipande (2002) set out to define these languages, discussed their status, presented factors accounting for retention or loss and described speakers' attitudes to the language. He proposed a definition based on functional load (the number of domains in which a variety is used) and functional transparency (the autonomy and power of a variety within a domain).

The Indian Constitution does not define minority languages, but lists in Schedule VIII, Articles 343–51, eighteen scheduled languages:[11] the rest are minority languages, but the Supreme Court's stated criterion of a language spoken by less than 50 per cent of a community does not work (Hindi for instance is spoken by a third of the population of India). The important factors which account for the attrition of minority and indigenous languages, Pandharipande said, were formal language policies, modernisation, speakers' attitudes and the contribution of the variety to identity.

The division of India into states after independence was aimed at producing linguistically homogenous communities where over 50 per cent spoke one language, which could then be used for official, educational and commercial purposes. In education, a three-language formula was proposed and partially implemented, with the mother tongue or the official language at the primary level, a regional language and Hindi (or English) added at the secondary level and all three at higher educational levels (Mohanty, 2019a). One effect of this policy was to reduce the use of minority languages in public domains. Many communities chose to assimilate with the larger majority community, but a number of indigenous communities especially in the north-east managed to maintain their languages. In general, minority languages lost power and status.

In spite of the fact that the constitution guarantees minority language maintenance, implementation was often unsuccessful. One factor was multilingualism: 13 per cent of the Indian population has more than one variety in their linguistic repertoire and over 40 per cent of the minority population is bilingual, meaning that they have a more powerful language available for use in public domains. Modernisation has also contributed to the shift. English and Hindi are seen as a way to achieve economic success, lowering the value of minority languages. Reduced functional load, Mohanty argues, is the main cause of minority language attrition.

Ethnologue[12] classifies listed Indian languages on the Expanded Graded Intergenerational Disruption Scale (EGIDS), the scale of probability of loss. A cautionary note is called for. The fact that many languages have not been studied and the fact that most have several names means that there are problems, recognised especially in the categories marked in the listing with * which are said to be educated guesses. *Ethnologue* has the authority of the International Organization for Standardization and is the most complete attempt at listing the languages of the world, but Hammarström (2015) in a comprehensive review raises many questions, noting especially the lack of detailed references, the weakness of the criteria and the many cases of missing and non-existent languages. Thus, not only do we lack reliable information on the number and nature of users of many varieties, but we also cannot be sure about their names and how many varieties exist.

With this initial proviso, I explored the nature of what are classified as endangered languages (see Table A.1 for classifications). In its section on India, *Ethnologue* starts by listing fourteen *extinct* languages whose last known native speaker died in the twentieth century, then goes on to list two languages with only second language speakers and then half a dozen *dormant* languages, with no known first language speakers (see Table A.2 in the Appendix). It classifies three Indian languages as *nearly extinct* ('The only remaining users of the language are members of the grandparent generation or older who have little opportunity to use the language'). Four languages are classified as *moribund* (defined as 'the only remaining active users of the language are members of the grandparent generation and older'). The next category is *shifting*, in which adults are reported to use the language but do not pass it to their children. *Ethnologue* lists a dozen Indian languages in this category. In the *threatened* (6) category, the language is still used by all generations, but there is said to be evidence of fewer users. *Ethnologue* classifies thirty-one languages in this category, seven of them with more than 10,000 speakers. There is also a *threatened* (6b*) category, with over seventy languages listed. The level marked with an asterisk are editorial best guesses, where there is no reported information on whether or not children are speaking the language. Those with an estimated 10,000 speakers or more in this category are listed in Table A.2 in the Appendix.

In spite of this uncertainty, we can note some general features. Threatened languages are reported to be threatened not by Hindi and English (though educated speakers are likely to know both), but by larger local languages, state languages and others included in the Eighth Schedule to the Constitution of India which obliges the government to develop them so that 'they grow rapidly in richness and become effective means of communicating modern knowledge': Hindi of course, but among the twenty-two now scheduled, Assamese, Bengali, Gujarati, Malayalam, Nepali, Odia, Santali, Telegu and Urdu are all listed as languages to which speakers of other languages are shifting. Many of the threatened varieties are listed as spoken by scheduled castes, the Depressed groups of Hindus (and others) once called *Dalit* or untouchable and making up 16 per cent of the population. Many others are varieties brought by immigrants from neighbouring countries like Nepal or China. Many are described as tribal languages. There are reported to be over 100 million tribal people (*Adivasi*), forming over 600 communities of indigenous or aboriginal people who generally exist outside the mainstream of Indian Hindu and Muslim society, living in the impoverished belt of central and north-east India and assumed to have been resident before the arrival of the Aryan invaders. They make up 8 per cent of the Indian population. In spite of government efforts, their economic position remains poor (Neff et al., 2019) and they remain the target of land grabs.[13] These then are the languages with over 10,000 speakers which show serious evidence of shift in culture and language.

The next level, called *vigorous* in the *Ethnologue* section on language status, is a classification for the lowest level where there is still use by all generations and therefore continued natural intergenerational transmission, the criterion that Fishman (1991) set as a minimum condition for language survival.[14] There are about fifty languages listed as 6a (based on information the editors received, though details are not given) and another seventy-eight as 6a* (an editorial guess). Here, it seems most interesting to give details about smaller languages that are assumed by *Ethnologue* to not be threatened, so I list in Table A.2 those under 10,000. A language with fewer than this number of speakers can be recognised by the Indian Government as a 'lesser known language' or endangered or about to be and so eligible to be documented under the Scheme for Protection and Preservation of Endangered Languages which was instituted by the Ministry of Human Resource Development in 2013; 117 such varieties have so far been documented, which means provided with a dictionary and a grammar.

These last cases make clear the fragility of GIDS and EGIDS, for they classify as *vigorous* languages like Kom, reported to be 'highly endangered', as well as the large number of 6a* languages for which there is presumably no reliable information and cases like Sartang which may not be a language. A number of these languages also seem to be part of a bilingual or multilingual repertoire, the stability of which is uncertain. In other words, they illustrate the kind of evolution that Mufwene has noted and show the difficulty of dealing with the dynamism of changing situations. If we look for certainty, it can only be found in the politically determined government classification in India in scheduled languages; what we have in *Ethnologue* are more or less informed guesses at the status of the varieties used by scheduled castes and tribes.

Mohanty (2019b) in a new book helps to account for this. In a study of multilingualism, he starts with a description of his own linguistic history. He grew up in Puri, a city of 200,000 on the Bay of Bengal in Odisha state, and economically dependent on the location there of the Shree Jagannath Temple, one of the major Hindu temples for pilgrimage. When pilgrims arrived, they were greeted by a *panda* (a temple servant) who recognised their language and origin and escorted them during their time there; a *panda* had professional competence in languages and varieties. Mohanty grew up speaking Odia and would use it to reply to the Hindi- or Bengali-speaking friends he visited. This acceptance of multilingualism[15] was normal in the many places he visited in India, so that he was surprised when he later moved to North America as a student; there, he found that the various language-speaking communities were isolated and that being a plurilingual individual was noticeable. In India, on the other hand, managing several languages was normal: Kond tribal speakers of Kui and non-tribal Odia speakers maintained their identity while communicating with each other and in markets with Hindu and Telegu speakers; code-mixing and borrowing from each of these languages and also from English was normal. Later, when he lived in Delhi, he spoke Odia at home, English at work, Hindi for television and informal communication, Bengali with domestic help and Sanskrit for religious observance; on a research project in Assam, he added communication in Assamese and Bodo.

On this basis, Mohanty argues that the diversity of languages in India is comparatively stable,[16] and in a series of studies that echo the work of Gardner and Lambert (1972) in Québec, he used questionnaires to assess attitudes to language and culture maintenance among the Kond in Odisha. Basically, Kond who were bilingual in Kui and Odia also show positive integrative attitudes to their heritage Kui variety, but they saw Odia as instrumentally more valuable. Kond who were monolingual in Odia had negative attitudes to Kui, showing that practical concerns had encouraged their language shift. In discussions among members of the *Kui Samaj* (the Society of the Kui People), Mohanty heard strong support for the Kui language, but nobody suggested that it be used in the educational system. Only after international pressure persuaded the Odisha State Government to develop mother tongue education around 2000 were books developed for initial teaching for Kui and other tribal languages, but although this did improve attitudes, it was not enough to overcome the threat to these languages. School was not enough (Spolsky, 2009c), it seems, to overcome economic values; when forced to make a choice between a heritage identity language and a dominant language with instrumental benefits, the latter usually wins out.[17]

In a later series of studies, Mohanty looked at the 1,350,000 Bodo people in Assam, recognised as a Scheduled Tribe and living in concentrated settlements. By 1952, political activity supported language maintenance, but in 1954 the Bodo were included in a state with Assamese as its dominant and official language. Bodo became a minority language and was marginalised and many Bodo individuals chose to assimilate by accepting Assamese and English education for their children. However, continued activism led by *the Bodo Maha Sanmilani* (formed in 1921) and the All Bodu Students' Union and strengthened by the violent resistance of the Bodo Liberation Tigers resulted in an agreement in 2003 that granted partial autonomy to the Bodos and recognition of the Bodo language as a constitutionally scheduled language. Gradually, this new status led to revitalisation of Bodo, its use as a medium of instruction even at the tertiary level and publications of newspapers and books in it.

India is a multilingual country that, in spite of the recent strengthening of Hindu nationalism, still recognises its many minority languages formally, allowing each state to choose its local state language and teaching many of them at various levels of education. But as Mufwene (2001) argues, there is a natural evolution taking place, with many speakers shifting to larger and more economically attractive languages and children picking up local varieties from neighbours and peers.

Smaller threatened languages are being documented by a government sponsored programme, the Scheme for Protection and Preservation of Endangered Languages, which is developing dictionaries (often trilingual) and grammars for languages for which writing systems also need to be chosen. Although documentation is a necessary first step in reversing language shift, I have so far not found evidence that speakers of these languages are alarmed; language activism in India comes, it seems, with larger languages such as those chosen for official state use and resisting the pressure from Hindi. And it seems clear that the more important pressures for intervention are those aimed not at language but at the social and economic status of the under-privileged castes and tribes that speak them. These are the groups that account for India having in 2011 the largest percentage of its population living below the World Bank's international poverty line and for the fact that a third of India's children are underweight (World Bank, 2016).

We can expect to find some of the same problems in looking at endangerment of varieties in other countries. I will look at similar borderline cases in multilingual countries on other continents, choosing Vanuatu for the Pacific (with 113 languages), Brazil for the Americas (with 237 languages, of which 217 are living and 20 are extinct and of the living languages, 201 are indigenous and 16 are non-indigenous; furthermore, 7 are institutional, 31 are developing, 39 are vigorous, 40 are in trouble and 100 are dying), Nigeria (which according to *Ethnologue* has 507 indigenous and 10 non-indigenous languages, of which 19 are institutional, 76 are developing, 299 are vigorous, 81 are in trouble and 42 are dying) for Africa and the Russian Federation for Europe (with 117 languages). In each country, I will select a sample of vigorous, threatened and dying languages, looking for larger threatened varieties and smaller vigorous languages.

Minority languages in Vanuatu

Vanuatu possibly has more indigenous languages per head of population than any other country on earth. It is an archipelago with over eighty islands. It is steep-sided hills mean that under 10% is used for agriculture; 90 per cent of the households continue to fish even though stocks are being depleted; logging is leading to deforestation; and most families have been forced into a subsistence economy. Bislama, a pidgin in rural and a creole in urban areas, is encroaching on the multitude of small language varieties. Education is in Bislama and the other two official languages, English and French, which were the languages of the British–French Condominium of New Hebrides before independence in 1980.

As Table A.3 in the Appendix shows, there are differences between rural and urban areas. In urban areas like Port Vila, most people are shifting to Bislama as a second or even first language. But in rural areas, plurilingual linguistic repertoires are common, as François (2012) shows in a study of the seventeen languages spoken in the fifty villages of the Torres and Banks islands of Northern Vanuatu. There have been shifts – moribund varieties not passed on, speakers of a language with five speakers reduced to two – and one growing variety with 2,100 speakers of all ages, but most have an average of about 500 speakers. A few are spoken in a single village and none in more than six. But many villages are multilingual, as a result of exogamy (men as well as women marrying into other villages) and of trade, exchange and social alliances. A social bias towards linguistic and cultural differentiation is common, leading to an ideological tendency to heterogenisation: 'each community will end up having its own word form for a given meaning, often highly divergent from its neighbours' (p. 92), which has produced diversity, made possible also by a willingness to learn each other's languages. Egalitarianism means that no one language is considered better than any other, but multilingualism means that children of intermarried parents grow up speaking more than one language. In one family with whom François stayed, four languages were spoken daily and three others were known. But there are counterforces: post-contact social changes such as missionaries and blackbirding; local migration and changes in demography; changes in power structure; schooling in English and French and by non-local teachers; and the so far limited spread of Bislama in rural areas. Thus, the future of linguistic diversity in Vanuatu is not guaranteed.

Minority languages in Brazil

For the Americas, I have chosen Brazil, although its dominant language is Portuguese and not the English of North America or the Spanish of Latin America, because I have already studied the colonial and postcolonial linguistic history of the multilingual nation (Spolsky, 2018b). Colonial policy was established there by 1757 when the rulers banned the 180 indigenous languages and made Portuguese obligatory (Massini-Cagliari, 2004: 8), a policy they continued to apply to many later immigrant languages like German, Italian and Japanese. However, the constitution of 1988 recognised Indian rights and promised the use of native languages in education (Hornberger, 1998).

Guilherme (2015) discusses the application of the Universal Declaration of Human Rights and of the 1988 Brazilian Constitution to the education of the 220 indigenous peoples and 178 indigenous languages still recognised, in the 2,323 indigenous schools listed in a 2005 school census. Of the 8,431 teachers employed in these schools, 90 per cent had a native background, but only 13 per cent had a degree, 64 per cent had completed secondary school and 12 per cent had only elementary education. There were a number of programmes aiming to remedy this problem, but they were relatively weak. The dropout rate of pupils remained high: only 12,000 of 89,000 indigenous children in elementary school went on to the secondary level. However, some 78 per cent of the Indian schools used native languages or had bilingual programmes; a few did not teach Portuguese at all. But fewer than half had access to pedagogical material in the native language. Only two-thirds had their own school buildings.

Affected by these policies are only those natives whose tribes have been contacted. There are still many tribes that remain isolated in the jungles. Current policy is to leave the uncontacted tribes alone, assuming that contact will be unwelcome or would be harmful. But Guilherme worries that schooling may not benefit either contacted or uncontacted indigenous tribes. Table A.4 in the Appendix presents details of selected endangered or surviving languages, starting with some indigenous languages with more secure status, *educational* (4), meaning vigorous use, standardisation and institutionally supported education and *developing* (5), vigorous use and standardisation but not yet widespread. Another twenty-seven languages are classified as (5a*), probably *developing*. I also list a few classified as 7, *shifting*, with over 1,000 speakers.

Survival of indigenous languages in Brazil depends first on being uncontacted, of which there are between forty and ninety such peoples, being reduced by genocide carried out by those exploiting the natural resources of the Amazon, by religious conversion – originally Roman Catholic but now likely to be Protestant – by anthropological and linguistic incursions (such as SIL International), by educational programmes and by the campaign of President Bolsonaro who favours appropriation of indigenous land and regrets the failure of genocide.[18] Contact means exposure to a nationalist policy aiming to have everyone speak Portuguese. Although some bilingual–bicultural programmes were developed, they were mainly transitional and are likely to have reduced support under the current government. Tribes more recently contacted, provided they were not wiped out by disease or violence, are more likely to have maintained their heritage languages; language loss is a mark of exposure and assimilation to the Portuguese-dominated environment.

Minority languages in Nigeria

A country of Africa, Nigeria has over 500 living indigenous languages, 3 of which are recognised as de facto provincial languages. These are Hausa in the north with over 38 million speakers, Yoruba in the south-west with over 37 million speakers and Igbo in the south-east with 27 million speakers. But the colonial language, English, was so well established that a recent paper dealing with the extinction of indigenous languages chooses to focus on one of the big three, Yoruba, as a language under threat (Olajo and Oluwapelumi, 2018). The paper deals with the decline of the Yoruba language, finding the main causes to be 'prominence of English language, love for western culture and failure of parents to train their wards to speak Yoruba' (p. 24); it is no longer a compulsory language in secondary schools and many parents no longer speak it to their children. Igboanusi (2008) found that the Nigerian National Policy on Education which calls for learning the child's first language or one of the three provincial languages alongside English has not been implemented even though parents want bilingual education with the mother tongue taught beyond the first three years of primary education.

Looking at endangered languages in Nigeria listed in Table A.5 in the Appendix, one realises the complexity as well as the uncertainty of the notion: half a dozen varieties with over 10,000 speakers are classified in *Ethnologue* as threatened and a dozen with under 6,000 speakers are considered vigorous; this includes two with under 300 speakers. But closer study of those for which there are independent published or unpublished reports of visits suggests that the critical difference is isolation. In most cases, the shift was to a local language, though the official national language after independence continued to be English, spoken by many, or Nigerian Pidgin and its higher form Nigerian English (Jowitt, 2018). Hausa is still spoken in Nigeria as a first language by 33 million and as a second by another 15 million and is the de facto provincial language in the North.

Minority languages in the Russian Federation

Finally, for Europe I have selected the Russian Federation, which provides an example of a totalitarian nation with a hegemonic national language enforced by government language policy (see Table A.6 in the Appendix). As a result, the only languages other than Russian classified as vigorous (6a) are Aghul, the provincially recognised constitutional language of the Dagestan Autonomous Region and spoken as a home language by 98 per cent of the population (a total reported in the 2010 census of 29,300) and used in local schools and classified as 6a*, and Siberian or Eastern Tatar, an unwritten language spoken by 100,000, with a dictionary published in the twenty-first century. Siberian Tatar is considered endangered by UNESCO and current dialect studies show considerable Russification (Fayzullina et al., 2017). There are seven provincial languages recognised by statute: Adyghe, Avar, Southern Altai, Chechen, Kalmyk-Orak, Tatar and Yakut, ranging from 57,000 to 4 million speakers. Bashkort, Dargha, Ingush, Lak, Lezgi and Tuval are also provincial languages, but classified as *educational* (4) along with English and Meadow Mari. Other provincial languages classified as *developing* (5) are Buriat, Khakas, Nogai and Rutul, which share the classification with Bezhta, Livvi-Karelian, Russian Sign Language and Selkup.[19]

The Russian Federation, after a few signs of recognition of diversity, now continues the Russification imposed by Stalin and continuing the trend of Czarist Russia. However, the fact that local languages are recognised if only in secondary status means that they might still compete with Russian as attractive to the evolution of the linguistic repertoires of speakers of smaller minority varieties.

The fate of endangered languages

Essentially, looking at these selected cases of minority languages in five regions, there seems to be support for Mufwene's case for seeing language shift as a normal evolutionary phenomenon, as speakers first add to their repertoires from the larger varieties spoken where they live, influenced both by needs to do business and obtain jobs and by the demographic pressures of their changing environment. In addition, once their children are provided with schooling, it is most likely to be in the dominant regional or national language to which they shift, speeding up the process and only counter-balanced where there is strong enough pressure from an ideology of identity leading to internally accepted or externally imposed socioeconomic isolation preventing integration in the wider community. From the point of view of speakers, this seems an inevitable result, hastened by globalisation and improved communication. But it does not necessarily lead to the loss of linguistic diversity that many fear, for the expansion of linguistic repertoires and the mixture of varieties appears to encourage the development of new varieties such as the Navlish that Webster (2010b) sees as replacing Navajo, or the multiple varieties of English that Kachru (1986; Kachru et al., 2009) recognise.

To summarise the situation of endangered languages, it is generally far from easy to be sure about the language practices of a community; often even the name and the uses and number of speakers of a variety are not reliably documented, so that lists like that of *Ethnologue* and other publications are derived from estimates.[20] However, from such published material as I have consulted, there is good evidence that many language varieties are under threat, whether as the result of direct external intervention, such as the Chinese policies towards Tibetan and Uyghur, or the Turkish killing of Kurds, or the Myanmar treatment of Rohingya, or the Brazilian destruction of the Amazon forests, or the continuing policy of Russification, or of the neglect of needed educational policies affecting 40 per cent of the world's children, or as a result of greater economic value and attraction of larger languages.

Given this situation, the maintenance of a language variety depends on the existence of either isolation, something that is decreasingly likely with modern communication and globalisation, or of the ideological commitment of speakers to their heritage and identity.

Ideally, language management needs to consider the interests of the community. But even a good plan, it must always be remembered, can be influenced or blocked by such non-linguistic events as civil war, poverty, disease and corruption. And it is generally the case that the speakers of endangered languages are poorer and less powerful than the average: the result, as William Labov stated, is that saving the people becomes as important as or more important than documenting and saving the language. In most cases, however, activists and governments who tackle the issue are likely to concentrate their efforts on the latter. Linguists have argued that preserving endangered indigenous languages, like the varieties spoken by the tribal peoples of India, is a way of preserving indigenous knowledge. As the Vice-Chancellor of the Indira Gandhi National Tribal University, Professor T. V. Kattimani, told me, a twelve-year-old tribal boy probably knows more about local plants and trees and their uses than his professor of botany! Saving the language saves that knowledge, he agrees, but he added that he sees the mission of the university as finding a way to save the people too, by converting that knowledge to a livelihood.

Recognition of the close relation between language policy and economic policy is rare. Commins (1988) and Ó Riágain (1997) pointed out the effects of socioeconomic development in the Gaeltacht in Ireland: government support for development did not prevent emigration and language loss and later encouraged immigration of non-Irish speakers. Kattimani's suggestion was that the two interests must somehow be combined: the indigenous knowledge of endangered speakers monetised and so balancing economic and heritage values. To deal with the threat to indigenous languages, there are many non-governmental organisation (NGO) and government supported schemes underway in many parts of the world. Commonly, they are undertaken by linguists and educators, the former aiming to document the language (develop a writing system, preparing grammars and dictionaries) and the latter opening schools and classes to teach the language to those whose heritage is at risk.

There are schemes such as some in India, where resettlement has strong effects on the linguistic repertoire of those involved. Mathur (2012) reports that the government of India announced a first resettlement plan in 2004, revised in 2007, but implementation has been uneven and generally unsuccessful. The linguistic effects of one such scheme are described by Kumar (2019; Kumar et al., 2015). Indigenous tribal peoples (two large tribes, Pawra and Bhil, and two smaller ones, Bhoi and Adivasi) in the Narmada Valley have been brought into contact with non-tribals and they continue to use only their tribal indigenous languages in the home, but in the public domain (the marketplace and with the police) they expand their repertoires, adding the local state languages (Marathi, Hindi and Gujarati) and other dialects. Again, the lack of fit between the economic and social goals interferes with the attainment of either.

I conclude then with this: language management in the case of endangered languages should ideally be part of a unified scheme to solve the socioeconomic problems of the community concerned. Simply documenting the language or even introducing it into the school system, desirable as both are, will not lead to successful language management.

Notes

1. I will deal with the human and linguistic rights arguments and the international organisations that support them in Chapter 11.
2. An expanded scale (Expanded Graded Intergenerational Disruption Scale; EGIDS) was proposed in Lewis and Simons (2010) and is now reported in *Ethnologue* for every listed language.
3. In India, too, it is usually a local or state language that attracts speakers of minority languages.
4. Not an easy distinction, but depending usually on assumed time of arrival.
5. This view was expressed strongly by Labov (2008), who believed that African-American Vernacular English would continue as long as so many young Blacks were in jail.
6. One example is the development of a rich and complex Jewish religious literature in English in the United States; the shift from Yiddish and Hebrew did not block continuation of the culture.
7. A Navajo student of mine who had settled in Albuquerque said that although she would have liked her son to grow up speaking Navajo, to move back to the Reservation would require her to carry several gallons of water a few miles every day.
8. Fishman's work with language loyalty followed from his attempt to understand the loss of his own secular Yiddish (Spolsky, 2011b).
9. In a move rare in scholarship, Fishman (2001) revisited the topic, inviting a dozen scholars to evaluate his own earlier analyses and conclusions.
10. I have mentioned Fishman's GIDS and the *Ethnologue* EGIDS. Others

they describe are Stephan Wurm's scale and other scales derived from it including Michael Krauss's scale, the index of vitality developed by the *Osservatorio linguistico della Svizzera italiana*, the European Language Diversity for All Barometer, and the University of Hawaii Catalogue of Endangered Languages Index.

11. There are, however, over 1000 scheduled castes and nearly 750 Scheduled Tribes, referred to as Depressed Classes and given Reservation status, which reserves access to seats in various legislative bodies, to government jobs and to admission to higher education. There is a distinction made in India between mother tongues and languages, the latter requiring recognition by a state government and qualifying for financial support. The problem was highlighted for me when a senior Indian linguist remarked that a variety with a million speakers was too small to expect a special script.

12. Most of the details that follow are taken from *Ethnologue.* I have checked the cases listed whenever I could find a source. But to make clear the problems involved, a paper by Professor Awadhesh K. Mishra, a professor at the English and Foreign Languages University, Shillong Campus at the 2019 Linguistic Society of India annual conference focused on exposing errors in status of a long list of Indian languages.

13. 'More than 40% of all land-related conflicts involve forest lands, mostly concentrated in regions where customary rights of tribal communities are not recognised.' 'A village chief and a gang of higher-caste men opened fire on poor farmers in northern India and killed at least 10 of them in a land dispute, police officials said on Thursday' (*The New York Times,* 19 July 2019).

14. Ignoring the way that religious languages like Hebrew, Latin and Sanskrit were maintained by educational systems.

15. Now called translanguaging by García and Li (2013) and others.

16. It is currently threatened by the increasing Hindu nationalism of Narendra Modi, leader of the Bharatiya Janata Party, the ideology of which is support for Hindi hegemony.

17. Fishman (1966) points to two US exceptions: the Hasidim and the Amish. In both cases, the religious groups made an effort to maintain social isolation, giving up on economic cultural assimilation and so rejecting the instrumental value of the dominant language.

18. See 'What Brazil's President, Jair Bolsonaro, has said about Brazil's Indigenous Peoples', available at <https://www.survivalinternational.org/articles/3540-Bolsonaro> (last accessed 29 September 2020). Other reports suggest that if present government policies continue, the Amazon and the peoples living there are under serious threat.

19. Another thirty-five varieties are classified as 8a (*moribund*) or 8b (nearly extinct) and two as *dormant* (no known speakers).

20. I recall some years ago attending a meeting at which a scholar suggested

preparing a highly reliable sample of the Human Relations Area Files, a collection of data on cultures of the world, by which he meant those cultures which had been described by a trained anthropologist who had been in residence for at least two years. Demanding anything like this for the 6,000 or so language varieties would be in vain.

10 Management Agencies and Advocates

Advocates and managers

The theory of language policy that I have proposed distinguishes between language practices (what people do), language beliefs (what they think they should do) and language management (when someone tries to change the practices or beliefs of others). Discussing language management, I added that managers – individuals or institutions, internal to the community or outside it – assume that they have authority over members of the community.[1] In this chapter, I will focus on a distinction between managers who do have authority (parents in a family or school boards and education ministries, for instance) and advocates and advocacy groups without authority, who must rely on persuasion. Lacking authority, advocates need to convince members of the relevant speech community or a powerful manager to adopt a proposed policy and implement it. Individual managers at the state level are dictators or prime ministers. At other levels, they are those who can control others – a grandfather in a family, a priest or religious leader, the owner of a business, the head of a hospital, a teacher in a classroom. At the level of the nation state, the most obvious managing agency is the government; the most common advocacy groups are supporters of a specific language variety. We will be comparing the language policing functions of government institutions such as those in Latvia and Québec with the advocacy of the Gaelic League or the Hebrew Language Committee before independence.

In his classic study of language policy, Cooper (1989: 98) proposed an 'accounting scheme for language planning' which he then summarised in a table. The table had the following key elements: 'what *actors* . . . attempt to influence what *behaviours* . . . of which *people* . . . for what *ends* . . . under what *conditions* . . . by what *means* . . . through which *decision-making* . . . process with what *effect*'. Dealing with actors, earlier in the chapter, he accepted a differentiation between '*formal elites, influential and authorities*', the latter being those who 'actually make policy decisions' (1989: 88). In the model in Spolsky (2001, 2003, 2004, 2009a), it is authorities who are the managers. But what about the elites and the influential? In his listing of means, Cooper added a clue to the distinction between the kinds of actors, by listing four examples of their activity: 'authority, force, promotion, persuasion' (1989: 98). Authority and force suggest managers (presidents, government ministers, governments, parliaments, business managers, school principals, teachers, parents and religious leaders). But promotion and persuasion refers to what I am calling advocacy. Advocates are individuals or groups who, without the authority assigned by government or institutions, wish to promote a language variety or persuade others to use it.[2]

Where do advocates and managers fit into language policy? There is a basic division recognised by scholars[3] between *status planning* (selecting which variety should be the norm in a society) and *corpus planning* (codifying and elaborating the language variety). Planning occurs, Neustupný (1970) suggested, when someone identifies a language problem, where there is a conflict of norms.[4] Selection, Einar Haugen wrote, is a social decision, that may be arrived at by a majority or enforced by a totalitarian leader. Codification, on the other hand, may be the work of a single person (such as the language reformers listed later in this chapter) who invents or modifes a writing system, or proposes new grammar rules and lexicon. Generally, as they are self-selected, language reforming individuals are best classified as advocates. The actual implementation of their proposals depends on the willingness of a speech community to accept their proposals or its acceptance by an individual or institution with authority over the community. Schools are the major institutions that implement language policy, choosing which variety to use for instruction or to teach. But an individual or group of reformers may be able to persuade a school system or parents to support a different norm, producing the grassroots programmes found in many countries to teach endangered languages. Advocates without authority may propose modifications in status or corpus, but must either become managers by setting up their own institutions or persuade managers to implement them.

Advocacy and management at different levels

Language policy occurs at different levels and in different domains, ranging from the individual (self-management) and the home to the supranational (groups and institutions proclaiming and supporting language and human rights). At each of these levels, we may find advocates and managers attempting to modify the language practices and beliefs of others. At the family level, it is usually the parents who set policy not just for themselves but also for their children, both by example and environment, in persuading or attempting to enforce language choice. But often there is an external agent, a school teacher or a religious leader or a political authority, who tries to influence family language policy.[5] In the business world, company managers often establish language policy by their hiring practices; they may enforce it by banning employees from using languages that customers do not know. In hospitals, there are often rules against doctors and nurses speaking a foreign language in the presence of patients. In the legal field, the language proficiency of police (set by hiring policies) determines the likelihood that victims and suspects can be understood without an interpreter.[6] In courts, judges determine what is acceptable language practice.[7] In religious institutions, the religious leadership decides what languages are acceptable for different functions – for sacred texts, prayers, sermons or confession.[8] In schools, the authority decides on the language of instruction and which other varieties are to be taught. Although these local policies may determine practices and beliefs, at the same time they interfere with central government policies. For example, school systems usually lay down that the standard language should be taught and used, but teachers will often use an informal local variety to make sure they are understood.

Two cases of Indian language activism

Describing nineteenth-century language policy in the Indian state of Odisha (formerly Orissa[9]) under the British, Mohanty (2002) said that the Oriya (now Odia) language spoken by 75 per cent of the population was finally recognised by the British Government, after a long struggle with Persian and Bengali,[10] as a result of the activism of the Oriya Language Movement. This is a prime example of the process I am describing through which an advocacy group achieves the implementation of a language policy that it proposes.

Those determining language policy in India in the nineteenth century were divided between Orientalists, who argued for the use of local vernaculars, and Anglicists, whose position in favour of English was set out most clearly by Macaulay (1920), whose 1835 Minute argued that modernisation depended on education in the imperial language. In Odisha, the Anglicist approach was dominant and the only officials hired apart from British were Bengali; two Bengali school inspectors proposed in 1864 using only Bengali in schools. The Odia resistance first appeared in a new weekly magazine, *Utkala Dipika*, three years later, after two years of famine. The weekly helped to raise funds for textbooks in Odia. In the same year, *Utkala Bhasoddipani Sabha*, The Society for the Development of the Odia language, was formed. Over the next few years, a passionate public debate between supporters of Bengali and of Odia took place, the former claiming that Odia was a corrupt form of Bengali. During this period, sales of Bengali textbooks rose and of Odia textbooks fell. Many of the members of the Odia Society were textbook writers, giving them even stronger motivation to call for recognition of their language. By 1870, Odia activism had won the struggle and the British reported that more Odia was being used in schools than Bengali and that Odia teachers were taking over the schools. The struggle for Odia outside

Odisha continued until, finally in 1936, Odisha Province was formed, uniting Odia-speaking areas by an act of the British Parliament.[11] This case shows how a movement lacking authority but building popular support was able to produce a major change in language policy by influencing the authorities.

Another example of effective advocacy in India is shown in a comparison of the fate of two languages studied by Mohanty (2019b), Kui in Odisha state and Bodo in Assam state, as described in Chapter 9 above. Each was the language of a scheduled tribal group and each had over a million speakers. But Kui without active support remains threatened, while Bodo, with the support of activism led by the *Bodo Maha Sanmilani* (formed in 1921) and the All Bodu Students' Union and strengthened by fear of the violent resistance of the Bodo Liberation Tigers, obtained an agreement in 2003 granting partial autonomy to the Bodos and recognition of the Bodo language as a constitutionally scheduled language.

Language academies

One of the earliest language advocacy institutions in Europe was the *Accademia della Crusca*, founded in Florence in 1582. It was a voluntary group of independent scholars whose initial goal was to describe the lexicon and grammar of the best Tuscan writers such as Dante, Petrarch and Boccaccio (Tosi, 2011). The scholars who founded the society believed that the Florentine dialect was the purest and most elegant variety of Italian and so should be chosen over the many other dialects, each of which had as long a history as it. To implement their philosophy, the scholars began to edit and publish a series of dictionaries, the first in 1561. The third, published in 1691 in three volumes, included not just classic and archaic terms but also words from contemporary writers and scientific terminology.

The dictionary was the first in modern Europe, prepared not by a group with authority but by a set of independent academicians. The debate over norms continued in Italy throughout the eighteenth century and there was criticism of the archaic nature of the lexicography. The status of Tuscan declined and when Napoleon conquered Tuscany, French became the official language. However, the position of the Academy improved after the unification of Italy in 1861, so that the first volume of the fifth edition of the dictionary was dedicated to the King of Italy. By the beginning of the First World War, only the tenth volume (up to the letter O) had appeared and in 1923 the Fascist government stopped funding the Academy and set up the *Commissione per l'Italianità della Lingua* (Commission for the Purity of the Italian Language), with a Roman bias. But this had no effect on the continuation of the dialects as spoken forms.[12]

The Crusca Academy was reborn after the Second World War with support from the Allied military government. The Academy was transformed into an activist group, with new technical means to support lexicography. With collected public funds, the Academy launched a number of publications and began to serve as a resource for lexical and linguistic information. By the 1990s, it was stressing the importance of Italian in resisting the spread of English, arguing for European multilingualism and encouraging the reform of language education. From a purely literary society, the Academy has now developed into a centre for language policy that recognises the political relevance of its activities. All this has happened without formal government authority, although the government does make a small grant.

In contrast, the *Académie française* was established by the Cardinal Richelieu for political reasons, to support the centralisation of France under the king located in Paris. The King, Louis XIII, was young but wise enough to appoint a strong minister, Cardinal Richelieu, who spent the next eighteen years working to consolidate royal power and to defeat adversaries abroad and at home. His mission was to fight against disorder, which he saw not just in the political situation but also in art and language. He became a patron of the arts and set out to seek the support of writers. By this time, Paris had become not just the political but also the cultural centre of the nation and many nobles, artists and writers moved there. The intellectual elite of France, educated as they were in the classics, were ready for conservatism in style and language. Purism and correctness were part of the classical model. French was taking over from Latin as the language of learning. The literary language was expanding rapidly, incorporating classical and regional lexicon. An instrument for policy was found by Richelieu in the salon, sessions at which aristocratic women entertained nobles and writers. One such salon met at the Hotel de Rambouillet, out of which grew a small group of writers who would meet once a week. Their club was secret, but Cardinal Richelieu learnt about it and persuaded the group to become official under government sponsorship. They agreed and in 1634 met for the first time as the *Académie française*. A year later, they were incorporated by the Paris parliament, with authority over the French language and books submitted to them for judgement. The academy's principal function was 'to give explicit rules to our language and to render it pure, eloquent and capable of treating the arts and sciences'. The main activity was the editing of a dictionary, although the first edition did not appear until 1694 (Cooper, 1989).

The French academy, unlike the Italian, began with government authority to manage the language. But in time, continuing to possess a public image as an institution of power (Estival and Pennycook, 2011), it turned out to have '*irréprochable inutilité*' (irreproachable uselessness) (Robitaille, 2002), taking more interest in the awarding of prizes and needing to be supplemented by the *Délégation générale à la langue française et aux langues de France* (DGLFLF) and by the formation of large numbers of language committees in the various departments of government.

Language management agencies

In addition, language management has been implemented in France by a number of laws (Ager, 1996, 1999). Often cited are the edicts of Villers-Cotterêt which in 1539 mandated replacing Latin in courts with the vernacular. More generally applicable were the decrees during the French Revolution, which in 1794 replaced church schools with state schools that were required to use French as language of instruction: German in Alsace was banned as were other regional languages. But finding French-speaking teachers took a long time, so that again in 1881 the Minister of Education had to repeat the requirement that French must be used in all schools; this policy was to be enforced also in the colonies (Spolsky, 2019c).

A law in 1975 laid down that French must be used in commerce, public places, the media and public service. Only in 1980 was the French Constitution amended, in preparation for the Maastricht Treaty, to require French. Going further, in 1994, the Toubon Law made French compulsory in consumer affairs, employment, education and congresses held in France (this last was overruled by the Constitutional Court). Terminology committees were established in each government ministry to control the lexicon needed by the ministry and since 1993 to disseminate the official terminology (Spolsky, 2004). Nevertheless, in spite of all this enforcement and of a general acceptance of ideology of monolingual hegemony, regional languages continue to exist: Alsatian, Basque, Breton, Catalan, Corsican, Flemish and the several varieties of Occitan (Judge, 2000).

The situation in Germany was different. There, in the seventeenth century, a number of language advocacy societies were formed to purify and spread the language. The first of these was the *Fruchtbringende Gesellschaft* (Fruitful Society), founded in 1617 and with 890 members, that aimed to replace foreign words. Its members were princes and noblemen who published various works and discussed how to purify the language. It was known as a noble order (*Palmordern*) and was active until 1680. Limited to ten members, another society, the *Aufrichtige Tannengesellschaft* (Sincere Fir Tree Society), was active from 1633 to 1670. Other seventeenth-century societies were the *Deutschgesinnte Genossenschaft* (German-minded Cooperative) and *Elbschwanordern* (Elb Swan Order). Their work was continued in the nineteenth century by half a dozen associations including the *Allgemeiner Deutscher Sprachverein* (Langer and Davies, 2011). A government-sponsored organisation, *Gesellschaft für deutsche Sprache* (Association for the German Language), was founded in 1947 to replace the *Allgemeiner Deutscher Sprachverein* (General Association for the German Language), which had been set up in 1885. It answers questions about spelling, grammar and punctuation, advises the German Government and has fifty branches in German states and fifty-nine in other countries. In 1996, major reform in German orthography was agreed by the governments of Germany, Liechtenstein,

Austria and Switzerland; after opposition, which included the work of over a dozen anti-reform societies, the Council for German Orthography in 2006 overturned the most radical changes. Thus, in Germany, a tradition of advocacy groups continued, as new groups were formed to oppose the reforms proposed by government management agencies.

More effective than the French Academy was the *Office québécois de la langue française* (OQLF), with 240 employees enforcing the policies of Bill 101 in Québec.[13] The Office was set up by the Québec Government in response to pressures from language activists, who were concerned about what they saw as a threat to the French language in the Province. There was a drop in the birth-rate of Francophones and assimilation among Francophones outside the Province. In Québec, Anglophones dominated the commercial world and new immigrants (especially Italian Catholics) were showing a preference for English schools. Support for French became a political platform, a more moderate form of separatism. The first step of the new government was Bill 22, which established that only the children of English Anglophones could register for English-medium schools. Bill 101, passed in 1977, added a number of more radical measures: all immigrants had to send their children to French-medium schools, Francophones had the right to be served by public agencies and in retail stores in French, and business firms with more than fifty employees had to be certified as using French as the language of work. Only French could be used in public signage.[14] The Office was empowered and required to implement these and any new language laws.

The most obvious effect of this was a change in the demographic balance of the Province as many English speakers moved to Ontario: Anglophones dropped from 13 per cent of the population of Québec in 1971 to 8.3 per cent in 2011. Further, between 1972 and 2012, enrolment in English-medium schools (which now offer strong bilingual programmes including French) dropped by 59 per cent. The implementation of the Québec language policy is supported by the federal bilingual programme, established under the Official Languages Act of 1969, which set up the Office of the Commissioner of Official Languages, which means English and French (Bourhis and Sioufi, 2017). Thus, Québec achieved what Fishman (1991) labelled as a successful case of reversing language shift, where a powerful well-funded government agency replaced advocacy groups and served as 'language police' to implement language laws.

The Quechua Academy

Not all academies succeed. In the introduction to his detailed history and account of the workings of the Quechua Academy, Coronel-Molina (2015) explains the importance of academies and sketches briefly the history and accomplishments of the traditional academies (Italian, French and Spanish) and of more recent academies for Hebrew, Arabic, Basque, Navajo and

Mayan, all similar in their concerns for both corpus and status planning, with the traditional academies concentrating on the former and those of endangered languages working on the latter. Additionally, he notes that those hiring professional linguists appear to be more successful. In Peru, he points out, since independence, there have been a number of movements among the indigenous to improve their position and, after a military coup in 1968, the new president, Velasco, encouraged the codification of the various dialects of Quechua and the development of bilingual education.

The High Academy of the Quechua Language was formed in 1990 and recognised by the government. The founding members of the Academy were bilingual in Quechua and Spanish and it was funded by the government although never formally established as an autonomous public organisation. A change of government in 1990 led to the loss of state funding and, over the next twenty years, there was modification in the nature of its recognition; it is currently under the authority of the Minister of Culture and in spite of reports of mismanagement and of infighting among members, does once again have the promise of a budget.

Part of the problem that faced the academy was the ideological division over varieties of Quechua, with conflict between those who believe that Cusco, the seat of the academy associated with the Inca past of Peru, should dominate and those who favour Lima, the capital city with its attraction to European culture. The academy is committed to the Cusco variety of Quechua, believing it to be the purest variety of the language. Thus there is conflict not just with Spanish but also with other dialects. Members of the Academy claim expertise, but this is disputed by other linguists. This too makes it difficult for the academy's work to be accepted. There continue to be disputes over spelling and over codification and modernisation. There has been an attempt to teach Quechua in schools, but with less success than hoped. Taking all this into account, it seems that the good intentions of the founders of the Academy have not been realised.

Hebrew language activism

A case of successful reversal of language shift according to Fishman (1991: 289–91) was what is often called the miraculous example of Modern Hebrew. But, as he points out, it was not a miracle but a 'rare and largely fortuitous co-occurrence of language-and-nationality ideology, disciplined collective will and sufficient societal dislocation from other competing influences' that permitted the revernacularisation and re-standardisation of the language, accompanied by the restoration of intergenerational transmission – revitalisation, as Spolsky (1991a) labels it.

The process started in Eastern Europe as part of the Zionist movement; Eliezer Ben Yehuda, mythologised as its founder (Fellman, 1973; St John, 1952), was a believer in the return to Zion (Mandel, 1993), before he took on the struggle for Hebrew. But Ben Yehuda settled in Jerusalem, where he had no one who would talk Hebrew with him and where he was excommunicated for heresy. The significant first steps in re-establishing Hebrew as a daily language took place in the schools of new agricultural settlements, first in Rishon Le Zion where David Yudelovich began to teach all subjects in Hebrew in 1886 and then in other farming settlements. By 1892 there were nineteen Hebrew-medium teachers who met and agreed to use Hebrew as medium of instruction. In 1895, fifty-nine members of the Hebrew Teachers' Association agreed to use Hebrew with Sephardi pronunciation for instruction, but to allow prayer with Ashkenazi pronunciation; Ashkenazi script was also to be used.

In 1890, Ben Yehuda set up a four-member Hebrew Language Council, which lasted six months, with task of developing vocabulary and correcting pronunciation.[15] It was revived in 1904 by the Teachers' Union, with a set of fundamental principles drafted by Ben Yehuda. Another major development was the founding of the city of Tel Aviv, defined in a 1906 prospectus as near Jaffa, pure, clean and 100 per cent Hebrew speaking! In 1911, the Council issued a pamphlet listing ninety-eight mistakes in spoken Hebrew, but Fellman (1973: 88) said that most were still used in informal Hebrew speech.

The Hebrew Language Council did not meet during the First World War but, afterwards, met twice a week to develop terminology for business, carpentry and the kitchen (Saulson, 1979). After the war, the Council was reactivated with the name Hebrew Language College and in 1922 its offer to handle all official translation for the British Mandatory Government was not taken up. Hebrew had, however, been included in the three official languages of Mandatory Palestine; the regulation made clear that this was a somewhat limited provision, requiring that inscriptions on postal stamps and currency must be in both languages (Saulson, 1979: 65). It also applied to other government public notices and communications, but implementation remained slow and even Zionist organisations found it necessary to continue to use English (Halperin, 2014: 101).

There was a long dispute over telegrams in Hebrew script and the Hebrew advocacy group, the *Gedud lemeginei hasafa* (Legion to Defend the Language) was involved. The society had been founded at the first Hebrew-medium high school, Herzlia Gymnasia, in Tel Aviv in 1923 and followed the leadership of Menahem Ussishkin, the Zionist leader, who criticised those Jews who used Yiddish or English (Schorr, 2000). The Legion sued the Post Office asking for permission to send telegrams in Hebrew written in Latin letters, but this too was denied. Israel Amikam, a clerk at the Electric Company, continued the fight. In 1922, he published a letter in a Hebrew newspaper; in 1929 after the failure of the Legion's court case, he wrote to the High Commissioner and a year later to the League of Nations; in 1933 he collected signatures in Palestine and at the Zionist Congress to send to the League of Nations; and finally in 1934, the British Government somewhat reluctantly agreed to permit Hebrew telegrams at twenty-four post offices beginning in 1935 (Halperin, 2014: 109).

It was during the period of the British Mandate that Hebrew was established as the language of the Yishuv (the Jewish community in Palestine), with growing (if reluctant) recognition by the Mandatory Government as one of the three official languages. Most important was the British decision to save money by leaving control of education to the two communities: during this period, the Jews set up a framework of Hebrew-medium schools from kindergarten to university level. But as Halperin (2014: 182) notes, instruction in other languages was important in Jewish schools: English was taught in all, Arabic and French in many.

Hebrew linguists continued their efforts to purify, standardise and modernise the language, but had only minor influence on the widespread vernacular use by Palestine-born and immigrant Jews (Reshef, 2019). Hebrew activists worked to influence the authorities to recognise the language and to influence Jews to use it in place of English or the Jewish varieties like Yiddish or Ladino or Judeo-Arabic that were their heritage languages. Shohamy (2007) reports efforts in 1939 of a 'Central Authority for the protection and encouragement of Hebrew in the Jewish community' to have all Jews to speak pure Hebrew; in 1941 they called on towns to establish Hebrew agents in all industries and institutions, shift all newspapers to Hebrew and close theatres not using Hebrew; they also called for public signs and advertisements to be in Hebrew. But lacking authority other than their name, these advocates could not enforce their decisions.

One of the first important decisions of a committee with authority was made by the pre-independence Education Committee set up by the *Vaad Hale'umi* (National Council) to plan for the new state. The committee met for several months in 1948, debating proposals to teach Arabic in Jewish schools and Hebrew in Arab schools. The day before independence was declared, the committee decided that the mother tongue of the majority of pupils in each school should become the language of instruction, reflecting a policy established in the Treaty of Versailles for multilingual areas. Later decisions added the teaching of Hebrew in Arab schools and of Arabic in Jewish schools (Spolsky and Shohamy, 1999: 108).

After independence in 1948, the Israeli Government dropped English as one of the three official languages. It also recognised the Academy of the Hebrew Language as the successor to the Hebrew Language Council, but there was controversy over the use of a foreign word, *Akademia*, in its title, so that it was only in 1953 that an act of the Knesset set it up and the first fifteen members were selected. Its task was to research Hebrew lexicon in all periods, to study the history of the language and 'guide the natural development of the language'.

The official status of the language having been already established, most of the work of the Academy has been corpus planning, with decisions on lexicon, grammar, punctuation, spelling and transliteration. In the 1980s, the Academy did take a policy position when it expressed concern to the Minister of Education that a proposed experiment of teaching physical education in English in a dozen elementary school classes might threaten Hebrew, but the Academy's website now limits its concerns to written texts and formal speech, denying any attempt to police spontaneous speech. Although sharing in what Joshua Fishman (1991) called the 'new monolingual, national secular culture', it played no role in the call by Kodesh (1972) to make Hebrew the only official language for radio and television, nor in the recent nationalistically initiated law lowering the status of Arabic from official to special. To sum up, while early advocacy groups encouraged the revernacularisation of Hebrew and supported what was a grassroots movement, and although there was official recognition of the status of Hebrew after the establishment of the State, the organisations involved never took on the role of language police as happened in Québec.

Language police

The term language police is also applied to the State Language Centre of Latvia. Latvia was multilingual, but once it was incorporated in the Soviet Union, the immigration of large numbers of Russian speakers led to a major change in the language situation. The percentage of Latvian speakers was reduced from 77 per cent in 1935 to 53 per cent in 1979 and the percentage of Russian speakers increased during the same period from 10 per cent to 40 per cent (Priedīte, 2005). Towards the end of Soviet rule, a series of laws were enacted raising the status of Latvian, which became the only official language in 1992, its position strengthened by further laws in 1999 (the State language law) and continued amendments. In 1992, the State Language Centre was established to implement the laws, and commissions were later formed to certify the Latvian proficiency of citizens. The State Language Inspectorate was set up to monitor implementation of the laws. Regulations replaced the parallel school system with a Latvian–Russian bilingual programme, laying down that most subjects were to be taught in Latvian. Levels of Latvian proficiency were established for the professions. A series of surveys showed a large increase in Latvian proficiency among younger participants. There continues to be controversy: in 2012, a referendum to make Russian a second official language was rejected by three-quarters of the voters but political pressure continues (Druviete and Ozolins, 2016).

Soviet language management

In the Soviet Union, language policy was under the central government. During the leadership of Lenin, a policy of equality of languages permitted the development of ethnic (national) languages but this policy changed under Stalin who called for cyrillisation of all languages and Russification as a goal (Grenoble, 2003). Each of the nationalities had its own development pattern, but it is worth looking at Yiddish for an example of Soviet language management.

Although both Lenin and Stalin were unhappy with Jewish cultural autonomy, some development of Yiddish was permitted. It was coordinated by the *Evsektsiya*, the Jewish section of the Communist Party, set up in 1918 and largely made up of former members of the Bund, a Jewish anti-Zionist socialist workers party which was dissolved in 1921. The organisation supported Yiddish but agreed to the banning of Hebrew, with its Zionist associations; Hebrew was not to be taught and publication in Hebrew was not permitted. Yiddish was to be dehebraised: a spelling reform, starting in 1918 and approved by the Jewish Subdivision of the Commissariat of Enlightenment, required that the many Hebrew words in Yiddish, until then written in their Hebrew spelling, should be written in phonetic form: thus, the Hebrew word שבת Sh*BT* should be spelled שאבאת *SHaBoS*. In 1919, a Yiddish Philological Commission was approved at the First All-Russian Culture Conference with the goal of standardising Yiddish. Yiddish research centres were subsequently established in Kiev, Minsk and elsewhere. In 1928, the Second All-Russian Culture Conference approved the new de-Germanised and dehebraised orthography and set up a Central Orthographic Conference which in 1930 approved a proposal for Latinisation; however, the Central Conference was replaced by an All-Union Orthography Conference in 1931 at which Latinisation was not considered (Shneer, 2004).

In the 1930s, then, there was much publication in reformed Yiddish, but this stopped as a result of Stalin's antisemitic activities: many Yiddish writers and leaders were murdered in the Purges from 1948 to 1952; the Yiddish theatres were closed, Yiddish publication halted and Yiddish schools closed or shifted to Russian. In the Soviet Union, language policy was under central control by the Party and the dictator, but various organisations, established usually by the Party, were able for a number of years to implement corpus planning: their pre-revolutionary ideology – anti-Zionist and secular – was applied to changes in Yiddish orthography, working to break links both with its German and its Hebrew components. But Stalin's pro-Russian antinationalist and antisemitic ideology led to the murder of the leadership of the Yiddish movement and the end of publication in the language. The lack of power of advocacy groups was thus shown again.

Language management in the People's Republic of China

Another totalitarian central government that has made use of committees and institutes to implement its ideologically motivated language policy is the People's Republic of China (Li and Li, 2015a; Spolsky, 2014). The PRC continued the 2,000-year-old programme to establish the centrality of the Mandarin topolect, which it recognises as Putonghua (common speech) and which is the basis of the writing system. But this is only one of the language management tasks being undertaken by the PRC: others include simplification and standardisation of Chinese script, design and use of Pinyin[16] as an auxiliary script, identification and mapping of regional language varieties, recognition and description of official minority varieties, creation of scripts for non-Sinitic varieties, translation of names and terms from other languages, language pedagogy and diffusion, bilingualism, foreign language instruction and language testing.

One early goal of PRC language management was to increase popular literacy and this task was assigned to the Commission for the Reform of the Chinese Written Language. The Commission issued a list of simplified characters in 1957, which was expanded in 1965. In 1980, the Committee on Script Reform was reorganised and proposed a Second Scheme. Strong political opposition emerged, however, and in 1986, at the Second National Conference on Language and Script, it was announced that the Second Scheme had been terminated and the revised list was to be withdrawn; although minor modification might still be made, there would no further attempts at large-scale simplification.

Zhao and Baldauf (2008) provide a detailed analysis of the struggles leading to the abandonment of the Second Scheme. They trace the problems produced by the mixed nature of the membership of committees and participants in conferences, which included linguists, language policy and informational technology experts as well as the non-specialist Party and government officials who had the final word. In 1986, the reform committee, renamed State Language Commission (its Chinese name was *Guojia Yuwen Wenzi Gongzuo Weiyuanhui* (The National Committee on Language and Script Work)), came under the authority of the State Educational Commission (Rohsenow, 2004: 30). At a conference in January 1986, the decision was announced that Pinyin would not become an independent writing system, but could be used as a tool in the learning of Chinese. There was some disagreement, but effectively the promotion of Putonghua became the principal goal of Chinese language management. Putonghua was to become the language of instruction in all schools, the working language of government, the language of media and the common language for speakers of all topolects and dialects.

The 2001 Language Law laid down this status of Putonghua and simplified spelling, but recognised the necessary but limited use of the topolects and the maintenance of some minority languages; these too were the subject of extensive linguistic research by appropriate institutes. In 1958, it had been agreed to develop alphabets for those minorities that had no writing system. The new phonetic alphabets were based on Pinyin and not on Cyrillic or other systems, taking into account the wishes of the minority groups, and were enforced after appropriate research and experimentation. The first burst of linguistic activity in the 1950s and 1960s resulted in the development and approval of fourteen scripts for eleven ethnic minorities, including Zhuang, Bouyei, Miaou, Hani and Yi peoples.[17] Others developed later included Lahu and Yi. Together with the pre-existing systems (Mongolian, Tibetan, Uyghur, Kazak, Korean, Kirghiz and Xibe already had scripts), by 2004 there were over thirty different writing systems being used.[18]

In 1950, a Committee for Unifying Academic Terms was set up, reassigned to the *Academica Sinica* in 1956, but work ceased during the Cultural Revolution. In 1996 a National Committee for Terms in Sciences and Technologies was established to replace earlier committees: it aims to develop basic terminology, offering consensus findings and proposing alternatives used in other Chinese speaking areas but not imposing its own solution. With this process in place, standard written Chinese is said to be able to function as the language of a modern state.

The task of language diffusion has been assigned to Confucius Institutes under the authority of the Office of Chinese Language Council (*Hanban*) affiliated with the Ministry of Education, and operated in over 440 universities and secondary schools by the end of 2013 in over ninety countries and regions around the world (Hartig, 2015). And new initiatives with foreign languages and overseas have been initiated as a result of the One Belt One Road strategy covering more than 68 countries and 100 languages.[19]

A central feature of PRC language management has been the combination of professionals such as linguists and IT experts on the various committees and commissions with politicians and representatives of the Communist Party. Thus, advocates work closely with managers in developing policy and monitoring its implementation. When decisions are reached, they are commonly announced by senior Party and government officials. In the minority regions, nationalist activists complain that there are not sufficient resources to support their languages and, in Hong Kong, Cantonese speakers have held demonstrations against the emphasis given to Mandarin. The enormous size and linguistic complexity of China makes clear the need for continued development of language management activities and the associated problem of allowing for diversity when building a national policy.

Successful advocacy for regeneration of Māori

Having looked at cases comparing advocacy and management, whether by individuals or institutions, it becomes clearer that the distinction is not binary: advocates can influence authorities and can carry out actions such as corpus planning that might be accepted by a target audience. At the same time, management institutions with authority, including dictators and governments, may find it difficult to implement their language policies, as they are often dealing with other forces[20] and with large complex populations. As a result, one might conclude that it is useful to include the category of advocates in a language policy model, but that it will not be a simple clear-cut distinction from other managers. To clarify this, it will be useful to look at a case of reasonably successful reversing of language shift, the regeneration of the Māori language in New Zealand (Spolsky, 2005).

Until the middle of the nineteenth century when European settlement in New Zealand started to increase, the Māori language was safe and thriving, spoken in the villages and taught in the missionary schools. Māori literacy was probably higher than English literacy among the settlers.[21] In the 1870s, the New Zealand Wars led to a major change in policy, as the British soldiers supported the settlers in seizing land occupied by Māori tribes; at the same time, the missionary schools were replaced by state schools requiring English as the language of instruction. After the First World War, urbanisation increased and the Māoris who left their home villages were exposed to English in their new communities and in the schools. Intermarriage and bilingualism became common. The school system and the pre-school teachers pressured parents to stop speaking Māori with their children and shift to English. By the 1970s, when Richard Benton (Benton, 1997; Benton and Smith, 1982) carried out a language survey, natural intergenerational transmission of the language had virtually ceased: few Māori children were speaking their language at home.

In the 1970s, concern for ethnic identity was a worldwide phenomenon (Fishman et al., 1985). In New Zealand, some political action had started earlier but the main language revival efforts date from the end of the 1970s. The first significant activity was an effort by a handful of Māori students at university to learn the language that their parents had not taught them. Because few Māori reached the tertiary level, the gap needed to be filled by a grassroots movement. This was *Te Ataarangi*, an activist group formed in 1980 and still active, which taught the language to an unknown number of adults (Browne, 2005). A second initiative, envisioned by individual Māori language advocates with interest in education, led to the creation by interested parents of pre-school programmes: meeting initially in church buildings or private homes, Māori-speaking grandparents would teach the language to their grandchildren. In 1982, the first *Kōhanga Reo* was opened near Wellington and by the end of the year there were programmes in other areas. The grassroots movement spread rapidly: by the end of 1983, there were 148 programmes, each with between twenty and forty pupils, in 1988 there were 520, and by 1994 there were 819 programmes. These programmes were initially under the control of the parents who selected and paid teachers. As time went by, a national coordinating group was set up and gradually the government accepted responsibility (J. King, 2001).

The third initiative was a Māori independent school programme, *Kura Kaupapa Māori* (Education Review Office, 1995). The first Māori immersion primary school was opened in 1985 near Auckland, followed in 1987 by two schools in Auckland. The procedure was similar: parents of children finishing

Kōhanga Reo asked if any state school would continue Māori immersion for their children; when this initiative failed, they started their own school. Again, advocacy became action! The government was finally persuaded to support this and the 1989 Education Amendment Act made it possible for these schools to be an option within the state system; by 1997, there were fifty-four *Kura Kaupapa Māori* offering Māori immersion to children at the elementary level.

At the same time, there were influences on the state system, with bilingual and immersion programmes set up when school principals acceded to local community pressure (Spolsky, 1989). Grassroots pressure built up, as evidenced by 30,000 signatures on a petition for an improved Māori language policy. The important action came when the New Zealand Government in 1975 passed the Treaty of Waitangi Act, setting up the Waitangi Tribunal to adjudicate Māori claims of breaking the 1840 Treaty that granted sovereignty to Queen Victoria. Most of the claims involved land, but an activist group, *Kaiwhakapūmau i Te Reo Māori*, claimed that the government had failed to protect the Māori language. The Tribunal approved the claim and, in 1987, the government passed the Māori Language Act, declaring the language official, allowing its use in law courts and setting up *Te Taura Whiri i te Reo Māori*, the Māori Language Commission. The Commission set out to purify the language, to monitor progress of regeneration and to develop a strategy (Te Puni Kokiri, 1998a, 1998b, 1998c, 1998d, 1998e, 1998f). A series of short cabinet papers set goals and in 1999 the government approved a strategy to increase the number of speakers, the use of the language and the standard of the language used. A major campaign began to establish Māori Television which started to broadcast in 2004.

As part of the policy of the Commission, tribes have been urged to develop their own language strategies, including home language use and use of the tribal dialect. Gradually, then, the Māori advocacy groups have been gaining authority and facing the need to take responsibility for successful restoration of language proficiency and use. The boundary between advocacy and management is blurring, raising new challenges for activists, who are uncomfortable that the funder (the government) wants to set policy. In 2018, Victoria University of Wellington's Deputy Vice-Chancellor (Māori) Professor Rawinia Higgins was appointed as chairperson of *Te Taura Whiri i te Reo Māori*. In a keynote presentation at the 2018 Sociolinguistics Symposium, she described the new Māori Language Act of 2016 which redefines the relationship between the government and the Māori people and commented on the problems being faced as advocacy groups dealt with institutionalisation and the challenge of the effects of government funding and authority.

Advocacy

The case of Māori in New Zealand shows how a grassroots movement, working through advocacy groups, can influence the managers (government and other institutions) to implement their policy aims. But as Williams (2007b, 2008a, 2017a) has shown in studies of Welsh language policy, successful language management cannot depend on central management alone, but needs to be supported by a whole network of implementing agencies at different levels. It is the complex nature of language policy, produced and implemented in the many different speech communities at different social levels and in different domains which constitutes a modern society, that sets the challenges both for advocates and managers. Mohanty (2002: 71) makes this point clearly: 'This case clearly suggests that however strong and powerful a government and its bureaucracy may be, their language policies should ensure support for the masses in order to be successful.'

For many years, the Joint National Committee for Languages, linguistic groups and Native American language activists have been advocating US recognition of Native American languages. In December 2019, the US House of Representatives passed the Esther Martinez Native American Languages Preservation Reauthorisation Act, passed by the Senate in June 2019, authorising funding for efforts to revitalise and maintain their heritage languages. Again, an advocacy group finally influenced a manager with authority.

Language reformers as advocates

Raising the status of a named language variety is what Haugen calls codification, which involves standardisation, the development of a fixed writing system and the agreement on purist rules of grammar, spelling, lexicon and pronunciation. Jones and Mooney (2017: 10) confirm that the creation of a standardised writing system is a challenging but key component of revitalising an indigenous language.

For many modern standard languages, this critical step is often attributed (correctly or mythically) to the work of a single language reformer. For example, the standardisation of Tibetan is commonly agreed to be the work of the seventh-century scholar Thonmi Sambotha (Miller, 1963), a minister sent to India by the king, Srongsten Campo, with sixteen attendants to study Indian scripts. It was the choice of Tuscan dialect by Dante Alighieri to write *The Divine Comedy* in the fourteenth century that led to its acceptance as the norm for standard Italian; it was accepted by the national government after the unification of Italy in the nineteenth century but only included in the constitution in 2007. It was the tasking of the *Académie française*, founded originally as a literary and artistic private club, with responsibility for the spread of the Parisian dialect by Cardinal Richelieu in 1635 that established the primacy of the French language (Cooper, 1989: 10).

Many of the language reformers associated with the standardisation of European vernaculars in the eighteenth, nineteenth and twentieth centuries were educators, grammarians or literary figures. Born in 1773, Josef Jungmann, together with his teacher Josef Dobrovský, a philologist, was the founder of modern Czech. He was Rector of Charles University and published important translations and a five volume German–Czech dictionary (Hroch, 2004). Johannes Aavik was an educator and grammarian who wrote in literary magazines arguing for the standardisation of Estonian (Tauli, 1974: 54). Author, poet and philologist, Ferenc Kazinczy (1759–1831) was important for the reformation and acceptance of Hungarian, recognised as official a decade after his death (Reményi, 1950). Educated as a medical doctor, Adamantios Korais or Koraïs was in Paris during the French Revolution and set out to restore demotic Greek to its classical origins, producing the Katharevousa that was the H variety until the colonels lost power in the 1980s (Mackridge, 2009: 102–25). In the early nineteenth century, Vuk Stefanović Karadžić collected folklore and published a dictionary of Serbian; he standardised the Serbian Cyrillic alphabet (Wilson, 1970). A nineteenth-century 'philosopher, academic educator, writer, translator, printer, publisher, entrepreneur, reformer and philanthropist' (as Wikipedia defines him), Ishwar Chandra Vidyasagar was responsible for the development of modern Bengali (Hatcher, 1996). Publishing much literature in Flemish in the first half of the nineteenth century, Jan Frans Willems is credited with the revival and establishment of the language (Hermans, 2015).

Pompeu Fabra, a professor of chemistry, engineer and grammarian, was considered the leader of the revival and reform of Catalan and he was one of the organisers of the First International Congress of the Catalan Language held in 1906 (Castell, 1993); he later became Professor of Philology and published grammars (Fabra, 1912) and a dictionary. Exiled by Franco, he died in a Catalan speaking area of France in 1948. Philosopher, writer and for a time Chinese Ambassador in Washington, Hu Shih was a leader of the May Fourth Movement and later the New Culture Movement and a major figure in the development of a written version of vernacular Mandarin which became the basis of Putonghua. He died in 1970 and his reputation was reestablished in the 1980s (Grieder, 1970). Shire Jama Ahmed who wrote many books on Somali culture developed a Latin-based orthography which formed the basis of a literacy campaign in the 1970s (Makina, 2011).

These non-governmental creators of standardised writing systems were all influential advocates who promoted their chosen languages.

Inventing writing systems

There were also reformers for some indigenous languages. Among them, the Cherokee silversmith Sequoya developed a syllabary for his language in the early nineteenth century which, once it was adopted, led to a high level of literacy. A similar reformer was the twentieth-century farmer, Shong Lue Yang, who invented (having seen it in a vision) the Pahawh script used for writing Hmong (among the people he is called 'Mother of Writing') and Khmu. He was assassinated by order of the communist forces in 1971. Cooper (1991) gives details of a number of other scripts created in dreams. One was Momulu Duwalu Bukele who discovered a syllabary for Vai in the eighteenth century; another script for a West African indigenous language was for Loma, a syllabary devised by Wido Zomo. In 1910, Afaka Atumisi developed a script for Djuka, spoken by West African slaves in Surinam. Alphabets were similarly discovered for Yupik by Uyakoq and for the same language by Qiatuaq. For Western Apache, Silas John Edwards invented in 1904 a writing system for the religion he founded (Basso and Anderson, 1977). Neither Somali nor Cherokee have a tradition of divine inspiration, but Cooper notes that over half of the twenty-one scripts for indigenous languages developed in the nineteenth and twentieth centuries do.

The invention of a writing system for an indigenous language, something commonly undertaken by missionaries and linguists, added the codification and the standardisation that helped to establish the status of the variety. There are three volumes reporting papers from conferences on the topic (Hanzeli, 2014; Zwartjes and Hovdhaugen, 2004; Zwartjes et al., 2009). Jones and Mooney (2017) deal with the problems of creating orthographies for endangered languages and give details of a number of attempts to do this.

Often the creator of a writing system is identified as a significant contributor to the language. There were three attempts by outsiders to develop a script for Navajo, two by anthropologists (Reichard, 1974; Sapir, 1942) and one by Roman Catholic missionaries (Franciscan Fathers, 1910; Haile, 1926) but the current system was the work of a linguist (John P. Harrington from the Bureau of American Ethnology) assisted by two young men, a student, Robert Young, and his Navajo co-worker, William Morgan (Young, 1977). These latter two produced the Navajo dictionary (Young and Morgan, 1943, 1980); in the 1940s, they published a newspaper in Navajo and a number of pamphlets for the government and some books.[22]

Literacy in Fijian was introduced by missionaries in the early nineteenth century and supported in local churches for a century (Mangubhai, 1987). Mugler (2001) reports efforts to teach literacy in Tamil and Telugu in the early twentieth century to the descendants of Indian forced labourers brought to Fiji by the British colonial government to work on the sugar plantations. Fijian and Fijian Hindi are both still spoken, but colonial rule led to their replacement as a written language by the English required in schools.

Individuals as advocates

There were language activists who argued for revival, a task they often passed later to an advocacy group. For Irish, one of the leading early advocates was Douglas Hyde (1860–1949), a Church of Ireland clergyman, who founded the Society for the Preservation of the Irish Language around 1880 and the *Conradh na Gaeilge* (Gaelic League) three years later; he became active in politics, but after the failure of the Protestant Party in 1923, returned to academic life as Professor of Irish at University College, Dublin; in 1938 he was elected the first President of Ireland (Dunleavy and Dunleavy, 1991), but his advocacy was effective even before he held a government position.

Acclaimed by the American journalist Robert St John as the principal force in the revival of Hebrew (St John, 1952), Eliezer Ben Yehuda became a symbol of what was called a miracle. St John ignored the fact that Hebrew had been used as a written language for the 2,000 years of exile, was spoken by some East European Zionists and was introduced as language of instruction in village schools in Ottoman Palestine. David Yudelovich was the first teacher to do this. Living in Jerusalem where there were few to converse with in Modern Hebrew, Ben Yehuda was excommunicated by the ultra-orthodox; he taught for a few months, but his dictionary was published only after his death (Fellman, 1973). But the responsibility for the development of Modern Hebrew as dominant language of the Jewish community in Ottoman and British Palestine and in the independent State of Israel must be shared by the early settlers in the agricultural villages and the teachers who formed the language committee that later became the Hebrew Language Academy, and by the founders of Tel Aviv who advertised it as 'clean and Hebrew-speaking'. The work of these advocates who gained authority in their own communities was taken over by state language management in 1948 (Spolsky, 2014).

Developing in the early nineteenth century as a literary language and proclaimed by writers who wrote in it as well as in Hebrew as '*a* Jewish language' (Fishman, 1993), secular Yiddish was maintained and standardised by YIVO (*Yidisher Visnshaftlekher Institut*), founded in Wilno by a number of scholars including Max Weinreich who brought it to New York in 1940 where he became Professor of Yiddish at City College of New York and published a two volume history of the language (Weinreich, 1980, 2008). The maintenance and spread of Hasidic Yiddish, on the other hand, must be attributed to the influence and authority of the rebbes who see it as a way of maintaining separateness (Katz, 2004).

The independence of Norway from Danish rule in 1814 produced an opportunity to create a Norwegian language. One advocate was Ivar Aasen (1813–96), a philologist, playwright and poet, who collected and published a dictionary of Norwegian dialects in 1850, labelling the language he had created *Landsmål* (country language) which was later modified into one of

Norway's official language, *Nynorsk* (Linn, 1997). His work was supported by Knud Knudsen (1812–95), an educator, philologist and writer, who proposed that writing should reflect speech and agued for Norwegianisation and *Landsmål*. For a while, this influenced Bjørnstjerne Martinius Bjørnson (1832–1910), playwright, poet and novelist, who wrote one work in *Landsmål* but later denounced the farmers and their language and clothing! Spokesman for the left was Henrik Arnold Thaulow Wergeland (1808–45); he wore homespun clothes (like a farmer) and was a highly controversial and influential poet and writer. Marius Nygaard (1838–1912) was an educator and linguist who shared responsibility for *Bokmål*, a Norwegianised variant of Danish, the orthography of which (under the name *Riksmaal*) was adopted in 1907. The development of the two varieties of written Norwegian is traced by Haugen (1959, 1961, 1966), showing how the conflict was political as much as linguistic. Trudgill (1978) pointed out that although students were required to study both versions, they were to be allowed to continue to speak in their local dialects.

Advocacy played an important role in both the loss and regeneration of Māori. Comfortably maintained until the 1870s, with a high level of bilingualism and Māori literacy, the decision at the end of the New Zealand Wars[23] to close missionary schools and to insist on English as language of instruction marked the beginning of the shift, made worse by urbanisation and the army service in the First World War. But a significant influence was the advocacy of bilingualism by Sir Apirana Ngata (1874–1950), politician and lawyer, who supported Māori culture (promoting the *haka* and *poi* dancing) and literature (publishing folk songs) but argued against separatism, encouraging a bilingualism that was not able to resist the forces of shift. By the 1960s, there were few Māori children being brought up to speak the language (Benton and Smith, 1982). An important figure who contributed to the regeneration of the language was Dame Katarina Mataira who together with Te Kumeroa Ngoingoi Pēwhairangi supported the *Te Ataarangi* movement which taught Māori to young adults and *Kōhanga Reo*, the parent-supported language nests in which pre-school children were exposed to the language by their grandparents (Spolsky, 2005, 2009b).

Lacking any direct authority, all these advocates depended for any success in establishing their chosen languages on acceptance by more powerful managers or agencies, often after a spell of support by an activist group such as the Gaelic League or a political party as in Norway or adoption by a government as with Irish or Hebrew. It is thus difficult to judge the effectiveness of an advocate, for some other agent or agency made the decisions relevant to language change, such as the parents who had their children taught in Hebrew or Māori, or the government that made the teaching of Irish in schools compulsory, or tried to replace French by Arabic in North Africa. Their contribution to language shift or maintenance is hard to estimate or remains controversial.

Managers

But managers, individuals or groups with authority do not need to wait for others to implement their decisions. Thus Cardinal Richelieu, as Chief Minister to King Louis XIII, was able to empower a literary society, the *Académie française*, to recognise and promote Parisian French as standard, a step later supported by the Jacobins during the Revolution and by Napoleon and gradually enforced by ministers of education[24] and more recently by a host of government committees.[25] Irish and Hebrew were both recognised by governments, the former at independence in 1917 and the latter after the British Government was persuaded by Zionist leaders to add it to the Mandatory list of three official languages, reaffirmed by action of the independent government of the State of Israel in 1948.[26]

Another powerful and successful individual manager was Kemal Ataturk (1881–1938), Turkish Army officer and revolutionary leader, who became first President of the Republic. Among his many reforms, he made elementary education free and compulsory. In accordance with his intention to break with Ottoman tradition and to secularise the nation, he switched the alphabet from Perso-Arabic to Latin, at the same time aiming to purge the language of its Arabic loanwords, replacing them often with borrowing from French.[27] The result was a major language shift, making earlier writing incomprehensible to modern Turks (Brendemoen, 1998, 2015; Lewis, 1999). The emphasis of his policy, though outwardly secular, was a continuation of the Ottoman policy to expel or kill Christians, 20 per cent of the population in 1860 and 2 per cent in 1920.[28]

A similar effort by a powerful autocrat and language manager to purge a language of Arabic influence was undertaken by Reza Shah Pahlavi (1878–1944), appointed by the British to rule Persia in 1925 and forced to abdicate by the Anglo-Soviet invasion of 1941. Among his many reforms aimed at the clergy, he banned the *chador* and required Western dress. Influenced by Ataturk, he set out to remove Arabic loanwords in Persian, though with somewhat less success (Perry, 1985).

Two Soviet leaders were also famous (or infamous) for language management. Lenin was willing to recognise most local languages, assuming this was the fastest way to teach communism. Even before the Revolution, Lenin had discussed the language and nationality issues with his fellows; in a letter written in 1914, he included freedom and equality of language in the rights of large nations and minorities, including use of national languages in schools and public institutions. The Soviet Constitution echoed this right. Lenin saw this as a necessary intermediate stage to full assimilation and Communism (Grenoble, 2003: 35). Stalin carried on this policy for a while, but shocked by the failure of the Ukrainian wheat harvest, took an increasingly Russian hegemonic view. In 1930, he attacked what he called 'local nationalism' which included 'exaggerated respect for national languages', which affected many local languages (especially in Turkestan, the Caucasus, Tartaria, Ukraine and Belorussia (Lewis, 1972: 71).[29] From 1938, the policy of Russification included replacing Roman and Perso-Arabic script with Cyrillic.

Lee Kuan Yew, elected as first Prime Minister of independent Singapore in 1959 (he served in that capacity until 1990 and continued in a senior role in government until 2011 and as member of parliament until his death in 2015) considered language reform to be one of his major tasks in modernising Singapore. A native speaker of Baba Malay, a Hokkien-influenced Creole, he was educated in English but gained electoral support from the Chinese majority by learning and using Hokkien and Mandarin. Once elected, he set out to reduce the thirty or so spoken languages to four, selecting Malay as national language, English and Mandarin as principal languages of government and education and Tamil. English was stressed and in 1979 a 'Speak Mandarin' campaign began; the actual topolects that were mother tongues of Chinese speakers were stigmatised as dialects. The economic success of Singapore is widely attributed to the success of Lee as a language manager (Chew, 2014).

Two more political leaders who managed language policy were Manuel L. Quezon, President of the Philippines, and Kim Il-sung, North Korean Head of State.[30] In 1936, Quezon called for the establishment of an Institute of National Language, using, Sibayan (1974: 224) points out, arguments similar to those presented by the Norwegian reformer Ivar Aasen in 1936, and a year later proclaimed that Tagalog should be the national language. In 1940, he ordered the publication of a grammar and dictionary. As a result, he is known as the father of the Filipino language.[31]

Language ideology and policy in North Korea has been monopolised, Song (2001) claims, by Kim Il-sung, the first Supreme Leader, who ruled from the establishment of the state in 1948 until he died in 1994. The underlying ideology of *Juche* (self-reliance) presented in two talks attributed to him declares the Pyongyang dialect to be the best representation of *munhwao* (cultured language), calls for the use of Korean and not foreign (for instance Chinese) lexicon and mandates teaching the improved language to all children and revising published work that uses the older forms (Terrell, 2007).

These authoritative language managers were totalitarian in character, often dictators without opposition.[32] This helps to explain why those I have identified as language advocates, operating in more liberal or democratic situations, have been less able to make major changes in national language choice. Canada helps us to understand this.

The Québec Charter of the French Language (Bill 101, passed in 1977) was a major achievement of the government headed by René Lévesque, but it appears that Lévesque himself was not extreme in his language views. The Canadian Official Languages Act, passed in 1969 on the recommendation of the Royal Commission on Bilingualism and Biculturalism set up by Prime

Minister Elliot Trudeau, made French official throughout Canada alongside English. But Canada is democratic and federally organised, so that enforcement is partial, with only Québec trying to enforce French hegemony and much of the rest of the country maintaining English dominance. In the USA, attempts to establish English as the official language continue to fail at the federal level. In Israel, similar efforts to lower the status of Arabic failed until a right-wing government recently passed a nation-state law. But policy in democratic societies depends on political parties and governments, which advocates (individuals and groups) attempt to influence; in more totalitarian situations, a strong leader can easily become a language manager at the state level.

The distinction between individual advocates and managers is reflected in the potential for effective action of groups and institutions. Language activist groups, such as the Gaelic League in Ireland and *Te Ataarangi* in New Zealand, remain advocates, as do many academies, until they are granted formal authority by governments (Spolsky, 2011a). An official academy, like the *Académie française*, or the Hebrew Language Academy, or the High Academy of the Quechua Language described by Coronel-Molina (2015) as powerless to overcome the hegemony of Spanish, lacks the authority of a totalitarian ruler or even of a minister of education to have real effects on a language policy entrenched by its past and blocked by political, social, ethnic and economic forces (Spolsky, 2018b). Even a major centralised programme of language management like that of France failed to eradicate the peripheral varieties like Breton and Occitan, allowing a basis on which to build language revival programmes and in addition to face the challenge of the new wave of immigration that added half a million Arabic speakers between 2010 and 2016. Nor did Stalin wipe out Ukrainian.

Looking at the work of individual advocates, then, one needs ask again the basic question: can language be managed? Advocates must persuade managers, but there are many factors that work against even authoritarian management, such as strong ideologies with different groups in a society, for example the oft-cited cases of Yiddish and Amish, who add language resistance to social isolationism. Thus, diversity continues, even in the face of linguistic hegemony and economic globalisation.[33]

Notes

1. An earlier form of this chapter appeared in Spolsky (2020b).
2. The need to distinguish between advocates and managers was suggested to me by an invitation to participate in a colloquium organised by Piet Van Avermaet and Elana Shohamy (Spolsky, 2018a, 2020b). I had earlier explored one aspect of the topic in a consideration of the nature of language academies and agencies (Spolsky, 2008a).

3. The distinction between status and corpus was proposed by the one-time Nazi linguist Kloss (1969). The model presented follows Fishman (1974), agreeing with Haugen (1966).

4. The examples that Haugen (1987: 590) cited were the decisions to replace English with Irish in Eire and Yiddish with Hebrew in Israel.

5. It was social workers and early childhood teachers who finally ended Māori mothers speaking the language to their children in the 1950s and 1960s; it is the Hasidic rebbes who persuade their cult followers to speak Yiddish with their children; it was the prime minister of Singapore who by example and proclamation led to the major changes in family language repertoires.

6. LanguageLine Services began as voluntary programme in San Diego to provide the police with interpreters when dealing with immigrants.

7. US courts have held that the true record of evidence is the English language translation and not the jury members' ability to understand a witness using another language. And laypeople are often confused by what is an acceptable question and answer.

8. Islam requires Classical Arabic for all public functions, but allows teaching in the local language. Vatican II switched a thirteenth-century requirement of Latin for the mass to the vernacular, a feature of Protestant churches. Orthodox Judaism uses Hebrew in public worship (but allows Aramaic in a few prayers) and assumes that spoken sermons are in the vernacular. Though they favour Hebrew for prayer and most writing, some Hasidic rebbes urge their followers to use Yiddish for teaching and as a vernacular to mark their separateness.

9. One notable case of language management in India has been the change of name of many cities and languages; thus, Calcutta is now Kolkata, Bombay is now Mumbai and Madras is now Chennai.

10. Four million Bengalis in Assam are currently being threatened with expulsion as foreigners, irrespective of how long they have been there (*The Hindu*, 19 July 2019).

11. According to the 1950 constitution, it is the statutory provincial language in Odisha, where it is spoken by over 90 per cent of the population. It is also spoken in four neighbouring states and in Bangladesh and elsewhere in a widespread diaspora.

12. As late as 1990, an Italian inspector of schools told me that Italian children came to school speaking a regional dialect and not the standard language. Tosi (2000: 44) cites an estimate that only half of Italians speak a standard variety as a native language.

13. The activities of the Office, set up in 1961 were characterised in a *Sixty Minutes* TV programme as 'language police'.

14. After years of controversy, Bill 86 modified this by requiring that French be twice as dominant as other languages on signs.

15. The Council (at first called the Literature Council) worked within the

framework of the Pure Language Society, whose goal was to 'uproot from among the Jews living in Palestine the jargons, the Ashkenazic, the Sephardic and so on' which divided the community. In other words, it opposed Yiddish and Ladino (Saulson, 1979: 24).

16. Pinyin is a version of Mandarin in Latin letters and so is useful for computer input and for teaching initial literacy.

17. This matched the involvement of US linguists in the classic language policy work (Jernudd and Nekvapil, 2012) of the same period.

18. Zhou (2004) discusses many of the problems of the teaching and use of Tibetan. Wang and Phillion (2009) write about the endangerment of minority languages in China as a result of the stress on Putonghua. Phillipson and Skutnabb-Kangas (2013: 513) report a plan to assimilate Uyghur speakers to Mandarin, which unfortunately has been implemented (Shir, 2019).

19. *The Washington Times* (Tuesday, 11 September 2018) reports a backlash to the strategy from a number of smaller nations.

20. For example, the existence of managers and advocates at other levels (family, business, schools, religion, regions) sets up pressures that may work against the state level and account for failure (Spolsky, 2006b) and many non-linguistic factors (wars, civil strife, natural disasters, corruption) may interfere with implementation of state policies (Spolsky, 2019e).

21. Colenso (1872) wrote *Willie's first English book, written for young Maoris who can read their own Maori tongue, and who wish to learn the English language.*

22. Both Young and Morgan were recognised by the Navajo Nation and the University of New Mexico for their work in standardising the language; see Holm (1996).

23. From 1854 until 1872, Māori tribes fought against British settlers and soldiers to try to keep their land (Belich, 1986).

24. Although it was only much later that there were enough teachers to carry this out.

25. As it was realised that the *Académie* was more interested in the award of prizes than functioning as language police.

26. In 1948, the provisions of the King's Order-in-Council making English, Arabic and Hebrew official under the Mandatory government (a more limited status than most assume, for it left choice of school language of instruction to the independent Jewish and Muslim sectors) was maintained except that English was dropped. But it continued to be used in publishing laws and for other legal and commercial functions. Then, in 2018, a law moved Arabic from official to special status, adding (probably correctly) that this was not a change.

27. This was justified by the Sun Language Theory, propagated by Austrian linguist Hermann F. Kvergić, who proposed that all languages (includ-

ing French) were descended from a primal Turkish; Ataturk accepted and helped develop this pseudoscientific notion.

28. See for example Akçam (2013).
29. Stalin's 1932 decree 'On the procurement of grain in Ukraine, North Caucasus and the Western Region' which produced the Holodomor, the famine which killed 4 million Ukrainians, also ordered local officials to switch official documents and education from Ukrainian to Russian and to stop publishing Ukrainian newspapers (Applebaum, 2017).
30. I am grateful to Robert Kaplan for drawing my attention to these two examples.
31. Filipino, Lewis et al. (2016) explain, is based on Tagalog with some lexicon added from other regional varieties.
32. Haugen (1987: 58) used the term 'omnipotent'.
33. This will be the theme of a planned collection (Or et al., 2021).

11 Treaties, Charters and Other Supranational Sources of Rights

Human rights and language

There are a number of scholars, such as May (2012), Phillipson and Skutnabb-Kangas (1995) and Romaine (2008), who argue for the existence and significance of linguistic or language rights. Skutnabb-Kangas and Phillipson (1995) take it as axiomatic that linguistic rights are one kind of universal human right, the absence of which leads to conflict. Kibbee (1998), however, in the introduction to a collection of papers from a 1996 conference on language legislation and linguistic rights, notes that because language is a social construct developed within a speech community and not an inherited characteristic like skin colour or gender, it is not universal but local in conditions and policies. Arzoz (2007) points out the difference between human rights, commonly now accepted as universal, and the much weaker case that can be made for recognition of linguistic rights. There are others like Pavlenko (2011) who deny that languages have rights, but agree that speakers do; this was a position taken also by Labov (2008). Avoiding this controversy, I shall simplify my approach by concentrating on rights to choose and speak language as they are set out in international charters and treaties, depending as they do for implementation on the language management of national states, which will be the topic of the next chapter.

Richter et al. (2012) recognise the problem of establishing any general model of linguistic rights. In the introduction, Ingo Richter notes language-related rights were not included in either the Universal Declaration of Rights on the United Nations (1948) or the European Convention of Human Rights two years later; however, minority language rights are included in International Covenant on Civil and Political Rights of 1966 and the United National Declaration of Rights belonging to National or Ethnic, Religious or Linguistic Minorities 1992 and the European Charter for Regional or Minority Languages of the same year. The UN Declaration of the Rights of Indigenous Peoples of 2007 also calls for protection of threatened languages.

Skutnabb-Kangas and Phillipson (1995) summarise treaties and international covenants with provision for linguistic rights up until the year of publication. They first note that universal human rights declarations have moved through five periods. First were statements of personal freedom, with civil and political rights developing from the rights of individuals to the decolonisation phase that expressed rights of peoples to self-determination. The second added economic, social and cultural rights and third, 'solidarity rights', such as peace and an unspoiled environment. These were the first three periods; two more are mentioned later. Before 1815, there were some bilateral treaties which protected religious but not linguistic minorities. During this time, national languages were commonly imposed and minority languages were stigmatised. The 1815 Congress of Vienna protected national minorities; an exception was protection for Polish in Poznan, but there was no other recognition of linguistic minorities. The 1867 Austrian Constitution did recognise all the languages used in the state.

In the third period between the world wars, there was some protection for linguistic minorities. The Peace Treaties after the First World War included clauses protecting minority language rights, specifically the right of language use in private conversation, in business, in religion, in the press and in other publications. Citizens also were granted the right to use their language in speech or writing in court. Where numbers justified it, primary school instruction was to be in the minority language, alongside the compulsory learning of the national language. These provisions were applied to Hungary, Rumania and Yugoslavia and to minorities inside Turkey. There was also provision for complaint to the League of Nations for non-implementation, but this had little if any effect. The League of Nations in 1922 expressed the hope that other countries would follow suit, but rejected proposals in the early 1930s to make the protection universal.

In the fourth period, after the Second World War, there were a number of declarations of universal human rights but none of minority or linguistic rights (Capotorti, 1979). Only after 1975 was attention paid to minorities, but linguistic rights were still not included.

In the fifth period, there was recognition of minority linguistic rights in some national constitutions and laws but less concern for language in regional and universal covenants; commonly, as in European policies, immigrant minorities were excluded, so that migrant workers, refugees and asylum seekers were not considered true minorities. Although Kloss (1971) dealt with the rights of immigrants, it is generally assumed that 'migrants will learn the dominant language of their new country and this is a requirement to gain citizenship in most Western countries' (Kymlicka and Patten, 2003: 7). Only a few countries, like Canada and Israel, consider teaching the national language a reasonable component of activities for immigrant absorption and set up special language courses for immigrants.

Minority language rights

Skutnabb-Kangas and Phillipson (1995) list some international efforts to list language rights for autochthonous minorities. The European Bureau for Lesser-Used Languages (EBLUL) was an NGO set up by the European Parliament in 1982, supported by the Council of Europe and the European Commission, but discontinued in 2010 when its funding ceased. Its mission was to support national and regional minority groups in the European Community. A new organisation, the European Language Equality Network (ELEN), was set up in 2011, with representation from the member states of EBLUL to monitor relevant European Union (EU), Council of Europe and other European legislation and activities supporting national minorities. Together with the European Union, they monitor linguistic discrimination and support work for the digitalisation of minority languages and help them make use of educational exchange programmes like Erasmus.

The European Parliament passed a resolution encouraging national and regional government to promote the use of minority languages in education (including them in the system from kindergarten to university, using them in nursery schools when the population requested and including literature and community history in the curriculum) (Arfé, 1981). A second resolution a few years later called for promoting minority languages in education, local administration and mass media (Kuijpers, 1987). These two resolutions were a step towards the passing of the European Charter for Regional or Minority Languages in 1992, which has since been ratified by twenty-five European states. Part II of the Charter sets eight fundamental principles:

- Recognition of regional or minority languages as an expression of cultural wealth.
- Respect for the geographical area of each regional or minority language.
- The need for resolute action to promote regional or minority languages.
- The facilitation and/or encouragement of the use of regional or minority languages, in speech and writing, in public and private life.
- The provision of forms and means for the teaching and study of regional or minority languages at all appropriate stages.
- The promotion of relevant transnational exchanges.
- The prohibition of all forms of unjustified distinction, exclusion, restriction or preference relating to the use of a regional or minority language and intended to discourage or endanger its maintenance or development.
- The promotion by states of mutual understanding between all the country's linguistic groups.

Part I of the Charter lists sixty-eight concrete undertakings, from which each ratifying nation must select thirty-five clauses. For example, they may agree to set a language as school language of instruction, or to teach the language at some school levels; similarly, they may agree to establish a radio or television station for the language, or to encourage programmes. The Charter uses terms that weaken the agreement, such as 'as far as possible' or 'where the numbers warrant' or 'where there are enough pupils'. Every five years ratifying states must submit a report of implementation and plans; this goes to a committee of experts and to the Council of Ministers. Skutnabb-Kangas and Phillipson (1995: 92–3) point out that these directives and charters are 'fraught with difficulties of interpretation and implementation' and the initiatives and plans regularly have 'no follow-up' or 'did not take place'. They also describe the decisions of the Council of Europe as not legally binding on members and full of escape clauses ('as far as possible', 'where appropriate').

They next mention the Organization for Security and Cooperation in Europe, set up in the early 1950s and leading to the Helsinki Accords in 1975.[1] The Accords and subsequent documents such as the Copenhagen Document of 1990 maintain that national minorities should have the right to maintain ethnic, cultural, linguistic and religious identity, to ask for voluntary and public assistance to establish educational institutions and not to be forcibly assimilated. It expresses willing to consider at future meetings the rights of migrant workers. Among its many concerns, the Organization includes minority rights and in 2003 published guidelines on the use of minority languages in the broadcast media.

In 1992, the United Nations General Assembly adopted a Declaration on the Rights of Persons belonging to National or Ethnic, Religious and Linguistic Minorities. In Article 2, it affirms that

> Persons belonging to national or ethnic, religious and linguistic minorities (hereinafter referred to as persons belonging to minorities) have the right to enjoy their own culture, to profess and practice their own religion and to use their own language, in private and in public, freely and without interference or any form of discrimination.

Most of the provisions use the term 'shall' but Skutnabb-Kangas and Phillipson (1995: 97) point out that the formulation is weaker in the case of education: 'States should take appropriate measures, so that, where possible . . .'

Stronger are the provisions of the United Nations Declaration on Indigenous Rights, adopted in 2007. Passing with a heavy majority, the Declaration was initially rejected by Australia, Canada, New Zealand and the United States, though they later changed their position, still holding that as a 'declaration', it has no legal authority in international law. Green (2019) also argues that the declaration is flawed and lists examples in Australia where the rights have been abrogated. The basic problem, she concludes, is that the Declaration is 'Western-normative' and allows too much power to the state.

In sum, then, with all the complications it takes to negotiate them and the time it takes to persuade national government to sign on to declarations and international treaties, the fact that the international organisations recognise state sovereignty means that they do not write enforcement into the agreements; they function in other words more like advocates than managers. Their advocacy can help to persuade governments to act; the appeal by a group suffering discrimination to a regional or international statement of principles and rights can help.

Green (2019) traces the genesis of the UN Declaration on Indigenous Rights from its inception as the idea of a Guatemalan lawyer, Augusto Willemsen Diaz, who wanted to separate indigenous from minority issues. This led to the establishment in 1982 of a working group, which consisted of independent experts and not government officials. A first draft was approved by the working group in 1988, revised and edited by 1993. A sub-commission submitted a proposal to the Commission on Human Rights in 1994, which set up a new working group the following year made up of member states, with some input from indigenous peoples. After eleven years of negotiation, the modified Declaration was adopted by the Human Rights Council, which next entered negotiations with African States who had not realised that it applied to them. The Declaration was adopted by the UN General Assembly in 2007, with the four major abstentions mentioned above, after twenty-five years of discussion and compromise. Although Australia finally signed the Declaration, Green (2019) points out that there are no cases of indigenous people there using the Declaration as defence against the numerous reported cases of lack of consultation, human rights violations and seizure of tribal land.

Regional recognition of rights for language

The issue of state sovereignty interfering with supranational charters of rights is made clearer by looking at regional policies. Hamel (1995) notes that the notion of universal human rights runs counter to the South American ideology of monolingual and monocultural nation states (see also Spolsky, 2018b). The fundamental approach has been to 'de-Indianise' the indigenous peoples. Most constitutions do not mention indigenous minorities, even when they are based on liberal and positivist ideologies. There are some local provisions for education, including support for indigenous languages, as there is an increase in respect for law and human rights, but it is not tied to any regional agreements.

Looking at indigenous language policy in the Americas, McCarty (2012) starts by citing the UN Declaration of 2007 as illustrating a change in mood, but finds that it is not the basis of the localised central and grassroots initiatives for partial recognition; she concludes (p. 568) that 'throughout the Americas, linguistic repression, racial discrimination and economic injustice are lived realities' and only indigenous self-empowerment will make a difference.

The Soviet Union controlled a centralised language policy, increasingly favouring the imposition of Russian on regions using other languages (Grenoble, 2003), but since the break-up, the newly independent states have worked to establish the status and use of their own national languages (Hogan-Brun and Melnyk, 2012), transforming languages that were downgraded by Russification, but not yet recognising all minority languages.

In Asia and the Pacific, as Baldauf and Nguyen (2012) describe the highly multilingual region, the main language issue is the spread of globalising English, supported by the language practice of a regional organisation like the Association of Southeast Asian Nations (ASEAN) (Kirkpatrick, 2017).

The European Union

The exception to this insistence on state sovereignty is the European Union, which came into existence with the Treaty of Maastricht in 1993, according to which the member states cede part of their autonomy. As the Union moves towards a federation, the central administration of the Union has taken over an increasing number of functions. But critically, for the purpose of language policy, member states retain autonomy in culture (Ammon, 2012) and so in issues concerning language.

A central principle of the Union is multilingualism, as laid down in Article 217 of the founding treaty, which requires that language policies of the institutions of the Union must be determined by unanimous votes of all member states. For each of its institutions, the Union has developed specific rules. For the European Council, the assembly of heads of government and the European Parliament and Council of Ministers, any member may use its national language.

This requirement sets up major strains on resources, requiring interpreters to work with the twenty-four official languages and demanding provision of a large number of booths for interpreters in the meeting rooms.[2] All official documents must be translated in all twenty-four languages, often delaying the meeting of committees. All languages of member nations are considered 'official languages' of the Union, but three, English, French and German, are 'procedural languages' used in the daily working of the institutions of the Union.

Gazzola (2006) studied various potential language regimes and found that the multilingual approach was consistent with the goals of the Parliament and did not produce an unsustainable increase in expenditures. Two autonomous

EU institutions have simpler policies: the Court of Justice uses French and the European Central Bank uses English.

This maintenance of the status of national languages comes, Ammon (2012) believes, from the fact that most European nations accept the notion of one state, one nation, one language. Besides national-official languages, the Union contains regional-official languages like Catalan. There are also 'indigenous (or autochthonous) minority languages' under the protection of European Charter for Regional or Minority Languages described above and some not under protection of the Charter because a state has not ratified the Charter or included the language in their list. There are also exogenous minority languages and immigrant languages, for which existing covenants provide no protection. Faingold (2020) summarises the situation of minority languages in the European Union, to some extent affected by EU law such as the 2004 EU draft constitution and the Treaty of Lisbon, but mainly dependent on national laws and policies, showing the varied fate of the claims for recognition of large language minorities like Catalan, Basque and Galician in Spain.

The EU mainly leaves language and education policy to its sovereign member states, but it does recommend the teaching of two foreign languages. The second is included to rule out the tendency of nations to teach only Global English as a foreign language, something strongly opposed by some scholars (Phillipson, 2003, 2017). There is speculation on the status of English in the Union after Brexit: Modiano (2017) speculates that this may allow the development of a European English, but most assume it will continue its role in the institutions.

The Council of Europe

The European Union was preceded by the Council of Europe, established in 1949 by a treaty signed by the foreign ministers of Belgium, Denmark, France, Ireland, Italy, Luxembourg, the Netherlands, Norway, Sweden and the United Kingdom. In 2019, the Council had forty-seven member states. It was founded to uphold human rights, democracy and the rule of law in Europe.

Although the Council cannot make laws, it can enforce some international agreements; it has established the European Court of Rights which can enforce the European Convention on Human Rights. Under the heading of the right to a fair trial is included the right to an interpreter. Article 14 on discrimination includes discrimination based on language. Article 2 of Protocol 1 includes the right to an education according to the choice of parents' religious and other views, but does not go into details. Skutnabb-Kangas and Phillipson (1995: 86) interpret the Court ruling on education as giving each member state the right to decide what should be the languages of education.

The Council did, however, establish in 1954 a Cultural Convention which has been ratified by the states. Its purpose is to

develop mutual understanding among the peoples of Europe and reciprocal appreciation of their cultural diversity, to safeguard European
culture, to promote national contributions to Europe's common cultural heritage respecting the same fundamental values and to encourage
in particular the study of the languages, history and civilisation of the
Parties to the Convention.

Thus, the Council moved away from the policy of earlier international
organisations which restricted themselves to French and, after the First
World War, English, and other regional associations like the Arabic league
(Arabic only), the Association of Southeast Asian Nations (English) and the
Monetary Community of Central Africa (French). The Council of Europe
has only two official languages (English and French) and three additional
working languages (German, Italian and Russian), but it made a major effort
to encourage the teaching of foreign languages.

There are two agencies working with language: the European Centre for
Modern Languages (created in 1994 in in Graz, Austria) and the Language
Policy Program acting as the secretariat of the European Charter for
Regional or Minority Languages and located in Strasbourg. The major
activity of the Council has been the development of the *Common European
Framework of Reference for Languages* (CEFR) (Council of Europe, 2001,
2018). Written under the leadership of an authoring group of British, Swiss
and French scholars[3] who consulted a group of representatives of twenty
member countries, the framework was intended to define common standards
for the teaching and assessment of foreign languages and has become a major
instrument for this purpose in Europe (Nikolaeva, 2019) and beyond (Read,
2019). Thus, although the Council has no legislative power, it has played a
significant role in the teaching and assessment of school languages.

In a discussion of the difference in treatment of the Basque language in
Spain and France, Palacín et al. (2015) note that, persecuted by Franco, it
is now constitutionally protected in Spain. In France, on the other hand,
the constitutional hegemony of French means that the only protection is
European policies on rights and they wonder whether this will be enough.

Rights as advocacy

But in terms of management, the work of the European Union and the
Council of Europe has been mainly concerned with state official languages
and in spite of the emphasis in many documents on multilingualism and the
inclusion of state-recognised languages in the European Charter for Regional
or Minority Languages, the practical result has been increasing monolingualism combined with growing dominance of English within the institutions
(Varennes, 2012: 161). The fact that such a high proportion of children do not
understand the language of instruction when they start school makes clear

that the increasing support for linguistic human rights among scholars has not been reflected in actual practice. As with the failure to deal with climate change, so in language policy, philosophical, academic and scientific opinions and evidence have been largely ineffective in modifying practice.

Notes

1. Supporting the Accords, the Commission for Security and Cooperation in Europe, also known as the US Helsinki Commission, an independent US government commission, was established in 1976 and controlled by eighteen US congressmen and senators and three US assistant secretaries appointed by the president to advance 'American national security and national interests by promoting human rights, military security and economic cooperation in 57 countries'.
2. The Parliament employs about 270 staff interpreters and can also regularly draw on more than 1,500 external accredited interpreters. Between 700 and 900 interpreters are on hand for plenary sessions. The Parliament employs about 600 translators and about 30 per cent of the translation work is outsourced to freelance translators.
3. John L. M. Trim (formerly of Cambridge University), Danielil Coste (École Normale Supérieure de Fontenay-Saint Cloud), Brian North (Eurocentres, Switzerland) and Joseph Sheils (Council of Europe Secretariat).

12 The Nation State as Language Manager

But who cares?

During what Jernudd and Nekvapil (2012) call the period of classical language planning in the 1960s, most studies began and many ended with language policy and management (which they called planning)[1] at the level of the nation state in newly independent states. By changing the order of presentation, and starting as I have in this book with the individual and the family before moving on to other levels and in this way exploring the development of individual and collective sociolinguistic repertoires, I have been able to show the many factors in play and the many competing attempts at language management that set up counterforces to the state's intervention. But the nation state remains of course potentially a major player in the development of a national language policy. I say potentially to recognise that there are nations, especially the core English-speaking states, that take language choice for granted; it is in the nations with two or more competing languages that the issue is most likely to be important and disputed.

I have shown that the best way to look at national policy is using the three-component model, language practice, language beliefs and language management, and asking how fitting the management is to the practices and how it has been biased by beliefs and ideology. Finally, we can ask how successful intervention has been and how any national policy has been weakened by failure to recognise the actual practices of the population, the policies favoured at the various levels and in the many domains, and the non-linguistic factors that interfere with implementation.

The nation state's attempts at language management should ideally be based on the government's knowledge of the language practices of the nation as a speech community and its beliefs about the role and value of the individual language varieties. This was the reason that the Ford Foundation's concern for some newly independent African states (Ford Foundation, 1975) resulted in support for detailed language surveys of Ethiopia where Amharic is now the official language, Kenya where English remains statutory national language alongside Swahili, Tanzania where Swahili is the de facto national language, Uganda where English is the statutory national language and Swahili is a statutory working language and Zambia, where English remains the statutory national language.

Although it seems obvious that the language policy of a nation state should be based on, or at least consider, the language repertoire of the population, it turns out in practice to be difficult to decide with any accuracy what this is. Even to determine how many varieties are involved is made difficult by the problem of deciding what counts as a language. As was noted earlier, the recognised listing of the languages of the world in the source approved by the International Organization for Standardization is more political than linguistic, for though the stated criterion is mutual unintelligibility of the listed languages, the rapid recognition of the newly established languages of former Yugoslavia shows that the definition is political: a language is a variety with a flag. Additionally, many of the actual names of the languages are uncertain: for most languages, *Ethnologue* (Eberhard et al., 2019) lists its own choice first and then provides a set of several alternative names.

To handle one part of this confusion, the International Organization for Standardization has set ISO 15924 to list the nearly 500 scripts in which languages are written. This is under the authority of the Unicode Consortium, an NGO with a registrar and six expert members who decide a four-letter code based on the most common language name (for instance, *Hebr* for Hebrew and *Latn* for Latin) and a numeric code for each script (100–199 for right-based alphabets, 200–299 for left-based alphabets and 993 for Emoji). For languages, the three classification systems, ISO 639-1, 639-2 and 639-3 which list two and three letter codes for recognised languages,[2] are under the authority of SIL International (formerly, the Summer Institute of Linguistics, an organisation of linguists set up in Texas with the goal of translating the Bible into all the languages of the world). There has been criticism of both the methods and the choice of a Christian missionary organisation to run the system (Morey et al., 2013).[3]

In addition to the problem of uncertainty of language names, there are questions about the status or kind of language. When linguists started to work with language policy and planning in the 1960s, Stewart (1968) proposed a typology for describing national multilingualism. Using four attributes (standardisation,[4] historicity,[5] autonomy[6] and vitality[7]), he set out a number of language types ranging from standard languages (with all four attributes) to artificial language (with none of the four). He then listed ten functions for which the named language may be used in the community: official, provincial, wider communication, international, capital, group, educational, school subject, literary and religious. The final category in his typology was degree of use, ranging from below 5 per cent to above 75 per cent.

But, given the confusion over naming and even without the problem of getting accurate counts of language proficiency, there can be variation in beliefs about the extent of variety use and knowledge. One such case of a mythic belief in the widespread acceptance of a national language is Thai. According to Smalley (1994), there are eighty languages spoken in Thailand (the *Ethnologue* count is seventy-three), but it is widely believed that Thailand is monolingual, with over 90 per cent speaking and understanding the national language. But Smalley points out that the varieties of Tai languages include dialects and others which are mutually incomprehensible. Standard Thai, he argues, is not a native language for most people, but a variety learned at school. He estimates there are no more than 10 million speakers; *Ethnologue* reports 60 million. Similar confusion is treating the mutually unintelligible topolects as a single language called Chinese.

And how are numbers of speakers determined? One obvious answer seems to be language censuses. Kertzer et al. (2002), however, point out how counts are distorted by political considerations. National language censuses can ask several different questions; first language can mean the first learned or the most used; speaking does not include reading or writing and is seldom quantified; not all agree on a name; many parents have no accurate knowledge of their children's language proficiency. As a result, reports of the number of speakers even when included in authoritative sources like *Ethnologue* cannot be relied on.

It is therefore safer to treat number of languages and speakers as beliefs and not as facts. This is true also of such important characteristics as domains of language use, level of speaking and reading proficiency and proportion of children who learn a language from their parents. And censuses can be distorted by the questions asked (What is the language of your home? What language did you learn first? What is the language you use most of the time?) and by the respondents' names for their varieties.[8]

A good starting point might be to recognise the wide range of potential and actual national sociolinguistic repertoires, ranging from the rare monolingual (but still multivariety) nations like Japan to the superdiverse multilingual states like Papua New Guinea with its 832 living languages. Lambert (1999) suggests treating as a distinct group dyadic or triadic nations with two or three competing varieties like Switzerland and Belgium with their special problems. In another approach, Fishman (1968, 1969) classified countries according to the number of Great Traditions (national ideological identities) that they have: he suggested recognising former colonies with no Great Tradition that found it acceptable to continue with the imperial language, countries with a single Great Tradition that, like Tanzania, could work on standardising and modernising an indigenous language and countries like India with a number of competing Great Traditions. This latter group which includes dyadic and triadic Belgium and Switzerland often seek a territorial solution to avoid conflict (McRae, 1975; Spolsky, 2006c; Williams, 2012).

For each of the language varieties used in a nation state, the most relevant characteristics are the number and percentage of speakers as a first or second language,[9] the nature of each language (ranging from international to dying),[10] the history and degree of literacy (ranging from long-established languages with a large historical literature to unwritten varieties) and the level of standardisation (written grammars and dictionaries and supporting agencies like academies). More detailed classifications might be built by listing the domains in which a variety is used, ranging from use only in the home to use in government, science and higher education.[11]

Pool (1991), who defines an official language as one designated as required or permitted to be used in the official business of a state or other institution, goes on to cite Kloss (1966) as saying that the maximum number of official languages that a nation can manage efficiently is three. He sees the choice as one between efficiency and fairness, proposing a compromise that gives financial returns to minority language groups to cover the cost of translation. Typically, an official language (in Soviet and some other countries called a state language) is designated by the government as the language to be used in government functions: the legislature,[12] administration and the judiciary.

The official language is not necessarily that spoken by the majority of the people: many former colonies have maintained imperial languages as official languages and do not grant the status to spoken vernaculars. There are cases like Pakistan where the national language is the mother tongue of a minority. The term national language, used in over 150 national constitutions, is not necessarily official, but refers to some connection to the territory in which it is spoken. Brann (1994) suggests a distinction for national languages between the territorial language of an ethnic group, a regional language, a community language and a central or government language.

For example, India has two official languages, Hindi and English, but does not identify a national language; it recognises twenty-two scheduled languages in the constitution. Five languages are considered classical languages. Indian states may raise mother tongues to the status of languages. The Indian census reports the number of speakers of a language as first, second and third language: it lists 1,369 mother tongues and 1,474 names which were treated as unclassified and relegated to mother tongue category.

It was Paulston (1998: 1) who reminded us that linguistic minorities or minority languages are a misnomer. The word minority suggests that it is a numerical issue: instead, it is a distinction in status, with a minority language subordinate to a dominant or majority language.

Classification and assignment of a category is not enough and one needs details of the functional use of a variety, ranging from the personal (dreaming or counting, for instance) to the use in public and government and higher educational domains.[13] To account for likelihood of maintenance or shift, critical aspects are use with children, the language of instruction in school and the use by the government. Language censuses do not produce this degree of detail, but at best give the answers to a single question such as how many people claimed the language. Nor are governments normally prepared to mount complex surveys of language use like those the Ford Foundation funded in Eastern Africa. As a result, national language policies are more likely to be driven by ideologies and beliefs than by accurate estimates of language practices.

Walter and Benson (2012) proposed a typology of languages based on national and international salience and level of development, adding the percentage of the world that use languages at this level: international languages (English, French; used by 17 per cent), major languages (Dutch, Russian, Mandarin; 23 per cent), developed national languages (Hindi, Swedish; 21 per cent), undeveloped national languages (Malagasy, Quechua; 18 per cent), underdeveloped national languages (lingua francas and trade languages; 20 per cent), underdeveloped sub-national languages (Illocano, Karen; 20 per cent) and localised oral languages (Tuyuca in Colombia, Borana in Kenya; 1 per cent). They also provide estimates for languages of instruction in schools: forty-five out of ninety-seven languages with over 10 million speakers are not used as languages of instruction, 109 of 771 languages spoken by between 250,000 and 10 million people are used in education. Summing up, 40 per cent of the world's children (2.3 billion) lack access to education in their first language.

State sovereignty and linguistic ideologies

A description of the sociolinguistic profile of a nation will help to explain the values allocated to the varieties and so suggest the likely national ideology underlying central government management efforts. Cobarrubias (1983: 63) lists four typical language ideologies: linguistic assimilation (associated particularly with colonialism), linguistic pluralism (such as the special status granted to French in Louisiana before statehood and to Samoan in American Samoa), vernacularisation (Modern Hebrew) and internationalisation (English in India).

But it is rare that a sociolinguistic analysis leads to a national language policy: the Canadian Royal Commission on Bilingualism and Biculturalism in 1963 was a response to the Québec nationalist threat to secede and ignored the seventy-nine indigenous and the seventeen immigrant languages spoken in the country, and the major Ford-supported studies in Africa (Ford Foundation, 1975) did not lead to the adoption of language policies that reflected existing sociolinguistic repertoires. Nationalist or religious or economic arguments are usually what influence the language policies expressed in national constitutions or laws.

The development of the nation state in Europe supported calls for a common language once legitimacy for government was assumed to be based on the sovereignty of the people (Wright, 2012: 59). As long as the power of the Emperor lasted, the Austro-Hungarian Empire could handle multilingualism, using interpreters and translations as Ahasuerus was reported to do in the Biblical book of Esther. But even before the French Revolution led to democratic rule combined with a hegemonic language policy, Cardinal Richelieu had recognised the importance of a single standardised language to guarantee the power of the king (Cooper, 1989). Thus, the nineteenth-century definition of a nation as marked by 'one land, one people, one language' arose,[14] and was accepted by most nations, not just in Europe.[15] The belief in monolingualism, though not necessarily supported by the facts, as for instance in Thailand (Smalley, 1994), is an important feature of a nation-state's linguistic ideology.

This belief was encapsulated in the German-speaking world in a model of *Volk* and ethno-linguistic nationalism, a mystical combination of blood and language, driving not just German policy but also accepted in the creation of new nations at the Treaty of Versailles (Wright, 2012: 62–3). But although there have been many disagreements about the nature of nationalism, Wright concludes that all nationalisms accentuate monolingualism; 'nationalism requires the citizen to use the national language to display loyalty'; and the conduct of cultural, economic and political life is more easily managed in a monolingual nation (Wright 2012: 64). Both communicative and ethnonationalist ideologies agree on monolingualism, but can lead to different policies: as Ammon (2012) observed, the French required that any metropolitan or colonial territory under their control should use French, but the Germans argued that any territory where German was spoken should come under their rule.

The counter-arguments come from ethnic or religious groups on the one hand, arguing that their heritage or ethnic identity depends on diversity and permission to maintain their traditional languages, and, on the other hand, the supranational demand for language rights, the linguistic aspects of human rights supported by international covenants that were discussed in Chapter 11. Ideologies supporting diversity – heritage languages for ethnic identity, multilingualism maintaining the rights of minority languages – conflict with the political desire for national unity, the economic-based concern for communicative efficiency and the nationalist ideology of monolingual hegemony. At the national level, this choice is often nominally resolved in a constitution or in language laws, but implementation is interfered with by the language policies of the various levels ranging from individual to region and ethnic group and the force of non-linguistic factors that have been discussed in the Introduction.

Given this complexity, whose belief or ideology best captures the national consensus? In a totalitarian state, the head or dictator is in a position to act freely as he or she wishes, though he or she may not have any interest in language or language-related matters. The managers described in Chapter 10 fit this definition: starting with Richelieu and including the leadership of Soviet, Nazi, fascist and communist states, governments could ignore popular opinions and enforce their own beliefs about the appropriate language policy. In the colonial governments described in Chapter 7, it was the imperial government which set and administered choice of language for government and education. Although in the early days of the Portuguese Empire, the Church, which was responsible for such education as there was, saw an advantage in using the local languages to convert the natives, much as Lenin in the early days of the Soviet Union permitted the maintenance of languages other than Russian to build socialism, the secular colonial rulers made rules requiring the use of the imperial language. Stalin, too, mistrusting what he believed was the result of diverse nationalism, chose to return to the Czarist support for Russian, first lowering the status of Ukrainian as punishment for low wheat crops, then favouring Russian over other languages including his own Georgian. In the People's Republic of China, the Party, in spite of recognising other issues in language, continued the two millennium old traditional Chinese priority for Mandarin which it called Putonghua, launching brutal campaigns against Tibetan, Uyghur and most recently Mongolian, and favouring Putonghua over the other topolects. In Nazi Germany, the government used speaking German as evidence for the need to add territory. In Fascist Italy, the government was committed to linguistic unification, bordering it is suggested on dialectophobia and ideology of 'one nation, one language' (Klein, 1989). In North Korea, under the leadership of Kim Il-sung from 1948 until 1994, language policy promoted unification and purification of Korean from Chinese influence (Song, 2001).

Democracies are more complex, with changes of ruling parties shifting emphasis and direction even of language issues. But in many nations, since the growth of nationalism in the nineteenth century, a national consensus now accepts the dominant official language. This is especially true of the core English-speaking nations, where only activist minorities pressure the government to recognise and permit their heritage language. In New Zealand, for instance, where in the 1960s children no longer spoke Māori, an activist movement beginning in the 1980s finally persuaded the government to support education and television in the language, leading to a slow and reluctant public acceptance of the language; at about the same time, Sign was legally recognised.[16] The task of persuading the government to make Māori official followed activist pressure and was facilitated by a bureaucrat in the Department of Māori Affairs who prepared a number of brief position papers for Cabinet (Spolsky, 2009b). Recognition of Sign in New Zealand followed a similar path, with pressure by the Deaf community starting in the 1990s; in 2002, the government established an Office of Disability Issues under a minister; an act was prepared and passed in 2006 (McKee and Manning, 2019). However, in the case of the Polynesian languages spoken by the 200,000 Pacific Islanders, recognition took longer and a thirty-year struggle by Pasifika activists only led to its inclusion in the budget in 2019. A national language policy drafted by a Treasury official in 1992 (Waite, 1992) has never been accepted (East et al., 2013).

In Australia, language policy could be established at a state or federal level. After development of a policy in the state of Victoria, a series of federal policies were formulated and published in succession, ranging from one calling for language diversity to another arguing economic motivation to support Asian languages. In Canada, the struggle between the colonising languages, English and French, led to a federal bilingual policy which ignored other languages and continued the neglect of indigenous languages; at the same time, the Province of Québec worked to restore the status of French at the expense of English. The ending of apartheid in South Africa led to token recognition of a handful of African languages in the constitution, but did not resolve the historical struggle between English and Afrikaans. The increase in local nationalism in Great Britain did not threaten the hegemony of English, but activist movements supported Gaelic in Ireland, Scots and Scottish Gaelic in Scotland and even a post-vernacular Cornish revival. Only in Wales was there serious support for Welsh, spoken now by about 20 per cent of the population (Williams, 2008b) and official in the national assembly. In the United States, immigration introduced a large number of languages other than English, but apart from discussion of language choice in the early days and a brief flourishing of support for bilingualism, the continuance of Spanish in USA with its over 40 million speakers depends on continued immigration. At the same time, the defence and intelligence communities have at times encouraged the teaching of strategic languages.

To understand the effect of national ideology, then, a first question is whose beliefs are to be counted, the political leaders, the bureaucrats and officials, the activists and advocates, or the population as a whole?[17] The answer seems to be the potential managers, the political leaders who can set national policy and order funding and other implementation.

Popular belief can encourage advocacy groups but only when they manage to convince government to act does management occur. Thus, in the USA, the long campaign of the Official English Movement has been successful in a number of states in having English declared official and in leading to local success in attacks on bilingual education, but has not yet led to a policy decision at the federal level. In Israel, an anti-Arabic campaign that wanted Hebrew to be the only official language finally succeeded in 2019, in a nationalist bill in the Knesset, to change the status of Arabic from an undefined official to an equally undefined special status. In 2012, a Latvian referendum rejected a proposal to make Russian, the language of about a third of the population, an official language. In Belarus, Belarusian was made the official language but, after 1994, the increasingly authoritarian government has worked to restore the status of Russian, leaving Belarusian as language of opposition (Goujon, 1999).

Besides other arguments for choosing a single language for official status, in many postcolonial states one critical factor has been that it maintains the personal status of the leadership who support the continuation of the colonial language that they were able to acquire through access to the limited colonial educational system. This phenomenon, identified and named elite closure by Myers-Scotton (1990, 1993), occurs when the elite who lead the newly independent postcolonial state, previously leaders of the independence movement, choose language policies which use their own language patterns to block access to political power and economic advancement for the uneducated masses. This usually involves continuing the official status of the colonial languages in which they were schooled and helps to explain why most African nations continue to use as official languages the non-African languages brought in by colonial governments. Their argument that this language promotes unity as well as providing access to the global economy is because of the fact that the boundaries of African colonies and independent states ignore ethnic and linguistic factors, as a result of the agreements made in the nineteenth-century imperial European partition of Africa (Förster et al., 1988).

We lack many detailed studies of the process by which governments accept advocacy, so we rely on speculative suppositions about the beliefs of legislators and government ministers about language policy based on their actions.[18] Essentially, this topic goes beyond language, because it concerns the whole question of the status of ethnic minorities, so that it focuses on the claims for autonomy of Québec, Catalonia, the Basque Country and Celtic regions of Britain. Generally, central government ideology favours and works to establish or maintain the hegemony of a single national language, considered vital to the maintenance of national unity and the easy flow of communication among all its citizens.

National language management – laws

How is this achieved? By law, or regulation, or enforced by delegated agencies or institutions. The first step might be the highest national law, the constitution. There are a few nations without a written constitution – the United Kingdom, Canada, New Zealand, Saudi Arabia and Israel – but most have a codified constitution with complex methods of amendment. A report of the Constitution.org titled 'Language provisions' in 2009 found that 50 per cent of the 800 or so national constitutions established since 1789 designate an official or a national language and 10 per cent list both. Another 9 per cent specify a particular language for use in state organisations (law courts or schools) or as a requirement for holding public office. Some 45 per cent do not mention language. French is official in twenty-six countries and fifty-four constitutions, Arabic in twenty-three countries and thirty-nine constitutions, English in twenty countries and thirty constitutions and Spanish in fifteen countries and thirty-nine constitutions. A single official language is designated in nintey-two countries, two are designated in twenty-nine countries, and South Africa lists eleven. Some typical language clauses are as follows:

The State language[19] of the Azerbaijan Republic is the Azerbaijan language. (Azerbaijan 2002, Article 21.1)

The language of the Republic is French. (France 2005, Article 2)

The Irish language as the national language is the first official language. The English language is recognised as a second official language. (Ireland 2002, Article 8)

Arabic shall be the official national language. A law shall determine the cases in which the French language can be used. (Lebanon 1990, Article 11)

The official languages of the Republic are Sepedi, Sesotho, Setswana, siSwati, Tshivenda, Xitsonga, Afrikaans, English, isiNdebele, isiXhosa and isiZulu. (South Africa 2003, Article 6.1)

A person shall not be qualified to be nominated or elected as a member of the Parliament unless that person . . . (b) is able to speak and to read the English language well enough to take an active part in the proceedings of Parliament. (Malawi 1999, Article 51.1.b)

In the Socialist Republic of Romania judicial procedure shall be conducted in the Romanian language. (Romania 1975, Article 109)

The state adopts and implements effective plans for strengthening and developing all languages of Afghanistan. (Afghanistan 2004, Article 16)

The freedom of language is guaranteed. (Switzerland 2002, Article 18)

In other cases, the status of language is set by laws and acts of the parliament. Leclerc (1994, 1994–2018) gives details of a number of such laws. In Albania, there were laws concerning school language; in Algeria, laws on the status of Arabic; in Andorra, a law making Catalan official; in Belgium fourteen federal laws about language; in Canada, twenty-nine federal and provincial laws about language; in China, a 2001 law made Putonghua the national language; in Croatia, there were laws on minority languages; in Denmark, laws required teaching Danish to immigrants; in Spain, a dozen federal laws concerned language federally and in the autonomous communities; in Estonia, there were four basic laws and regulations; in the United States, the defunct Bilingual Education Act and the No Child Left Behind Act controlled federal funding for school language management; in Finland, half a dozen laws deal with the status of Finnish, Swedish and Sámi; in France, some twenty-two laws and regulations set the hegemony of French; in Hungary, there is a basic education law and laws on minorities; in Italy, a number of laws concern language; in Latvia, the basic law establishes Latvian; in Lithuania, there are laws on the official language and ethnic minorities; in Moldova, a law making Moldavan official and others on minorities; in New Zealand, two official languages are established by law, Māori and New Zealand Sign; in Poland, a law protects the Polish language; in Rumania, a similar law protects Rumanian and another protects twenty minority languages; in the United Kingdom, there are some laws concerning immigration and language laws in the autonomous regions (Wales, Scotland and Northern Ireland); in Russia, a post-Soviet law makes Russian the official language of the Federation; in what was formerly Yugoslavia, laws in Serbia, Slovakia, Slovenia and Kosovo establish official languages to replace Serbo-Croatian; in Sweden, there are laws on minority languages; and in Switzerland, there are some federal and many cantonal laws on language. These are the marked cases; many nations establish language use by practice and consensus.

Besides laws concerning choice of official and national language status, there is also significant legislation dealing with spelling and language reform. One of the best known was the major reform of Turkish, when Kemal Atatürk set out to remove Arabic and Ottoman elements from the language and shift to the Latin alphabet (Lewis, 1999). In Norway, a struggle between two systems resulted in a compromise accepting both (Haugen, 1966). German spelling reform was a major topic for much of the twentieth century and remains an issue (Johnson, 2002).

But passing laws does not mean implementing them. Even politicians and bureaucrats may continue using another language instead of the official one. Shortly after the break-up of the Soviet Union a group of ministers and politicians visited Israel; a friend of mine, who was present at a dinner, reported that they gave speeches in newly recognised Ukrainian, but conducted private conversations in the Russian that had been favoured during Soviet rule. The implementation of constitutional and legal language policies depends often on court decisions. In France, the 1994 Toubon Law required French in all public events including international conferences, though this later provision was cancelled by the Constitutional Court. In Israel, many court decisions about language use ignored the law concerning official bilingualism, basing decisions calling for Arabic on road signs on safety needs. In South Africa in 2018 the High Court upheld the right of the University of South Africa to offer English-only courses, ignoring the constitutional recognition of eleven languages.

Although constitutions and laws regularly establish the official use of the national language, there are some common exceptions. The first is a human rights-related provision that a person being investigated or charged by the police should be able to understand the nature of the charges against him; this occurs in some forty constitutions. The second is the provision of protection for the language rights of ethnic and linguistic minorities, common in former Soviet bloc countries, increasing in Latin American constitutions and present in some Asian nations including China, India, Pakistan, Indonesia and the Philippines.

But there are many gaps between policies and implementation. The requirement set by the French Revolutionary Assembly for all teaching to be in French took nearly 100 years to implement because of the limited language proficiency of teachers in the periphery. In Cameroon, Kouega (2007) found that the 1966 constitutional provision for support of indigenous languages had still not been implemented. In India, English continued to be used after the ten years laid down in the Constitution.

In many cases, the implementation of language laws and regulations, intended to support centralisation and unity, has led to a conflict with peripheral groups; this is true of Spain and to a lesser extent of France. One solution to this is territorial. The states of India had their borders set to reflect local languages. Switzerland and Belgium, although nominally bilingual or multilingual, in effect apply monolingual policies to specific regions. In Finland, Finnish has replaced Swedish except in the southern coastal region. In a number of states recently, the granting of some autonomy to certain regions has promoted local languages – French in Québec, Catalan and Basque in Spain, the Celtic varieties in Great Britain. And, as has already been noted, the break-up of the Soviet Union and Yugoslavia has been followed by the increased status of titular languages.

National language management – agents and agencies

There is common belief that the implementation of national language policy is the principal work of language academies. But in effect, academies are institutions that advocate the use and form of a chosen language. If they are formally authorised to manage language policy, it tends to be through advising the minister or department of education on the nature and choice of the school language of instruction. Because the curriculum, funding and staffing of schools is often under centralised government control, the school is perhaps the most available institution to implement language policy; although its success is not guaranteed, it is a powerful instrument (Hornberger, 2008; Spolsky, 2009c).

It is for this reason that language activist and advocacy groups endeavour to gain control of school systems. The revitalisation of the Māori language was initiated by grassroots-sponsored pre-school language nests, which later developed into independent immersion schools before the government was persuaded to fund and run them. The revernacularisation of Hebrew was made possible by the British Mandatory Government saving money by leaving education to the Arab and Jewish communities in Palestine. The establishment of French as hegemonic language followed the secularisation and central control of schools after the Revolution. In post-independence Israel, the failure of the Education Department to enforce its own regulations on the teaching of Arabic in Jewish schools left the policy to be administered by the Defence establishment (Mandel, 2014). In Québec, the separation of the education system into Catholic French and Protestant English prepared the way for later divisions. In Thailand, the claims of ministries for control of education, with the Defence Ministry holding responsibility for elementary schools, permitted the teaching of valued English by unqualified teachers. Many indigenous language maintenance programmes depend on communities having taken responsibility for schools (Coronel-Molina and McCarty, 2016; McCarty et al., 2015). In Indonesia, as in many countries, the choice for schools of Bahasa Indonesia over Dutch (the colonial language) and Javanese (the most widely spoken local language) was the principal reason for its spread and establishment as main second language (Zein, 2020). Thus, the education system becomes a major agency for implementation of language policy and when it is starved of funds because of low economic development, wars and civil strife, disease and starvation and corruption, there is little chance of supporting a language policy.

Another government agency with power to implement language policy is the ministry responsible for radio and television. State radios are controlled by the government. Fishman and Fishman (1974) documented the refusal of the Israeli Minister of Education, in charge of radio broadcasting, to add news broadcasts in Yiddish. Any government agency can take on the task of trying to manage language choice. One obvious way to do this is by choosing the languages used by their clerks or online sites or telephone operators. Commonly, this is limited to the official or national language, with sometimes the addition of another major language or a language like English intended for tourists.

In France, although the status of French was established by Cardinal Richelieu, who gave authority over the language to the *Académie française*, a status reinforced by laws passed in 1794 by the National Assembly during the Revolution, in the twentieth century there proved to be a need for other agencies. The *Office de la langue française* was set up in 1937 and replaced twenty years later by the *Office du vocabulaire français*, replaced from 1989 until 2006 by the *Conseil supérieur de la langue française*, presided over by the prime minister and established to advise the government on usage, management, diffusion of the French language in France and overseas, with its first task to reform French spelling. There are similar councils in Belgium and Québec. It is under the *Délégation générale à la langue française et aux langues de France*, set up in 1989 as part of the Ministry of Culture. It has had responsibility since 1994 to administer the Toubon Law and later decrees and for an online terminological dictionary, for teaching French to immigrants and to support regional languages (Breton, Basque, Occitan and Catalan). There are more than a dozen other government and semi-government agencies dealing with Francophonie.

There are a number of key studies of national efforts at language management. One set looks at the Canadian example, where in response to threats
of Québec independence, the federal government set out to implement a
bilingual policy. In an attempt to deal with the problems created by the submersion of French Canada into an English-dominant federation, a Royal
Commission on Bilingualism and Biculturalism was established in 1963
which reported in 1965 that there was a national crisis and recommended in
1969 that Canada become officially bilingual; the government under Prime
Minister Trudeau passed the Official Languages Act, which required the government to serve its citizens in both English and French, in the hope that this
would improve employment chances for Francophones and reduce the pressure for independence for Québec. The difficulty of implementation became
clear in the armed services; the navy and air force were reluctant and despite
the establishment of a Bilingual Secretariat, after twenty years the results
were minimal: only senior officers are required to be bilingual and three-
quarters of the military are Anglophones with low proficiency in French; the
other quarter are Francophones who know English and fill positions requiring both languages (Spolsky, 2009a: 133–5). In a detailed study of the efforts
to build national bilingualism, Williams (2008a: 301–60) concludes that
although the attempts of Québec 'to institute the widespread legitimisation of
the French language have been largely successful within the public domain',
at the federal level and in other provinces the policy has been much less successful, so that instead of developing a national bilingual community, there
has been protection of French minority rights 'where numbers warrant'. And
of course, the attempt at multiculturalism has not led to equal protection for
Canada's many other indigenous and immigrant languages.

Williams (2008a: 127–30) also describes the efforts at a territorial solution
to language planning in Ireland. Starting in 1927, Irish speakers were given
priority in public service hiring and in 1937 the Constitution made Irish the
first official language which led to policies to stabilise Irish-speaking communities; but this did not work, as many Irish speakers left the Gaeltacht to
find work in anglicised towns and cities. The policy failed; in spite of government strategy, sixty years of reforms and initiatives did not produce a self-
sustaining Irish-speaking community.

The approach in Wales was different. Native speakers of Welsh continued
to age and decline, but since the Welsh Language Act of 1993 and the establishment of the Welsh Language Board, there has been growing support for
maintenance. Altogether, from 1995 until 2008, some 350 language schemes
have been approved, establishing in effect a bilingual public sector. Recent
efforts, tied to the movement for devolution, aim to encourage use of these
bilingual resources. But, Williams concludes, there is still a great deal to be
done and no strong central consensus supporting these efforts. To show the
complexity of developing a successful strategy for national language policy,
Williams (2007a) lists issues that need to be tackled: creation of a National

Data Centre for data on socioeconomic trends, establishment of a National Language Planning and Resource Centre, a review of the way Welsh is taught and used as language of instruction in statutory school, a review of teacher training for bilingual and Welsh-medium schools, priority action in designated Welsh homeland districts once they have been defined, action on the concordats on policy with various agencies, expansion of bilingual education in the university and further education sector and extension of the Welsh Language Act to deal with the rights of consumers and workers in the private sector. There has been weakening in the strategy, he says, such as the abolishment of the Welsh Language Board in 2004 and the defeat of the proposed timetable for implementation in the National Assembly. He notes also the weakness of the authority granted to the Board and its executive, the *Dyfarnydd*. Reviewing the situation in Wales after a new strategy was announced in 2016, Williams (2017b) is not convinced that the goal of a million speakers will be achieved by 2050, citing uncertainties in planning and implementation.

Both the Canadian and the Welsh cases deal not so much with national policy seeking hegemony but with minority language speakers fighting back, taking advantage of the existence of territorial localisation and a degree of devolution – a nationally recognised regional government able to manage language policy within its boundaries. Territorialism is the first line of treatment to divided ethnicity. Federal Canada granted a degree of power to its provinces, providing the basis for claims of independence for Québec and for its current efforts to establish the status of French; devolution in the United Kingdom provides similar scope for Wales to work on Welsh language maintenance.

There are other examples. Nominally bilingual, Switzerland and Belgium both recognise local monolingual policies, permitting residents to have highly biased linguistic repertoires. India on independence divided off Pakistan on a linguistic as well as ethnic and religious basis; and drew the boundaries of its constituent states in recognition of the major local languages. Although the Indian Constitution lays down this territorial linguistic autonomy, the history of language policy disputes in India has been an ongoing conflict between the nationally favoured Hindi, bolstered by Hindu nationalism, and the state languages, providing an opening for the seemingly unbiased English that the 1948 Constitution aimed to eliminate to continue as a useful second language. There were similar pressures in Yugoslavia under Tito, with the proclamation of Serbo-Croatian as a unifying language, shown by the speed with which the new states made local varieties official – Serbian, Croatian, Macedonian, Slovene, Montenegrin, Albanian. South Africa has a historic language struggle between Dutch, renamed Afrikaans, and English which ignored the African languages until nine were included in the 1996 Constitution.

All of these are cases where two or more language varieties, each with their own history and Great Tradition, have struggled for primacy. There were cases like this in the newly independent states in the 1960s, but more complex were those new states where the colonial language had blocked the many local indigenous languages from access to official status for government or education. The problem was how to develop a consensus among all the various interests competing over choice of language variety. Commonly, a first claim for selection among varieties had been made by missionaries; in Fiji, for instance, the choice of Bauan over the other dialects set its dominant status as Fijian (Schütz, 1985).

Recognising the conflicts arising from the fact that more than 7,000 languages are squeezed into just under 200 political entities, Lo Bianco (2017; Lo Bianco and UNICEF, 2015) has been using facilitated dialogue, a technique developed in psychiatry, education, landscape and political conflict, to help develop language policy in Malaysia, Myanmar, Sri Lanka, Thailand and other cases sponsored by the United Nations Children's Fund (UNICEF). He gives an example:

> One focused on populations displaced from Myanmar now living in Thailand, bringing together 68 participants from 22 different organisations, for a 3-day retreat conducted in 6 languages. The outcome was a 35-page position statement on ethnic rights for minority Myanmar displaced populations, creation of a coordinated grassroots representative council and training in how to advocate effectively for language rights with public authorities. The representative council remains active in what has since grown into a nationwide movement to introduce a national language policy to recognise and support Myanmar's many language minorities. (Lo Bianco, 2017)

He goes onto say that

> Key features include: collective establishment of the rules of discourse; problem naming and ranking by participants; identification of different ways participants have knowledge of problems, identification of knowledge needed to tackle the problems; reflection on available research, commissioning or conducting of original research; speech to writing sequences; and collective building of new words and phrases to give life to new perspectives and interpretations of problems.

Other important conditions are the institutional and funding support of UNICEF, the wise selection of participants and the facilitating skills and recognised knowledge and neutrality of Lo Bianco, who has so far conducted forty-five such dialogues (personal communication).

The question remains, how successful is national language policy?

Notes

1. It was the many failures of economic as well as language planning in the 1960s that led me to prefer the term management to planning. Also used by Czech linguists like Neustupný and Nekvapil (2003), the term management has the added attraction of suggesting the possibility of modification and change. But with the stubbornness of experts, many continue to prefer Language Policy and Planning or its abbreviation LPP.
2. ISO 639-3 includes 7,707+ codes.
3. Morey et al. (2013) list other problems: the codes are mnemonic (*eng* for English); some minority codes enshrine offensive designations; *Ethnologue* does not cite sources; it ignores some published studies; and it assumes permanence, so that Chaucerian and Modern English have the same code.
4. Standardisation means that there is a generally accepted writing system and published grammars and dictionaries; it also refers to the belief that there is a correct form of the language.
5. Historicity refers to the belief that the language has a long history, or a Great Tradition.
6. Autonomy refers to the belief that the variety is not a dialect of another named language.
7. Vitality is the fact that children are brought up speaking the language and that there is natural intergenerational transmission, or the belief (as part of family language policy) that this should be so.
8. In the details of languages in India in Chapter 9, it was shown both that many speakers do not have a name for their language and that many languages have multiple names. In a US survey (Shin and Kominski, 2010), it was estimated that there were just over 200,000 speakers of Hebrew and just under 200,000 speakers of Yiddish. But only thirty speakers of Ladino were reported, presumably because they reported Spanish as their language.
9. De Swaan (1998a, 1998b, 2001) argues convincingly that it is second language use that sets the value of an international language; English does not have the most first language speakers in Europe or Asia or Africa, but it has the most second language speakers.
10. Fishman (1991) proposed a Graded Intergenerational Disruption Scale ranging from a variety with only vestigial and isolated speakers to a variety with some higher educational and governmental use. Lewis et al. (2016) use an expanded scale, ranging from extinct to international.
11. Fishman (1967) argues, and in Fishman et al. (1971) demonstrates, the assignment of language varieties to specific domains, such as in Jersey City where the use of Spanish at home and in church and of English for public functions supported stable bilingualism.

12. Many constitutions such as those of Caribbean nations set proficiency in the national language as a condition for election to political office.
13. And this too will need to recognise the fact that some subjects are taught in other languages; for example, science is often taught in English even where the national language is the language of instruction for other subjects.
14. A notion and formula, according to Piller (2016), mistakenly attributed to Johan Herder by Bauman and Briggs (2003).
15. In studying Japanese nationalism, Doak (2006) shows that the term has two different translations in Japanese, distinguishing *kokuminshugi* (statism) from *minzokushugi* (ethnic nationalism); Western scholars too now recognise many kinds of nationalism.
16. Meulder et al. (2019) describe the success of similar campaigns advocating the legal recognition of Sign languages in eighteen countries.
17. Spolsky (2009a: 184) mentioned 'the undefined "they" who constitute "government"', regretting the absence of detailed studies.
18. A useful exception is the detailing of the position papers that led to the recognition of official status for Māori in New Zealand (Spolsky, 2005). Another important account of legislative and bureaucratic activities leading to language policies is in Williams (2008a) who deals with Celtic, Spanish and Canadian cases.
19. In the Soviet Union, state language was the term used instead of official language.

13 Some National Language Policies

Recognising the importance of evidence on effectiveness, I have in this book given many details of national language policies and their implementation. In this penultimate chapter, I will describe a number of specific cases as a first attempt at summing up the results of rethinking the model. Essentially, they can be read as trying to answer the question: can language be managed?

Language policy in Singapore and Malaysia

Singapore is often cited as a successful case of national language planning in the service of economic progress (Chew, 2006, 2014; Dixon, 2009; Wee, 2003; Xu and Li, 2002). Early in his life, Lee Kuan Yew, a native speaker of Baba Malay creole educated in an English-medium school, came to believe that English (which he and his wife spoke well) and Mandarin were the way to achieve economic success in the West and the East. He set out to master both Hokkien (the main topolect of Singapore Chinese) and Mandarin and used this new proficiency in the election campaign that led to his election as prime minister in 1959. His first language policy was multilingual, choosing not mother tongues but the symbolic languages of the four races: English, Mandarin (instead of Hokkien),[1] Malay (instead of Malayalam) and Tamil. Malay, spoken by 15 per cent (Rappa and Wee, 2006), was declared a 'national language' in which the national anthem is sung. The four languages became the languages of instruction in schools, replacing the vernacular languages that had been recognised by the British colonial government. By 1972, Lee's party had won all the seats in parliament and he proclaimed a bilingual policy for schools, with English as the first language and the other three defined as second languages. By 1983, 99 per cent of schools were English-medium. In 1978, a new campaign began to replace the Chinese topolects with Mandarin and by 2010 nearly half of the Chinese homes were reported to use Mandarin, following the example of Lee and his family. But English has continued to grow in private and public domains and this has been accompanied by the progress of Singapore into first world status, with a gross domestic product (GDP) of around US$2,200 in 1959 growing to more than US$60,000 by the 1990s (Rappa and Wee, 2006). But, as Chew (2014) notes, this has been accompanied by mother tongue abandonment, perhaps helping to explain why Singapore's 'Happiness' score is below that of thirty nations with lower GDPs. One explanation may be the continued sense of attachment to the topolects, evidence of which is given in their use in church services and by younger people (Rappa and Wee, 2006: 93–4). A second major campaign launched in 2000 was the Speak Good English Movement, intended to fight the continued popularity of the local variety know as Singlish. However, given the high instrumental value of English, Rappa and Wee (2006: 90) see little opposition to the movement.

In Malaysia, on the other hand, Malay has been the de facto and *de jure* preferred language since independence in 1963, as part of the function of nation-building and the maintenance of traditional Malay culture. Ethnic Malays make up 60 per cent of the population; another quarter speak various Chinese topolects and just over 7 per cent are Eurasian and Indian (Rappa and Wee, 2006). The main linguistic issue is a balance between Bahasa Melayu, which represents tradition, and English, which provides access to modernity and economic development. The 1961 Education Act made Malay compulsory for primary and secondary education and for government institutions including the army and police. But Chinese Malaysians continue to send their children to Chinese-medium schools and to non-Malay universities. The high failure rate in Bahasa Melayu was also a cause for concern.

The conflict has moved to the tertiary level. Gill (2005, 2006) reports the 2005 modification of policy in Malaysian higher education when the first cohort of students affected by the 2002 switch to English for the teaching of science and mathematics arrived as undergraduates. There was confusion in the absence of any clear direction of implementation: universities first learned of the change from mass media and developed their own policies. The lack of documentation followed a decision by the former Prime Minister, Tun Dr Mahatjir Mohd, and his cabinet to avoid the controversy that an announcement would lead to given the strong support of Malay intellectuals for the continued use of Bahasa Melayu. Thus, the government avoided claiming ownership and responsibility for a policy that worked against the established support for Bahasa Melayu. Gill (2006) goes on to report discussions of the issue in the universities. Again, in the minutes of the senate meetings, there is no identification of attitudes or debate, but summary statements of decisions, with plans for implementation left to the faculties: in practice, this meant that 30 per cent of the first-year courses would be taught in English. But this led to concern by parents, for the sciences and mathematics had been entirely taught at secondary school in English: why did they need to revert to Bahasa Melayu? Only in 2005 did the minister of higher education overrule the universities' plans to shift gradually and require all science teaching in English. But in contrast to Singapore, Bahasa Melayu remains the dominant language in Malaysia, with the pragmatic attraction of English starting to weaken its hold.

Swahili in East Africa

As part of its support for language studies in the 1970s, the Ford Foundation (Ford Foundation, 1975; Fox, 2007) funded sociolinguistic surveys of five Eastern African nations, Uganda, Kenya, Ethiopia, Tanzania and Zambia. What is noteworthy about these counties is their different choices of national languages: Uganda and Kenya selected both English and Swahili, Tanzania made Swahili a de facto national language and English a de facto working language, Zambia made only English official nationally, but recognised seven official regional languages, while Ethiopia chose Amharic. It should first be noted that these are rare cases of sub-Saharan African languages as national languages.

How does one account for the status of Swahili? Whiteley (1969: 1) pointed out the rapid increase in the importance and recognition of Swahili; by the time he wrote, it was 'the most widely known, taught, discussed and spoken African language on the Continent' and had been selected as the national language of Tanzania. He traced its history from a coastal Bantu language first described by Salt (1814) as a jargon spoken by some sailors on an Arab boat, that spread up-country during the nineteenth century, becoming a widely spoken and written language during the colonial period, used and recognised by governments and missionaries and standardised in the 1930s by an interterritorial language committee. He noted the problems of developing it as a national language and wondered whether it will become 'Africa's most virile language, supporting a full educational programme, a mastery over modern technology and a creative literature' (p. 126). Tanzania, he noted, had gone further than its neighbours (p. 99).

The United Republic of Tanzania was made up of Tanganyika and the island of Zanzibar in 1964. With over 120 indigenous languages, there are 15 million native speakers of Swahili and another 32 million second language speakers. English is a working language reported to be spoken by 4 million. Swahili, a Bantu language with many lexical borrowings from Arabic – it used to be written in Arabic script – was standardised at a conference in 1928, with the Zanzibar dialect chosen as the standard. Its use was supported by the Tanganyika African National Union (TANU) which became the ruling party after independence. Under the presidency of Julius Nyerere, in 1967 an educational policy, Education for Self-reliance, emphasised primary education for the rural masses and expressed rejection of Western influence. But over time, this position weakened and in 1982 and again in 1995 English became the medium for secondary education. Many private English-medium schools were set up, in which the speaking of English was encouraged (Vavrus, 2002).

Swahili is described as the de facto national language, but there is no mention of language in the 1977 Constitution nor in the 1985 amended version. In 2015, the secretary of the Department of Education announced plans to ditch English at all levels of education, but this does not seem to have happened. The difficulty and cost of developing Swahili to fill all the tasks of a modern language predicted by Whiteley (1969) has even in Tanzania, the nation most committed to the language, made it hard for the language to compete with English.

Although Uganda has more than thirty languages, three are the main competitors for dominance: English, Luganda (spoken by 6 million as a lingua franca) and Kiswahili (spoken as a second language by most). English is the national statutory language and Swahili is the national working language. At independence in 1965, a policy for schools was adopted: six Ugandan languages were to be used as medium of instruction at the primary level: Luganda, Akarimojong/Ateso, Lugbara, Luo, Runyoro/Rutooro and Runyankole/Rukiga. Secondly, children were to be taught in their own language in the early years of school. Thirdly, English was to be introduced as a subject in the first year and continue as a subject for all seven years of primary school. In the fourth year, mathematics and physical education were to be taught through the medium of English. English as a medium of instruction would be gradually extended to science and some other subjects in the fifth year and in the sixth and seventh year all subjects would be taught in English. However, implementation of this elaborate plan proved difficult (Mukama, 2009). Nakayiza (2013) writes that initially there was opposition to Swahili, but under President Museveni, Swahili was proclaimed second official language and military lingua franca. Since 1992, the government has been encouraging the use of Swahili in schools, but this is delayed by the lack of teachers with proficiency in the language. Its use as lingua franca in eastern Africa has also raised its attractiveness. At the same time, few of the other indigenous languages are being developed – only half have satisfactory orthographies and, in spite of some NGO and grassroots activities, the chance of maintenance remains weak.

In a study comparing three British colonies, Powell (2002) gives an interesting analysis of the development of language policy in Kenya. The government took over control of Kenya from the Imperial British East Africa Company, a commercial association which was created after the Berlin Conference of 1885, inheriting eight education officers among the 369 British officers. Unlike Uganda, there were no existing elites with whom to cooperate, so that the government needed to invent and appoint new chiefs and develop new codes of practice that they claimed were traditional. There was also growing white settlement, whose requests for local rule were blocked by the Colonial Office's decision in 1923 to reserve Kenya for the Africans. Colonial education in Kenya began with missionaries, who chose English, Swahili or local vernaculars. The colonial system favoured vocational education in the vernacular, but after the Second World War, a policy of four years in the vernacular followed by Swahili and gradual introduction of English was replaced in 1949 by a recommendation to switch from the vernacular to English, lowering the status of Swahili. A political struggle developed between those who called for white-biased home rule and those who wanted to develop African elites. The conflict continued with the radical nationalism of the Mau Mau movement, which supported African languages, but by 1966 half of primary schools were English-medium. In 1964, Kenya became independent, with Jomo Kenyatta as President and British administrators were replaced by English-educated Africans. In 1985, the educational policy called for four years of a local language (eighteen languages including Swahili which was also a compulsory exam subject) followed by English medium. Kikuyu at first was the dominant language of government under Kenyatta but, by 1974, Swahili was recognised as the national language and is so named in the constitution; Swahili and English are named official languages and the constitution also calls for the development and use of indigenous language and Sign. In practice, though, the emphasis in schools continues to be on English, even though research (Piper et al., 2016) shows that comprehension is better in the local indigenous language. Mose (2017) found that teachers do not agree with the policy, preferring English to the local languages, so that the official policy is not widely implemented. Again, the status of English as a global language and its economic value appears to outweigh the government's proclamation of the importance of the national language.

Swahili is listed in *Ethnologue* as a language of wider communication in Zambia, but Ohannessian and Kashoki (1978) estimated there were under 8,000 mother tongue speakers; there is no neutral language not associated with an ethnic group or region apart from the colonial language. Bemba with over 3 million speakers and Tonga with over 1 million are listed as provincial languages, as is Luvale with under 200,000. Until the British colonial government took over in 1924, the missions were responsible for the limited education offered to Africans. There was teaching in local languages, but a lack of materials, teachers and standardisation. The goal of colonial education was to teach English whenever a competent teacher was available; by the late 1950s, education was begun in the mother tongue, with a shift to one of seven approved languages in the third year and to English from Standard V if not earlier. In practice, teachers did not have proficiency in the locally approved African language and the Zambian languages were not of high priority. There were plans to train more teachers able to teach in a local language. However, teachers continued to use English, the language in which they had been trained, most of the time. In many regions, only half the children were speakers of an approved language. Some improvement was offered by a new primary course started in the 1970s, but major problems remained at the time of the survey. Current reports suggest that schools are under-resourced and standards are low. Mwanza (2017) thinks that part of the problem is that Zambian teachers hold purist attitudes to Zambian languages and to informal English. A recent paper (Banda and Mwanza, 2017) argues that the monolingual approach of school language education programmes in Zambia is mistaken and suggests they would do better to recognise the multilingualism of the pupils by adopting a translanguaging approach.

Summing up these Eastern African examples, those nations where Swahili is widely used and seen as a potential unifying force still face major problems to implement its acceptance and use as a unifying language and are challenged by the pull towards economically advantageous Global English, with its long entrenchment under colonial rule, its power in elite closure and its use in higher education and government.

National policy in former Soviet nations

Under Soviet rule, the many countries that had been brought into the empire were subjected to national language policies that 'fundamentally changed the nature of language use within its borders' (Grenoble, 2003: 1). In the first years of Soviet rule, there were two competing approaches: one aimed to use the many national languages to establish socialism and produce a sense of identity; the other promoted Russian as the state language to be used in government, law and education throughout the empire. Given the multi-ethnic and multilingual nature of the state, with 286 million people, 130 ethnic groups and between 150 and 200 languages, such a combined policy seemed inevitable. It involved, Grenoble proposes, setting four levels of language status: the lowest were languages without any support. At the next level were languages like Kazakh with some support, a writing system, but no official status. At the second level were titular languages with official status within each Union Republic, but little or no use outside the republic. The highest level was Russian, the only lingua franca, being developed as the official language of a new Soviet nation, the sole official language of all administration, law and education. For seventy-five years, this policy was in effect, in fifteen Union Republics, divided not ethnolinguistically but to create new national identities.

The three largest ethnic groups were Slavic, making up the Russian, the Belorussian and the Ukrainian republics and including nearly 80 per cent of the population. Three were Turkic – Uzbek, Tatar and Kazakh. Three were genetically unrelated languages of the Caucasus, Azerbaijani, Georgian and Armenian. The demography changed, partly because of different birthrates and family size, partly because of urbanisation and partly because of forced deportation, such as the deportation of Crimean Tatars, Greeks and Bulgarians to Central Asia. In addition, many ethnic Russians moved to Baltic nations, especially to Latvia, where they came to constitute half the population, Estonia where they were nearly 40 per cent and Lithuania where they reached 9 per cent in 1989 (Grenoble, 2003).

A major step in the newly established Soviet Union was the literacy campaign, which involved both development of new writing systems and teaching people to read; a result was an increase of literacy from 24 per cent in 1897 to 81 per cent in 1939 (Grenoble, 2003). Initially, the emphasis was on Cyrillic, but in 1930s many languages were given Latin-based scripts in place of earlier Arabic and Mongolian. Another emphasis was lexical development, with commissions set up to Russify as well as modernise the local languages. Up until 1950, the national languages were supported, but after that there was a move to Russification: in the Education Reforms of 1958–9, mother tongue education was no longer compulsory and there was a move to make Russian the second mother tongue. The 1936 Constitution had stated the right of all to mother tongue education but this was unevenly implemented. Emphasis moved to Russian which was introduced in early school years, so that by 1981 the nationwide average highest grade with languages other than Russian as medium was down to 2.6 (Grenoble, 2003).

The collapse of Soviet rule gave an opportunity to re-establish the place of the local languages (Hogan-Brun and Melnyk, 2012). Some successor countries passed laws on state languages even before independence: Ukraine in 1986, Kyrgyzstan in 1989, Uzbekistan in 1992, Armenia in 1993, Azerbaijan and Lithuania in 1995; others passed such laws soon after, with the Russian Federation last in 2005. Three successor states classified Russian as a foreign language: Estonia, Latvia and Lithuania. Kyrgyzstan and Kazakhstan kept it official. Belarus made it a second state language. Tajikistan, Turkmenistan and the Ukraine defined it as a language of interethnic communication. And four did not mention it in the law or constitution. Most former Soviet states have now made the local state language a compulsory language of education, with some provision to maintain minority languages. There are variations in school language policy, some with the national language the medium at all levels, some bilingual, with Russian at the highest level. Tertiary education is often partly at least in Russian.

In the Baltic region, the titular national languages have regained their status and use. In the Russian Federation, the position of Russian has become stronger, but in the Ukraine, Ukrainian and Russian are balanced. In Belarus, Russian remains strong. In the Caucasus, the titular language, Russian, and minority languages share. In Central Asia, Kazakhstan and Kyrgyzstan are working to raise the status of the titular language, but Russian is still used in government and higher education. In Tajikistan, Russian is still required for higher education.

To sum up, political independence has freed the successor states from Russian hegemony, but they have shown various degrees of success in establishing new language policies. Generally, the titular languages have regained their place, but the effect of seventy-five years of Russification remains strong.

China and the Koreas

A recent magazine article (Charlemagne, 2020) reports that Chinese schol-ars now describe China as a civilisation-state and not a nation state; other candidates are Russia, India, USA, Turkey and the European Union. This shows the dynamism of language policy; just as there is constant shift, chang-ing political and economic patterns are likely to be influential; for example, Brexit changes the status of languages in the European Union and of English. China continues its 2,000-year-old policy of unification, with language a central focus.

Since its creation, the People's Republic of China with its linguistic diver-sity has been active in tackling the major tasks of language management: sim-plification and standardisation of Chinese script, promotion of Putonghua as a national language, design and use of Pinyin as an auxiliary script, identification and mapping of regional language varieties, recognition and description of official minority varieties, creation of scripts for non-Sinitic varieties, translation of names and terms from other languages, language pedagogy and diffusion, bilingualism, foreign language instruction and lan-guage testing (Spolsky, 2016a).

Some of these were older endeavours: the establishment of the status of Mandarin, as the major and leading topolect goes back 2,000 years. There was important terminology development under the Han, Tang and Ming dynasties and the simplification of writing started under the Republic in 1935. But building on and expanding this tradition, there have been a large number of centrally controlled activities under the PRC, starting soon after it came to power but suspended during the Cultural Revolution.

Established to solve problems of popular illiteracy, the first Commission for the Reform of the Chinese Written Language issued a list of simplified characters in 1957, which was expanded in 1965. Mandarin was selected as Putonghua, the national standard language, and Pinyin was developed as a method of writing it phonetically. Originally conceived by some as a replace-ment for traditional characters, Pinyin was finally defined as a learning tool. The 2001 Language Law laid down the status of Putonghua and simplified spelling, but recognised the necessary but limited use of the topolects like Hokkien and Shanghainese and allowed for the maintenance of some minor-ity languages; these too were the subject of extensive linguistic research. But the shift to Putonghua continues, hastened by the large-scale urbanisation of the population. Many minority languages have been formally recognised, but this remains a topic of some concern as there might be nearly 300 such varieties, some associated like Tibetan and Uyghur with politically unre-solved issues. By 2004, there were writing systems for thirty of the minority languages.

Since 1996, a National Committee for Terms in Sciences and Technologies has worked to develop new terminology. An extensive programme for Chinese language diffusion has been undertaken, focused on the Confucius institutes operating in ninety countries of the world. Recognition of bilingualism has followed the grassroots reluctance of speakers of other varieties to shift to Putonghua. There has been progress in foreign language teaching and expansion in the public and private teaching of English. Building on the 2,000-year history of the Chinese Imperial Examination system, Chinese and English are required subjects in the *Gaokao* (National College Entrance Examination) taken by over 9 million high school students annually competing for limited university places. More recently, studies have begun of family language policy.

From this brief sketch of the areas of Chinese language management in the PRC, one can see that the field is well developed. There is strong centralised political control, with ideological and leadership changes leading to modification of goals. There has been a serious attempt to take into account the counterforces of the periphery – the strength of the topolects and the minority and regional communities. There have been difficulties in implementation, an inevitable result of bureaucratic complexity and centralised planning in such a huge country, that might well benefit from appreciation of the differences in levels and domains (Spolsky, 2009a). Given the enormous complexity of Chinese sociolinguistic communities, even a strong central government faces serious problems in central planning. As in economic and other planning processes, the assumption that all that is involved is implementation of centrally determined plans has been shown to be invalid. There is great variety in the language practices of the various ethnic and social groups, differences of ideology within and between groups and resulting conflicts in management.

Even without the major problems of modern Chinese history and the gaps in qualified manpower produced by the horrors of the Cultural Revolution and the major problems associated with central economic planning, the enormous complexity of the task and the potential conflicts between goals would have blocked any easy success. The changes produced by globalisation and information technology have exacerbated these difficulties. What has been important has been a willingness to consult (there has been extensive use of conferences and committees of experts and politicians) and an openness to experiment and reform.

In the field of language management, it is hard to assess results, and failure is more common than success. This is true in economics, too, as we stagger from one crisis to another, in international politics, as one war succeeds another, and in public health policy. So we cannot expect the complex tasks tackled by Chinese language management to do much better. We can note the Chinese success in increasing literacy, in maintaining a sense of national identity, in satisfying some but not all minority concerns, in spreading Mandarin outside China and in starting to build a cadre of people with foreign language mastery. But each of these remains an unfinished task, with problems produced by tension between contradictory goals (maintaining traditional script at the same time as dealing with demands of the computer age, recognising regional and heritage languages even though encouraging use of Putonghua, teaching Chinese overseas while strengthening the teaching of English inside China) as well as the difficulty of implementation of policies that require resources and support at all levels of a complex system. The size of China and the multiplicity of language issues make it a fascinating case for the study of language management. But it also shows the regrettable effects of the willingness to use violent means to achieve management goals: the use of boarding schools to shift Tibetans to Putonghua (Postiglione, 2009) and the million Uyghur adults in 'political re-education camps' in Xinyang shows the extremes to which a totalitarian government can go to try to enforce language management.

The two Koreas have different language policies. After years of persecution, with Korean banned during the Japanese occupation, the language has been restored in both South and North Korea. In North Korea, the language reform – such as cleansing the language of Chinese influence and characters – has been intended to meet the needs of a socialist state (Song, 2001; Terrell, 2007). In South Korea, on the other hand, acceptance of globalisation as a goal has led to a high status for English, with public and private teaching as well as individuals willing to send their families overseas to an English-speaking country in order to achieve proficiency (Song, 2011). In each, then, national ideology has driven language management.

The European Union

Whether it is seen as a civilisation-state or a confederation of nation states, the European Union combines recognition of the rights of the sovereign states to their own languages and language policies (the European Council, the Council of Members and the European Parliament use all twenty-three official languages, regardless of technical difficulties and expense (Gazzola, 2006)), but also has its own working languages (the European Commission uses English, French and German, the Court of Justice only French and the European Central Bank only English) and its support for diversity and minority languages in some charters and treaties (Faingold, 2020; Nic Shuibhne, 2001). The official languages of the Union are selected by the member states: Ireland has two and Luxembourgish is omitted. French is selected by France, Belgium and Luxembourg. The cost of providing interpreting (there are not enough booths) and translation is high (the first item on committee agendas is said to be the lack of a full set of translations), so that the limitation to working languages is needed. There has been debate about the place of English after Brexit, but it is widely known and listed in any case by Ireland as one of its national languages (Ammon, 2012).

Some regional languages official in the nation are recognised but others, like Catalan, Scots and Sorbian, are not. Indigenous autochthonous languages can be protected by Charter, but only if nominated by the appropriate nation. How many are involved is hard to determine. Exogenous (which means immigrant) languages have no protection. Institutions of the Union can specify in which language they will receive or answer communications. The cost of the policy is high: the Commission has 1,500 translators and the Parliament has 500 full-time and 2,700 freelance interpreters (Gazzola, 2006).

European Union language policy also applies to language teaching. The central goal is trilingualism in the national language, English and one other foreign language. In spite of the efforts to achieve balanced results, the use and level of proficiency remain uneven, with English gaining most. Numbers of speakers of minority languages continue to decline, with some exceptions depending on local conditions and not the result of European Union policy.

Four I's – India, Israel, Indonesia and Ireland

In a pioneering (and somewhat rare) attempt to evaluate the success of what they labelled language planning processes and what I prefer to call language management, Rubin et al. (1977) selected three nations starting with 'I', India, Indonesia and Israel, and in addition Sweden. In an echo, Lo Bianco (2012) presents his reflection on four national language revival efforts: the same three I's plus one more, Ireland. Here, I choose to concentrate on Indonesia, which seems to show successful handling of a complex highly multilingual nation, followed by brief remarks on some other nations also beginning with the same letter.

Indonesia: selecting a new national language

With a population of over 250 million people and 600 ethnic groups, Indonesia has over 700 languages and over 1,000 dialects. The national language is Bahasa Indonesia and over forty indigenous languages serve as regional languages of wider communication. With a tradition of internal migration and the diversity of languages, individual plurilingualism is common. But a long programme of encouraging Bahasa Indonesia has, without replacing indigenous languages in all domains, provided a working national language.

The languages that make up Indonesian superdiversity are Bahasa Indonesia, developed from the Riau dialect of Malay, recognised as a unifying language by the 1928 Youth Conference and as the national language in the 1945 National Constitution, the many indigenous languages, the Malayic and non-Malayic regional lingua francas, the heritage languages of immigrant communities (for instance Chinese, Arabic), sign languages and the major educational languages (for instance Arabic, English, French). Fewer than 5 per cent of the population spoke Malay in 1928 but it was chosen over the colonial Dutch (in which the conference was conducted) and Javanese spoken by nearly 50 per cent (Zein, 2020). Nowadays, Indonesian is the most important language, with proficiency required in the workplace; it is the official language in politics, the media and education. The 2011 census claimed that 20 per cent of the population speak it as their native language and that literacy in it reaches over 90 per cent.

The status of Indonesian after the initial proclamation in 1928 was strengthened at the First Congress of Indonesian language in 1938 with the adoption of the slogan 'One language, Bahasa Indonesia'. This was confirmed in the 1945 proclamation of independence and strengthened after recognition as a national language in 1954 and by the New Order regime under President Soeharto. At the same time, there continued to be recognition of indigenous languages, although under President Sukarno, Indonesian was required in order to show loyalty to the nation. Current status planning recognises the role of indigenous languages for individual and ethnic and regional identity. It does not include recognition of languages like Chinese or of languages of religion. Foreign languages (including Arabic) have been recognised since 2009 as important for international communication.

The corpus planning required to make Indonesian 'a stable sophisti-cated national and official modern language' (Zein, 2020) has been the work of the *Badan Bahasa*, founded in 1947 as The Language and Culture Research Institute and recently renamed the Agency for Language and Book Development. Orthography was under Dutch influence, but the second Congress recommended it be replaced. A new spelling system was proposed in 1967 but never implemented; however, there were changes in 1987 and again in 2009. Terminological expansion began during the Japanese occupa-tion and continued afterwards. There have been many borrowings, some from indigenous languages but most from heritage or foreign languages, especially Dutch followed by English and Arabic. There were controversies over the standardisation of Indonesian grammar, with major influences from Arabic and from structural linguistics. There has not been similar interest in research into the languages other than Indonesian.

Several hundred Indonesian languages are now endangered. Several factors account for the shift to Indonesian: one is the relocation of people to less intensively settled areas; a second is the use of Indonesian as language of instruction in schools; and the third is the use of the language in media. Some of the larger languages are also threatened: for example, there is a shift from Javanese with its complex pattern of registers. Smith-Hefner (2009) reports a noticeable shift from Javanese (and lower proficiency in the high language) to Indonesian among younger Javanese in Yogyakata in Central Java. This is truer of women, reflecting changed ideology. There are also shifts from smaller indigenous languages to regional lingua francas. Religious conversion migration is another factor. There has been genocide as a result of tribal wars, and violent conflicts especially in western New Guinea have led to militaristic government and suppression of some of the languages.

Although the Badan Bahasa has done some work in documentation, it is estimated that fewer than 10 per cent of the indigenous languages of Indonesia have been documented (Zein, 2020). For many languages, there is no data on vitality or use. There have been a few studies of language attitudes and few localised efforts at building sustainability. Education has been variously administered, with a distinction between secular and religious (Zein, 2020). Since 2014, secular elementary and secondary schools have been under the Ministry of Education and Culture and religious schools under the Ministry of Religious Affairs. Universities, except for religious universities, are under a separate ministry.

Major emphasis in the early years after independence was on teaching Indonesian, chosen as language of instruction, but lacking qualified teachers. Under the New Order, some mother tongue education was allowed until the third year. The policy continues, with emphasis on moving to the national language by the fourth year. There is controversy about the degree of Indonesian literacy achieved. There is some mother tongue literacy, but the general goal is to shift to Indonesian. Indonesian and English are favoured. But there is evidence of local variation, with some resistance to official policy. Arabic and Asian languages are taught, but English is the dominant foreign language.

Paauw (2009) presents evidence for the claim of success of Bahasa Indonesia as a national language. At the outset, Indonesians had three choices: Dutch, the colonial language, lacked the status of English or French; Javanese, spoken by just under half of the population, was resented by others; and Malay, spoken by about 5 per cent, was considered easier to learn than Javanese with its complex social registers. Dutch was banned by the Japanese, with the result that Indonesian made major advances during the occupation. Lowenberg (1990) argued that

> its central role as a vehicle and symbol of the movement for political independence, its ethnically neutral status in not being the first language of any prominent ethnic group and the freedom it provides from encoding in all utterances distinctions in rank and status.

Given the ethnic and linguistic diversity of Indonesia, the choice of language was basic to unification. This provided a strong ideological basis for the legal status of the language. The development of education and literacy was a major part of implementation. Diglossia (with the elite using the H variety) and urbanisation have also been significant factors. Apart from weakness of implementation in higher education, the widespread acceptance of the language has been remarkable:

no other post-colonial nation has been able to develop and implement a national language with the speed and degree of acceptance which Indonesia has. No other national language in a post-colonial nation is used in as wide a range of domains as Indonesian, a feat made more impressive by the size and ethnic, linguistic and cultural diversity of Indonesia. (Paauw, 2009: 7)

Wright (2004) wonders whether Indonesian may not have reached its apogee, as result of problems of the state including corruption, ethnic tension and the loss of Timor, and pressure for Global English on the one hand and resurgent vernaculars on the other. But essentially, Paauw concludes that Indonesian has been a successful example of language planning.

In 1959, President Sukarno suspended the constitution and established Guided Democracy, a state controlled by the supreme leader. In 1965, power moved to Soeharto who became president in 1967 and instituted the New Order. There was emphasis on the teaching of ideology in schools, involving the teaching in Indonesian of the thirty-six values drawn form the *Pancasila* (five principles). Indonesian was not just a unifying force but a sacred symbol of the state. Morfit (1981) observed that in 1979 Indonesian civil servants including senior ones were required to attend a two-week 'upgrading' course on Pancasila. Attendance every day was compulsory. Classes went from 8 a.m. to 6 p.m. and there was homework and a final exam. The five principles are belief in one supreme being, commitment to just and civilised humanitarianism, commitment to the unity of Indonesia, the idea of wise policies and consensus, and commitment to social justice. The principles derived from Sukarno's Guided Democracy are seen as derived from the past, but also as the basis for future policy. The Badan Bahasa developed terminology in support of this ideology, adding many words from Javanese. Development became a central slogan. Nominalisation led to abstraction. Euphemism was common. The discourse policy of the bureaucracy strengthened the dictatorship and weakened opposition. Soeharto's goal was a uniform citizenry using a uniform culture achieved through a single language. Indigenous languages were permitted but not over-encouraged. Language policing involved fines for signs written in other than Standard Indonesian. One form of resistance was the development of a vernacular non-standard variety of Indonesian by students and youth, developing in a variety of Indonesian which included wider repertory of borrowing from indigenous languages and English (Zein, unpublished). All these developments show the importance of discourse planning, supporting Lo Bianco's assertion that 'The planning of discourse is what every powerful institution has always sought: armies, political parties, religions, ideological movements; all want to influence human mental states' (Lo Bianco, 2001: 52).

Lo Bianco (2012) agrees that Indonesia among comparable Asian countries has achieved good success. He cites Dardjowidjojo (1998) as attributing this to four factors: the past colonial policy, the nationalist response, the rivalry between the national language and the vernaculars or colonial language, and the successful cultivation of the national language once it was adopted. Early writings on the topic such as Alisjahbana (1974) stressed successful development of modern terminology as well as the effects of the Japanese occupation. Also the sharing of Malay with Malaysia after the British withdrawal helped. The 1928 Youth Pledge made Bahasa Indonesia a symbol of resistance to colonial Dutch and of nationalism. Diffusion was through the school system with the development of literacy. This has led to bilingualism and multiple language competence with English added. The result is diglossia, with Indonesian as the language of official use, and vernaculars used for local commercial and cultural life.

Israel: revernacularising and revitalising a classical heritage literary language

In earlier chapters, I have referred on a number of occasions to the restoration of Hebrew, after 2,000 years of use as a written language passed on by a religious educational system, to the status of a normal national language. The outline is clear: exile and invasions added to the Hebrew spoken in the Holy Land two other varieties, Aramaic and Greek, and they were the main spoken varieties after the destruction of the Temple and in the Diaspora. Both were Hebraised and used by a community that added and modified new spoken varieties alongside a steady maintenance of Hebrew taught to children and used and respected as a written language. With the growth of political Zionism and the return to the traditional homeland starting at the end of the nineteenth century, a Hebrew revival programme began.

Lo Bianco (2012) recognises two stages: revernacularisation followed by revitalisation, the first being introduction of the language into some village schools whose graduates took the language home and used it with their own children. Strong nationalistic activism supported by an adult language teaching programme meant that most of the large numbers of new immigrants arriving over the next half-century, whether survivors of the Holocaust or speakers of Judeo-Arabic expelled from Muslim countries, also adopted Hebrew as a vernacular and their children, too, acquired it in Jewish and state schools. These pressures also affected non-Jewish residents, so that Palestinian Arabic was in time Hebraised and used by Palestinians as a strong second language. Although Yiddish was maintained by some Hassidim and some immigrants kept up use of heritage languages, especially when there was dense settlement, Modern Israeli Hebrew is now the dominant language.

Ireland and the shift to English

After independence and with the 1937 Constitution and adoption of many laws, Irish conquered, Lo Bianco (2012: 518) stated, 'all areas of formal recognition' but failed to achieve 'domain normalisation'. The policy stressed territorialism, but inconsistency of economic and language policy meant that even the Gaeltacht continued to shift to the English that dominated the rest of the country. Thus a national language revival movement that was older than Indonesia and contemporary with Hebrew failed to lead to vernacular and vital revival.

Indian diversity and revivals

While India shares the linguistic diversity of Indonesia, the constitutional recognition of many major languages, Lo Bianco (2012: 506) explains, is accompanied also by local state revival movements which have blocked the full imposition of Hindi and encourage the maintenance of English well beyond the fifteen years allowed in the constitution. As a result, India manages with a highly complex and multilingual linguistic repertoire, something that was more or less allowed for in the original plans but that does not satisfy the current aspirations of the Hindu nationalists.

Note

1. Other topolects spoken in Singapore were Khek, Hainanese, Cantonese, Hakka, Teochew and Hoklo.

14   Rethinking a Theory

The examples presented earlier help us understand why nation states find forming and implementing a national language policy so difficult. There is commonly a conflict between two major goals: the desire to choose a language with maximum economic advantage and the desire to choose the national heritage-identifying language. When the two overlap, as they do in English-speaking nations and to a lesser extent in nations with a developed international language, nations still face the problems of the existence of disparate and varied language goals at each level from the individual to international rights. Implementation is complex, easier in a totalitarian than in a democratic state and requires resources to support a high level of education and recognition of minority languages. In some cases, a workable national language policy has been selected and largely put in practice, but usually at the cost of ignoring the demands and needs of recognised and unrecognised linguistic minorities.

The success or failure of a national language policy depends on the complexity of the language situation: a simple case like virtually monolingual Japan is easier to manage than a highly complex case like Indonesia. A second major factor is the political and economic strength of the nation: totalitarian governments like the People's Republic of China or the Soviet Union have greater prospects of imposing a policy than democracies, and a sound economy permits allocating sufficient funds to education to implement a policy. Ideology is also important: a single Great Tradition or popular acceptance of national identity leads to a simpler language policy, while competing traditions can be best managed by territorial solutions. Some policies like in Pakistan take on the difficult task of working against the language practices and beliefs of the majority of the population. Most find it difficult to deal with the challenge of diversity and the existence of minority groups, whether indigenous or immigrant. And few can deal with the need to find a consensus and a way of managing the competing demands of different domains and groups.

The fundamental problem in language policy is the lack of resources for education. Global education monitoring report team (2020) makes this clear.

There are a number of relevant findings. In moderately wealthy nations, only 18 of the poorest students compared to 100 of the richest finish high school. Marginalised groups (indigenous or immigrant) are commonly ignored. Even in middle income countries many pupils are not learning the basics, which includes reading the dominant language. Immigrant students in the Organisation for Economic Development and Co-operation (OECD) countries are usually in schools where half the pupils are immigrants and so do not have a chance to learn the dominant language from peers. Even in OECD countries, teachers of disadvantaged pupils are less qualified. The failures of language education policy then reflect the failures of national education systems and ultimately of misguided national policies that fail to recognise diversity and disparity of resources.

The current model of language policy

Summing up, I have found that language practices can be managed, but this is made more difficult because management occurs on many different levels. At the individual level, a speaker can choose which language variety, or which item out of their repertoire, they use, depending both on their proficiency and their assumption of what is appropriate to their intended audience or readers. This is what Bell (1984) called audience design which he proposed to account for the various styles adopted by radio announcers on the various programmes in New Zealand, but expanded to allow for the code-switching or translanguaging now assumed in multilingual communities. This usage may or may not accord with the variety expected in the various communities (family, educational, neighbourhood, work, media, local or national) or domains (home, friends, shopping, employment, official). The variety expected in a community or domain may be influenced by internal or external advocates or managers, varying in power that may be assigned by religious, educational, political, economic, historical, sociological or psychological factors. It is this very complexity that makes it difficult to know which factor will be strongest in predicting maintenance or shift of the current practices of an individual or a group. Commonly, it is the family or home that accounts for the initial individual language repertoire, but it can be modified when there are significant others (such as more recent immigrants) in the family or by elder siblings already at school or by peers from the neighbourhood speaking another variety. The school is the next major influence, depending usually on a governmentally chosen language of instruction (but limited by the teacher's proficiency); parental choice of a school (based often on their belief about the economical value of a language) is sometimes a factor. As individuals move into new communities (perhaps because of immigration or urbanisation) or add domains, their language repertoire is likely to be expanded or modified. Any national management, ideally but seldom recognising diversity and aiming at equality, should recognise all these forces and influences, but implementation still depends on the availability of resources to support any plans. Within these limits, a workable national language policy can be developed and, with ample funding, implemented.

Should language be managed?

Until recently, I saw my study of language policy as part of a larger project, which I labelled 'Can language be managed?' But as I continue my rethinking and notice my discomfort with the term language planning, arguing that the Soviet economic plans which provided a model for social and linguistic planning were largely unsuccessful, I wonder if that is the right question.[1] A Christmas essay in *The Economist*, 'Beware of the Borg' (Anonymous, 2019) discusses the comparative merit of planned and market-driven models in economics, noting that increasingly powerful computers and bigger and bigger data sources suggest the possibility of technological control not just of the economy but even of the ballot box. The article notes that the argument is commonly not about the desirability of machine-like efficiency, but of how to achieve it, offering two unrelated comparisons: the suppression of Uyghur in Xinjiang and the willingness of busy people to surrender data and decisions to Alexa and Siri. It offers as a more favourable model Project Cybersyn, built by a British consultant, Stafford Beer, for Chile's President Salvador Allende in the 1970s to control the country's newly centralised and socialised economy and abandoned in 1973 when Allende killed himself after a coup. But new attempts at computer control can be even more powerful, with the possibility of gathering and processing enormous quantities of data. As a result and with the possibilities of the cloud to handle data from billions of servers, there may well be a technology that outperforms the market in prediction. And as a result, more and more people are trusting technology to replace personal judgement. So the answer to 'Can language be planned?' might be 'not yet, but soon'.[2]

But is this a good thing? Should we assume that the uniformity and hegemony of the most efficient language variety is what we want? Or can we imagine a system that recognises and permits the kind of diversity that occurs in the complex linguistic repertoires of individuals and speech communities? Is the dictatorship of a national language plan, whether forcing everyone to shift to the common language that maintains the national unity and communicative efficiency that governments prefer, or the alternative offered by linguists who argue that everyone should keep using their heritage variety and not shift to a socially or economically more desirable language, to be aimed at? And are we trapped in the kind of Northern view of the world that fails to allow for other approaches? My own bias, I now realise, is a combination of diversity that comes from allowing choice, whether at the individual or the community level. And we have plenty of examples showing that multilingualism works, in families or cities or even nations, with India providing a good example (Agnihotri and Sachdeva, 2021).

The recent growing sentiment for allowing diversity in the classroom, celebrated by the new term translanguaging (García and Li, 2013), suggests that the linguists who appealed to us to leave our language alone (Hall, 1950) were more on the right line than those who argued for prescriptive purity (Fishman, 2006). In a discussion of the question of the extent to which a community should try to maintain its traditional language, Li (2018b) first considers the problem of diasporic communities, which is part of what he calls the post-multilingual challenge and offers translanguaging as a grass-roots response (García and Li, 2013) 'whereby multilingual language users mediate complex social and cognitive activities through strategic and creative employment of multiple semiotic resources to act, to know and to be'. It is a marked feature of the language practices of individuals and communities with expanded language repertoires to be able to take advantage of them to go beyond the limits of monolingualism.

The idea is appealing, but as my wife keeps reminding me and as Rubinstein (2018: 92) notes at the end of a review of a book on translanguaging,

> Despite the general tone of the book being strongly optimistic on the benefits and opportunities of bringing translanguaging into the class-rooms, it concludes with a not-so-positive tone regarding the social acceptance – especially by policy makers but also teachers – of translan-guaging as a legitimate educational practice.

Policy makers at the national level and teachers generally prefer certainty, holding a belief like that of Fishman (2006) that there is a correct and desir-able version of named languages, and are uncomfortable with the openness of translanguaging and the notion that linguists only describe and should not prescribe.

Nor is there widespread popular acceptance of the notion of diversity and of multilingualism that many linguists favour. Thus, the first task that supporters of language diversity and of minority languages face is finding out how to modify popular beliefs and ideologies in the hope of persuading powerful language managers and the general public to accept the positions they advocate. Language policy remains a disputed issue, just like economic and political policies. The complex set of levels at which it occurs, with each speech community varying in language practices, ideologies and attempts at management, means that there is no simple resolution. No one level, whether the individual, the family, the business, religion, international agreements or the nation, is likely to have the final word, although one must recognise the power of totalitarian states. Failure to recognise this complexity works against the selection and implementation of management efforts. Rethinking language policy makes clear how much more there is to be done in understanding it.

Rethinking

I remember the presentations I heard when I was a linguistics student, usually about a phonological problem, when at the end the speaker announced a solution and wrote it on the blackboard. There were disagreements and doubts and uncertainties, but it seemed that I was getting into a field where one could reach conclusions. It was later when I started to tackle questions about language teaching, a field where one method after another was tried, tested and discarded, that I was prepared for the long years that I have struggled to develop a working model for language policy.

I started thinking about the topic four decades ago (Spolsky, 1977). Writing a first paper for a collection entitled *Frontiers of Bilingual Education* that I edited with Robert Cooper, I cited a model that I had worked out with a group of young associates from the Navajo Reading Study (Spolsky et al., 1976) to describe bilingual education. The model consisted of half a dozen factors labelled psychological, sociological, economic, religio-cultural, political and linguistic, working on three levels: the situation of the language community before a bilingual programme was introduced, the factors that were under the control of the administrators of the programme and the perceptions that those responsible had for the outcomes of the programme. It was this three level multi-factor model that I later extended beyond language education to consider all levels of a language policy.

Ten years later, I was meeting regularly with Robert Cooper who was writing what became his major work on language policy (Cooper, 1989), a book that started with four challenging cases of language planning: the establishment of the *Académie française* by Cardinal Richelieu, the revitalisation of Hebrew in Ottoman Palestine, the American feminist movement and the mass literacy campaign in Ethiopia. On the basis of these cases, he set out a study of language planning and social change that incorporated the work of the sociolinguists responsible for what Jernudd and Nekvapil (2012) called classical language planning.

So I had already been thinking about language policy for some years when in 1996 I first ventured to propose a model, writing a paper claiming to set out prolegomena (Spolsky, 1996) that followed some months of discussions with Elana Shohamy about an Israeli language education policy (Spolsky and Shohamy, 1998, 2000). In the first of these papers, I noted the current linguistic situation of Israel, the state and status of the various languages, the number of other problems that the young state faced and the need to consider the role of languages other than Hebrew. In the second, we were already making a division of language policy into practice, ideology and policy. This was expanded to language practices, language beliefs or ideologies and management and planning in my first book-length study (Spolsky, 2004). A few years later, made more comfortable with the use of the word management by acquaintance with the work of the Prague group (Nekvapil and Sherman, 2009), I wrote a second book (Spolsky, 2009a), the major innovation of which was division into levels and domains, starting with the family and leading up to the supranational level. Over the next few years, I built on this model, looking more closely at the family level (Spolsky, 2012a), language academies and activism, PRC language policy (Spolsky, 2014) and two detailed studies of colonial language policies (Spolsky, 2018b, 2019c). Taking these data into account, I modified the model and added consideration of the individual (Spolsky, 2019b, 2019e). While many questions remain, I have found the ordering of the chapters in this book, starting with the individual and ending with the state or nation, to be much more useful in accounting for the difficulty of formulating a workable and equable language policy and of implementing it.

The difficulties of naming and counting

Learning a new discipline at school was a matter not just of adding concepts but at recognising new terminology.[3] Language policy has many terminological problems, starting with its name: I have earlier dealt with the polysemy of 'language' and the reason to prefer 'variety' and the ambiguity of 'policy' as either a field of study or as a plan or programme. Language practices may also be repertoires, or in older usage, landscape, thought that term is now preferred for urban public signage. The second component of my model is either beliefs (a looser term) or ideology (suggesting a more organised system supported by a movement). I still prefer 'management' to the common 'planning', but have to recognise that, for many, the field is 'LPP, Language Policy and Planning'.

A second level of confusion is in the distinction between various kinds of language: language, vernacular, topolect, dialect, pidgin, creole and the application of this classification to named varieties. Treating the mutually incomprehensible varieties of Chinese as dialects rather than topolects produces a huge language whose speakers cannot understand each other. Language names produce a number of problems: should Modern Israeli Hebrew have a different name to recognise its difference from Biblical or Mishnaic or Medieval varieties? And is Old English as much a kind of English as Texan English? Should we use native or foreigner names – French or *français*? And which version should we use for varieties with many names – Ladino or Judezmo or Spaniolit?

Even when we agree on a name, it is, as I noted earlier, far from simple to agree on numbers, whether of speakers or users. As a result, building a working model of the current state of language use, or of the beliefs and ideologies of users of a language, is far from easy and does not offer the possibility of straightforward prediction. If we could obtain accurate figures of these factors over time, which we usually approximate by age of proficient speakers, we could do better at determining what we blithely label language endangerment, the likelihood that the speakers of one language will shift to another. With the difficulties of collecting data, we have to depend on guesses and estimates that are often anonymous, as in the major lists such as *Ethnologue* (Eberhard et al., 2019) or Leclerc (1994–2018).

It is these many uncertainties that condemn those of us who study language policy to thinking and rethinking rather than counting and measuring and calculating and deciding. We are dealing with a dynamic and indefinite phenomenon, so that we may disagree honestly and rethink and continue to propose revised models and theories that help to add to our understanding of language policy and that enables the development of wise and effective management policies.

Notes

1. Chew (2014: 12) reminds me that I asked the 'should' question already in Spolsky (2009a).
2. For example, a big data analysis based on the language chosen on messages or phone calls would help to answer the question of language use more precisely.
3. I recall the problems we had with a science teacher who lisped: it took a long time to work out that what we heard as 'felthpar' was feldspar.

Appendix

Table A.1 EGIDS

Level	Label	Description	UNESCO
0	International	The language is used internationally for a broad range of functions.	Safe
1	National	The language is used in education, work, mass media, government at the nationwide level.	Safe
2	Regional	The language is used for local and regional mass media and governmental services.	Safe
3	Trade	The language is used for local and regional work by both insiders and outsiders.	Safe
4	Educational	Literacy in the language is being transmitted through a system of public education.	Safe
5	Written	The language is used orally by all generations and is effectively used in written form in parts of the community.	Safe
6a	Vigorous	The language is used orally by all generations and is being learned by children as their first language.	Safe
6b	Threatened	The language is used orally by all generations but only some of the child-bearing generation are transmitting it to their children.	Vulnerable
7	Shifting	The child-bearing generation knows the language well enough to use it among themselves but none are transmitting it to their children.	Definitely Endangered
8a	Moribund	The only remaining active speakers of the language are members of the grandparent generation.	Severely Endangered
8b	Nearly Extinct	The only remaining speakers of the language are members of the grandparent generation or older who have little opportunity to use the language.	Critically Endangered
9	Dormant	The language serves as a reminder of heritage identity for an ethnic community. No one has more than symbolic proficiency.	Extinct
10	Extinct	No one retains a sense of ethnic identity associated with the language, even for symbolic purposes.	Extinct

Endangered languages in five countries[1]

Table A.2 Some endangered languages of India

Language	EGIDS	State	Number of speakers	Use	Shift	Source?
Khamyang	8a	Assam	50 out of 800	Grandparents	Assamese	
Ralte	8a	Misoram	90 (1981) 170 (1961)	Old people	Miso	Yes[a]
Ruga	8a	Meghalaya	A few born before 1950	Old people	Garo	Yes[b]
Turi (caste)	8a	Chotanagpur	2,000 out of 350,000		Sadri and other local varieties	No
Allar	7	Kerala	350 hunter-gatherers		Malayalam	No
Atong	7	Meghala	4,600 Meghalaya; 5,400 Bangladesh	Impossible to estimate	Garo	Yes[c]
Eastern Baloch	7	Balochistan	800 out of 95,000; Pakistan 3,500,000	Mainly second language	Urdu	No
Bazigar (Goaar) (former nomadic performers)	7	Haryana and others	58,000 out of 800,000	Over 40	Hindi, Punjabi	Yes[d]
Bellari (caste)	7	Haryana	1000			No
Irula (tribe)	7	Tamilnadu and others	5,000 to 11,900 out of 200,000	All domains Nightly news	Badaga, Kannada and other local varieties	Yes[e]
Majhi	7	Jharkhand	11,000 out of 55,000; 25,000 in Nepal	Not home, religion	Nepali	No
Majhwar tribe	7	Chhattisgarh	34,000 out of 174,000	?	Chhattisgarhi	No
Rawat tribe	7	Uttarakhand	700	Poor, few	Kumaoni	No
Sansi (former criminal caste)	7	Haryana, Punjab and others	60,000	Home, not children	Hindi, Punjabi, Gujarati	No
Yakkha	7	Sikkim and West Bengal	800 out of 6,300; 19,000 in Nepal	Adults	Nepalese	No

Table A.2 *continued*

Language	EGIDS	State	Number of speakers	Use	Shift	Source?
Zakhring (tribe)	7	Arunachal Pradesh	300	Adults and children multilingual	Central Tibetan, Nefamese	No
Balti	6b	Jammu and Kashmir	13,800 out of 38,000	All adults and some children	Purik, Urdu	No
Bantawa	6b	Sikkom and West Bengal	14,400	Adults	Nepali	No
Godwari	6b	Gujurat	3,000,000	Adults and children; most domains	Hindi (educated)	No
Kachari (tribe)	6b	Assam	16,000	Second language	Assamese	No
Koraga (Korra)	6b	Karnataka	14,000	Adults and some children	Tulu	No
Kumbaran	6b	Kerala	10,000	Adults and some children	Malayalam	No
Newar	6b	Pradesh	14,000	Home, religion (especially Buddhist)	Central Tibetan, English, Hindi	No
Andh (tribe)	6b*	Madhya Pradesh and Telangana	100,000 out of 420,000		Marathi	No
Apatani	6b*	Arunachal Pradesh	44,000	Some villages	Assamese, Hindi	Yes[f]
Brokstat	6b*	Jammu and Kashmir	10,000		Ladakh	No
Dekharu (caste)	6b*	Jharkhand and West Bengal	10,000?	?		Yes[g]
Dubli	6b*	Gujarat and others	250,000 out of 791,000		Gurjurati	No
Groma	6b*	Sikkim	14,000		Tibetan?	No
Gurung	6b*	Sikkim	33,000	All use Nepali	Gurkhas	No
Kanauji	6b*	Uttar Kadesh	9,500,000	Adults	Hindi and upper class English	Yes[h]
Kodaku	6b*	Kamataka	15,000	Home, children	Hindi	No
Kui	6b*	Odisha	600,000 to 900,000	Bilingual programmes	Oriya	Yes[i]
Kurichiya tribe	6b*	Kerala	29,000	High caste?	Malayalam	No
Lepcha	6b*	Sikkim	43,000	Adults and children	Taught in primary school	No
Lyngngam	6b*	Assam and others	11,600		Assamese	No

Table A.2 *continued*

Language	EGIDS	State	Number of speakers	Use	Shift	Source?
Eastern Magar	6b*	Sikkim	70,000 out of 280,000	Migrants from Nepal	Nepalese	No
Mahali tribe	6b*	West Bengal and Odisha	26,000 out of 260,000	Home	Local languages	No
Mal Paharia	6b*	Jharkhand and West Bengal	Half of 100,000 ethnic and not linguistic	Cultural adaptation	Bengali, Hindi, Santali	Yes[j]
Malavedan, poor tribe	6b*	Kerala and Tamil Nadu	12,000	Home?	Malayalam	No
Pardhan	6b*	Andhra Pradesh and others	135,000		Hindi and local	No
Parsi	6b*	Gujurat and others	11,600	Religious	Gujarati, English and others	No
Northern Pashto	6b*	Many states	21,700		Urdu	No
Pattani	6b*	Himachal Pradesh	20,000	Home	English, Hindi	No
Powari (Rajput clan)	6b*	Himachal Pradesh and Maharashtra	2,000,000	Quarter use it at home, half children use it	Hindi, Marathi	No
Reli (scheduled caste)	6b*	Andhra Pradesh and Odisha	13,000	Home and internal	Telegu with outsiders	No
Sherpa	6b*	Sikkim and West Bengal	13,000	Villagers, some children	Nepali and others	No
Tinani	6b*	Himachal Pradesh	11,600	Home, village	Hindi, Pattani	No

Notes

a Mehrotra (1999).
b Burling (2003).
c Van Breugel (2014).
d Deb et al. (1987).
e Das (2013).

f Kala (2005).
g Hammarström (2015)
h Dwivedi and Kar (2016).
i Mohanty (1990).
j Manna and Ghosh (2015).

Table A.3 Some endangered languages of Vanuatu

Language	EGIDS	Number of speakers	Use	Shift	Source?
Whitesands	7	7,500	Children still speak it at home	Bislama	Yes[a]
Aulua	6a	750	Most domains; adults and children; Church support	Bislama, English, French	Yes[b]
Avava	6a	400	Most domains; adults and children	Bislama	Yes[c]
Dorig	6a	200	Most domains	Lakon and Tume (3 generations)	Yes[d]
Eton	6a	500	Adults and children	Bislama and others	No
Hiw	6a	150	Adults and children	Bislama (emigration)	No
Koro	6a	160	Adults and children; most domains	Dorig (high degree of multilingualism)	Yes[e]
Lelepa	6a	400	Adults and children	Bislama, English and other local varieties	Yes[f]
Löyöp	6a	250	Adults and children; most domains	Vatrata; population moved in 1958, but survived	Yes[g]
Mwotlap	6a	1,800+	Adults and children	Bislama	No
Port Vato (Daakie)	6a	1,300	Adults and children, and taught in primary school	Bislama	No
Sa	6a	4,000	Adults and children, and taught in primary school	4 dialects, penis wrappers; Bislama	Yes[h]
Sakao	6a	2,000	Home, adults and children	Bislama, Tolomako	Yes[i]
Unua	6a	1,000	Home, adults and children	Bislama for church	Yes[j]
Central Maewo	6b	1,400	Adults, some young people	Bislama	No
Neverver	6b	1,250	Adults, some young people	Bislama	No
Ninde, Labo	6b	1,100	Adults, some young people		

Notes

a Hammond (2009).
b Crowley (2000).
c Crowley and Lynch (2006).
d François (2011).
e François (2011).

f François et al. (2015).
g François et al. (2015).
h Cheer et al. (2013).
i Guy (1974).
j Pearce (2015).

Table A.4 Selected endangered indigenous languages of Brazil

Language	EGIDS	Number of speakers	Use	Shift	Source?
Guajajara (also Tenetehára)	4	14,000 out of 20,000 in 11 indigenous lands	Adults and children in villages, but unknown in cities	Portuguese as lingua franca	No
Hixkaryána	4	600	Adults and children; school and literature	Portuguese	No
Jamamadí	4 (other sources say endangered)	1,000	Adults and children; people want a school	Portuguese	No
Xavánte	4	19,000 (7,000 monolinguals)	Adults and children; all domains, school	Portuguese	No
Kayapó	5	7,000 in 20+ communities	Adults and children; all domains, initial education	Some use Portuguese	Yes[a]
Maxakalí	5	1,270	Young population, 30% literate in L1	Some use Portuguese	No
Araweté	6a	340	Mainly monolingual, discovered 1970	Some under 20 use Portuguese	Yes[b]
Asurini do Xingu	6a	120	Over 40; adults support school teaching	Under-14 year olds	Yes[c]
Dâw	6a	120	Adults and children; school teaches Dâw literacy	Old also use Nheengatu; young use Portuguese	Yes[d]
Himarimã	6a	40? 1,000?	Adults and children	Uncontacted	No
Kadiwéu	6a	1,590	Adults and children	Some Portuguese	No
Karo (Arara Tupi)	6a	200	Adults and children, in 2 villages	Portuguese for contact	Yes[e]
Maquiritari	6a	430 (also 6,000 in Venezuela)	Adults and children		No
Mehináku	6a	200	Adults and children		Yes[f]
Ninam	6a	470	Adults and children	Some (especially children) use Portuguese	No
Suruahá Zuruahá	6a	140	Adults and children	Isolated	Yes[g]

Table A.4 *continued*

Language	EGIDS	Number of speakers	Use	Shift	Source?
Suruí	6a	250–1,000	Adults and children	Some use Portuguese	No
Uru-Eu-Wau-Wau	6a	87–183	Adults and children	Little contact	No
Waimiri-Atroarí	6a	1,000–2,000	Adults and children	20% of males use Portuguese for contact	No
Yanomami	6a	4,000–6,000	Adults and children	May be endangered	Yes[h]
Zo'é	6a	180	Adults and children	Contact recent; monolingual in 1997	No
Aikanã	6b	150/200 (relocated)	Adults	Some children use Portuguese	Yes[i]
Awetí	6b	170 (relocated)	Adults, some children	Kamayurá; also Portuguese	Yes[j]
Borôro	6b	1,390	Adults, some children	Children use Portuguese	Yes[k]
Jabutí (Djeoromitxí)	6b	5–50/170	Adults, some children	Portuguese	Yes[l]
Mamaindê	6b	300	Adults, some children	Shift in 1 of 4 villages	Yes[m]
Iatê	7	1,000/2,300	Adults	Adults bilingual, children use Portuguese	Yes[n]
Ingarikó	7	1,000 in Brazil (same as Guyana)	Adults and children (good transmission)	Some children use Portuguese	No
Nhengatu	7	3,000–10,000	Elderly in some areas; adults but not children	Tukano; was lingua franca under Jesuits; many use Portuguese	Yes[o]
Terêna	7	16,000/20,000	Adults; taught in school	Portuguese	Yes[p]
Wapishana	7	4,000/7,000 in Brazil, 6,000 in Guyana	Some children	Portuguese	No

Notes

a Zanotti (2016).
b De Castro (1992).
c Pereira (2009).
d Martins (2004).
e Gabas (1999).
f Gregor (2009).
g Feitosa et al. (2010).
h Borofsky and Albert (2005).

i Anonby (2009).
j Drude (2011).
k Crocker and Maybury-Lewis (1985).
l Van der Voort (2007).
m Eberhard (2009).
n Ribeiro (2009).
o Moore et al. (1994).
p Ferreira (2010).

Table A.5 Some endangered languages of Nigeria

Language	EGIDS	Number of speakers	Use	Shift	Source?
English	1				
Hausa	2				
Yoruba	2				
Igbo	2				
Bura-Pabir	6b over 10,000	250,000	Adults, some children	English	No
Duguri	6b	65,000	Adults, some children	Hausa	No
Dza	6b	100,000	Adults, some young people	Also use Hausa, Nigerian Pidgin	No
Nzanyi	6b	77,000	Adults, some children	Schools, Fufulde	No
Olulumo-Ikom	6b	30,000	Adults, some children	Also use Nigerian Pidgin, Ejagham	No
Tangale	6b	200,000	Adults, some children	Young men and Muslims use Hausa	No
Ake	6a under 6,000	2,000–3,000	Adults and children	Shift to Hausa noticed	No
Bali	6a	2,000 (SIL) –100,000	Adults and children	Also Bacama, Hausa, Pidgin	No
Cakfem-Mushere	6a	5,000	Adults and children	Also Hausa, Piin	No
Horom	6a	1,500	Adults and children	Remote; surprisingly vigorous	Yes[a]
Iceve-Maci	6a	5,000 in Nigeria; also Cameroon	Home, village; adults and children	Pidgin	No
Iko	6a	5,000	Adults and children	Also Ibibio	No
Kpasham	6a	3,000	Adults and children; village primary schools, one junior secondary	Also Bacama, Hausa, Fufulde	No
Mvanip	6a	100	Adults and children	Fulfulde	Yes[b]
Ndunda	6a	300	Adults and children	Fulfulde, Mambila and Ndoro	Yes[c]
Nnam	6a	3,000	Adults and children	Pidgin; English in schools	No
Pe	6a	4,000	Adults and children		No
Rogo	6a	?	Adults and children	?	No
Vori	6a	3,000	Adults and children		No
Yotti	6a	3,000	Adults and children	Mumuye	No

Notes

a Blench (1998).
b Blench (2012).
c Blench and Dendo (2003).

Table A.6 Russian minority languages

Language	EGIDS	Number of speakers	Use	Shift	Sources?
Avar	3	715,000	Dagestan provincially recognised; language of wider communication; primary and secondary education	Russian	Yes[a]
Akhvakh	6b	200/8,000 (or more)	Some children as well as adults	Avar for literature and newspapers, Russian for education	No
Northern Altai	6b	57,000/74,000	Home, community, few children	Russian, but high vitality	Yes[b]
Andi	6b	5,800/40,000	Some children	Russian	No
Archi	6b	970/2,000	Urbanisation, few children	Russian, Avar	Yes[c]
Botlikh	6b	210/7,000	Some children, few domains	Russian, Avar	No
Chamalal	6b	500/2,000	Some young children	Russian, Avar	No
Chukchi	6b	5,100/15,900	Reindeer herders, few children	Even and Yakut, nomad resist Russian	No
Chuvash	6b	1,243,000/1,440,000	Provincial language	Few young people, shifting to Russian	Yes[d]
Dido	6b	12,500/20,000	Stronger in highlands, 50% of children	Primary school, Russian	No
Dolgan	6b	1,050/20,000	Home domain, adults over age 30, some children	Russian	Yes[e]
Evenki	6b	4,800/38,400	Adults, few children	Unsuccessful school teaching, Russian	Yes[f]
Hinukh	6b	5/600	Few children	Dido, Russian	No
Hunzib	6b	1,000/2,000	Few children	Avar and Russian in school	No
Karelian	6b	25,600/60,800	Children learn but shift	Russian	Yes[g]
Khanty	6b	9,580/30,900	Some children but shift later	Tatar and Russian	Yes[h]
Khvarshi	6b	1,740/4,000	Some children	Avar, Russian	No
Komi-Permyak	6b	63,100/94,500	Some children in some villages	Russian	No

Language	EGIDS	Number of speakers	Use	Shift	Sources?
Komi-Zyrian	6b	156,000/228,000	Provincial language; learnt by some children	Nenets, Russian	No
Koryak	6b	1,670/7,950	Few domains, primary school, some children	Russian; catastrophic decline	No
Mansi	6b	940/12,300	Very few children	Russian as school language	No
Hill Mari	6b	30,000	Very few children	Meadow Mari in school, Russian	Yes[i]
Moksha	6b	2,030/4,770	Some children speak with elderly	Russian	No
Nenets	6b	21,900/44,600	In Siberia, young people fluent	Russian	No
Nganasan	6b	130/860	Some semi-nomads	Russian	No
Tat. Muslim	6b	2010	Provincial language	Azerbaijani, Russian	No
Tindi	6b	2,150/10,000	Few children	Avar and Russian	No
Udmurt	6b	324,000/554,000	Some young children	Russian	No
Veps	6b	1,640/5,940	Efforts at revival	Russian	Yes[j]
Baglaval	6b*	1,450/4,000			
Judeo-Tat	6b*	2,000/10,000			
Karata	6b*	260/6,400			
Romani	6b*	128,000/205,000			
Even	7 (shifting)	5,660/21,800			
Ghodoberi	7	130/3,000			
Ludian	7	3000			
Shor	7	2,840/12,900	50 monolingual		
Yiddish	7	200/1,680			
Yupik	7	200/1,200			

Notes

a Mustafina et al. (2014).
b Yagmur and Kroon (2006).
c Chumakina (2009).
d i Font (2014).
e Krivonogov (2013).

f Mamontova (2014).
g Pyoli (1998).
h Jordan (2003).
i Morova et al. (2015).
j Siragusa (2015).

Note

1. These tables present data selected from the online edition of *Ethnologue* (Eberhard et al., 2019). In each case, I have used the first name for the variety, though there are others. I have added notes of any published reports that deal with the status of the variety. In other cases, I rely on the *Ethnologue* reports based on their usually anonymous experts, often SIL linguists.

References

Abela, A. and Walker, J. (eds) (2014). *Contemporary Issues in Family Studies: Global Perspectives on Partnerships, Parenting and Support in a Changing World*. Malden, MA and Oxford: Wiley Blackwell.

Adams, J. N. (2003). *Bilingualism and the Latin language*. Cambridge: Cambridge University Press.

Adegbija, E. (2001). Saving threatened languages in Africa: a case study of Oko. In J. A. Fishman (ed.), *Can Threatened Languages Be Saved?* (pp. 284–308). Clevedon, Avon: Multilingual Matters Ltd.

Adkins, M. (2013). Will the real Breton please stand up? Language revitalization and the problem of authentic language. *International Journal of the Sociology of Language, 2013*(223), 55–70.

Ager, D. E. (1996). *Language Policy in Britain and France: The Processes of Policy*. London and New York: Cassell.

Ager, D. E. (1999). *Identity, Insecurity and Image: France and Language*. Clevedon, Philadelphia and Adelaide: Multilingual Matters Ltd.

Ager, D. E. (2001). *Motivation in Language Planning and Language Policy*. Clevedon and Buffalo, NY: Multilingual Matters Ltd.

Agnihotri, R. K. and Sachdeva, R. (eds) (2021). *Being and Becoming a Multilingual*. Hyderabad: Orient BlackSwan.

Ahmed, S. (2008). Censorship. In E. W. Rothenbuhler, K. Jensen, J. Pooley and R. T. Craig (eds), *The International Encyclopedia of Communication*. Hoboken, NJ: John Wiley and Sons.

Ahmed, S. M. O. (2012). *Aspects of Bilingualism in a Mauritanian Context*. Masters thesis, Aboubekr Belkaid University, Tlemcen, Algeria.

Akçam, T. (2013). *The Young Turks' Crime against Humanity: The Armenian Genocide and Ethnic Cleansing in the Ottoman Empire* (Vol. 17). Princeton: Princeton University Press.

Alidou, H., Boly, A., Brock-Utne, B., Diallo, Y. S., Heugh, K. and Wolff, H. E. (2006). Optimizing learning and education in Africa – the language factor, <https://www.heart-resources.org/doc_lib/optimizing-learning-and-education-in-africa-the-language-factor/> (last accessed 2 October 2020).

Alisjahbana, S. T. (1974). Language policy, language engineering and literacy in Indonesia and Malaysia. In J. A. Fishman (ed.), *Advances in Language Planning* (pp. 391–416). Berlin: Walter de Gruyter.

Alt, J.-C. (2013). L'esclavage en Mauritanie. Enquête menée par Amnesty International. *ILCEA. Revue de l'Institut des langues et cultures d'Europe, Amérique, Afrique, Asie et Australie* (17), <http://ilcea.revues.org/1735> (last accessed 23 September 2020).

Ammon, U. (ed.) (2001). *The Dominance of English as a Language of Science: Effects on Other Languages and Language Communities.* Berlin and New York: Mouton de Gruyter.

Ammon, U. (2012). Language policy in the European Union (EU). In B. Spolsky (ed.), *Handbook of Language Policy* (pp. 570–91). Cambridge: Cambridge University Press.

Amos, H. W. (2017). Regional language vitality in the linguistic landscape: hidden hierarchies on street signs in Toulouse. *International Journal of Multilingualism, 14*(2), 93–108.

Andall, J. and Duncan, D. (2005). *Italian Colonialism: Legacy and Memory.* Bern: Peter Lang.

Anderson, C. (2004, October). The Long Tail. *Wired.*

Aneesh, A. (2012). Negotiating globalization: men and women of India's call centers. *Journal of Social Issues, 68*(3), 514–33.

Angelelli, C. V. (2004). *Medical Interpreting and Cross-Cultural Communication.* Cambridge: Cambridge University Press.

Anonby, S. (2009). Language Use on the Tubarão-Latundê Reserve, Rondônia, Brazil. Electronic Survey Report.

Anonymous. (2019). Beware of the Borg, 21 December, *The Economist, 433*(9174), 59–64.

Antonini, R. (2002). Irish language used in the community and family domains in two Gaeltacht areas: a comparative analysis. *Durham Working Papers in Linguistics, 8,* 1–12.

Applebaum, A. (2017). *Red Famine: Stalin's War on Ukraine.* New York: Doubleday.

Appleyard, D. and Orwin, M. (2008). The Horn of Africa: Ethiopia, Eritrea, Djibouti and Somalia. In A. Simpson (ed.), *Language and National Identity in Africa* (pp. 267–90). Oxford: Oxford University Press.

Arfé, G. (1981). *On a community charter of regional languages and cultures and on a charter of rights of ethnic minorities.* European Parliament: Strasbourg

Arviso, M. and Holm, W. (2001). Tsehootsooidi Olta'gi Dine Bizaad Bihoo'aah: a Navajo immersion program at Fort Defiance, Arizona. In L. Hinton and K. Hale (eds), *The Green Book of Language Revitalization in Practice* (pp. 203–15). New York: Academic Press.

Arzoz, X. (2007). The nature of language rights. *JEMIE Journal on Ethnopolitics and Minority Issues in Europe, 6,* 1–35.

Aspinall, A. (1946). The circulation of newspapers in the early nineteenth century. *The Review of English Studies, 22*(85), 29–43.

Associated Press News. (2019). Census: Louisiana remains 1 of nation's poorest states, 27 September, <https://apnews.com/article/1068e41cc2374eb9a3457b807de011f0> (last accessed 12 October 2020).

Aunger, E. A. (1993). Regional, national and official languages in Belgium. *International Journal of the Sociology of Language, 104,* 31–48.

Austin, P. K. (2013). Language documentation and meta-documentation. In M. C.

Jones and S. Ogilvie (eds), *Keeping Languages Alive: Documentation, Pedagogy and Revitalization* (pp. 3–15). Cambridge: Cambridge University Press.

Austin, P. K. and Sallabank, J. (eds) (2011). *The Cambridge Handbook of Endangered Languages*. Cambridge: Cambridge University Press.

Austin, P. K. and Sallabank, J. (eds) (2014). *Endangered Languages. Beliefs and Ideologies in Language Documentation and Revitalisation*. Oxford: Oxford University Press for the British Academy.

Avineri, N. R. (2012). *Heritage language socialization practices in secular Yiddish educational contexts: The creation of a metalinguistic community*. PhD, UCLA.

Azam, M., Chin, A. and Prakash, N. (2013). The returns to English-language skills in India. *Economic Development and Cultural Change, 61*(2), 335–67.

Backhaus, P. (2005). Signs of multilingualism in Tokyo – a diachronic look at the linguistic landscape. *International Journal of the Sociology of Language, 175/176*, 103–21.

Backhaus, P. (2006). Multilingualism in Tokyo – a look into the linguistic landscape. *International Journal of Multilingualism, 3*(1), 52–66.

Backhaus, P. (2007). *Linguistic Landscapes: A Comparative Study of Urban Multilingualism in Tokyo*. Clevedon: Multilingual Matters Ltd.

Bae, S. H. (2013). The pursuit of multilingualism in transnational educational migration: strategies of linguistic investment among Korean jogi yuhak families in Singapore. *Language and Education, 27*(5), 415–31.

Bahalwan, Y. (2015). The acquisition of English as a second language by mixed-marriage children in Sydney. *Language Horizon, 3*(1), 117–24.

Bailey, B. (1997). Communication of respect in interethnic service encounters. *Language in Society, 26*(3), 327–56.

Bailey, M. J. H. and Cooper, B. S. (2009). The introduction of religious charter schools: a cultural movement in the private school sector. *Journal of Research on Christian Education, 18*(3), 272–89.

Baldauf Jr, R. B. and Nguyen, H. T. M. (2012). Language policy in Asia and the Pacific. In B. Spolsky (ed.), *The Cambridge Handbook of Language Policy* (pp. 617–38). Cambridge: Cambridge University Press.

Ball, S. J. (2012). *Politics and Policy Making in Education: Explorations in Sociology*. London: Routledge.

Bamgbose, A. (2004). *Language of Instruction Policy and Practice in Africa*. Dakar: Regional Office for Education in Africa, UNESCO.

Banda, F. and Mwanza, D. S. (2017). Language-in-education policy and linguistic diversity in Zambia: an alternative explanation to low reading levels among primary school pupils. In M. K. Banja (ed.), *Selected Readings in Education* (pp. 109–32). Lusaka: University of Zambia Press.

Barron-Hauwaert, S. (2004). *Language Strategies for Bilingual Families: The One-Parent-One-Language Approach*. Clevedon: Multilingual Matters.

Bartsch, R. (1987). *Norms of Language: Theoretical and Practical Aspects*. London and New York: Longman.

Basso, K. H. and Anderson, N. (1977). A Western Apache writing system: the symbols of Silas John. In J. A. Fishman (ed.), *Advances in the Creation and Revision Of Writing Systems* (pp. 77–104). The Hague and Paris: Mouton.

Bauman, R. and Briggs, C. L. (2003). *Voices of Modernity–Language Ideologies and the Politics of Inequality*. Santa Fe: School of American Research Press.

Becker, K. and Newlin-Lukowicz, L. (2018). The myth of the New York City Borough accent: Evidence from perception. *University of Pennsylvania Working Papers in Linguistics, 24*(2), 9–17.

Belich, J. (1986). *The New Zealand Wars*. Auckland: Auckland University Press.

Bell, A. (1984). Language style as audience design. *Language in Society, 13*(2), 145–204.

Ben-Rafael, E., Shohamy, E., Amara, M. H. and Trumper-Hecht, N. (2006). Linguistic landscape as symbolic construction of the public space: the case of Israel. *International Journal of Multilingualism, 3*(1), 7–30.

Benally, A. and Viri, D. (2005). Diné Bizaad [Navajo language] at a crossroads: extinction or renewal? *Bilingual Research Journal, 29*(1), 85–108.

Beniamino, M. (1996). *Le français de la Réunion Inventaire des particularités lexicales*. Malakoff, France: Edicef.

Benmaman, V. (1992). Legal interpreting as an emerging profession. *Modern Language Journal, 76*(10), 445–9.

Benor, S. B. (2010). Ethnolinguistic repertoire: shifting the analytic focus in language and ethnicity. *Journal of Sociolinguistics, 14*(2), 159–83.

Benor, S. B., Krasner, J. and Avni, S. (2020). *Hebrew Infusion: Language and Community at American Jewish Summer Camps*. New Brunswick, NJ: Rutgers University Press.

Benrabah, M. (2004). Language and politics in Algeria. *Nationalism and Ethnic Politics, 10*, 59–78.

Benrabah, M. (2013). *Language Conflict in Algeria: From Colonialism to Post-Independence*. Bristol, Buffalo and Toronto: Multilingual Matters.

Benson, C. (2000). The primary bilingual education experiment in Mozambique, 1993 to 1997. *International Journal of Bilingual Education and Bilingualism, 3*(3), 149–66.

Benton, R. A. (1997). *The Maori language: Dying or reviving*. Wellington: New Zealand Council for Educational Research.

Benton, R. A. and Smith, L. (1982). *Survey of language use in Maori households and communities: A report to participants in the initial investigation 1973–1978*. Wellington: New Zealand Council for Educational Research.

Berman, P. (ed.) (2011). *Debating PC: The controversy over Political Correctness on College Campuses*. New York: Delta.

Bernier, S. and Pariseau, J. (1994). *French Canadians and Bilingualism in the Canadian Armed Forces* (Vol. II: Official languages). Ottawa: Ministry of Supply and Services.

Bhat, C. and Bhaskar, T. (2007). Contextualising diasporic identity. In G. Oonk (ed.), *Global Indian Diasporas* (pp. 89–118). Amsterdam: Amsterdam University Press.

Bhuiyan, A. A. M. (2017). Indigenous languages in Bangladesh: loopholes behind the scene. *Indigenous Policy Journal, 27*(3), 1–16.

Bingbing, J., Jianhua, S. and Yijia, W. (2015). A survey of the language use in the migrant schools in Shanghai. In Y. Li and W. Li (eds), *The Language Situation in China* (Vol. 2, pp. 120–36). Berlin and Beijing: De Gruyter Mouton and Commercial Press.

Blanc, H. (1964). *Communal Dialects in Baghdad*. Cambridge, MA: Harvard University Press.

Blench, R. (1998). Recent fieldwork in Nigeria: report on Horom and Tapshin. *Ogmios: Newsletter of the Foundation for Endangered Languages, 9*, 10–11.

Blench, R. (2012). *An Atlas of Nigerian Languages*. Jos, Nigeria: Kay Williamson Educational Foundation.

Blench, R. and Dendo, M. (2003). *Language death in West Africa*. Paper presented at the Round Table session on Language and Endangerment, Bad Godesborg.

Block, D. (2018). *Political Economy and Sociolinguistics: Neoliberalism, Inequality and Social Class*. London: Bloomsbury Publishing.

Blommaert, J. (2013). *Ethnography, Superdiversity and Linguistic Landscapes: Chronicles of Complexity*. Bristol: Multilingual Matters.

Bogoch, B. (1999). Gender, literacy and religiosity: dimensions of Yiddish education in Israeli government-supported schools. *International Journal of the Sociology of Language, 138*, 123–60.

Bokamba, E. G. (1991). French colonial language policies in Africa and their legacies. In D. F. Marshall (ed.), *Language Planning* (Vol. III of Focusschrift in honor of Joshua A. Fishman on the occasion of his 65th birthday, pp. 175–214). Amsterdam and Philadelphia: John Benjamins Publishing Company.

Bokamba, E. G. (2008). DR Congo: language and 'authentic nationalism'. In A. Simpson (ed.), *Language and National Identity in Africa* (pp. 214–34). Oxford: Oxford University Press.

Bordia, S. and Bordia, P. (2015). Employees' willingness to adopt a foreign functional language in multilingual organizations: the role of linguistic identity. *Journal of International Business Studies, 46*(4), 415–28.

Borofsky, R. and Albert, B. (2005). *Yanomami: The Fierce Controversy and What We Can Learn From It*. Berkeley: University of California Press.

Botticini, M. and Eckstein, Z. (2012). *The Chosen Few: How Education Shaped Jewish History*. Princeton: Princeton University Press.

Boulet, J. R., Zanten, M. V., McKinley, D. W. and Gary, N. E. (2001). Evaluating the spoken English proficiency of graduates of foreign medical schools. *Medical Education, 35*(8), 767–73.

Bourhis, R. Y. (1984). Cross-cultural communication in Montreal: two field studies since Bill 101. *International Journal of the Sociology of Language, 46*, 33–48.

Bourhis, R. Y. and Sioufi, R. (2017). Assessing forty years of language planning on the vitality of the Francophone and Anglophone communities of Quebec. *Multilingua, 36*(5), 627–61.

Bowe, R., Ball, S. J. and Gold, A. (2017). *Reforming Education and Changing Schools: Case Studies in Policy Sociology*. London: Routledge.

Bradley, D. and Bradley, M. (2019). *Language Endangerment*. Cambridge: Cambridge University Press.

Brann, C. M. B. (1994). The national language question: concepts and terminologies. *L'ogos 14*.

Brecht, R. D. and Rivers, W. P. (2000). *Language and National Security in the 21st Century: The Role of the Title VI/Fulbright-Hays in Supporting National Language Capacity*. Dubuque, IA: Kendall-Hunt Publishing Company.

Brecht, R. D. and Rivers, W. P. (2005). Language needs analysis at the societal level. In M. Long (ed.), *Second Language Needs Analysis*. Cambridge: Cambridge University Press.

Brecht, R. D. and Rivers, W. P. (2012). US language policy in defence and attack. In B. Spolsky (ed.), *The Cambridge Handbook of Language Policy* (pp. 262–77). Cambridge: Cambridge University Press.

Brecht, R. D. and Walton, A. R. (1994). National strategic planning and less commonly taught languages. *The Annals of the American Academy of Political and Social Science, 532*, 190–212.

Brendemoen, B. (1998). The Turkish language reform. In L. Johanson and É. Á. C. Johanson (eds), *The Turkic Languages* (1st edn). Abingdon: Routledge.

Brendemoen, B. (2015). The Turkish language reform. In L. Johanson and É. Á. C. Johanson (eds), *The Turkic Languages* (2nd edn). Abingdon: Routledge.

Browne, M. H. (2005). *Wairua and the Relationship It Has with Learning te reo Maori within te Ataarangi.* Master of Educational Administration thesis, Massey University, New Zealand.

Bruthiaux, P. (2008). Language education, economic development, and participation in the Greater Mekong Subregion. *International Journal of Bilingual Education and Bilingualism, 11*(2), 134–48.

Bührig, K. and Meyer, B. (2004). Ad-hoc-interpreting and the achievement of communicative purposes in doctor-patient-communication. *Multilingual Communication, 3*, 43–62.

Bumpass, L. L. and Sweet, J. A. (1989). National estimates of cohabitation. *Demography, 26*(4), 615–25. doi:10.2307/2061261

Burhanudeen, H. (2003). Factors influencing the language choices of Malay Malaysians in the family, friendship and market domains. *Journal of Language and Linguistics, 2*(2), 224–45.

Burling, R. (2003). *The Language of the Modhupur Mandi, Garo: Vol. I: Grammar.* Ann Arbor: The Scholarly Publishing Office, University of Michigan.

Byram, M. (2018). Language education in and for a multilingual Europe. In A. Bonnet and P. Siemund (eds), *Foreign Language Education in Multilingual Classrooms* (Vol. 7, pp. 33–56). Philadelphia and Amsterdam: John Benjamins Publishing Company.

Cadora, F. I. (1970). Some linguistic concomitants of urbanization. *Anthropological Linguistics, 12*(1), 10–19.

Caldas, S. J. (2006). *Raising Bilingual-Biliterate Children in Monolingual Cultures.* Clevedon, Buffalo and Toronto: Multilingual Matters Ltd.

Caldas, S. J. (2008). Changing bilingual self-perceptions from early adolescence to early adulthood: empirical evidence from a mixed-methods case study. *Applied Linguistics, 29*(2), 290–311.

Caldas, S. J. (2012). Language policy in the family. In B. Spolsky (ed.), *Handbook of Language Policy* (pp. 351–73). Cambridge: Cambridge University Press.

Caldas, S. J. and Caron-Caldas, S. (2000). The influence of family, school, and community on bilingual preference: results from a Louisiana/Quebec case study. *Applied Psycholinguistics, 21*(3), 365–81.

Caldas, S. J. and Caron-Caldas, S. (2002). A sociolinguistic analysis of the language preferences of adolescent bilinguals: shifting allegiances and developing identities. *Applied Linguistics, 23*(4), 490–514.

Cameron, D. (2000). Styling the worker: gender and the commodification of language in the globalized service economy. *Journal of Sociolinguistics, 4*(3), 323–47.

Capotorti, F. (1979). *Study on the Rights of Persons Belonging to Ethnic, Religious and Linguistic Minorities.* New York: United Nations.

Cardozier, V. R. (1993). *Colleges and Universities in World War II.* Westport, CT: Praeger.

Carrière, J.-M. (1941). The phonology of Missouri French: a historical study. *French Review*, 410–15.

Castell, J. M. I. (1993). The First International Catalan Language Congress, Barcelona, 13–18 October, 1906. In J. A. Fishman (ed.), *The Earliest Stage of Language Planning: 'The First Congress' Phenomenon* (pp. 47–68). Berlin: Mouton

Central Intelligence Agency. (2017). *The World Factbook.* Washington, DC: Central Intelligence Agency.

Cerqueglini, L. (2018). *Intergenerational transmission of traditional Arabic dialects in Israel.* Paper presented at the Fourth Intergenerational Transmission of Minority Languages Symposium: Language and Identity.

Chabal, P. and Birmingham, D. (2002). *A History of Postcolonial Lusophone Africa.* Bloomington: Indiana University Press.

Chang, T., Rasyid, Y. and Boeriswati, E. (2018). Similarities and differences of honorific systems between Indonesian and Korean languages (Perbedaan dan Persamaan Honorifik Bahasa Indonesia dan Korea). *Indonesian Language Education and Literature, 3*(2), 212–26.

Charlemagne. (2020). Huntington's disease. *The Economist, 434(9175)*, 20.

Cheer, J. M., Reeves, K. J. and Laing, J. H. (2013). Tourism and traditional culture: land diving in Vanuatu. *Annals of Tourism Research, 43*, 435–55.

Chen, I.-C. (2020). *Government Internet Censorship Measures and International Law* (Vol. 26). Cologne: LIT Verlag Münster.

Cheng, K. K. Y. (2003). Language shift and language maintenance in mixed families: a case study of a Malaysian-Chinese family. *International Journal of the Sociology of Language, 161*, 81–90.

Chew, P. G.-L. (2006). Language use and religious practice: the case of Singapore. In T. Omoniyi and J. A. Fishman (eds), *The Sociology of Language and Religion: Change, Conflict and Accommodation* (pp. 213–34). Basingstoke: Palgrave Macmillan.

Chew, P. G.-L. (2014). From multilingualism to monolingualism. Linguistic management in Singapore. In K. Sung and B. Spolsky (eds), *Conditions for English Language Teaching and Learning in Asia* (pp. 1–16). Newcastle upon Tyne: Cambridge Scholars Publishing.

Chiswick, B. R. (ed.) (1992). *Immigration, Language and Ethnicity: Canada and the United States.* Washington, DC: American Enterprise Institute.

Chiswick, B. R. (1994). Language and earnings among immigrants in Canada: a survey. In S. Zerker (ed.), *Essays in Canadian Social Science* (pp. 247–64). Jerusalem: Magnes Press.

Chiswick, B. R. and Miller, P. W. (1992). Language in the immigrant labor market. In B. R. Chiswick (ed.), *Immigration, Language and Ethnicity: Canada and the United States* (pp. 471–6). Washington, DC: American Enterprise Institute.

Chiswick, B. R. and Miller, P. W. (2002). Immigrant earnings: language skills, linguistic concentrations and the business cycle. *Journal of Population Economics, 15*(1), 31–57.

Chiswick, B. R. and Repetto, G. (2000). *Immigrant Adjustment in Israel: Literacy and Fluency in Hebrew and Earnings*. Bonn: Institute for the Study of Labor.

Chumakina, M. (2009). Loanwords in Archi, a Nakh-Daghestanian language of the North Caucasus. In M. Haspelmath, U. Tadmor (eds), *Loanwords in the World's Languages. A Comparative Handbook* (pp. 430–43). The Hague: De Gruyter Mouton.

Coates, J. (2005). *Women, Men and Language: A Sociolinguistic Account of Gender Differences in Language* (3rd edn). Harlow, UK: Longman.

Cobarrubias, J. (1983). Ethical issues in language planning. In J. Cobarrubias and J. A. Fishman (eds), *Progress in Language Planning: International Perspectives* (pp. 41–85). The Hague: Mouton.

Cohen, S., Moran-Ellis, J. and Smaje, C. (1999). Children as informal interpreters in GP consultations: pragmatics and ideology. *Sociology of Health and Illness, 21*(2), 163–86.

Colenso, W. (1872). *Willie's first English book, written for young Maoris who can read their own Maori tongue, and who wish to learn the English language*. Wellington: G. Didsbury, Government Printer.

Coles, F. A. (1993). Language maintenance institutions of the Isleiio dialect of Spanish. *Spanish in the United States: Linguistic Contact and Diversity, 6,* 121–33.

Collier, V. P. and Thomas, W. P. (2004). The astounding effectiveness of dual language education for all. *NABE Journal of Research and Practice, 2*(1), 1–20.

Commins, P. (1988). Socioeconomic development and language maintenance in the Gaeltacht. *International Journal of the Sociology of Language, 70,* 11–28.

Conklin, A. L. (1997). *A Mission to Civilize: The Republican Idea of Empire in France and West Africa, 1895–1930*. Stanford, CA: Stanford University Press.

Conrick, M. and Regan, V. (2007). *French in Canada: Language Issues*. Bern: Peter Lang.

Conteh, J. (2012). Families, pupils and teachers learning together in a multilingual British city. *Journal of Multilingual and Multicultural Development, 33*(1), 101–16.

Conteh, J., Riasat, S. and Begum, S. (2013). Children learning multilingually in home, community and school contexts in Britain. In M. Schwartz and A. Verschik (eds), *Successful Family Language Policy* (pp. 83–102). Dordrecht: Springer.

Cooper, R. L. (ed.) (1982). *Language Spread: Studies in Diffusion and Social Change*. Bloomington: Indiana University Press.

Cooper, R. L. (1989). *Language Planning and Social Change*. Cambridge: Cambridge University Press.

Cooper, R. L. (1991). Dreams of scripts: writing systems as gift of God. In R. L. Cooper and B. Spolsky (eds), *The Influence of Language on Culture and Thought: Essays in honor of Joshua A. Fishman's Sixty-Fifth Birthday* (pp. 219–26). Berlin: Mouton de Gruyter.

Cooper, R. L. and Carpenter, S. (1976). Language in the market. In M. L. Bender, J. D. Bowen, R. L. Cooper and C. A. Ferguson (eds), *Language in Ethiopia*. London: Oxford University Press.

Corne, C. (1993). Creole French: of continuity, change, and creation. *Prudentia, 25*(2), 47–71.

Coronel-Molina, S. (2008). Language ideologies of the High Academy of the Quechua

Language in Cuzco, Peru. *Latin American and Caribbean Ethic Studies, 3*(1), 319–40.

Coronel-Molina, S. (2015). *Language Ideology, Policy and Planning in Peru*. Bristol: Multilingual Matters.

Coronel-Molina, S. and McCarty, T. L. (2016). *Indigenous Language Revitalization in the Americas*. New York and London: Routledge.

Council of Europe. (2001). *Common European Framework of Reference for Languages: Learning, Teaching, Assessment*. Cambridge: Cambridge University Press.

Council of Europe. (2018). *Common European Framework of Reference for Languages: Learning, Teaching, Assessment: Companion Volume with New Descriptors*. Strasbourg: Council of Europe Publishing.

Coupland, N. (2011). *The Handbook of Language and Globalization*. Malden, MA and Oxford: John Wiley and Sons.

Covell, M. (1993). Political conflict and constitutional engineering in Belgium. *International Journal of the Sociology of Language, 104*, 65–86.

Crawford, J. (1999). *Bilingual Education: History, Politics, Theory and Practice* (4th edn). Los Angeles, CA: Bilingual Education Services.

Crocker, J. C. and Maybury-Lewis, D. (1985). *Vital Souls: Bororo Cosmology, Natural Symbolism, and Shamanism*. Tucson, AZ: University of Arizona Press.

Crowley, T. (2000). The language situation in Vanuatu. *Current Issues in Language Planning, 1*(1), 47–132.

Crowley, T. and Lynch, J. (2006). *The Avava Language of Central Malakula (Vanuatu)*. Canberra: Australian National University.

Curdt-Christiansen, X. L. (2013). Negotiating family language policy: doing homework. In M. Schwartz and A. Verschik (eds), *Successful Family Language Policy* (pp. 277–95). Dordrecht: Springer.

Curdt-Christiansen, X. L. (2016). Family language policy in the Chinese community in Singapore: a question of balance? In W. Li (ed.), *Multilingualism in the Chinese Diaspora Worldwide* (pp. 255–75). Abingdon: Taylor & Francis.

Curtin, P. D. (1972). *The Atlantic Slave Trade: A Census*. Madison, WI: University of Wisconsin Press.

Damari, R. R., Rivers, W. P., Brecht, R. D., Gardner, P., Pulupa, C. and Robinson, J. (2017). The demand for multilingual human capital in the US labor market. *Foreign Language Annals, 50*(1), 13–37.

Daoud, M. (2011). The sociolinguistic situation in Tunisia: language rivalry or accommodation? *International Journal of the Sociology of Language, 211*, 9–34.

Dardjowidjojo, S. (1998). Strategies for a successful national language policy: the Indonesian case. *International Journal for the Sociology of Language, 130*, 35–47.

Darquennes, J. (2013). The contribution of the ecology of language to the advancement of linguistic profiling: some notes and some preliminary suggestions on further improvements. In W. Vandenbussche, E. H. Jahr and P. Trudgill (eds), *Language Ecology for the 21st Century: Linguistic Conflicts and Social Environments* (pp. 94–114). Oslo: Noovus.

Das, P. (2013). The Irula Language and Literature. *The Criterion, 4*(2), 1–7.

David, D. (2016). Reconciliation in Australia: achieving transparency through the theatre. *Cultures of the Commonwealth* (19/20/21), 35–52, <https://search.informit.

com.au/documentSummary;dn=796520699105469;res=IELLCC> (last accessed 23 September 2020).

De Castro, E. V. (1992). *From the Enemy's Point of View: Humanity and Divinity in an Amazonian Society*. Chicago: University of Chicago Press.

De Klerk, V. (2001). The cross-marriage language dilemma: his language or hers? *International Journal of Bilingual Education and Bilingualism, 4*(3), 197–216.

De Swaan, A. (1998a). A political sociology of the world language system (1): the dynamics of language spread. *Language Problems and Language Planning, 22*(1), 63–78.

De Swaan, A. (1998b). A Political sociology of the world language system (2): The unequal exchange of texts. *Language Problems and Language Planning, 22*(2), 109–28.

De Swaan, A. (2001). *Words of the World: The Global Language System*. Cambridge and Malden, MA: Polity Press and Blackwell Publishers.

Deane, S. (2016). Syria's lost generation: refugee education provision and societal security in an ongoing conflict emergency. *IDS Bulletin, 47*(3).

Deb, P. C., Ram, B. and Lal, J. (1987). *Bazigars of Punjab: A Socio-Economic Study*. Delhi: Mittal Publications.

Delafosse, M. (1904). *Vocabulaires comparatifs de plus de 60 langues ou dialectes parlés à la Côte d'Ivoire et dans les régions limitrophes: avec des notes linguistiques et ethnologiques, une bibliographie et une carte*. Angers, France: E. Leroux.

Desai, G. (1990). Theater as praxis: discursive strategies in African popular theater. *African Studies Review, 33*(1), 65–92.

Diamond, J. (1997). *Guns, Germs, and Steel: The Fates of Human Societies*. New York and London: W. W. Norton & Co.

Diamond, J. (2005). *Collapse: How Societies Choose to Fail or Survive*. London: Penguin Books.

Diamond, J. (2013). *The World Until Yesterday: What Can We Learn From Traditional Societies?* London: Penguin.

Diki-Kidiri, M. (1998). *Dictionnaire orthographique du sängö*. Bangui: BBA Editions.

Dixon, L. Q. (2009). Assumptions behind Singapore's language-in-education policy: implications for language planning and second language acquisition. *Language Policy, 8*(2), 117–38.

Doak, K. (2006). *A History of Nationalism in Modern Japan: Placing the People*. Leiden: Brill.

Doherty, M. A. (2000). *Nazi Wireless Propaganda: Lord Haw-Haw and British Public Opinion in the Second World War*. Edinburgh: Edinburgh University Press.

Döpke, S. (1992). *One Parent, One Language: An Interactional Approach*. Amsterdam and Philadelphia: John Benjamins Publishing Company.

Dörnyei, Z. (1999). Motivation. In B. Spolsky (ed.), *Concise Encyclopedia of Educational Linguistics*. Amsterdam and New York: Elsevier.

Dörnyei, Z. (2009). The L2 motivational self system. In Z. Dörnyei and E. Ushiodo (eds), *Motivation, Language Identity and the L2 Self* (Vol. 36, pp. 9–11). Bristol: Multilingual Matters.

Dörnyei, Z. and Clément, R. (2001). Motivational characteristics of learning different target languages: results of a nationwide survey. In Z. Dörnyei and R. Schmidt (eds),

Motivation and Second Language Acquisition (Vol. 23, pp. 399–432). Honolulu, HI: University of Hawai'i Press.

Dörnyei, Z. and Ushioda, E. (2009). *Motivation, Language Identity and the L2 Self.* Bristol: Multilingual Matters.

Dossou, C. (2002). *Langue française et langues nationales dans le contexte des pluri-linguismes d'Afrique noire : le cas du Bénin.* Doctorat en Sciences du langage, Université de Cergy-Pontoise.

Drori, I. (2009). *Foreign Workers in Israel: Global Perspectives.* Albany, NY: SUNY Press.

Drude, S. (2011). 'Derivational verbs' and other multi-verb constructions in Aweti and Tupi-Guarani. In A. Y. Aikhenvald, P. Muysken and J. Birchall (eds), *Multi-Verb Constructions* (pp. 213–54). Leiden: Brill.

Druviete, I. and Ozolins, U. (2016). The Latvian referendum on Russian as a second state language, February 2012. *Language Problems and Language Planning, 40*(2), 121–45.

Duchêne, A. and Heller, M. (eds) (2008). *Discourses of Endangerment: Ideology and Interest in the Defence of Languages.* London and New York: Continuum.

Duchêne, A. and Heller, M. (2012a). *Language in Late Capitalism: Pride and Profit.* London: Routledge.

Duchêne, A. and Heller, M. (2012b). Language policy in the workplace. In B. Spolsky (ed.), *Handbook of Language Policy* (pp. 322–34). Cambridge: Cambridge University Press.

Dunleavy, J. E. and Dunleavy, G. W. (1991). *Douglas Hyde: A Maker of Modern Ireland.* Berkeley: University of California Press.

Dunmore, S. (2019). *Language Revitalisation in Gaelic Scotland.* Edinburgh: Edinburgh University Press.

Duranti, A., Ochs, E. and Schieffelin, B. B. (2011). *The Handbook of Language Socialization.* Malden, MA and Oxford: John Wiley and Sons.

Dwivedi, P. and Kar, S. (2016). Kanauji of Kanpur: a brief overview. *Acta Linguistica Asiatica, 6*(1), 101–19.

Dzialtuvaite, J. (2006). The role of religion in language choice and identity among Lithuanian immigrants in Scotland. In T. Omoniyi and J. A. Fishman (eds), *The Sociology of Language and Religion: Change, Conflict and Accommodation* (pp. 79–85). Basingstoke: Palgrave Macmillan.

East, M., Chung, H. and Arkinstall, C. (2013). A fair go for all: a contribution to the call for a national languages policy in Aotearoa New Zealand. *The New Zealand Language Teacher, 39.*

Eberhard, D. M. (2009). *Mamaindê Grammar: A Northern Nambikwara Language and Its Cultural Context.* Amsterdam: Netherlands Graduate School of Linguistics.

Eberhard, D. M., Simons, G. F. and Fennig, C. D. (eds) (2019). *Ethnologue: Languages of the World.* Dallas, TX: SIL International.

Education Review Office. (1995). *Kura Kaupapa Maori.* Wellington: Education Review Office.

Edwards, J. (1992). Sociopolitical aspects of language maintenance and loss. In W. Fase, K. Jaspaert and S. Kroon (eds), *Maintenance and Loss of Minority Languages* (pp. 37–54). Amsterdam and Philadelphia: John Benjamins Publishing Company.

Edwards, J. (2019). Language typology in contemporary perspective. In J. Darquennes, J. Salmons and W. Vandenbussche (eds), *Language Contact*. Berlin: Mouton de Gruyter.

Elder, C., Pill, J., Woodward-Kron, R., McNamara, T., Manias, E., Webb, G. and Mccoll, G. (2012). Health professionals' views of communication: implications for assessing performance on a health-specific English language test. *TESOL Quarterly, 46*(2), 409–19.

Elman, B. A. (2000). *A Cultural History of Civil Examinations in Late Imperial China*. Berkeley, Los Angeles and London: University of California Press.

Englebert, P. (1996). *Burkina Faso: Unsteady Statehood in West Arica*. Boulder, CO: Westview Press.

Estival, D. and Pennycook, A. (2011). L'Académie française and Anglophone language ideologies. *Language Policy, 10*(4), 325–41.

Ewans, M. (2017). *European Atrocity, African Catastrophe: Leopold II, the Congo Free State and Its Aftermath*. London: Routledge.

Ezzamel, M. (1997). Accounting, control and accountability: preliminary evidence from ancient Egypt. *Critical Perspectives on Accounting, 8*(6), 563–601.

Fabra, P. (1912). *Gramática de la lengua catalana*. Barcelona: Massa, Casas & Ca.

Faingold, E. D. (2020). *Language Rights and the Law in the European Union*. London: Palgrave Macmillan.

Fairclough, N. (2003). Political correctness: the politics of culture and language. *Discourse Society, 14*(1), 17–28.

Fasold, R. (1987). Language policy and change: sexist language in the periodical news media. In P. Lowenberg (ed.), *Georgetown University Round Table on Languages and Linguistics 1987* (pp. 187–206). Washington, DC: Georgetown University Press.

Fayzullina, G. Z., Ermakova, E. N., Fattakova, A. A. and Shagbanova, H. S. (2017). The problem of fixation of Siberian endangered languages in the multimedia corpus: evidence from the Siberian Tatars Tyumen region dialect. *Pertanika Journal of Social Sciences and Humanities, 25*, 59–72.

Feitosa, S. F., Garrafa, V., Cornelli, G., Tardivo, C. and Carvalho, S. J. d. (2010). Bioethics, culture and infanticide in Brazilian indigenous communities: the Zuruahá case. *Cadernos de saúde pública, 26*, 853–65.

Feldmann, H. (2016). The long shadows of Spanish and French colonial education. *Kyklos, 69*(1), 32–64.

Fellman, J. (1973). *The Revival of a Classical Tongue: Eliezer Ben Yehuda and the Modern Hebrew Language*. The Hague: Mouton.

Ferguson, C. A. (1959). Diglossia. *Word, 15*, 325–40.

Ferguson, C. A. and Gumperz, J. (eds) (1960). *Linguistic Diversity in South Asia*. Bloomington: Indiana University Research Centre in Anthropology, Folklore, and Linguistics.

Ferreira, J.-A. S. (2010). Bilingual education among the Karipúna and Galibi-Marwono. In B. Migge, I. Léglise and A. Bartens (eds), *Creoles in Education: An Appraisal of Current Programs and Projects* (Vol. 36, pp. 211–36). Amsterdam and Philadelphia: John Benjamins Publishing Company.

Ferreira, M. P. (2005). *Cantus Coronatus D'El-Rei Dom Dinis: 7 Cantigas by King Dinis of Portugal* (Vol. 10). Kassel: Edition Reichenberger.

Fishman, J. A. (ed.) (1966). *Language Loyalty in the United States: The Maintenance and Perpetuation of Non-English Mother Tongues by American Ethnic and Religious Groups.* The Hague: Mouton.

Fishman, J. A. (1967). Bilingualism with and without diglossia; diglossia with and without bilingualism. *Journal of Social Issues, 23*(2), 29–38.

Fishman, J. A. (1968). Language problems and types of political and sociocultural integration: a conceptual postscript. In J. A. Fishman, C. A. Ferguson and J. Das Gupta (eds), *Language Problems of Developing Nations* (pp. 491–8). New York: John Wiley and Sons.

Fishman, J. A. (1969). National languages and languages of wider communication in the developing nations. *Anthropological Linguistics, 11*, 111–35.

Fishman, J. A. (ed.) (1974). *Advances in Language Planning.* The Hague: Mouton.

Fishman, J. A. (1990). What is reversing language shift (RLS) and how can it succeed? *Journal of Multilingual and Multicultural Development, 11*(1–2), 5–36.

Fishman, J. A. (1991). *Reversing Language Shift: Theoretical and Empirical Foundations of Assistance to Threatened Languages.* Clevedon: Multilingual Matters Ltd.

Fishman, J. A. (1993). Reversing language shift: successes, failures, doubts and dilemmas. In E. H. Jahr (ed.), *Language Conflict and Language Planning* (pp. 69–81). Berlin: Mouton de Gruyter.

Fishman, J. A. (ed.) (2001). *Can Threatened Languages Be Saved? Reversing Language Shift, Revisited: A 21st Century Perspective.* Clevedon: Multilingual Matters Ltd.

Fishman, J. A. (2006). *Do Not Leave Your Language Alone: The Hidden Status Agendas within Corpus Planning in Language Policy.* Mahwah, NJ: Lawrence Erlbaum Associates.

Fishman, J. A. and Fishman, D. E. (1974). Yiddish in Israel: a case-study of efforts to revise a monocentric language policy. *International Journal of the Sociology of Language, 1*, 126–46.

Fishman, J. A. and Lovas, J. (1970). Bilingual education in a sociolinguistic perspective. *TESOL Quarterly, 4*, 215–22.

Fishman, J. A., Cooper, R. L. and Ma, R. (1971). *Bilingualism in the Barrio.* Bloomington: Research Center for the Language Sciences, Indiana University.

Fishman, J. A., Gertner, M. H., Lowy, E. G. and Milan, W. G. (1985). *The Rise and Fall of the Ethnic Revival: Perspectives on Language and Ethnicity.* Berlin: Mouton de Gruyter.

Fleming, L. (2016). Linguistic exogamy and language shift in the northwest Amazon. *International Journal of the Sociology of Language, 2016, 240*, 9–27.

Footitt, H. and Kelly, M. (2012a). *Languages at War: Policies and Practices of Language Contacts in Conflict.* Basingstoke: Palgrave Macmillan.

Footitt, H. and Kelly, M. (eds) (2012b). *Languages and the Military: Alliances, Occupation and Peace Building.* Basingstoke: Palgrave Macmillan.

Footitt, H. and Tobia, S. (2013). *WarTalk: Foreign Languages and the British War Effort in Europe, 1940–47.* Basingstoke: Palgrave Macmillan.

Ford Foundation. (1975). *Language and Development: A Retrospective Survey of Ford Foundation Language Projects, 1952–1974.* New York: Ford Foundation.

Förster, S., Mommsen, W. J. and Robinson, R. E. (1988). *Bismarck, Europe and Africa: The Berlin Africa Conference 1884–1885 and the Onset of Partition.* Oxford: Oxford University Press.

Foster, B. R. (1982). Education of a bureaucrat in Sargonic Sumer. *Archív Orientální, 50*, 238–41.

Foucault, M. (1975). *Surveiller et punir: naissance de la prison*. Paris: Gallimard.

Fox, M. J. (2007). Ford Foundation: personal reflection. In C. B. Paulston and G. R. Tucker (eds), *The Early Days of Sociolinguistics* (pp. 271–2). Dallas, TX: The Summer Institute of Linguistics.

Franciscan Fathers. (1910). *Ethnologic Dictionary of the Navaho Language*. St. Michaels, AZ: Franciscan Fathers.

François, A. (2011). Social ecology and language history in the northern Vanuatu linkage: a tale of divergence and convergence. *Journal of Historical Linguistics, 1*(2), 175–246.

François, A. (2012). The dynamics of linguistic diversity: egalitarian multilingualism and power imbalance among northern Vanuatu languages. *International Journal of the Sociology of Language, 214*, 85–110.

François, A., Franjieh, M., Lacrampe, S. and Schnell, S. (2015). The exceptional linguistic density of Vanuatu. In A. François, M. Franjieh, S. Lacrampe and S. Schnell (eds), *The languages of Vanuatu: Unity and Diversity* (pp. 1–21). Canberra: Australian National University.

Freyre, G. (1938). *Casa-grande and senzala: formação da familia brasileira sob o regimen de economia patriarchal*. Köln: Schmidt.

Gabas, N. J. (1999). *A grammar of Karo, Tupi (Brazil)*. PhD, University of California Santa Barbara, Santa Barbara.

Gagnon, A. and Montcalm, M. B. (1990). *Quebec: Beyond the Quiet Revolution*. Scarborough, ON: Nelson Canada.

Gal, S. (1978). Peasant men can't get wives: language change and sex roles in a bilingual community. *Language in Society, 7*(1), 1–16.

Galisson, M.-P., Malonga-Moungabio, F. and Denys, B. (2016). The evolution of mathematics teaching in Mali and Congo-Brazzaville and the issue of the use of French or local languages. In A. Hallai and P. Clarkson (eds), *Teaching and Learning Mathematics in Multilingual Classrooms* (pp. 249–66). Rotterdam: Sense Publishers.

García, O. and Li, W. (2013). *Translanguaging: Language, Bilingualism and Education*. Berlin: Springer.

García, O., Morin, J. L. and Rivera, K. M. (2001). How threatened is the Spanish of New York Puerto Ricans? Language shift with vaiven. In J. A. Fishman (ed.), *Can Threatened Languages Be Saved?* (pp. 44–73). Clevedon: Multilingual Matters Ltd.

Gardner, R. C. and Lambert, W. E. (1959). Motivational variables in second-language acquisition. *Canadian Journal of Psychology, 13*, 266–72.

Gardner, R. C. and Lambert, W. E. (1972). *Attitudes and Motivation in Second Language Learning*. Rowley, MA: Newbury House.

Gazzola, M. (2006). Managing multilingualism in the European Union: language policy evaluation for the European Parliament. *Language Policy, 5*(4), 393–417.

Genesee, F. (1988). The Canadian second language immersion program. In C. B. Paulston (ed.), *International Handbook of Bilingualism and Bilingual Education* (pp. 163–84). New York: Greenwood Press.

Gewald, J. B. (2003). The Herero genocide: German unity, settlers, soldiers, and ideas.

In M. Bechhaus-Gerst and R. Klein-Arendt (eds), *Die (koloniale) Begegnung: AfrikanerInnen in Deutschland (1880–1945), Deutsche in Afrika (1880–1918)* (pp. 109–27). Frankfurt am Main: Peter Lang.

Gibson, M. (2013). Dialect levelling in Tunisian Arabic: towards a new spoken standard. In A. Rouchdy (ed.), *Language Contact and Language Conflict in Arabic* (pp. 42–58). London and New York: Routledge.

Giles, H. (1971). *A study of speech patterns in social interaction: Accent evaluation and accent change*. PhD, Bristol University,

Giles, H. (1973). Accent mobility: a model and some data. *Anthropological Linguistics, 15*(2), 87–105.

Giles, H., Taylor, D. M. and Bourhis, R. Y. (1973). Towards a theory of interpersonal accommodation through language: some Canadian data. *Language in Society, 2*(2), 177–92.

Gill, S. K. (2005). Language policy in Malaysia: reversing direction. *Language Policy, 4*(3).

Gill, S. K. (2006). Change in language policy in Malaysia: the reality of implementation in public universities. *Current Issues in Language Planning, 7*(1), 82–94.

Glazer, N. (1966). The process and problems of language maintenance: an integrative review. In J. A. Fishman (ed.), *Language Loyalty in the United States* (pp. 358–68). The Hague: Mouton.

Glinert, L. (1987). Hebrew-Yiddish diglossia: type and stereotype implications of the language of Ganzfried's *Kitzur*. *International Journal of the Sociology of Language, 67*, 39–56.

Global education monitoring report team. (2020). Global education monitoring report, 2020: inclusion and education: all means all, <http://hdl.voced.edu. au/10707/553248> (last accessed 13 October 2020).

Gorter, D. (ed.) (2006). *Linguistic Landscape: A New Approach to multilingualism.* Clevedon: Multilingual Matters Ltd.

Gouin, F., Swan, H. and Bétis, V. (1892). *The Art of Teaching and Studying Languages.* London: G. Philip & Son.

Goujon, A. (1999). Language, nationalism, and populism in Belarus. *Nationalities Papers, 27*(4), 661–77.

Goyal, S. and Pandey, P. (2009). How do government and private schools differ? Findings from two large Indian states, <http://crossasia-repository.ub.uni-heidel berg.de/3465/> (last accessed 13 October 2020).

Green, S. (2019). A critical reading of the Declaration on the Rights of Indigenous Peoples. *Indigenous Policy Journal, 29*(3).

Gregor, T. (2009). *Mehinaku: The Drama of Daily Life in a Brazilian Indian Village.* Chicago: University of Chicago Press.

Grenoble, L. A. (2003). *Soviet Language Policy.* Dordrecht: Kluwer Academic Publishers.

Grenoble, L. A. (2011). Language ecology and endangerment. In P. K. Austin and J. Sallabank (eds), *The Cambridge Handbook of Endangered Languages* (pp. 27–45). Cambridge: Cambridge University Press.

Grenoble, L. A. and Whaley, L. J. (1998). Toward a typology of language endangerment. In L. A. Grenoble and L. J. Whaley (eds), *Endangered Languages* (pp. 22–54). Cambridge: Cambridge University Press.

Grieder, J. B. (1970). *Hu Shih and the Chinese Renaissance: Liberalism in the Chinese Revolution, 1917–1937* (Vol. 46). Cambridge, MA: Harvard University Press.

Grimes, B. A. (ed.) (1996). *Ethnologue: Languages of the World* (13th edn). Dallas, TX: Summer Institute of Linguistics.

Grin, F. (1996a). Economic approaches to language and language planning: an introduction. *International Journal of the Sociology of Language, 121*, 1–16.

Grin, F. (1996b). The economics of language: survey, assessment and prospects. *International Journal of the Sociology of Language, 121*, 17–44.

Grin, F. (1997). *Langues et différentiels de statut socio-économique en Suisse*. Berne: Office fédéral de la statistique.

Grin, F. (1998). *Language policy in multilingual Switzerland-Overview and recent developments*. Paper presented at the Cicle de confèrencies sobre política lingüística, Barcelona.

Grin, F. (1999). Economics. In J. A. Fishman (ed.), *Handbook of Language and Ethnic Identity* (pp. 9–24). New York and Oxford: Oxford University Press.

Grin, F. (2001). English an economic value: facts and fallacies. *World Englishes, 20*(1), 65–78.

Grin, F. (2003). Language planning and economics. *Current Issues in Language Planning, 4*(1), 1–66.

Grin, F. (2005). The economics of language policy implementation: identifying and measuring costs. In N. Alexander (ed.), *Mother Tongue-Based Bilingual Education in Southern Africa: The Dynamics of Implementation* (pp. 11–25). Paris: Multilingualism Network.

Grin, F. and Korth, B. (2005). On the reciprocal influence of language politics and language education: the case of English in Switzerland. *Language Policy, 4*(1), 67–85.

Grin, F. and Sfreddo, C. (1998). Language-based earnings differentials on the Swiss labour market: is Italian a liability? *International Journal of Manpower, 19*(7), 520–32.

Grin, F., Sfreddo, C. and Vaillancourt, F. (2010). *The Economics of the Multilingual Workplace*. New York and London: Routledge.

Grosjean, F. (2019). *A Journey in Languages and Cultures: The Life of a Bicultural Bilingual*. Oxford: Oxford University Press.

Guilherme, A. (2015). Indigenous education in Brazil: the issue of contacted and noncontacted Native Indians. *Diaspora, Indigenous, and Minority Education, 9*(4), 205–20.

Gumperz, J. J. (1958). Dialect differences and social stratification in a North Indian village. *American Anthropologist, 60*(4), 668–82

Gumperz, J. J. (1964). Linguistic and social interaction in two communities. *American Anthropologist, 66*(6, Part 2), 137–53.

Gumperz, J. J. (1965). *Linguistic repertoires, grammars, and second language instruction*. Paper presented at the Roundtable on languages and linguistics, Georgetown University, Washington, DC.

Gumperz, J. J. (1968). The speech community. In D. L. Sills (ed.), *International Encyclopedia of the Social Sciences* (Vol. 9, pp. 381–6). New York: The Macmillan Company.

Gumperz, J. J. (1983). *Language and Social Identity*. Cambridge: Cambridge University Press.

Gumperz, J. J. and Blom, J.-P. (1972). Social meaning in linguistic structures: code switching in northern Norway. In J. J. Gumperz and D. Hymes (eds), *Directions in Sociolinguistics*. New York: Holt, Rinehart, & Winston.

Guy, J. B. M. (1974). *A Grammar of the Northern Dialect of Sakao*. Canberra: Department of Linguistics, Research School of Pacific Studies, Australian National University.

Haile, B. (1926). *A Manual of Navaho Grammar*. St Michaels, AZ: Franciscan Fathers.

Halaoui, N. (2000). La législation constitutionnelle des langues au Bénin. *Revue juridique et politique: indépendance et coopération, 54*(3), 270–88.

Hale, K. (1992). On endangered languages and the safeguarding of diversity. *Language, 68*(1), 1–3.

Hall, R. A., Jr. (1950). *Leave Your Language Alone!* Ithaca, NY: Cornell University Press.

Halperin, L. R. (2014). *Babel in Zion: Jews, Nationalism, and Language Diversity in Palestine, 1920–1948*. New Haven, CT: Yale University Press.

Hamel, R. E. (1995). Linguistic rights for Amerindian peoples in Latin America. In R. Phillipson, M. Rannut and T. Skutnabb-Kangas (eds), *Linguistic Human Rights: Overcoming Linguistic discrimination* (pp. 289–304). Berlin and New York: Mouton de Gruyter.

Hamel, R. E. (2013). Language policy and ideology in Latin America. In R. Bayley, R. Cameron and C. Lucas (eds), *The Oxford Handbook of Sociolinguistics* (pp. 609–28). Oxford: Oxford University Press.

Hammarström, H. J. F. (2015). Ethnologue 16/17/18th editions: a comprehensive review. *Language, 91*(3).

Hammond, J. (2009). *The Grammar of Nouns and Verbs in Whitesands, an Oceanic Language of Southern Vanuatu*. (MA). University of Sydney.

Hamp-Lyons, L. and Lockwood, J. (2009). The workplace, the society, and the wider world: the offshoring and outsourcing industry. *Annual Review of Applied Linguistics, 29*, 145–67.

Hanzeli, V. E. (2014). *Missionary Linguistics in New France: A Study of Seventeenth- and Eighteenth-Century Descriptions of American Indian Languages*. Berlin: Walter de Gruyter GmbH & Co KG.

Haque, S. and Le Lièvre, F. (eds) (2019). *Politique linguistique familiale / Family Language Policy: Dynamics in Language Transmission under a Migratory Context*. Munich: Lincom.

Harrington, J., Palethorpe, S. and Watson, C. I. (2001). Does the Queen speak the Queen's English? *Nature, 408*(6815), 927–8.

Harris, J. R. (1995). Where is the child's environment? A group socialization theory of development. *Psychological Review, 102*, 458–89.

Harris, J. R. (1998). *The Nurture Assumption: Why Children Turn Out the Way They Do*. New York: Free Press.

Harris, J. R. (2011). *The Nurture Assumption: Why Children Turn Out the Way They Do* (2nd edn). New York: Simon & Schuster.

Hartig, F. (2015). *Chinese Public Diplomacy: The Rise of the Confucius Institute*. London: Routledge.

Hatcher, B. A. (1996). *Idioms of Improvement: Vidyāsāgar and Cultural Encounter in Bengal*. New York: Oxford University Press.

Haugen, E. (1959). Planning for a standard language in Norway. *Anthropological Linguistics, 1*(3), 8–21.

Haugen, E. (1961). Language planning in modern Norway. *Scandinavian Studies, 33*, 68–81.

Haugen, E. (1966). *Language Conflict and Language Planning: The Case of Modern Norwegian*. Cambridge, MA: Harvard University Press.

Haugen, E. (1972). The ecology of language. In A. Dil (ed.), *The Ecology of Language: Essays by Einar Haugen* (pp. 325–39). Stanford, CA: Stanford University Press.

Haugen, E. (1987). *Blessings of Babel: Bilingualism and Language Planning: Problems and Pleasures*. Berlin, New York and Amsterdam: Mouton de Gruyter.

Haugen, J. D. and Philips, S. U. (2010). Tongan Chiefly Language: the formation of an honorific speech register. *Language in Society, 39*(5), 589–616.

Heggoy, A. A. (1973). Education in French Algeria: an essay on cultural conflict. *Comparative Education Review, 17*(2), 180–97.

Heller, M. (2010a). The commodification of language. *Annual Review of Anthropology, 39*(1), 101–14. doi:10.1146/annurev.anthro.012809.104951

Heller, M. (2010b). The commodification of language. *Annual Review of Anthropology, 39*, 101–14.

Heller, M. and McElhinny, B. (2017). *Language, Capitalism, Colonialism: Towards a Critical History*. Toronto: University of Toronto Press.

Hermans, T. (2015). *The Flemish Movement: A Documentary History 1780–1990*. London: Bloomsbury Publishing.

Heugh, K., Benson, C., Bogale, B. and Yohannes, M. A. G. (2007). Final report. Study on medium of instruction in primary schools in Ethiopia, <http://ecommons.hsrc.ac.za/bitstream/handle/20.500.11910/6273/4379_Heugh_Studyonmediumofinstruction.pdf?sequence=1&isAllowed=y> (last accessed 13 October 2020).

Hilmes, M. (2002). Rethinking radio. In M. Hilmes and J. Loviglio (eds), *Radio Reader: Essays in the Cultural History of Radio* (pp. 1–19). New York and London: Routledge.

Hinton, L. (2011). Revitalization of endangered languages. In P. K. Austin and J. Sallabank (eds), *The Cambridge Handbook of Endangered Languages* (pp. 291–311). Cambridge: Cambridge University Press.

Hirvonen, V. (2008). 'Out on the fells, I feel like a Sámi': is there linguistic and cultural equality in the Sámi school? In N. H. Hornberger (ed.), *Can Schools Save Indigenous Languages? Policy and Practice on Four Continents* (pp. 15–41). Basingstoke: Palgrave Macmillan.

Hogan-Brun, G. (2017). *Linguanomics*. London: Bloomsbury.

Hogan-Brun, G. and Melnyk, S. (2012). Language policy management in the former Soviet sphere. In B. Spolsky (ed.), *Handbook of Language Policy*. Cambridge: Cambridge University Press.

Holm, W. (1996). On the role of 'YounganMorgan' in the development of Navajo literacy. In E. Jelinek, S. Midgette, K. Rice and L. Saxon (eds), *Athabaskan Language Studies: Essays in Honor of Robert W. Young* (pp. 391–406). Albuquerque, NM: University of New Mexico Press.

Holm, A. and Holm, W. (1995). Navajo language education: retrospect and prospect. *Bilingual Research Journal, 19*(1), 141–67.

Holm, W. and Holm, A. (1990). Rock Point: a Navajo way to go to school: a valediction. *Annals, AASSP, 508*, 170–84.

Holmes, J. and Stubbe, M. (2015). *Power and Politeness in the Workplace: A Sociolinguistic Analysis of Talk at Work*. Abingdon: Routledge.

Holton, G. (2011). The role of information technology in supporting minority and endangered languages. In P. K. Austin and J. Sallabank (eds), *The Cambridge Handbook of Endangered Languages* (pp. 371–99). Cambridge: Cambridge University Press.

Hornberger, N. H. (1998). Language policy, language education, language rights: indigenous, immigrant, and international perspectives. *Language in Society, 27*(4), 439–58.

Hornberger, N. H. (ed.) (2008). *Can Schools Save Indigenous Languages? Policy and Practice on Four Continents*. Basingstoke: Palgrave Macmillan.

Horne, A. (2012). *A Savage War of Peace: Algeria 1954–1962*. London: Pan Macmillan.

Hornsby, D. (2007). Regional dialect levelling in urban France and Britain. *Nottingham French Studies, 46*(2), 64–81.

Horvath, B. and Sankoff, D. (1987). Delimiting the Sydney speech community. *Language in Society, 16*(2), 179–204.

Hourigan, N. (2007). The role of networks in minority language television campaigns. In M. J. Cormack and N. Hourigan (eds), *Minority Language Media: Concepts, Critiques and Case Studies* (pp. 52–8). Bristol: Multilingual Matters.

Hroch, M. (2004). From ethnic group toward the modern nation: the Czech case. *Nations and Nationalism, 10*(1–2), 95–107.

Huillery, E. (2011). The impact of European settlement within French West Africa: did pre-colonial prosperous areas fall behind? *Journal of African Economies, 20*(2), 263–311.

Huss, L. (2008). Revitalization through indigenous education: a forlorn hope? In N. Hornberger (ed.), *Can Schools Save Indigenous Languages?* (pp. 125–35). Basingstoke: Springer.

Hymes, D. (1974). *Foundations in Sociolinguistics: An Ethnographic Approach*. Philadelphia: University of Pennsylvania Press.

i Font, H. A. (2014). Chuvash language in Chuvashia's instruction system: an example of educational language policies in post-Soviet Russia. *Journal on Ethnopolitics and Minority Issues in Europe, 13*(4), 52.

Igboanusi, H. (2008). Mother tongue-based bilingual education in Nigeria: attitudes and practice. *International Journal of Bilingual Education and Bilingualism, 11*(6), 721–34.

Irvine, J. T. (1989). When talk isn't cheap: language and political economy. *American Ethnologist, 16*(2), 248–67.

Jacobs, B., Ryan, A. M., Henrichs, K. S. and Weiss, B. D. (2018). Medical interpreters in outpatient practice. *The Annals of Family Medicine, 16*(1), 70–6.

Jacobs, J. (ed.) (1893). *The Jews of Angevin England: Documents and Records from Latin and Hebrew Sources Printed and Manuscript for the First Time Collected and Translated*. London: David Nutt.

Jan, J.-S., Kuan, P.-Y. and Lomeli, A. (2016). Social context, parental exogamy and Hakka language retention in Taiwan. *Journal of Multilingual and Multicultural Development, 37*(8), 794–804.

Jernudd, B. H. and Nekvapil, J. (2012). History of the field: a sketch. In B. Spolsky (ed.), *Handbook of Language Policy* (pp. 16–36). Cambridge: Cambridge University Press.

Johansson, S. (1991). Language use in mixed marriage, University of Lund, Sweden, <hj.sel-lsj./bl/bl.pdf> (last accessed 17 June 2005).

Johnson, S. (2002). On the origin of linguistic norms: orthography, ideology and the first constitutional challenge to the 1996 reform of German. *Language in Society, 31*(4), 549–76.

Johnston, A. and Lawson, A. (2000). Settler colonies. In H. Schwarz and S. Ray (eds), *A Companion to Postcolonial Studies* (pp. 360–76): John Wiley & Sons.

Jones, J. P. (2002). *Constitution Finder*. Richmond, VA: T.C. Williams School of Law, University of Richmond.

Jones, M. C. and Mooney, D. (eds). (2017). *Creating Orthographies for Endangered Languages*. Cambridge: Cambridge University Press.

Jones, M. C. and Ogilvie, S. (eds) (2013). *Keeping Languages Alive: Documentation, Pedagogy and Revitalization*. Cambridge: Cambridge University Press.

Jones, S. (1983). Arabic instruction and literacy in Javanese Muslim schools. *International Journal of the Sociology of Language, 1983*(42), 83–94.

Jordan, P. (2003). Continuity and change in Eastern Khanty language and worldview. In E. Kasten (ed.), *Rebuilding Identities: Pathways to Reform in Post-Soviet Siberia* (pp. 63–88). Berlin: Dietrich Reimer Verlag.

Jowitt, D. (2018). *Nigerian English*. Berlin: Walter de Gruyter GmbH and Co.

Judge, A. (2000). France: 'One state, one nation, one language'? In S. Barbour and C. Carmichael (eds), *Language and Nationalism in Europe* (pp. 44–84). Oxford and New York: Oxford University Press.

Kachru, B. B. (1986). *The Alchemy of English: The Spread, Functions and Models of Non-Native Englishes*. Oxford: Pergamon Institute of English.

Kachru, B. B., Kachru, Y. and Nelson, C. (eds) (2009). *The Handbook of World Englishes*. Hoboken, NJ: John Wiley & Sons.

Kala, C. P. (2005). Ethnomedicinal botany of the Apatani in the Eastern Himalayan region of India. *Journal of Ethnobiology and Ethnomedicine, 1*(1), 1–11.

Kamen, H. (2004). *Empire: How Spain Became a World Power, 1492–1763*. London: Harper Collins.

Kamwangamalu, N. M. (2008). Commentary from an African and international perspective. In N. Hornberger (ed.), *Can Schools Save Indigenous Languages?* (pp. 136–51). Basingstoke: Springer.

Kamwangamalu, N. M. (2016). Why inherited colonial language ideologies persist in postcolonial Africa. In N. M. Kamwangamalu (ed.), *Language Policy and Economics: The Language Question in Africa* (pp. 125–55). London: Springer.

Kankaanranta, A., Karhunen, P. and Louhiala-Salminen, L. (2018). 'English as corporate language' in the multilingual reality of multinational companies. *Multilingua, 37*(4), 331–51.

Kapadia, P. (2016). Jatra Shakespeare: indigenous Indian theater and the postcolonial stage. In P. Kapadia (ed.), *Native Shakespeares* (pp. 101–14). London: Routledge.

Karliner, L. S., Pérez-Stable, E. J. and Gildengorin, G. (2004). The language divide. *Journal of General Internal Medicine, 19*(2), 175–83.

Katz, D. (2004). *Words on Fire: The Unfinished Story of Yiddish*. New York: Basic Books.

Keefers, L. E. (1988). *Scholars in Foxholes: The Story of the Army Specialized Training Program in World War II*. Jefferson, NC: McFarland & Company.

Kelly, M. and Baker, C. (2013). *Interpreting the Peace: Peace Operations, Conflict and Language in Bosnia-Herzegovina*. Basingstoke: Palgrave Macmillan.

Kendrick, M. and Elizabeth, N. (2016). Family language practices as emergent policies in child-headed households in rural Uganda. In J. Macalister and S. H. Mirvahedi (eds), *Family Language Policies in a Multilingual World* (pp. 56–73). London: Routledge.

Kent, J. (2015). Lumumba and the 1960 Congo crisis: cold war and the neo-colonialism of Belgian decolonization. In M. B. Jerónimo and A. C. Pinto (eds), *The Ends of European Colonial Empires: Cases and Comparisons* (pp. 218–42). London: Palgrave Macmillan.

Kerswill, P. (2003). Dialect levelling and geographical diffusion in British English. In D. Britain and J. Cheshire (eds), *Social Dialectology: In Honour of Peter Trudgill* (pp. 223–43). Amsterdam and Philadelphia: John Benjamins Publishing Company.

Kertzer, D. I., Kertzer, D. I., Arel, D. and Hogan, D. P. (2002). *Census and Identity: The Politics of Race, Ethnicity, and Language in National Censuses*. Cambridge: Cambridge University Press.

Kibbee, D. A. (ed.) (1998). *Language Legislation and Linguistic Rights*. Amsterdam and Philadelphia: John Benjamins Publishing Company.

King, J. (2001). Te Kohanga Reo: Maori language revitalization. In L. Hinton and K. Hale (eds), *The Green Book of Language Revitalization in Practice* (pp. 119–31). New York: Academic Press.

King, K. A. and Benson, C. (2003). Indigenous language education in Bolivia and Ecuador: contexts, changes, and challenges. In J. W. Tollefson and A. B. M. Tsui (eds), *Medium of Instruction Policies: Which Agenda? Whose Agenda?* (pp. 241–61). Mahwah, NJ: Lawrence Erlbaum Associates.

King, R. D. (2001). The poisonous potency of script: Hindi and Urdu. *International Journal of the Sociology of Language, 150*, 43–60.

Kingsley, L. (2013). Language choice in multilingual encounters in transnational workplaces. *Journal of Multilingual Multicultural Development, 34*(6), 533–48.

Kirkpatrick, A. (2017). Language education policy among the Association of Southeast Asian Nations (ASEAN). *European Journal of Language Policy, 9*(1), 7–25.

Klain, B. and Peterson, L. C. (2000). *Native media, commercial radio, and language maintenance: Defining speech and style for Navajo broadcasters and broadcast Navajo*. Paper presented at the Texas Linguistic Forum.

Klein, G. (1989). Language policy during the fascist period: the case of language education. In R. Wodak (ed.), *Language, Power and Ideology: Studies in Political Discourse* (pp. 39–55). Amsterdam and Philadelphia: John Benjamins Publishing Company.

Kloss, H. (1966). German-American language maintenance efforts. In J. Fishman (ed.), *Language Loyalty in the United States* (pp. 206–52). The Hague: Mouton.

Kloss, H. (1969). *Research Possibilities on Group Bilingualism: A Report*. Laval University, Quebec: International Center for Research on Bilingualism.

Kloss, H. (1971). Language rights of immigrant groups. *International Migration Review, 5*(2), 250–68.

Kodesh, S. (1972). *Me-'inyan le-'inyan ba-ulpan (Issues in the Ulpan)*. Tel Aviv: Hamatmid.

Kopeliovich, S. (2006). *Reversing language shift in the immigrant family: Case study of a Russian-speaking community in Israel.* PhD, Bar-Ilan University, Ramat-Gan.

Kopeliovich, S. (2009). *Reversing Language Shift in the Immigrant Family: A Case Study of a Russian-Speaking Community in Israel.* Saarbrücken, Germany: VDM Verlag Dr Müller.

Kopeliovich, S. (2011). Family language policy: a case study of a Russian-Hebrew bilingual family: toward a theoretical framework. *Diaspora, Indigenous, and Minority Education, 4*(3), 162–78.

Kopeliovich, S. (2013). Happylingual: a family project for enhancing and balancing multilingual development. In M. Schwartz and A. Verschik (eds), *Successful Family Language Policy* (pp. 249–75). Dordrecht: Springer.

Korsch, B. M., Gozzi, E. K. and Francis, V. (1968). Gaps in doctor-patient communication: I. Doctor-patient interaction and patient satisfaction. *Pediatrics, 42*(5), 855–71.

Kosonen, K. (2009). Language-in-education policies in Southeast Asia: an overview. In K. Kosonen and C. Young (eds), *Mother Tongue as Bridge Language of Instruction: Policies and Experiences in Southeast Asia* (pp. 22–43). Bangkok: Southeast Asian Ministers of Education Organization.

Kouadio N'Guessan, J. (2008). Le français en Côte d'Ivoire: de l'imposition à l'appropriation décomplexée d'une langue exogène. *Documents pour l'histoire du français langue étrangère ou seconde, 40–41*, 179–97.

Kouega, J.-P. (2007). The language situation in Cameroon. *Current Issues in language planning, 8*(1), 3–92.

Krashen, S. (1981). *Second Language Acquisition and Second Language Learning.* Oxford: Pergamon.

Krauss, M. (1991). *Endangered languages.* Paper presented at the Linguistic Society of America Annual meeting.

Krauss, M. (1992). The world's languages in crisis. *Language, 68*(1), 4–10.

Krivonogov, V. P. (2013). The Dolgans' ethnic identity and language processes. *Journal of Siberian Federal University. Humanities and Social Sciences, 6*(6), 870–81.

Kuijpers, W. (1987). *On the languages and cultures of regional and ethnic minorities in the European Community.* Strasbourg: European Parliament

Kulick, D. (1992). *Language Shift and Cultural Reproduction: Socialization, Self and Syncretism in a Papua New Guinean Village.* Cambridge and New York: Cambridge University Press.

Kumar, V. (2019). 'Resettlement' – adding new languages in the life of the Bhils and the Pawras of the West Central India. *International Journal of Innovations in TESOL and Applied Linguistics, 4*, 1–10.

Kumar, V., Hasnain, S. I. and Kulkarni-Joshi, S. (2015). Maintenance and shift among tribal migrants in Nandurbar. *International Journal of Innovations in TESOL and Applied Linguistics, 1*(1), 1–7.

Kweon, S.-O. and Spolsky, B. (eds) (2018). *The Asian EFL Classroom.* Abingdon: Routledge.

Kymlicka, W. and Patten, A. (2003). 1. Language rights and political theory. *Annual Review of Applied Linguistics, 23*, 3–21.

Labov, W. (1962). The social motivation of a sound change. *Word, 19*, 273–309.

Labov, W. (1966). *The Social Stratification of English in New York City.* Washington, DC: Center for Applied Linguistics.

Labov, W. (2008). Unendangered dialects, endangered people. In K. A. King, N. Schilling-Estes, L. Fogle, J. L. Lia and B. Soukup (eds), *Sustaining Linguistic Diversity: Endangered and Minority Languages and Language Varieties* (pp. 219–38). Washington, DC: Georgetown University Press.

Lambert, R. D. (1999). A scaffolding for language policy. *International Journal of the Sociology of Language, 137*, 3–25.

Lambert, W. E., Giles, H. and Picard, O. (1975). Language attitudes in a French-American community. *International Journal of the Sociology of Language, 4*, 127–52.

Lange, D. (1988). *Tomorrow's Schools: The Reform of Education Administration in New Zealand.* Wellington: Government Printer.

Langer, N. and Davies, W. (eds) (2011). *Linguistic Purism in the Germanic Languages.* Berlin: Walter de Gruyter.

Lastra, Y. (2001). Otomi language shift and some recent efforts to reverse it. In J. A. Fishman (ed.), *Can Threatened Languages Be Saved?* (pp. 142–65). Clevedon: Multilingual Matters Ltd.

Laitin, D. D. (1992). *Language Repertoires and State Construction in Africa.* Cambridge: Cambridge University Press.

Lawrence, A. (2016). *Colonial approaches to governance in the periphery: Direct and indirect rule in French Algeria.* Paper presented at the Conference on Colonial Encounters and Divergent Development Trajectories in the Mediterranean, Harvard University.

Leclerc, J. (1994). *Recueil des législations linguistiques dans le monde.* Quebec, Canada: Centre internationale de recherche en aménagement linguistique.

Leclerc, J. (1994–2018). L'aménagement linguistique dans le monde, <http://www.tlfq.ulaval.ca/axl/> (last accessed 23 September 2020).

Lee, T. and McLaughlin, D. (2001). Reversing Navajo language shift, revisited. In J. A. Fishman (ed.), *Can Threatened Languages Be Saved?* (pp. 23–43). Clevedon: Multilingual Matters Ltd.

Lee, Y.-J. and Koo, H. (2006). 'Wild geese fathers' and a globalised family strategy for education in Korea. *International Development Planning Review, 28*(4), 533–53.

Leibowitz, A. H. (1970). *The Imposition of English as the Language of Instruction in American schools.* (ED C47 321). Washington, DC: Center for Applied Linguistics and ERIC Clearinghouse for Linguistics.

Lemaire, H. B. (1966). Franco-American efforts on behalf of the French language in New England. In J. A. Fishman (ed.), *Language Loyalty in the United States* (pp. 253–79). The Hague: Mouton.

Léonard, S. D. (1996). Vernacular languages and education in New Caledonia. In F. Mugler and J. Lynch (eds), *Pacific Languages in Education* (pp. 76–91). Suva: Institute of Pacific Studies, University of the South Pacific.

Leventhal, T. and Brooks-Gunn, J. (2000). The neighborhoods they live in: the effects of neighborhood residence on child and adolescent outcomes. *Psychological Bulletin, 126*(2), 309.

Levin, T., Shohamy, E. and Spolsky, B. (2003). *Academic achievements of immigrants in schools: Report to the Ministry of Education.* Tel Aviv University.

Lewis, E. G. (1972). *Multilingualism in the Soviet Union.* The Hague: Mouton

Lewis, E. G. (1980). *Bilingualism and Bilingual Education: A Comparative Study.* Albuquerque, NM and Oxford: University of New Mexico Press and Pergamon.

Lewis, G. (1999). *The Turkish Language Reform: A Catastrophic Success.* Oxford: Oxford University Press.

Lewis, M. P. (ed.) (2009). *Ethnologue: Languages of the World* (16th edn). Dallas, TX: SIL International.

Lewis, M. P. and Simons, G. F. (2010). Assessing endangerment: expanding Fishman's GIDS. *Revue roumaine de linguistique, 55*(2), 103–20.

Lewis, M. P., Simons, G. F. and Fennig, C. D. (eds) (2013). *Ethnologue* (17th edn). Dallas, TX: SIL International.

Lewis, M. P., Simons, G. F. and Fennig, C. D. (eds) (2016). *Ethnologue* (19th edn). Dallas, TX: SIL International.

Li, M. (2005). The role of parents in Chinese heritage-language schools. *Bilingual Research Journal, 29*(1), 197–207.

Li, W. (2016a). Transnational connections multilingual realities: the Chinese Diaspora experience in a global context. In W. Li (ed.), *Multilingualism in the Chinese Diaspora Worldwide* (pp. 1–12). Abingdon: Taylor & Francis.

Li, W. (ed.) (2016b). *Multilingualism in the Chinese Diaspora Worldwide.* Abingdon: Taylor & Francis.

Li, W. (2018a). Community languages in late modernity. In J. W. Tollefson and M. Pérez-Milans (eds), *The Oxford Handbook of Language Policy and Planning* (pp. 591–609). New York: Oxford University Press.

Li, W. (2018b). Translanguaging as a practical theory of language. *Applied Linguistics, 31*(1), 9–30.

Li, Y. and Li, W. (eds) (2015a). *Language Planning in China.* Berlin: De Gruyter.

Li, Y. and Li, W. (eds) (2015b). *The Language Situation in China* (Vol. 2). Berlin and Beijing: De Gruyter Mouton and Commercial Press.

Liddicoat, A. J. (2009). Evolving ideologies of the intercultural in Australian multicultural and language education policy. *Journal of Multilingual Multicultural Development, 30*(3), 189–203.

Linn, A. R. (1997). *Constructing the Grammars of a Language: Ivar Aasen and Nineteenth-Century Norwegian Linguistics.* Münster: Nordus Publikationem.

Lo Bianco, J. (2001). *Officialising language: A discourse study of language politics in the United States.* (unpublished PhD) Australian National University, Canberra.

Lo Bianco, J. (2008). Educational linguistics and education systems. In B. Spolsky and F. M. Hult (eds), *The Handbook of Educational Linguistics* (pp. 113–26). Malden, MA and Oxford: Blackwell.

Lo Bianco, J. (2012). National language revival movements: reflections from India, Israel, Indonesia and Ireland. In B. Spolsky (ed.), *The Cambridge Handbook of Language Policy* (pp. 501–22). Cambridge: Cambridge University Press.

Lo Bianco, J. (2017). Resolving ethnolinguistic conflict in multi-ethnic societies. *Nature Human Behavior.* doi:10.1038/s41562-017-0085

Lo Bianco, J. and UNICEF. (2015). *Synthesis report: Language, education and social cohesion (LESC) initiative in Malaysia Myanmar and Thailand*. Bangkok: UNICEF EAPRO.

Lo Bianco, J. and Wickert, R. (eds) (2001). *Australian Policy Activism in Language and Literacy*. Canberra: Language Australia.

López, L. E. (2008). Top-down and bottom-up: counterpoised visions of bilingual intercultural education in Latin America. In N. H. Hornberger (ed.), *Can Schools Save Indigenous Languages? Policy and Practice on Four Continents* (pp. 42–65). Basingstoke: Palgrave Macmillan.

Lorente, B. P. (2017). *Scripts of Servitude: Language, Labor Migration and Transnational Domestic Work*. Bristol: Multilingual Matters.

Lowenberg, P. H. (1990). Language and identity in the Asian state: the case of Indonesia. *The Georgetown Journal of Languages and Linguistics, 1*(1), 109–20.

Lüdi, G. (2006). Multilingual repertoires and the consequences for linguistic theory. In K. Bührig and J. D. t. Thije (eds), *Beyond Misunderstanding: Linguistic Analyses of Intercultural Communication* (Vol. 144, pp. 11–42). Amsterdam and Philadelphia: John Benjamins.

Lyons, Z. (2004). Under two flags: national conflicts and the reconstruction of identity. *Language and Intercultural Communication, 4*(1–2), 109–20.

Lyons, Z. (2009). Imagined identity and the L2 self in the French Foreign Legion. In Z. Dörnyei and E. Ushioda (eds), *Motivation, Language Identity and the L2 Self* (pp. 248–73). Bristol: Multilingual Matters.

Ma, R. and Herasimchuk, E. (1971). The linguistic dimensions of a bilingual neighborhood. In J. A. Fishman, R. L. Cooper and R. Ma (eds), *Bilingualism in the Barrio* (pp. 349–464). Bloomington: Research Center for the Language Sciences, Indiana University.

Macalister, J. and Mirvahedi, S. H. (2016). *Family Language Policies in a Multilingual World: Opportunities, Challenges, and Consequences*. New York and London: Routledge.

McCarthy, D. M., Waite, K. R., Curtis, L. M., Engel, K. G., Baker, D. W. and Wolf, M. S. (2012). What did the doctor say? Health literacy and recall of medical instructions. *Medical care, 50*(4), 277–82.

McCarty, T. L. (2002). *A Place to Be Navajo: Rough Rock and the Struggle for Self-Determination in Indigenous Schooling*. Mahwah, NJ: Lawrence Erlbaum Associates.

McCarty, T. L. (2008). Schools as strategic tools for indigenous language revitalization: lessons from Native America. In N. H. Hornberger (ed.), *Can Schools Save Indigenous Languages?* (pp. 161–79). Basingstoke: Springer.

McCarty, T. L. (2012). Indigenous language planning and policy in the Americas. In B. Spolsky (ed.), *The Cambridge Handbook of Language Policy* (pp. 544–69). Cambridge: Cambridge University Press.

McCarty, T. L., Nicholas, S. E. and Wyman, L. T. (2015). 50 (0) years out and counting: Native American language education and the four Rs. *International Multilingual Research Journal 9*(4), 227–52.

Macaulay, T. B. (1920). *Minute by the Hon'ble T. B. Macaulay, dated the 2nd February 1835*. Calcutta: Superintendent, Government Printing

McEwen, E. and Anton-Culver, H. (1988). The medical communication of deaf patients. *The Journal of Family Practice, 26*(3), 289–91.

MacGregor, L. (2003). The language of shop signs in Tokyo. *English Today, 19*(1), 18–23.

Macias, R. F. (1997). Bilingual workers and language-use rules in the workplace: a case study of nondiscriminatory language policy. *International Journal of the Sociology of Language, 127*, 53–70.

McIvor, O. (2020). Indigenous language revitalization and applied linguistics: parallel histories, shared futures? *Annual Review of Applied Linguistics, 40*, 78–96. doi:10.1017/S0267190520000094

McKee, R. and Smiler, K. (2016). Family language policy for deaf children and the vitality of New Zealand Sign Language. In J. Macalister and S. H. Mirvahedi (eds), *Family Language Policies in a Multilingual World* (pp. 40–65). London: Routledge.

McKee, R. L. and Manning, V. (2019). Implementing recognition of New Zealand Sign Language: 2006–2018. In M. D. Meulder, J. J. Murray and R. L. McKee (eds), *The Legal Recognition of Sign Languages: Advocacy and Outcomes around the World* (pp. 224–37). Bristol: Multilingual Matters.

Mackey, W. (1970). A typology of bilingual education. *Foreign Language Annals, 3*(4), 596–608.

Makina, A. (2011). *The Impact of Globalization on Somali Culture*, <https://www.researchgate.net/publication/228432222_The_Impact_of_Globalization_on_Somali_Culture> (last accessed 13 October 2020).

Mackridge, P. (2009). *Language and National Identity in Greece, 1766–1976*. Oxford: Oxford University Press.

MacNaughton, J. C. (1994). *Nisei linguists and new perspectives on the Pacific War: Intelligence, race, and continuity*. Paper presented at the Conference of Army Historians, <http://www.army.mil/cmh-pg/topics/apam/Nisei.htm> (last accessed 4 October 2020).

McRae, K. D. (1975). The principle of territoriality and the principle of personality in multilingual states. *International Journal of the Sociology of Language, 4*, 33–54.

MacSwan, J. (2017). A multilingual perspective on translanguaging. *American Educational Research Journal, 54*(1), 167–201.

Magga, O. H., Nicolaisen, I., Trask, M., Dunbar, R. and Skutnabb-Kangas, T. (2005). Indigenous children's education and indigenous languages, <http://citeseerx.ist.psu.edu/viewdoc/download?doi=10.1.1.476.5279&rep=rep1&type=pdf> (last accessed 4 October 2020).

Mahapatra, B. (1990). A demographic appraisal of multilingualism in India. In D. P. Pattanayak (ed.), *Multilingualism in India* (pp. 1–14). Bristol: Multilingual Matters.

Maher, J. C. (2001). Akor Itak – our language, your language: Ainu in Japan. In J. A. Fishman (ed.), *Can Threatened Languages Be Saved?* (pp. 323–49). Clevedon: Multilingual Matters Ltd.

Mair, V. (1991). What is a Chinese 'dialect/topolect'? Reflections on some key Sino-English linguistic terms. *Sino-Platonic Papers, 29*.

Makoni, S. B. and Severo, C. (2015). Lusitanization and Bakhtinian perspectives on the role of Portuguese in Angola and East Timor. *Journal of Multilingual and Multicultural Development, 36*(2), 151–62.

Malinowski, D. (2009). Authorship in the linguistic landscape: a performative-multimodal view. In E. Shohamy and D. Gorter (eds), *The Linguistic Landscape: Expanding the Scenery* (pp. 107–25). London: Routledge.

Mallikarjun, B. (2004). Indian multilingualism, language policy and the digital divide. *Language in India, 4*(4), 109–13.

Maltby, W. S. (2008). *The Rise and Fall of the Spanish Empire.* Basingstoke: Palgrave Macmillan.

Mamontova, N. A. (2014). What language do real Evenki speak? Discussions surrounding the nomad preschool. *Anthropology and Archeology of Eurasia, 52*(4), 37–75.

Manan, S. A., David, M. K. and Dumanig, F. P. (2016). Language management: a snapshot of governmentality within the private schools in Quetta, Pakistan. *Language Policy, 15*(1), 3–26.

Mandel, G. (1993). Why did Ben-Yehuda suggest the revival of spoken Hebrew? In L. Glinert (ed.), *Hebrew in Ashkenaz* (pp. 193–207). New York and Oxford: Oxford University Press.

Mandel, Y. (2014). *The Creation of Israeli Arabic: Political and Security Considerations in the Making of Arabic Language Studies in Israel.* Basingstoke and New York: Palgrave Macmillan.

Mangubhai, F. (1987). Literacy in Fiji: its origins and its development. *Interchange, 18*(1–2), 124–35.

Manna, S. and Ghosh, A. (2015). *Endangered Culture and Dialects with Special Reference to Mal-Paharia- A Primitive Tribal Group of Jharkhand.* In G. K Bera and K. Jose, *Endangered Cultures and Languages in India.* Karachi: Spectrum Publications.

Manzano, F. (2004). Situation and use of Occitan in Languedoc. *International Journal of the Sociology of Language, 160*, 63–90.

Martin, W. (1817). *Tonga Islands: William Mariner's account.* London: John Murray.

Martins, M. d. L. (2014). Língua Portuguesa, globalização e lusofonia. In N. B. Bastos (ed.), *Língua portuguesa e lusofonia* (pp. 15–33). São Paulo: EDUC - Editora de PUC-SP.

Martins, S. A. (2004). *Fonologia e gramática Dâw.* PhD, Vrije Universiteit, Amsterdam.

Massini-Cagliari, G. (2004). Language policy in Brazil: monolingualism and linguistic prejudice. *Language Policy, 3*(1), 3–23. doi:10.1023/B:LPOL.0000017723.72533.fd

Mathur, H. M. (ed.) (2012). *Resettling Displaced People: Policy and Practice in India.* New Delhi: Routledge.

May, S. (2012). *Language and Minority Rights: Ethnicity, Nationalism and the Politics of Language* (2nd edn). New York and London: Routledge.

May, S. and Hill, R. (2008). Maori-medium education: current issues and challenges. In N. H. Hornberger (ed.), *Can Schools Save Indigenous Languages? Policy and Practice on Four Continents* (pp. 66–98). Basingstoke: Palgrave Macmillan.

Mays, T. M. (2002). *Africa's First Peacekeeping Operation: The OAU in Chad, 1981–1982.* Westwood, CT: Praeger.

Mbokou, L. M. (2012). A survey of bilingualism in multilingual Gabon. In H. S. Ndinga-Koumba-Binza and S. E. Busch (eds), *Language Science and Language Technology in Africa: A Festschrift for Justus C. Roux* (pp. 163–75). Stellenbosch: Sun Press.

Meadows, W. C. (2002). *The Comanche Code Talkers of World War II.* Austin, TX: University of Texas Press.

Meer, N. (2009). Identity articulations, mobilization, and autonomy in the movement for Muslim schools in Britain. *Race Ethnicity and Education, 12*(3), 379–99. doi:10.1080/13613320903178311

Mehrotra, R. R. (1999). Endangered languages in India. *International Journal of the Sociology of Language, 140*(1), 105–14.

Mehrotra, S. (ed.) (2006). *The Economics of Elementary Education in India: The Challenge of Public Finance, Private Provision and Household Costs.* New Delhi: Sage.

Mendel, Y. (2014). *The Creation of Israeli Arabic: Political and Security Considerations in the Making of Arabic Language Studies in Israel.* Basingstoke: Palgrave Macmillan.

Meulder, M. D., Murray, J. J. and McKee, R. L. (eds) (2019). *The Legal Recognition of Sign Languages: Advocacy and Outcomes around the World.* Bristol: Multilingual Matters.

Migge, B. and Léglise, I. (2010). Integrating local languages and cultures into the education system of French Guiana. In B. Migge, I. Léglise, and A. Bartens (eds), *Creoles in Education: An Appraisal of Current Programs and Projects* (pp. 107–32). Amsterdam and Philadelphia: John Benjamins Publishing Company.

Migué, J.-L. (1970). Le nationalisme, l'unite nationale et la theorie economique de l'information. [Nationalism, National Unity, and the Economic Theory of Information. With English summary.] *Canadian Journal of Economics, 3*(2), 183–98.

Mikkelson, H. (2016). *Introduction to Court Interpreting.* London: Routledge.

Miller, R. A. (1963). Thon-Mi Sambhoṭa and His Grammatical Treatises. *Journal of the American Oriental Society, 83*(4), 485–502.

Milroy, L. (1980). *Languages and Social Networks.* Oxford: Basil Blackwell.

Mirvahedi, S. H. (2016). Exploring family language policies among Azerbaijani speaking families in the city of Tabriz, Iran. In J. Macalister and S. H. Mirvahedi (eds), *Family Language Policies in a Multilingual World* (pp. 74–95). London: Routledge.

Mitchell, L. (2009). *Language, Emotion, and Politics in South India: The Making of a Mother Tongue.* Bloomington: Indiana University Press.

Mitchell, S. (2016). *Exploring the use of procedural policy instruments in the development and implementation of French second language policy in New Brunswick and Nova Scotia.* PhD, Université d'Ottawa/University of Ottawa.

Mizuno, T. (2000). Self-censorship by coercion: the federal government and the California Japanese-language newspapers from Pearl Harbor to internment. *American Journalism, 17*(3), 31–57.

Modiano, M. (2017). English in a post-Brexit European Union. *World Englishes, 36*(3), 313–27.

Mohanty, A. K. (1990). Psychological consequences of mother-tongue maintenance and the language of literacy for linguistic minorities in India. *Psychology and Developing Societies, 2*(1), 31–50.

Mohanty, A. K. (2019a). Language policy in education in India. In A. Kirkpatrick and A. J. Liddicoat (eds), *The Routledge International Handbook of Language Education Policy in Asia.* London: Routledge.

Mohanty, A. K. (2019b). *The Multilingual Reality: Living with Languages*. Bristol: Multilingual Matters.

Mohanty, A. K., Panda, M. and Pal, R. (2010). Language policy in education and classroom practices in India. In K. Menken and O. Garcia (eds), *Negotiating Language Policies in Schools: Educators as Policymakers* (pp. 211–31). London and New York: Routledge.

Mohanty, P. (unpublished). Wall, gate or door: English in Indian society and education.

Mohanty, P. (2002). British language policies in 19th century India and the Oriya language movement. *Language Policy, 1*(1), 57–73.

Moon, S. (2011). Expectation and reality: Korean sojourner families in the UK. *Language and Education, 25*(2), 163–76.

Moore, D., Facundes, S. and Pires, N. (1994). Nheengatu (Língua Geral Amazônica), its history, and the effects of language contact, <https://escholarship.org/uc/item/7tb981s1> (last accessed 23 September 2020).

Moore, L. C. (2016). Change and variation in family religious language policy in a West African Muslim community. *Language Policy, 15*(2), 125–39.

Morey, S., Post, M. W. and Friedman, V. A. (2013). The language codes of ISO 639: a premature, ultimately unobtainable, and possibly damaging standardization, <https://core.ac.uk/download/pdf/41237514.pdf> (last accessed 4 October 2020).

Morfit, M. (1981). Pancasila: the Indonesian state ideology according to the new order government. *Asian Survey, 21*(8), 838–51.

Morova, N. S., Lezhnina, L. V., Biryukova, N. A., Domracheva, S. A. and Makarova, O. A. (2015). Diversity and tolerance in a multi-ethnic region of Mari El Republic, Russia. *Review of European Studies, 7*(8), 171–81.

Morris, D. and Jones, K. (2007). Minority language socialisation within the family: investigating the early Welsh language socialisation of babies and young children in mixed language families in Wales. *Journal of Multilingual and Multicultural Development, 28*(6), 484–501.

Mose, P. N. (2017). Language-in-education policy in Kenya. *Nordic Journal of African Studies, 26*(3), 215–230.

Mufwene, S. S. (2001). *The Ecology of Language Evolution*. Cambridge and New York: Cambridge University Press.

Mufwene, S. S. (2005a). Globalization and the myth of killer languages: what's really going on. In G. Huggan and S. Klasen (eds), *Perspectives on Endangerment* (Vol. 5, pp. 19–48). Hildesheim: Olms.

Mufwene, S. S. (2005b). Language evolution: the population genetics way. In G. Hauska (ed.), *Gene, Sprachen und ihre Evolution* (pp. 30–52). Regensburg: Regensburg University Press.

Mugler, F. (2001). Dravidian languages in Fiji: survival and maintenance. In A. Abbi, R. S. Gupta and A. Kidwai (eds), *Linguistic Structures and Language Dynamics in South Asia: Papers from the Proceedings of SALA XVIII Roundtable* (pp. 21–40). Delhi: Motilal Banarsidass.

Mukama, R. (2009). Theory and practice in language policy: the case of Uganda. *Kiswahili, 72*(1).

Muller, K. (2012). Between Europe and Africa: Mayotte. In R. Adler-Nissen and

U. Gad (eds), *European Integration and Post-Colonial Sovereignty Games* (pp. 187–203). London: Routledge.

Mustafina, D., Bilyalova, A., Mustafina, L. and Slavina, L. (2014). Language policy and language situation in the Russian national regions. *European Journal of Science and Theology, 6*, 185–91.

Muth, S. (2014). Linguistic landscapes on the other side of the border: signs, language and the construction of cultural identity in Transnistria. *International Journal of the Sociology of Language, 2014*(227), 25–46.

Mwanza, D. S. (2017). Implications of teachers' attitudes towards unofficial languages on English language teaching in multilingual Zambia. *Zambian Journal of Language Studies, 1*(1), 101–24.

Myers-Scotton, C. (1990). Elite closure as boundary maintenance: the case of Africa. In B. Weinstein (ed.), *Language Policy and Political Development* (pp. 25–42). Norwood, NJ: Ablex Publishing Company.

Myers-Scotton, C. (1993). Elite closure as a powerful language strategy: the African case. *International Journal of the Sociology of Language, 103*, 149–63.

Nakayiza, J. (2013). *The sociolinguistics of multilingualism in Uganda: A case study of the official and non-official language policy, planning and management of Luruuri-lunyara and Luganda.* PhD, SOAS, University of London, London.

Navarro, D. and Macalister, J. (2016). Adrift in an Anglophone world: refugee families' language policy challenges. In J. Macalister and S. H. Mirvahedi (eds), *Family Language Policies in a Multilingual World* (pp. 115–32). London: Routledge.

Neff, D., Haasnoot, C. W., Renner, S. and Sen, K. (2019). The social and economic situation of Scheduled Tribes in India. In C. Fleming and M. Manning (eds), *Routledge Handbook of Indigenous Wellbeing.* London: Routledge.

Nekvapil, J. (2012). From language planning to language management. *Media and Communication Studies, 63*, 5–21.

Nekvapil, J. and Nekula, M. (2006). On language management in multinational companies in the Czech Republic. *Current Issues in Language Planning, 7*(2–3), 307–27.

Nekvapil, J. and Sherman, T. (eds) (2009). *Language Management in Contact Situations: Perspectives from Three Continents.* Frankfurt am Main, Berlin, Bern, Bruxelles, New York, Oxford and Wien: Peter Lang.

Neustupný, J. V. (1970). Basic types of treatment of language problems. *Linguistic Communications, 1*, 77–98.

Neustupný, J. V. and Nekvapil, J. (2003). Language management in the Czech Republic. *Current Issues in Language Planning, 4*(3–4), 181–366.

Ng, S. H. and He, A. (2004). Code-switching in trigenerational family conversations among Chinese immigrants in New Zealand. *Journal of Language and Social Psychology, 23*(1), 28–48.

Nic Shuibhne, N. (2001). The European Union and minority language rights. *International Journal on Multicultural Societies, 3*(2), 61–77

Nikolaeva, S. (2019). The Common European Framework of Reference for Language: past, present, and future. *Advanced Education, 6*(12), 12–20.

Nolan, J. S. (2008). School and extended family in the transmission and revitalisation of Gallo in Upper-Brittany. *Journal of Multilingual and Multicultural Development, 29*(3), 216–34.

Nolan, R. (2020). Language barrier. *The New Yorker,* 6 January, 26–31.

Noro, H. (1990). Family and language maintenance: an exploratory study of Japanese language maintenance among children of postwar Japanese immigrants in Toronto. *International Journal of the Sociology of Language, 86*, 57–68.

Novianti, E. (2013). Family communication in mixed-marriage between Sundanese and Minangkabau. *The International Journal of Social Sciences, 18*(1), 33–50.

Ó Riágain, P. (1997). *Language Policy and Social Reproduction: Ireland 1893–1993.* Oxford: Clarendon Press.

O'Donnell, P. E. (2000). Crossing the line in Quebec and Catalonia: the consequences of the linguistically 'mixed' marriage. *Language Problems and Language Planning, 24*(3), 233–47.

Obeng, S. G. and Adegbija, E. (1999). Sub-Saharan Africa. In J. A. Fishman (ed.), *Handbook of Language and Ethnic Identity* (pp. 353–68). New York and Oxford: Oxford University Press.

Ochs, E. (1986). Introduction. In B. B. Schieffelin and E. Ochs (eds), *Language Socialization across Cultures* (pp. 2–13). Cambridge: Cambridge University Press.

Ochs, E. (1988). *Culture and Language Development: Language Acquisition and Language Socialization in a Samoan Village.* Cambridge, Cambridge University Press.

Ochs, E. and Schieffelin, B. (2001). Language acquisition and socialization: three developmental stories and their implications. In A.Duranti (ed.), *Linguistic Anthropology: A Reader, 2001* (pp. 263–301). Oxford: Blackwell.

Ochs, E. and Schieffelin, B. B. (2011). The theory of language socialization. In A. Duranti, E. Ochs and B. B. Schieffelin (eds), *The Handbook of Language Socialization* (pp. 1–21). Malden, MA and Oxford: Wiley Blackwell.

Oellers-Frahm, K. (1999). European Charter for Regional and Minority Languages— minority group rights and compatibility with concepts of equality, nondiscrimination and national unity in French Constitution—reconciling official language with freedom of speech. *American Journal of International Law, 93*(4), 938–42.

Ohannessian, S. and Kashoki, M. E. (eds) (1978). *Language in Zambia.* London: International African Institute.

Olajo, A. S. and Oluwapelumi, A. M. (2018). A study on the extinction of indigenous languages in Nigeria: causes and possible solutions. *Annals of Language and Literature, 2*(1), 22–6.

Omissi, D. (2016). *The Sepoy and the Raj: The Indian Army, 1860–1940.* Berlin: Springer.

Omoniyi, T. and Fishman, J. A. (eds) (2006). *Explorations in the Sociology of Language and Religion.* Amsterdam and Philadelphia: John Benjamins Publishing Company.

Oni, J. B. (1995). Fostered children's perception of their health care and illness treatment in Ekiti Yoruba households, Nigeria. *Health Transition Review, 5*(1), 21–34.

Oonk, G. (2007a). *Global Indian Diasporas: Exploring Trajectories of Migration and Theory.* Amsterdam: Amsterdam University Press.

Oonk, G. (2007b). 'We Lost our Gift of Expression'. In G. Oonk (ed.), *Global Indian Diasporas* (pp. 67–88). Amsterdam: University of Amsterdam Press.

Or, I. G., Shohamy, E. and Spolsky, B. (eds) (2021). *Multilingual Israel: Language Ideologies, Survival, Integration, and Hybridization.* Bristol: Multilingual Matters.

Otheguy, R., García, O. and Reid, W. (2015). Clarifying translanguaging and deconstructing named languages: a perspective from linguistics. *Applied Linguistics Review, 6*(3), 281–307.

Oyero, O. (2003). Indigenous language radio for development purposes. In E. O. Soola (ed.), *Communicating for Developing Purposes* (pp. 185–95). Ibadan, Nigeria: Kraft Books.

Paauw, S. (2009). One land, one nation, one language: an analysis of Indonesia's national language policy. *University of Rochester Working Papers in the Language Sciences, 5*(1), 2–16.

Paia, M. and Vernaudon, J. (2016). Le défi de l'éducation bilingue en Polynésie fran-çaise. In C. Hélot and J. Erfurt (eds), *L'Education bilingue en France: Politiques linguistiques, modèles et pratiques* (pp. 87–99). Strasbourg: Lambert-Lucas.

Palacín, I., Martinez, A. and Ortuoste, L. (2015). Shouting against the silencing. A brief introduction to the minority struggles from the Basque Country. *Revista Eletrônica Direito e Sociedade-REDES, 3*(2), 55–63.

Pandharipande, R. V. (2002). Minority matters: issues in minority languages in India. *International Journal on Multicultural Societies, 4*(2), 213–34.

Pandharipande, R. V., David, M. K. and Ebsworth, M. E. (eds) (2020). *Language Maintenance, Revival and Shift in the Sociology of Religion.* Bristol: Multilingual Matters.

Paternost, J. (1985). A sociolinguistic tug of war between language value and lan-guage reality in contemporary Slovenian. *International Journal of the Sociology of Language, 52,* 9–29.

Paugh, A. L. (2005). *Acting adult: Language socialization, shift, and ideologies in Dominica, West Indies.* Paper presented at the Proceedings of the 4th International Symposium on Bilingualism.

Paul, D. A. (1998). *The Navajo Code Talkers.* Pittsburgh: Dorrance Publishing.

Paulston, C. B. (ed.) (1988). *International Handbook of Bilingualism and Bilingual Education.* New York: Greenwood Press.

Paulston, C. B. (1998). Linguistic minorities in Central and East Europe: an intro-duction. In C. B. Paulston and D. Peckham (eds), *Linguistic Minorities in Central and East Europe* (pp. 1–18). Clevedon and Philadelphia: Multilingual Matters Ltd.

Paulston, C. B. and Watt, J. M. (2011). Language policy and religion. In B. Spolsky (ed.), *Handbook of Language Policy.* Cambridge: Cambridge University Press.

Pavlenko, A. (2011). Language rights versus speakers' rights: on the applicability of Western language rights approaches in Eastern European contexts. *Language Policy, 10*(1), 37–58.

Pavlenko, A. (2017). Superdiversity and why it isn't: reflections on terminological innovation and academic branding. In S. Breidbach, L. Küster and B. Schmenk (eds), *Sloganizations in Language Education Discourse.* Bristol: Multilingual Matters Ltd.

Pearce, E. (2015). *A Grammar of Unua* (Vol. 647). Berlin: Walter de Gruyter GmbH and Co KG.

Pereira, A. A. (2009). *Estudio morfossintatico do Asurini do Xingu.* PhD, Universidade Estadual de Campinas, Campinas.

Perry, J. R. (1985). Language reform in Turkey and Iran. *International Journal of Middle East Studies, 17*(3), 295–311.

Phillipson, R. (1992a). Linguistic imperialism. In C. Chapelle (ed.) *The Encyclopedia of Applied Linguistics* (pp. 1–7): Wiley Online Library.

Phillipson, R. (1992b). *Linguistic imperialism*. Oxford: Oxford University Press.

Phillipson, R. (2003). *English-Only Europe?: Challenging Language Policy*. London: Routledge.

Phillipson, R. (2017). Myths and realities of 'global' English. *Language Policy, 16*(3), 313–31. doi:10.1007/s10993-016-9409-z

Phillipson, R. and Skutnabb-Kangas, T. (1995). Linguistic rights and wrong. *Applied Linguistics, 16*, 483–504.

Phillipson, R. and Skutnabb-Kangas, T. (2013). Linguistic imperialism and endangered languages. In T. K. Bhatia and W. C. Ritchie (eds), *The Handbook of Bilingualism and Multilingualism* (pp. 495–516). Hoboken, NJ: Wiley.

Piller, I. (2016). Herder: an explainer for linguists, <http://www.languageonthemove.com/herder-an-explainer-for-linguists/> (last accessed 4 October 2020).

Piper, B., Schroeder, L. and Trudell, B. (2016). Oral reading fluency and comprehension in Kenya: reading acquisition in a multilingual environment. *Journal of Research in Reading, 39*(2), 133–52.

Pizer, G. (2013). Bimodal bilingual families: the negotiation of communication practices between deaf parents and their hearing children. In M. Schwartz and A. Verschik (eds), *Successful Family Language Policy* (pp. 203–22). Dordrecht: Springer.

Pool, J. (1991). The official language problem. *American Political Science Review, 85*(2), 495–514.

Postiglione, G. A. (2009). Dislocated education: the case of Tibet. *Comparative Education Review*, 483–512.

Powell, R. (2002). Language planning and the British Empire: comparing Pakistan, Malaysia and Kenya. *Current Issues in Language Planning, 3*(3), 205–79.

Preston, D. R. (ed.) (1999). *Handbook of Perceptual Dialectology*. Amsterdam and Philadelphia: John Benjamins Publishing Company.

Preston, R. A. (1991). *To Serve Canada: A History of the Royal Military College since the Second World War*. Ottawa: Ottawa University Press.

Priedīte, A. (2005). Surveying language attitudes and practices in Latvia. *Journal of Multilingual and Multicultural Development, 26*(5), 409–24.

Pütz, M. and Mundt, N. (eds) (2019). *Expanding the Linguistic Landscape*. Bristol: Multilingual Matters.

Pyoli, R. (1998). Karelian under pressure from Russianinternal and external Russification. *Journal of Multilingual and Multicultural Development, 19*(2), 128–41.

Qy Research. (2019). *Global Digital English Language Learning Market Size, Status and Forecast 2025*. Market Insight Reports. Harrisburg, NC and Pune: Wise Guy Reports.

Rahman, T. (2009). Language ideology, identity and the commodification of language in the call centers of Pakistan. *Language in Society, 38*(2), 233–58.

Ramonienė, M. (2013). Family language policy and management in a changed sociopolitical situation: Russians and Russian speakers in Lithuania. In M. Schwartz and A. Verschik (eds), *Successful Family Language Policy* (pp. 127–43). Dordrecht: Springer.

Rampton, B. (2014). *Crossings: Language and Ethnicity among Adolescents.* Abingdon: Routledge.

Rappa, A. L. and Wee, L. (2006). *Language Policy and Modernity in Southeast Asia: Malaysia, the Philippines, Singapore, and Thailand.* New York: Springer Science.

Rautz, G., Toggenburg, G. N., Tomaselli, A. and Zabielska, K. (eds) (2008). *Material for Specialized Media EURASIA-Net Project.* Bolzano/Bozen: EURAC within the EURASIA-Net project.

Read, J. (2019). The influence of the Common European Framework of Reference (CEFR) in the Asia-Pacific region. *LEARN Journal: Language Education and Acquisition Research Network, 12*(1), 12–18.

Read, J., Wette, R. and Deverall, P. (2009). *Achieving English Proficiency for Professional Registration: The Experience of Overseas-Qualified Health Professionals in the New Zealand Context.* Canberra: IELTS Australia and British Council.

Recendiz, N. R. (2008). Learning with differences: strengthening Hñähñö and bilingual teaching in an elementary school in Mexico City. In N. H. Hornberger (ed.), *Can Schools Save Indigenous Languages? Policy and Practice on Four Continents* (pp. 99–124). Basingstoke: Palgrave Macmillan.

Regnault, M. (2009). Politique culturelle et départementalisation à Mayotte. *Revue juridique de l'Océan Indien* (NS-2009), 145–74.

Reichard, G. (1974). *Navaho Grammar.* New York: AMS Press.

Reid, C. (2004). *Negotiating Racialised Identities: Indigenous Teacher Education in Australia and Canada.* Canberra: Common Ground.

Remennick, L. (2002). Transnational community in the making: Russian-Jewish immigrants of the 1990s in Israel. *Journal of Ethnic and Migration Studies, 28*(3), 515–30. doi:10.1080/13691830220146581

Reményi, J. (1950). Ferenc Kazinczy, Hungarian critic and neologist (1759–1831). *The Slavonic and East European Review, 29*(72), 233–43.

Renan, E. (1882). Qu'est-ce qu'une nation? *Bulletin de l'Association Scientifique de France*, 26 March.

Reshef, Y. (2019). *Historical Continuity in the Emergence of Modern Hebrew.* Lanham, MD: Lexington Books.

Restall, M. (2007). The decline and fall of the Spanish Empire? *The William and Mary Quarterly, 64*(1), 183–94.

Revis, M. (2016). How religious ideologies and practices impact on family language policy: Ethiopians in Wellington. In J. Macalister and S. H. Mirvahedi (eds), *Family Language Policies in a Multilingual World* (pp. 135–53). London: Routledge.

Ribeiro, E. R. (2009). Tapuya connections: language contact in eastern Brazil. *LIAMES: Linguas Indígenas Americanas, 9*(1), 61–76.

Richter, D., Richter, I., Toivanen, R. and Ulasiuk, I. (2012). *Language Rights Revisited - The Challenge of Global Migration and Communication* (Vol. 4). Berlin: BWV Verlag.

Riley, K. C. (2011). Language socialization and language ideologies. In A. Duranti, E. Ochs and B. B. Schieffelin (eds), *The Handbook of Language Socialization* (pp. 493–514). Malden, MA and Oxford: Wiley Blackwell.

Robitaille, L.-B. (2002). *Le Salon des immortels: Une académie très française.* Paris: Denoël.

Rochette, B. (2011). Language policies in the Roman Republic and Empire. In

J. Clackson (ed.), *Blackwell Companion to the History of the Latin Language* (pp. 549–63). Malden, MA and Oxford: Blackwell.

Rodrigues, A. D. I. (1986). *Línguas Brasileiras: para um conhecimento das línguas indígenas*. São Paulo: Edições Loyola.

Rodríguez, C. and El Gazi, J. (2007). The poetics of indigenous radio in Colombia. *Media, Culture, Society, 29*(3), 449–68.

Rodríguez-Ordóñez, I. (2019). The role of linguistic ideologies in language contact situations. *Language and Linguistics Compass*, e12351. doi: https://doi.org/10.1111/lnc3.12351

Rohsenow, J. S. (2004). Fifty years of script and written language reform in the P.R.C.: the genesis of the language law of 2001. In M. Zhou (ed.), *Language Policy in the People's Republic of China: Theory and Practice since 1949* (pp. 21–45). Dordrecht: Kluwer Academic Publishers.

Romaine, S. (2008). Language rights, human development and linguistic diversity in a globalizing world. In P. v. Sterkenburg (ed.), *Unity and Diversity of Languages* (pp. 85–96). Amsterdam: John Benjamins Publishing Company.

Ronjat, J. (1913). *Le développement du langage observé chez un enfant bilingue*. Paris: H. Champion.

Rosen, L. (1977). The anthropologist as expert witness. *American Anthropologist, 79*(3), 555–78.

Rosenbaum, Y., Nadel, E., Cooper, R. L. and Fishman, J. A. (1977). English on Keren Kayemet Street. In J. A. Fishman, R. L. Cooper and A. W. Conrad (eds), *The Spread of English* (pp. 179–96). Rowley, MA: Newbury House Publishers.

Rosier, P. and Holm, W. (1980). *The Rock Point Experience: A Longitudinal Study of a Navajo School Program*. Washington, DC: Center for Applied Linguistics.

Rubin, J., Jernudd, B., Das Gupta, J., Fishman, J. A. and Ferguson, C. A. (1977). *Language Planning Processes*. The Hague: Mouton Publishers.

Rubinstein, C. V. (2018). Book review: translanguaging: language, bilingualism and education by Ofelia García and Li Wei (2014). *Bellaterra Journal of Teaching & Learning Language & Literature, 11*(1), 85–95.

Ryoo, H.-K. (2005). Achieving friendly interactions: a study of service encounters between Korean shopkeepers and African-American customers. *Discourse Society, 16*(1), 79–105.

Sacks, O. (2019). The machine stops. *The New Yorker, XCIV(48)*, 11 February, 28–9.

Sahgal, A. (1991). Patterns of language use in a bilingual setting in India. In J. Cheshire (ed.), *English around the World: Sociolinguistic Perspectives* (pp. 299–307). Cambridge: Cambridge University Press.

Salimbene, F. P. (1996). Court interpreters: standards of practice and standards for training. *Cornell Journal of Law and Public Policy, 6*, 645–72.

Sallabank, J. (2011). Language policy for endangered languages. In P. K. Austin and J. Sallabank (eds), *The Cambridge Handbook of Endangered Languages* (pp. 277–90). Cambridge: Cambridge University Press.

Salt, H. (1814). *A voyage to Abyssinia*. London: Rivington.

Samarin, W. J. (1986). French and Sango in the Central African Republic. *Anthropological Linguistics, 28*(3), 379–87.

Samarin, W. J. (1991). The origins of Kituba and Lingala. *Journal of African Languages and Linguistics, 12*(1), 47–78.

Samper-Padilla José, A. (2008). Sociolinguistics aspects of Spanish in the Canary Islands. *International Journal of the Sociology of Language, 2008*(193–4), 161–76. doi:10.1515/IJSL.2008.053

Sapir, E. (1942). *Navaho Texts*. Iowa City: Linguistic Society of America.

Saulson, S. B. (ed.) (1979). *Institutionalized Language Planning*. The Hague: Mouton.

Sawyer, J. F. A. (2001). Religion and language. In R. Mesthrie (ed.), *Concise Encyclopedia of sociolinguistics* (pp. 262–5). Oxford: Pergamon.

Schalley, A. C. and Eisenchlas, S. A. (2020). *Handbook of Home Language Maintenance and Development: Social and Affective Factors* (Vol. 18). Berlin: Walter de Gruyter GmbH and Co KG.

Schieffelin, B. B. and Doucet, R. C. (1998). The 'real' Haitian Creole: ideology, metalinguistics, and orthographic choice. In B. B. Schieffelin, K. A. Woolard and P. V. Kroskrity (eds), *Language Ideologies: Practice and Theory* (pp. 285–316). New York and Oxford: Oxford University Press.

Schlick, M. (2003). The English of shop signs in Europe. *English Today, 19*(1), 3–17.

Schorr, S. A. (2000). *Gedud Meginei Hasafah B'eretz Yisrael 1923–1936 (Legion for the Defense of the Language in Palestine 1923–1936)*. Haifa: Herzl Institute for Research on Zionism.

Schultz, K. (2001). *Tropical Versailles: Empire, Monarchy, and the Portuguese Royal Court in Rio de Janeiro, 1808–1821*. New York and London: Routledge.

Schüpbach, D. (2009). Language transmission revisited: family type, linguistic environment and language attitudes. *International Journal of Bilingual Education and Bilingualism, 12*(1), 15–30.

Schuster, M., Elroy, I. and Elmakais, I. (2017). We are lost: measuring the accessibility of signage in public general hospitals. *Language Policy, 16*(1), 23–38.

Schütz, A. J. (1985). *The Fijian Language*. Honolulu, HI: University of Hawaii Press.

Schwartz, M. (2008). Exploring the relationship between family language policy and heritage language knowledge among second-generation Russian-Jewish immigrants in Israel. *Journal of Multilingual and Multicultural Development, 29*(5), 400–18.

Schwartz, M. (2010). Family language policy. *Applied Linguistics Review, 1*(1), 171–91.

Schwartz, M., Moin, V., Leiken, M. and Breitkofy, A. (2011). Immigrant parents' choice of a bilingual versus monolingual kindergarten for second-generation children: motives, attitudes, and factors. *International Multilingual Research Journal, 4*(2), 107–24.

Seto, K. (2014). What should we understand about urbanization in China? *Yale Insights-Yale School of Management*, <https://insights.som.yale.edu/insights/what-should-we-understand-about-urbanization-in-china> (last accessed 4 October 2020).

Shabani, O. A. P. (2007). Language policy of a civic nation-state: constitutional patriotism and minority language rights. In D. Castiglione and C. Longman (eds), *The Language Question in Europe and Diverse Societies: Political, Legal and Social Perspectives* (pp. 37–59). Oxford: Hart.

Sharma, R. N. and Sharma, R. K. (1996). *History of Education in India*. New Delhi: Atlantic Publishers.

Shibata, S. (2000). Opening a Japanese Saturday school in a small town in the United

States: community collaboration to teach Japanese as a heritage language. *Bilingual Research Journal, 24*(4), 465–74.

Shin, H. B. and Kominski, R. A. (2010). *Language Use in the United States: 2007.* Washington, DC: US Census Bureau.

Shiohata, M. (2012). Language use along the urban street in Senegal: perspectives from proprietors of commercial signs. *Journal of Multilingual Multicultural Development, 33*(3), 269–85.

Shir, R. (2019). Resisting Chinese linguistic imperialism: Abduweli Ayup and the movement for Uyghur mother tongue-based education, <https://docs.uhrp.org/pdf/UHRP_Resisting_Chinese_Linguistic_Imperialism_May_2019.pdf> (last accessed 4 October 2020).

Shively, R. L. (2011). L2 pragmatic development in study abroad: a longitudinal study of Spanish service encounters. *Journal of Pragmatics, 43*(6), 1818–35.

Shneer, D. (2004). *Yiddish and the Creation of Soviet Jewish Culture: 1918–1930.* Cambridge: Cambridge University Press.

Shohamy, E. (2007). At what cost? Methods of language revival and protection: examples from Hebrew. In K. A. King, N. Schilling-Estes, J. J. Lou, L. Fogle and B. Soukup (eds), *Endangered and Minority Languages and Language Varieties: Defining, Documenting and Developing.* Washington, DC: Georgetown University.

Shohamy, E., Levin, T., Spolsky, B., Inbar, O., Levi-Keren, M. and Shemesh, M. (2002). *Assessment of academic achievement of immigrant students in Israeli schools.* Paper presented at the AILA World Congress, Singapore.

Sibayan, B. (1974). Language policy, language engineering and literacy in the Philippines. In J. A. Fishman (ed.), *Advances in language Planning* (pp. 221–54). The Hague: Mouton.

Silver, R. E. (2005). The discourse of linguistic capital: language and economic policy planning in Singapore. *Language Policy, 4*(1), 47–66.

Simon, J. (ed.) (1998). *Nga Kura Maori: The Native Schools System 1867–1967.* Auckland: Auckland University Press.

Siragusa, L. (2015). Metaphors of language: the Vepsian ecology challenges an international paradigm. *Eesti ja soome-ugri keeleteaduse ajakiri. Journal of Estonian and Finno-Ugric Linguistics, 6*(1), 111–37.

Siridetkoon, P. and Dewaele, J.-M. (2018). Ideal self and ought-to self of simultaneous learners of multiple foreign languages. *International Journal of Multilingualism, 15*(4), 313–28.

Sirles, C. A. (1999). Politics and Arabization: the evolution of postindependence North Africa. *International Journal of the Sociology of Language, 137*, 115–30.

Skutnabb-Kangas, T. (2000). *Linguistic Genocide in Education, or Worldwide Diversity and Human Rights?* Mahwah, NJ: Lawrence Erlbaum Associates.

Skutnabb-Kangas, T. and Phillipson, R. (1995). Linguistic human rights, past and present. In T. Skutnabb-Kangas, R. Phillipson and M. Rannut (eds), *Linguistic Human Rights: Overcoming Linguistic Discrimination* (pp. 71–110). Berlin and New York: Mouton de Gruyter.

Skutnabb-Kangas, T. and Phillipson, R. (2010). The global politics of language: markets, maintenance, marginalization, or murder. In N. Coupland (ed.), *The Handbook of Language and Globalization* (pp. 77–100). Malden, MA and Oxford: John Wiley & Sons.

Skutnabb-Kangas, T. and Phillipson, R. (2017). *Language Rights*. New York and London: Routledge.

Smalley, W. A. (1994). *Linguistic Diversity and National Unity: Language Ecology in Thailand*. Chicago: University of Chicago Press.

Smith, A. (2017). Indigenous languages on stage: a roundtable conversation with five indigenous theatre artists. *Theatre Research in Canada/Recherches théâtrales au Canada, 38*(2), 219–35.

Smith, J. (2016). *Maori Television: The First Ten Years*. Auckland: Auckland University Press.

Smith-Hefner, N. J. (2009). Language shift, gender, and ideologies of modernity in Central Java, Indonesia. *Journal of Linguistic Anthropology, 19*(1), 57–77.

Song, J. J. (2001). North and South Korea: language policies of divergence and convergence. In N. Gotieb and P. Chen (eds), *Language Planning and Language Policy. East Asian Perspectives* (pp. 129–58). London: Curzon.

Song, J. J. (2011). English as an official language in South Korea: global English or social malady. *Language Problems and Language Planning, 35*(1), 35–55.

Soukup, B. (2016). English in the linguistic landscape of Vienna, Austria (ELLViA): outline, rationale, and methodology of a large-scale empirical project on language choice on public signs from the perspective of sign-readers. *Views, 25*, 1–24.

Spolsky, B. (1970). Navajo language maintenance: six-year-olds in 1969. *Language Sciences, 13*, 19–24.

Spolsky, B. (1974a). Linguistics and the language barrier to education. In T. A. Sebeok, A. S. Abramson, D. Hymes, H. Rubenstein, E. Stankiewicz and B. Spolsky (eds), *Current Trends in Linguistics: Linguistics and Adjacent Arts and Sciences* (Vol. 12, pp. 2027–38). The Hague: Mouton.

Spolsky, B. (1974b). Navajo language maintenance: six-year-olds in 1969. In F. Pialorsi (ed.), *Teaching the Bilingual* (pp. 138–49). Tucson, AZ: University of Arizona Press.

Spolsky, B. (1975). Prospects for the survival of the Navajo language. In M. D. Kinkade, K. Hale and O. Werner (eds), *Linguistics and Anthropology, in Honor of C.F. Voegelin* (pp. 597–606). Lisse: The Peter de Ridder Press.

Spolsky, B. (1977). The establishment of language education policy in multilingual societies. In B. Spolsky and R. L. Cooper (eds), *Frontiers of Bilingual Education* (pp. 1–21). Rowley, MA: Newbury House Publishers.

Spolsky, B. (1978). Bilingual education in the United States. In J. E. Alatis (ed.), *Georgetown Roundtable on Language and Linguistics 1978* (pp. 268–84). Washington, DC: Georgetown University Press.

Spolsky, B. (1989). Maori bilingual education and language revitalization. *Journal of Multilingual and Multicultural Development, 9*(6), 1–18.

Spolsky, B. (1991a). Hebrew language revitalization within a general theory of second language learning. In R. L. Cooper and B. Spolsky (eds), *The Influence of Language on Culture and Thought: Essays in Honor of Joshua A. Fishman's Sixty-Fifth Birthday* (pp. 137–55). Berlin: Mouton de Gruyter.

Spolsky, B. (1991b). The Samoan language in the New Zealand educational context. *Vox, 5*, 31–6.

Spolsky, B. (1993). Language conflict in Jerusalem – 1880 and 1980. In E. H. Jahr (ed.), *Language Conflict and Language Planning* (pp. 179–92). Berlin: Mouton de Gruyter.

Spolsky, B. (1995). The impact of the Army Specialized Training Program: a reconsideration. In G. Cook and B. Seidelhofer (eds), *For H.G. Widdowson: Principles and Practice in the Study of Language: A Festschrift on the Occasion of His Sixtieth Birthday* (pp. 323–34). Oxford: Oxford University Press.

Spolsky, B. (1996). Prologemena to an Israeli language policy. In T. Hickey and J. Williams (eds), *Language, Education and Society in a Changing World* (pp. 45–53). Dublin and Clevedon: IRAAL/Multilingual Matters Ltd.

Spolsky, B. (1998). *Sociolinguistics*. Oxford: Oxford University Press.

Spolsky, B. (ed.) (1999). *Concise Encyclopedia of Educational Linguistics*. Amsterdam and New York: Elsevier.

Spolsky, B. (2001). Language in Israel: policy, practice and ideology. In J. E. Alatis and A.-H. Tan (eds), *Georgetown University Roundtable on Language and Linguistics* (pp. 164–74). Washington, DC: Georgetown University Press.

Spolsky, B. (2003). *Language policy*. Paper presented at the ISB4: Proceedings of the 4th International Symposium on Bilingualism, Tempe, AZ.

Spolsky, B. (2004). *Language Policy*. Cambridge: Cambridge University Press.

Spolsky, B. (2005). Maori lost and regained. In A. Bell, R. Harlow and D. Starks (eds), *Languages of New Zealand* (pp. 67–85). Wellington: Victoria University Press.

Spolsky, B. (2006a). Fallas en la politica del lenguaje (Failures of language policy). In R. Terborg and L. G. Landa (eds), *Los retos de la planificación del lenguaje en el siglo XXI (The Challenges of Language Policy in the XXI Century)* (Vol. 1, pp. 91–111). Mexico: Universidad Nacional autónoma de México.

Spolsky, B. (2006b). Language policy failures – why won't they listen? In M. Pütz, J. A. Fishman and J. N.-v. Aertselaer (eds), *'Along the Routes to Power': Explorations of Empowerment through Language* (pp. 87–106). Berlin and New York: Mouton de Gruyter

Spolsky, B. (2006c). *Territoriality, tolerance, and language education policy*. Paper presented at the 16th Annual Nessa Wolfson Colloquium University of Pennsylvania, Philadelphia.

Spolsky, B. (2008a). Family language management: some preliminaries. In A. Stavans and I. Kupferberg (eds), *Studies in Language and Language Education: Essays in Honor of Elite Olshtain* (pp. 429–50). Jerusalem: The Hebrew University Magnes Press.

Spolsky, B. (2008b). Riding the tiger. In N. H. Hornberger (ed.), *Can Schools Save Indigenous Languages? Policy and Practice on Four Continents* (pp. 152–60). Basingstoke: Palgrave Macmillan.

Spolsky, B. (2009a). *Language Management*. Cambridge: Cambridge University Press.

Spolsky, B. (2009b). Rescuing Maori: the last 40 years. In P. K. Austin (ed.), *Language Documentation and Descriptions* (Vol. 6, pp. 11–36). London: School of Oriental and African Studies.

Spolsky, B. (2009c). *School alone cannot do it, but it helps: Irish, Hebrew, Navajo and Maori language revival efforts*. Paper presented at the Visiting professor seminar, Institute for Advanced Studies, University of Bristol, UK.

Spolsky, B. (2011a). Does the United States need a language policy? *CAL Digests*, 1–6.

Spolsky, B. (2011b). Ferguson and Fishman: sociolinguistics and the sociology of language. In R. Wodak, B. Johnstone and P. Kerswill (eds), *The Sage Handbook of Sociolinguistics* (pp. 11–23). London: Sage Publications Ltd.

Spolsky, B. (2012a). Family language policy – the critical domain. *Journal of Multilingual and Multicultural Development, 33*(1), 3–11.

Spolsky, B. (ed.) (2012b). *The Cambridge Handbook of Language Policy*. Cambridge: Cambridge University Press.

Spolsky, B. (2014). Language management in the People's Republic of China. *Language, 90*(4), e165–e175.

Spolsky, B. (2016a). Language management in the PRC: an evaluation. *Chinese Journal of Language Policy and Planning, 1*(5), 6–8.

Spolsky, B. (2016b). The languages of diaspora and return. *Brill Research Perspectives in Multilingualism and Second Language Acquisition, 1*(2–3), 1–119. doi:10.1163/2352877X-12340002

Spolsky, B. (2018a). Family language policy: the significant domain. In S. Haque and F. Le Lièvre (eds), *Family Language Policy: Dynamics in Language Transmission under a Migratory Context* (pp. 16–32). Munich: Lincom.

Spolsky, B. (2018b). Language policy in Portuguese colonies and successor states. *Current Issues in Language Planning, 19*(1), 62–97.

Spolsky, B. (2019a). Family language policy: the significant domain. In S. Haque (ed.), *Politique linguistique familiale* (pp. 23–36). Munich: Lincom.

Spolsky, B. (2019b). The individual in language policy and management, 28 June, <https://catedra-unesco.espais.iec.cat/en/2019/06/28/37-the-individual-in-language -policy-and-management/> (last accessed 23 September 2020).

Spolsky, B. (2019c). Language policy in French colonies and after independence. *Current Issues in Language Planning, 19*(3), 231–315. doi:10.1080/14664208.2018. 1444948

Spolsky, B. (2019d). Linguistic landscape – the semiotics of public signage. *Linguistic Landscape, 6*(1), 2–15.

Spolsky, B. (2019e). A modified and enriched theory of language policy (and management). *Language Policy, 18*(3), 323–38. doi:10.1007/s10993-018-9489-z

Spolsky, B. (2019f). Some demographic aspects of language policy (in Chinese). *Chinese Journal of Language Policy and Planning, 4*, 12–18.

Spolsky, B. (2020a). Linguistic landscape: the semiotics of public signage. *Linguistic Landscape, 6*(1), 2–25.

Spolsky, B. (2020b). Language management agencies and advocates. In T. Rahman (ed.), *Alternative Horizons in Linguistics* (pp. 1–18). Hyderabad: Lincom Europa.

Spolsky, B. and Benor, S. B. (2006). Jewish languages. In K. Brown (ed.), *Encyclopedia of Language and Linguistics* (2nd edn, Vol. 6, pp. 120–4). Oxford: Elsevier.

Spolsky, B. and Cooper, R. L. (eds) (1977). *Frontiers of Bilingual Education*. Rowley, MA: Newbury House Publishers.

Spolsky, B. and Cooper, R. L. (eds) (1978). *Case Studies in Bilingual Education*. Rowley, MA: Newbury House Publishers.

Spolsky, B. and Cooper, R. L. (1991). *The Languages of Jerusalem*. Oxford: Clarendon Press.

Spolsky, B. and Holm, W. (1973). Literacy in the vernacular: the case of Navajo. In

R. W. J. Ewton and J. Ornstein (eds), *Studies in Language and Linguistics, 1972–3* (pp. 239–51). El Paso: University of Texas at El Paso Press.

Spolsky, B. and Hult, F. M. (eds) (2008). *Handbook of Educational Linguistics*. Oxford: Blackwell.

Spolsky, B. and Shohamy, E. (1998). Language policy in Israel. *New Language Planning Newsletter, 12*(4), 1–4.

Spolsky, B. and Shohamy, E. (1999). *The Languages of Israel: Policy, Ideology and Practice*. Clevedon: Multilingual Matters.

Spolsky, B. and Shohamy, E. (2000). Language practice, language ideology and language policy. In R. D. Lambert and E. Shohamy (eds), *Language Policy and Pedagogy, Essays in Honor of A. Ronald Walton* (pp. 1–42). Amsterdam and Philadelphia: John Benjamins Publishing Company.

Spolsky, B., Engelbrecht, G. and Ortiz, L. (1983). Religious, political, and educational factors in the development of biliteracy in the Kingdom of Tonga. *Journal of Multilingual and Multicultural Development, 4*(6), 459–70.

Spolsky, B., Green, J. and Read, J. (1976). A model for the description, analysis and perhaps evaluation of bilingual education. In A. Verdoodt and R. Kjolseth (eds), *Language in Sociology* (pp. 233–61). Louvain: Editions Peeters.

Spolsky, B., Holm, W., Holliday, B. and Embry, J. (1973). A computer-assisted study of the vocabulary of young Navajo children. *Computers in the Humanities, 7*, 209–18.

St John, R. (1952). *Tongue of the Prophets: The Life Story of Eliezer Ben Yehuda*. New York: Doubleday.

Stewart, W. (1968). A sociolinguistic typology for describing national multilingualism. In J. A. Fishman (ed.), *Readings in the Sociology of Language* (pp. 531–45). The Hague: Mouton.

Stroud, C. (1999). Portuguese as ideology and politics in Mozambique: semiotic (re) constructions of a postcolony. In J. Blommaert (ed.), *Language Ideological Debates* (pp. 343–80). Berlin: Walter de Gruyter.

Suleiman, Y. (1994). Nationalism and the Arabic language: an historical overview. In Y. Suleiman (ed.), *Arabic Sociolinguistics: Issues and Perspectives* (pp. 3–24). Richmond: Curzon Press.

Suleiman, Y. (1996). Language and identity in Egyptian nationalism. In Y. Suleiman (ed.), *Language and Identity in the Middle East and North Africa* (pp. 25–38). London: Curzon Press.

Sumien, D. (2009). Comment rendre l'occitan disponible? Pédagogie et diglossie dans les écoles Calandretas. In P. Sauzet and F. Pic (eds), *Politique linguistique et enseignement des langues de France* (pp. 67–86). Paris: L'Harmattan.

Takeda, K. (2009). The interpreter, the monitor and the language arbiter. *Meta: Journal des traducteurs/Meta: Translators' Journal, 54*(2), 191–200.

Tauli, V. (1974). The theory of language planning. In J. A. Fishman (ed.), *Advances in Language Planning* (pp. 49–67). The Hague: Mouton.

Tavárez, D. (2013). A banned sixteenth-century biblical text in Nahuatl: the proverbs of Solomon. *Ethnohistory, 60*(4), 759–62.

Taylor-Leech, K. (2009). The language situation in Timor-Leste. *Current Issues in Language Planning, 10*(1), 1–68.

Te Puni Kokiri. (1998a). *Maori Language Policy: An International Example of Private*

Sector Contribution to Minority Language Revitalisation. Wellington: Te Puni Kokiri Ministry of Maori Development.

Te Puni Kokiri. (1998b). *Maori Language Policy: Language Corpus Development.* Wellington: Te Puni Kokiri Ministry of Maori Development.

Te Puni Kokiri. (1998c). *Maori Language Strategy: Maori Language Corpus Development.* Wellington: Te Puni Kokiri Ministry of Maori Development.

Te Puni Kokiri. (1998d). *Maori Language Strategy: Public and Private Sector Activities and Options.* Wellington: Te Puni Kokiri Ministry of Maori Development.

Te Puni Kokiri. (1998e). *Monitoring the Health of the Maori Language and the Effectiveness of Maori Language Policies: Monitoring and Evaluation Mechanisms Used in the Basque Country (Euskadi).* Wellington: Te Puni Kokiri Ministry of Maori Development.

Te Puni Kokiri. (1998f). *Progress on Maori Language Policy.* Wellington: Te Puni Kokiri Ministry of Maori Development.

Te Puni Kokiri. (2002). *Survey of Attitudes, Values and Beliefs about the Maori Language.* Wellington: Te Puni Kokiri Ministry of Maori Development.

Terasawa, T. (2017). Has socioeconomic development reduced the English divide? A statistical analysis of access to English skills in Japan. *Journal of Multilingual Multicultural Development, 38*(8), 671–85.

Terrell, J. A. (2007). *Political ideology and language policy in North Korea.* Paper presented at the Annual Meeting of the Berkeley Linguistics Society.

Thibaut, J. W. and Kelley, H. H. (1959). *The Social Psychology of Groups.* London: Routledge.

Thirumalai, M. S. (2003). Lord Macaulay: the man who started it all, and his minute. *Language in India, 3*(4).

Thomas, W. P. and Collier, V. P. (2002). A national study of school effectiveness for language minority students' long-term academic achievement, <escholarship.org/uc/item/65j213pt> (last accessed 4 October 2020).

Tibategeza, E. R. and du Plessis, T. (2018). The prospects of Kiswahili as a medium of instruction in the Tanzanian Education and Training Policy. *Journal of Language and Education, 4*(3), 88–98.

Tosi, A. (2000). *Language and Society in a Changing Italy.* Clevedon: Multilingual Matters Ltd.

Tosi, A. (2011). The Accademia della Crusca in Italy: past and present. *Language Policy, 10*(4), 289–303.

Tossa, C.-Z. (1998). Phénomènes de contact de langues dans le parler bilingue fongbe-français. *Linx, 38,* 197–220.

Totten, S. and Hitchcock, R. K. (2011). *Genocide of Indigenous Peoples: A Critical Bibliographic Review* (Vol. 1). Piscataway, NJ: Transaction Publishers.

Tov, E. (2018). *Scribal Practices and Approaches Reflected in the Texts Found in the Judean Desert.* Leiden: Brill.

Trouche, L. (2016). The development of mathematics practices in the Mesopotamian scribal schools. In J. Monaghan, L. Trouche and J. M. Borwein (eds), *Tools and Mathematics* (pp. 117–38). Bern: Springer.

Trudgill, P. (1978). Norwegian as a normal language. In U. Rhyneland (ed.), *Language Contact and Language Conflict* (pp. 151–8). Volda, Norway: Ivar Aasen Institute.

Trudgill, P. (1986). *Dialects in Contact.* Oxford: Blackwell.

Tveit, J.-E. (2009). Dubbing versus subtitling: old battleground revisited. In J. D. Cintas and G. Anderman (eds), *Audiovisual Translation* (pp. 85–96). Basingstoke: Palgrave Macmillan.

United Nations Development Programme. (2015). 2015 Human development report, <http://hdr.undp.org/en/content/human-development-report-2015> (last accessed October 2020).

US Census Bureau. (2004). Public education finances: 2002, <https://www.census.gov/library/publications/2004/econ/gc024-1.html> (last accessed 2 October 2020).

Vaillancourt, F. (1980). *Difference in Earnings by Language Groups in Quebec, 1970: An Economic Analysis.* Quebec City: International Center for Research on Bilingualism.

Vaillancourt, F., Lemay, D. and Vaillancourt, L. (2007). Laggards no more: the changed socioeconomic status of Francophones in Quebec. *Backgrounder - C. D. Howe Institute, 1*(1)–13.

Valdman, A. (1968). Language standardization in a diglossia situation: Haiti. In J. A. Fishman, C. A. Ferguson and J. Das Gupta (eds), *Language Problems of Developing Nations* (pp. 313–26). New York: Wiley.

Valdman, A. (1997). *French and Creole in Louisiana.* New York: Plenum.

Valdman, A. (2001). Creole: the national language of Haiti. *Footsteps, 4,* 36–9.

Valdman, A. (2015). *Haitian Creole: Structure, Variation, Status, Origin.* Sheffield: Equinox.

Van Breugel, S. (2014). *A Grammar of Atong.* Leiden: Brill.

Van der Voort, H. (2007). Proto-Jabutí: Um primeiro passo na reconstrução da língua ancestral dos Arikapú e Djeoromitxí. *Boletim do Museu Paraense Emílio Goeldi. Ciências Humanas, 2*(2), 133–68.

Vanthemsche, G. (2006). The historiography of Belgian colonialism in the Congo. In C. Lévail (ed.), *Europe and the World in European Historiography* (pp. 89–119). Pisa: Edizioni Plus – Pisa University Press.

Varennes, F. d. (2012). Language policy at the supra-national level. In B. Spolsky (ed.), *Handbook of Language Policy.* Cambridge: Cambridge University Press.

Vavrus, F. (2002). Postcoloniality and English: exploring language policy and the politics of development in Tanzania. *TESOL Quarterly, 36*(3), 373–97.

Versteegh, K. (2001). Arabic in Europe: from language of science to language of minority. *Lingua e stile, 36*(2), 335–46.

Vertovec, S. (2007). Super-diversity and its implications. *Ethnic and Racial Studies, 30*(6), 1024–54.

Vicino, T. J., Hanlon, B. and Short, J. R. (2011). A typology of urban immigrant neighborhoods. *Urban Geography, 32*(3), 383–405.

Waite, J. (1992). *Aoteareo: Speaking for Ourselves: A Discussion on the Development of a New Zealand Languages Policy.* Wellington: Learning Media, Ministry of Education.

Wallace, M. (2019). Competency-based education and assessment: a proposal for US court interpreter certification. In E. Huertas-Barros, S. Vandepitte and E. Iglesias-Fernández (eds), *Quality Assurance and Assessment Practices in Translation and Interpreting* (pp. 112–32). Hershey, PA: IGI Global.

Walsh, F. (2012). *Normal Family Processes: Growing Diversity and Complexity.* New York: Guilford Press.

Walter, S. L. (2003). Does language of instruction matter in education? In M. R. Wise, T. N. Headland and R. M. Brend (eds), *Language and Life: Essays in Memory of Kenneth L. Pike* (pp. 611–35). Dallas, TX: SIL International and the University of Texas at Arlington.

Walter, S. L. (2008). The language of instruction issue: framing an empirical perspective. In B. Spolsky and F. M. Hult (eds), *Handbook of Educational Linguistics* (pp. 129–46). Malden, MA and Oxford: Blackwell Publishing.

Walter, S. L. and Benson, C. (2012). Language policy and medium of instruction in formal education. In B. Spolsky (ed.), *The Cambridge Handbook of Language Policy* (pp. 278–300). Cambridge: Cambridge University Press.

Walter, S. L. and Davis, P. M. (2005). *The Eritrea national reading survey*. Dallas, TX: SIL International.

Wang, H. (2014). *Writing and the Ancient State: Early China in Comparative Perspective*. Cambridge: Cambridge University Press.

Wang, Y. and Phillion, J. (2009). Minority language policy and practice in China: the need for multicultural education. *International Journal of Multicultural Education, 11*(1), 1–14.

Webster, A. K. (2010a). Imagining Navajo in the boarding school: Laura Tohe's No Parole Today and the intimacy of language ideologies. *Journal of Linguistic Anthropology, 20*(1), 39–62.

Webster, A. K. (2010b). On intimate grammars with examples from Navajo English, Navlish, and Navajo. *Journal of Anthropological Research, 66*(2), 187–208.

Webster, A. K. (2014). Dif'G'one'and semiotic calquing: a signography of the linguistic landscape of the Navajo Nation. *Journal of Anthropological Research, 70*(3), 385–410.

Wee, L. (2003). Linguistic instrumentalism in Singapore. *Journal of Multilingual Multicultural Development, 24*(3), 211–24.

Weinreich, M. (1945). Der YIVO un di problemen fun undzer tsayt (דער ייװאָ און די פּראָבלעמען פֿון אונדזער צײט "The YIVO Faces the Post-War World". *YIVO Bletter, 25*(1).

Weinreich, M. (1980). *History of the Yiddish Language* (J. A. Fishman and S. Noble, trans.). Chicago: University of Chicago Press.

Weinreich, M. (2008). *History of the Yiddish Language* (S. Noble and J. A. Fishman trans., P. Glasser ed.). New Haven and London: Yale University Press.

Weinreich, U. (1944). Di velshishe shprakh in kampf far ir kiyem. *Yivo-bletter, 23*, 225–48.

Weinreich, U. (1953). *Languages in Contact: Findings and Problems*. New York: Linguistic Circle of New York.

Werner, O., Austin, M. and Begishe, K. (1966). *The Anatomical Atlas of the Navaho*. Evanston, IL: Northwester University.

Westbrook, R. (1985). Biblical and cuneiform law codes. *Revue Biblique (1946–), 92*(2), 247–64.

Whiteley, W. H. (1969). *Swahili: The Rise of a National Language*. London: Methuen and Co.

Wille, C., de Bres, J. and Franziskus, A. (2015). Intercultural work environments in Luxembourg. Multilingualism and cultural diversity among cross-border workers at the workplace (Working paper). University of Luxembourg.

Williams, C. H. (2007a). *Language and Governance*. Cardiff: University of Wales Press.

Williams, C. H. (2007b). *When Mandarin gates yield*. Paper presented at the Babel in reverse: Language ideology in the 21st century conference, Duisburg.

Williams, C. H. (2008a). *Linguistic Minorities in Democratic Context*. Basingstoke and New York: Palgrave Macmillan.

Williams, C. H. (2008b). Welsh language policy and the logic of legislative devolution. In C. H. Williams (ed.), *Linguistic Minorities in Democratic Context* (pp. 245–301). Basingstoke: Palgrave Macmillan.

Williams, C. H. (2012). Language policy, territorialism and regional autonomy. In B. Spolsky (ed.), *Handbook of Language Policy* (pp. 174–202). Cambridge: Cambridge University Press.

Williams, C. H. (2017a). Policy review: wake me up in 2050! Formulating language policy in Wales. *Languages, Society and Policy*. doi:doi.org/10.17863/CAM.9802

Williams, C. H. (2017b). Policy review: wake me up in 2050! Formulating language policy in Wales. *Languages Society and Policy, Policy papers*. doi:doi:10.17863/CAM.9802

Williams, R. J. (1972). Scribal training in ancient Egypt. *Journal of the American Oriental Society, 92*(2), 214–21.

Wilson, D. (1970). *The Life and Times of Vuk Stefanović Karadžić: 1787–1864: Literacy, Literature, and National Independence in Serbia* (Vol. 27). Ann Arbor, MI: Michigan Slavic Publications.

Wilson, W. H. and Kawai'ae'a, K. (2007). I Kumu; I Lālā: 'let there be sources; let there be branches': teacher education in the College of Hawaiian Language. *Journal of American Indian Education, 46*(3), 37–53.

Winston-Allen, A. (2010). *Stories of the Rose: The Making of the Rosary in the Middle Ages*. University Park, PA: Penn State Press.

Wolf, E. (2003). The issue of language in democratization: the Niger experience in literacy and basic education. In A. Ouane (ed.), *Towards a Multilingual Culture of Education* (pp. 191–214). Hamburg: UNESCO Institute for Education.

World Bank. (2016). The international poverty line, September, <https://www.worldbank.org/en/programs/icp/brief/poverty-line> (last accessed 4 October 2020).

Wright, S. (2002). Language education and foreign relations in Vietnam. In J. W. Tollefson (ed.), *Language Policies in Education: Critical Issues* (pp. 225–44). Mahwah, NJ: Lawrence Erlbaum Associates.

Wright, S. (2004). *Language Policy and Language Planning: From Nationalism to Globalisation*. London and Basingstoke: Palgrave Macmillan.

Wright, S. (2012). Language policy, the nation and nationalism. In B. Spolsky (ed.), *The Cambridge Handbook of Language Policy* (pp. 59–78). Cambridge: Cambridge University Press.

Wright, S. (2016). *Language Policy and Language Planning: From Nationalism to Globalisation* (2nd edn). London and Basingstoke: Palgrave Macmillan.

Wylie, C. (1997). *Self-Managing Schools Seven Years On: What Have We Learnt?* Wellington: New Zealand Council for Educational Research.

Xu, D. (2004). The speech community theory. *Journal of Chinese Sociolinguistics, 2*, 18–28.

Xu, D. (2015). Speech community and linguistic urbanization: sociolinguistic theories developed in China. In D. Smakman and P. Heinrich (eds), *Globalising Sociolinguistics* (pp. 115–26). Abingdon: Routledge.

Xu, D. and Li, W. (2002). Managing multilingualism in Singapore. In W. Lei, J.-M. Dewaele and A. Housen (eds), *Opportunities and Challenges of Bilingualism* (pp. 275–96). Berlin: Mouton de Gruyter.

Yagmur, K. and Kroon, S. (2006). Objective and subjective data on Altai and Kazakh ethnolinguistic vitality in the Russian Federation Republic of Altai. *Journal of Multilingual and Multicultural Development, 27*(3), 241–58.

Yates, L. and Terraschke, A. (2013). Love, language and little ones: successes and stresses for mothers raising bilingual children in exogamous relationships. In M. Schwartz and A. Verschik (eds), *Successful Family Language Policy* (pp. 105–25). Dordrecht: Springer.

Young, R. J. (2016). *Postcolonialism: An Historical Introduction.* Malden, MA and Oxford: John Wiley & Sons.

Young, R. W. (1977). Written Navajo: a brief history. In J. A. Fishman (ed.), *Advances in the Creation and Revision of Writing Systems* (pp. 459–70). The Hague and Paris: Mouton.

Young, R. W. and Morgan, W. (eds) (1943). *The Navaho Language.* Phoenix, AZ: U.S. Indian Service.

Young, R. W. and Morgan, W. (1980). *The Navajo Language: A Grammar and Colloquial Dictionary.* Albuquerque, NM: University of New Mexico Press.

Zanotti, L. (2016). *Radical Territories in the Brazilian Amazon: The Kayapó's Fight for Just Livelihoods.* Tucson, AZ: University of Arizona Press.

Zein, S. (2020). *Language Policy in Superdiverse Indonesia.* Abingdon and New York: Routledge.

Zein, S. (unpublished). *Language Policy Apparatus.*

Zhao, S. and Baldauf Jr., R. B. (2008). *Planning Chinese Characters: Reaction, Evolution or Revolution?* Dordrecht: Springer.

Zhou, M. (ed.) (2004). *Language Policy in the People's Republic of China: Theory and Practice since 1949.* Dordrecht: Kluwer Academic Publishers; Springer Science.

Zouhir, A. (2013). *Language situation and conflict in Morocco.* Paper presented at the 43rd Annual Conference on African Linguistics, Tulane University.

Zug, M. A. (2016). *Buying a Bride: An Engaging History of Mail-Order Matches.* New York: New York University Press.

Zwartjes, O. and Hovdhaugen, E. (eds) (2004). *Missionary Linguistics/Lingüística misionera.* Amsterdam and Philadelphia: John Benjamins.

Zwartjes, O., Marín, R. A. and Smith-Stark, T. C. (2009). *Missionary Linguistics IV/ Lingüística misionera IV: Lexicography.* Selected papers from the Fifth International Conference on Missionary Linguistics, Mérida, Yucatán, 14–17 March 2007 (Vol. 114). Amsterdam and Philadelphia: John Benjamins Publishing.

Index of language varieties

Index of Topics